D1192352

Milestones A

HEINLE
CENGAGE Learning™

Australia • Brazil • Japan • Korea • Mexico • Singapore • Spain • United Kingdom • United States

Milestones A

Contributing Writer: Jill Korey O'Sullivan

Editorial Director: Joe Dougherty

Publisher: Sherrise Roehr

Managing Editor: Carmela Fazzino-Farah

Editorial Assistant: Jennifer Kuhnberg

Technology Development Manager:
Debie Mirtle

Executive Marketing Manager:
Jim McDonough

Director of Product Marketing:
Amy T. Mabley

Product Marketing Manager: Katie Kelley

Assistant Marketing Manager:
Andrea Bobotas

Director of Content and Media Production:
Michael Burggren

Content Project Manager:
Dawn Marie Elwell

Manufacturing Manager: Marcia Locke

Development Editor: Arley Gray

Composition and Project Management:
Nesbitt Graphics, Inc.

Illustrations/Photography:
see pages 451–452 for credits

Interior Design: Studio Montage

Cover Design: Page 2, LLC

Cover Image: Darrell Gulin/CORBIS

Library of Congress Control Number: 2007940574

Student Edition
ISBN-13: 978-1-4240-0887-2
ISBN-10: 1-4240-0887-5

International Student Edition (Not for Sale in the United States)
ISE ISBN-13: 978-1-4240-3350-8
ISE ISBN-10: 1-4240-3350-0

Heinle Cengage Learning
25 Thomson Place
Boston, Massachusetts 02210
USA

Cengage Learning products are represented in Canada by Nelson Education, Ltd.

Visit Heinle online at **elt.heinle.com**
Visit our corporate website at **www.cengage.com**

Printed in the United States of America
2 3 4 5 6 7   12 11 10 09 08

Program Authors

NEIL ANDERSON

Dr. Neil J. Anderson received his Ph.D. from the University of Texas at Austin, where he specialized in research in the teaching of reading. He has done significant work in the area of reading comprehension, reading strategies, and fluency. He has published several books in this area and continues to actively research and publish.

Dr. Anderson has been teaching English and teachers of English for over twenty-five years. He is a professor in the Department of Linguistics and English Language at Brigham Young University in Provo, Utah. He has received many awards for outstanding teaching and believes that everyone can learn to be a good reader.

Dr. Anderson helped to establish the pedagogical framework of the *Milestones* program with a particular focus on reading strategies and reading fluency.

JILL KOREY O'SULLIVAN

Jill Korey O'Sullivan holds a Masters Degree in Education from Harvard University. Her specific area of research and interest is language and literacy. Ms. Korey O'Sullivan is an experienced author and editor of educational materials with a background in curriculum development and teaching. She has taught and developed materials for students of a broad range of levels and in a variety of educational settings, including kindergarten, middle school, and community college programs.

Ms. Korey O'Sullivan has brought her classroom experience and creativity to the writing of several textbooks and has served as editor on many publications in the field of English language learning.

She helped to establish the pedagogical framework of the *Milestones* program, incorporating the latest in research and pedagogy.

The students she has taught and the students who use her materials serve as her inspiration.

JENNIFER TRUJILLO

Jennifer Trujillo received her Ed.D. in Educational Leadership and Change from Fielding Graduate University, Santa Barbara, CA. Dr. Trujillo grew up in a home where another language besides English was spoken. Her family moved back and forth between her mother's homeland and the United States. Her dedication to reading led her to earn degrees and teaching credentials in English (Fort Lewis College) and Reading from the University of Northern Colorado. She has been an ESL educator for fourteen years.

She is currently a professor in the Teacher Education Department at Fort Lewis College in Durango, Colorado. Her areas of specialization are reading and writing, ESL, home-school partnerships, professional development, cognitive coaching, differentiated instruction and diversity training.

Dr. Trujillo feels strongly about the importance of culturally responsive and universally relevant readings, with challenging activities, to help all students succeed. To that end, she helped to establish the pedagogical framework of the *Milestones* program and provided valuable feedback on each of the reading selections to ensure culturally responsive instruction for the pre and post reading activities.

Program Advisors

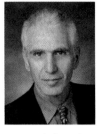

ROBERT J. MARZANO, Ph.D., Vocabulary Advisor

Dr. Robert J. Marzano is president and founder of Marzano & Associates, specializing in long term school reform efforts to enhance student academic achievement. His works guiding teachers to assist students in developing academic language can be found in the books *Building Background Knowledge for Academic Achievement* and *Building Academic Vocabulary*.

Over his 35 years in education, the central theme of his work has been translating research and theory into practical programs and tools for teachers and administrators. He is a Senior Scholar at Mid-continent Research for Education and Learning (McREL) and an Associate Professor at Cardinal Stritch University.

Dr. Marzano received his M.Ed. degree in Reading and Language Arts from Seattle University, and his Ph.D. in Curriculum and Instruction from the University of Washington.

He is the author of more than 20 books, 150 articles, and more than 100 curriculum guides and related materials for teachers and students. His most recent publication is *The Art and Science of Teaching: a Comprehensive Framework for Effective Instruction.*

KEITH LENZ, Ph.D., Differentiated Instruction/Universal Access Advisor

Dr. Keith Lenz specializes in adolescents with learning problems, teacher planning, and strategic instruction for teaching diverse groups. He has degrees in Special Education and Secondary Education from Bradley University and a Ph.D. from the University of Kansas. At the University of Kansas, Dr. Lenz is an Associate Professor, Director of the Institute for Effective Instruction, and Senior Research Scientist at the Center for Research on Learning.

Dr. Lenz is the founder and member of the Board of Trustees at the Strategic Learning Center, Inc., Seattle, WA. He is an adjunct professor at Seattle Pacific University, and a National Trainer of The Strategies Intervention Model.

Dr. Lenz's work with guiding teachers on effective differentiated instruction practices can be found in his co-authored book *Teaching content to all: Inclusive teaching in grades 4–12*, amongst others.

Dr. Lenz taught at Florida Atlantic University and serves as a Project Trainer for the Florida Department of Education.

ANNE KATZ, Ph.D., Assessment Advisor

Dr. Anne Katz has worked for 20 years as a researcher and evaluator for projects connected with the education of linguistically and culturally diverse students. As a teacher educator, she has provided and supported professional development in the areas of curriculum, assessment, and evaluation.

Dr. Katz co-directed a national study of successful leadership strategies to create more harmonious racial and ethnic environments in K–12 schools. She is co-author of *Leading for Diversity: How School Leaders Promote Positive Interethnic Relations* and author of numerous publications on diversity and the development of standards-based assessment systems.

Dr. Katz was instrumental in developing standards for English as a second language with the Teachers of English to Speakers of Other Languages organization, and she has assisted many school districts in developing more authentic assessments of student performance. In all her work, she promotes the links between research and the classroom to support meaningful school change.

Anne Katz holds a doctorate in second language education from Stanford University. She is a lecturer at the School for International Training's graduate teacher education program.

Teacher Reviewers

Sonia Abrew
Orange County Public Schools
Orlando, FL

Ruby Ali
H.L. Watkins Middle School
Palm Beach Gardens, FL

Jean Anderson
Broward County Public Schools
Ft. Lauderdale, FL

Teresa Arvizu
McFarland Unified School District
McFarland, CA

Maridell Bagnal
Fletcher Middle School
Jacksonville Beach, FL

Miriam Barrios-Chacon
Chipman Middle School
Alameda, CA

Cathy Bonner
Bowie High School
El Paso, TX

Irene Borrego
CA State University Bakersfield
Bakersfield, CA

Tanya Castro
Pharr-San Juan-Alamo Independent
School District
Alamo, TX

Nicole Chaput
Metro Nashville Public Schools
Nashville, TN

Vikki Chavez
San Bernardino High School
San Bernardino, CA

Anthony Colonna
Ocala Middle School
San Jose, CA

Catherine Cominio
Howell Watkins Middle School
Palm Beach Gardens, FL

Ayanna Cooper
DeKalb County Schools
DeKalb, GA

James Coplan
Oakland Technical High School
Oakland, CA

Alicia Cron
Austin Middle School
San Juan, TX

Libby Taylor Deleon
Plano ISD
Plano, TX

Farida Doherty
Boston Public Schools
Boston, MA

Mercedes A. Egues
Fort Lauderdale High School
Fort Lauderdale, FL

Karen Ernst
Highland High School
Palmdale, CA

Rafael Estrada
Lake Shore Middle School
Belle Glade, FL

Mary Ford
Pahokee Middle High School
Pahokee, FL

Beverly Franke
Palm Beach County Schools
Greenacres, FL

Helena Gandell
Duval County Public Schools
Jacksonville, FL

Linsey Gannon
Lawrence Cook Middle School
Santa Rosa, CA

Renee Gaudet
New River Elementary School
Wesley Chapel, FL

Nathalie Gillis-Rumowicz
Seminole Middle School
Seminole, FL

Evelyn Gomez
The Academy for New Americans
Middle School
Astoria, NY

Rafael Gonzalez
Wasco Union High School District
Wasco, CA

Vivian Kahn
I.S. 296 Halsey School
Brooklyn, NY

Sarah Harley
ALBA Elementary School
Milwaukee, WI

Renote Jean-Francois
Boston Public Schools
Boston, MA

Tony King
Boston Public Schools
Boston, MA

Christa Kirby
Pinellas Country School District
Largo, FL

Letitia Laberee
Angelo Patri Middle School
Bronx, NY

Gemma Lacanlale
Houston Independent School District
Houston, TX

Arthur Larievy
Boston Public Schools
Boston, MA

Alisa Leckie
Billy Lane Lauffer Middle School
Tucson, AZ

Chad Leith
Boston Public Schools
Boston, MA

Arnulfo Lopez
Delano High School
Delano, CA

Carmen Lopez
Cesar E. Chavez High School
Delano, CA

Lana Lysen
Multicultural, ESOL Education
Fort Lauderdale, FL

Vanessa MacDonna
Andries Huddle Middle School
Brooklyn, NY

Rita Marsh-Birch
Sandalwood High School
Jacksonville, FL

Lorraine Martini
Nova Middle School
Davie, FL

Jean Melby-Mauer
Valley High School
Las Vegas, NV

Patsy Mills
Houston Independent School District
Houston, TX

Amy Mirco
Charlotte-Mecklenburg Schools
Charlotte, NC

Gloria Pelaez
University of Miami
Miami, FL

Maria Pena
Doral Middle School
Doral, FL

Yvonne Perez
Alief Middle School
Houston, TX

Lunine Pierre-Jerome
Boston Public Schools
Boston, MA

Yolanda Pokaski
Boston Public Schools
Boston, MA

Diana Ramlall
School District of Palm Beach County
West Palm Beach, FL

Marlene Roney
New River Middle School
Fort Lauderdale, FL

Cheryl Serrano
Lynn University
Boca Raton, FL

Raynel Shepard
Boston Public Schools
Boston, MA

Michele Spohn
Fort Caroline Middle School
Jacksonville, FL

Ilza Sterling
Falcon Cove Middle School
Weston, FL

John Sullivan
Clark County School
District, East Region
Las Vegas, NV

Teri Suzuki
Lincoln Middle School
Alameda, CA

Daisy Torres
Marion County Schools
Ocala, FL

Matthew Trillo
Maxwell Middle School
Tucson, AZ

Heather Tugwell
Oakland Unified School District
Oakland, CA

Cassandra Vukcevic
Ridgewood High School
New Port Richey, FL

Sheila Weinstein
Deerfield Beach Middle School
Deerfield Beach, FL

MaryLou Whaley
Immigrant Acculturation Center
Tampa, FL

Jill Wood
Dr. John Long Middle School
Wesley Chapel, FL

Veronica Yepez
Washington Middle School
Pasadena, CA

Family Connections

Dreams
Page 130

UNIT 4

Conflict and Resolution
Page 192

Survival

Page 260

UNIT 5

Welcome to *Milestones!*
Your Steps to Success

The title of this book is *Milestones*. Milestones are rocks set on a road to show the distance from one place to another. Like milestones on a road, this book will help guide you from one step in your learning to the next. It will provide the support you need every step of the way.

There are four specific skills you will learn and practice in *Milestones*:

Reading Reading is the foundation of learning. This book will help you become a more effective reader in many ways. For example, you will learn important vocabulary words that come from the readings. You will also learn academic vocabulary. These are the words that are used frequently in all subject areas. Learning academic vocabulary will help you understand academic texts and succeed in subject areas. Reading Fluency activities will help you learn to read more fluently. Reading Strategies will teach you specific methods for comprehending readings more effectively.

Listening Effective listening requires you to be focused and attentive. This book will provide you with opportunities to practice and improve your listening skills.

Speaking You will have many opportunities to practice your speaking skills by discussing the readings, performing role plays, and working on projects with your classmates.

Writing This book will help you understand and practice the writing process. You will plan, draft, revise, and edit each of your writing assignments. You will learn how to evaluate your own writing and how to give feedback to your classmates on their writing.

Your teachers will provide important guidance as you work through this book. The assessment material at the end of each chapter and unit will help you and your teacher identify material you have successfully learned and areas where you may need more practice.

However, the most important ingredient for academic success is YOU! You are the one holding the book. You are the one reading these words. You have the power and ability to work toward academic success. As you open this book, open your mind by thinking carefully and critically.

With this book, help from your teacher, and your own determination, you will achieve wonderful academic milestones!

Family Connections

Explore the Theme

1. What is a family?
2. Talk about the people you see in the pictures.

Theme Activity

Work with a partner. Think about the people in your families or a family you know. Make a chart like the one here. Give one or two words for each person.

mother	father	sister	brother	?
friendly, helpful				

CHAPTER 1

Objectives

Reading Strategies
Visualize; Ask questions

Listening and Speaking
Role-play an interview

Grammar
Learn the simple present tense of **be** and the present progressive tense

Writing
Descriptive writing: Write a paragraph about a place

Academic Vocabulary

visualize	conclusion
image	recognize

Academic Content

Korean culture
History of ancient Greece

● Chapter Focus Question

How do families teach us about ourselves?

Reading 1 **Literature**
Short story
My Korean Name
by Leonard Chang

Reading 2 **Content:** Social Studies
Informational text (adapted)
HOME LIFE IN ANCIENT GREECE
by Melanie Ann Apel

My Korean Name

● About the Reading

You are going to read a short story about a Korean-American boy and his grandfather.

● Build Background

Calligraphy

The grandfather in "My Korean Name" is a calligraphy artist. Calligraphy is an art form that is hundreds of years old. It is an important part of many Asian cultures. Calligraphy artists use a brush and ink to write beautiful "characters." These characters are pictures or letters that stand for words.

Use your finger to trace the character for *mother*.

● Use Prior Knowledge

Tell About Your Experience

The boy in "My Korean Name" speaks English. His grandfather speaks Korean. It is difficult for them to communicate. Think about a time you tried to communicate with someone who did not speak your language.

1. Who did you try to communicate with?
2. Did you understand this person? Did he or she understand you?
3. Why did you need to communicate with this person?
4. What did you do to communicate?
5. How did you feel?

Key Vocabulary

- annoyed
- scared
- surprised
- traditional
- wise

Build Your Knowledge

Create a Vocabulary Log in a notebook. List new words you learn. Put the words in alphabetical order. Write the definitions and use the words in sentences.

● Vocabulary From the Reading

Learn, Practice, and Use Independently

Learn Vocabulary Read each sentence. Look at the **highlighted** word. Think about the context (the words around the highlighted word). Use the context to determine the meaning of the word.

1. I was **annoyed.** My little sister made noise and asked questions during the movie.

2. The little boy **scared** his sister. He jumped out of a closet and said, "Boo!"

3. John was **surprised.** He did not know we were having a party for him.

4. It is **traditional** to eat turkey on Thanksgiving Day in the United States.

5. My grandmother is a **wise** woman. Many people talk to her about their problems.

Practice Vocabulary Match a Key Vocabulary word to each picture.

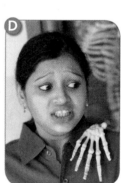

✓ Checkpoint

1. When do you get **annoyed**?

2. When do you get **scared**?

3. Who do you think is very **wise**?

Use Vocabulary Independently Write one sentence for each Key Vocabulary word. Read your sentences to a partner.

Vocabulary Log

Workbook page 29

Independent Practice CD-ROM/Online

● Academic Vocabulary

Vocabulary for the Reading Strategy

Word	Explanation	Sample Sentence	Visual Cue
visualize *verb*	to make a picture in your mind	When I am homesick, I **visualize** my mother cooking in our kitchen.	
image *noun*	a picture you make in your mind	I often have an **image** in my mind of my mother cooking.	

Draw a picture and write a sentence for each word.

● Reading Strategy

Visualize

When you **visualize,** you make an **image** of something in your mind. You also think about what you hear, taste, smell, and feel. **Visualizing** helps you enjoy the story more.

As you read "My Korean Name," **visualize** the story.

1. After you read each paragraph, close your eyes. Make **images** in your mind of people and things in the story.
2. Look at each paragraph again. Find the words that helped you **visualize** the paragraph.
3. Look at the chart. After you read, you will look at the reading again. Then you will complete the chart.

see	hear	taste	smell	feel

√Checkpoint

Explain the word **visualize** to a partner. Use your own words.

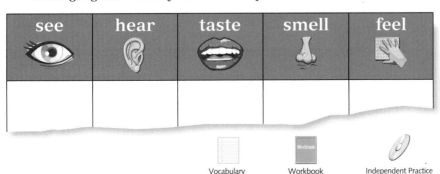

Text Genre

Short Story

"My Korean Name" is a **short story.** A short story is a form of **fiction**—stories that are not true. The purpose, or reason, for reading a short story is for enjoyment.

A short story has the features below. Look for these features as you read "My Korean Name."

Short Story		
characters	people in a story	
setting	where the story happens	
plot	events in a story that happen in a certain order 	
theme	the meaning or message of the story	

Meet the Author

Leonard Chang was born in New York City. His parents were from Seoul, South Korea. Chang was a quiet, shy child. He liked to read at his local library. When Chang was older, he traveled to his parents' homeland. He wanted to learn about the language and culture of Korea. Today, Chang lives in California. He is a writer and teacher.

Reading Focus Questions

As you read, think about these questions.

1. How does the reading relate to the theme of "family connections"?

2. What do you think was the author's purpose for writing "My Korean Name"?

3. Is it important to learn about family history and culture? Why?

Checkpoint
What does **plot** mean?

Workbook
page 31

Independent Practice
CD-ROM/Online

My Korean Name

by Leonard Chang

1   My grandfather left Korea to live with us in New York when he was almost eighty years old. My parents fixed up the **attic** so that he had his own room.

2   He wore **traditional** Korean clothes: shiny vests with gold buttons, and puffy pants that made his legs look fat even though he was really very skinny. He chewed on small dried fish **snacks** that smelled up everything. He coughed a lot.

3   My grandfather spoke only Korean, so I never understood what he was saying. He **scared** me. I had never seen anyone so old so close.

4   "Take this tea up to your **halabogee**," my mother told me soon after he had moved in.

5   "I don't want to," I said.

6   "He's your grandfather," she **scolded.** "Be nice to him."

Reading Strategy

Visualize Imagine you are in the attic. What do you see? What do you smell? What do you hear? What words help you imagine these things?

✓ **Reading Check**

1. **Identify** Who is the narrator (the speaker) of the story?

2. **Recall facts** Where does the grandfather live?

3. **Recall facts** What language does the grandfather speak? What language does the boy speak?

4. **Explain** How does the boy feel? Why?

---

attic room or space below the roof of a house

snacks small amounts of food eaten between meals

halabogee Korean word for *grandfather*

scolded told someone in an angry way that he or she did something wrong

7   I brought up the steaming cup of tea, hearing him cough once, twice, and again. I **peeked** around the corner and said, "Here's your tea." He looked up at me, chewing his dried fish snack, and smiled.

8   He began speaking Korean to me, but I didn't understand him. He waved me over and continued talking.

9   "What? What? I don't understand Korean," I said. "I never learned."

10   "*Aigoo*," he said, which was like "Oh my!" in Korean. My mother said that word to me all the time. He waved his finger at me and said, "Korean important. Yes?"

11   "I guess so," I said, **surprised.** So he *did* speak a little English.

12   He smiled and nodded and sipped his tea loudly. He began speaking to me in Korean again. He talked for a long time, and I didn't understand a single word. I said, "Grandpa, I *told* you I can't understand you!"

13   But he just smiled and nodded and kept on talking. After a while, I just listened. I liked the sound of his **raspy** voice filling the warm attic.

Reading Strategy

Visualize In which paragraph does the boy seem to be **annoyed**? In which paragraph do you imagine him enjoying his time with his grandfather?

---

peeked looked secretly at someone or something
raspy deep and rough

14 My mother gave my grandfather a colorful shiny hand fan that he used to keep himself cool during the hot afternoons.

15 My father gave him a small **transistor radio,** which my grandfather listened to late at night, tuned to the Korean **Gospel** station.

16 My mother also gave him a goat-hair brush, rice paper, an ink stick, and an **inkstone** to practice his calligraphy, a special kind of writing.

17 One day I was watching him draw lines on the paper. He looked up and said,

18 "You." I was **surprised.** Another English word.

19 "Me," I said.

20 He smiled, his face wrinkling.

21 "You," he said again. "Won Chul."

22 "Me," I said. "Won Chul is my middle name."

23 He nodded and dipped his brush in the inkstone, shaking off some of the extra ink. "You," he said. "Won Chul."

24 "I know my middle name," I said, getting **annoyed.**

25 He talked to me in Korean again for a long time, then motioned for me to come closer.

26 I walked to him. He smelled like **mothballs** and fish.

◀ **Reading Strategy**

Visualize Is Won Chul standing close to his grandfather? How do you know?

✓
Reading Check

1. **Recall facts** What is the boy's middle name?

2. **Analyze characters** Why do you think the grandfather speaks Korean to Won Chul?

---

transistor radio small radio that you can carry

Gospel Christian teachings from the Bible

inkstone stone used in calligraphy for making ink

mothballs strong-smelling balls used to keep moths away from clothing

27   He drew some stick figures **overlapping** each other, **swirling** his brush easily, quickly. "Won," he said, pointing.

28   He drew another figure, this time going slowly. The brush made a *swish* sound on the thin rice paper. He pointed to this second figure and said, "Chul." Bringing me nearer so that I could study the picture, he said, "Won Chul. You."

29   "That's my name?"

30   He nodded. "Won Chul."

31   "That looks neat," I said.

32   He pushed it toward me.

33   "For me?" I asked.

34   "For Won Chul," he said.

35   My mother later told me that this was *hanja*, a special Korean way of writing using the Chinese alphabet. This was the *hanja* **version** of my Korean name. She said, "Your grandfather was once a famous artist. All the people in his town wanted him to draw their names."

Reading Strategy

Visualize Imagine Won Chul looking at the drawing of his name. Does he seem interested? What words help you picture this?

36   "Wow," I said, holding the rice paper carefully.

37   "You know what your name means, don't you?" she said. "It means '**Wise** One.' Do you remember?"

38   "I remember," I said. I held up my Korean name to the light, the paper so thin it **glowed.**

---

overlapping having a part of something over part of something else

swirling moving in a twisting and turning motion

version different form of something

glowed gave off light

39 Not too long after that my grandfather went to a **nursing home,** and during the next summer he died while I was away at **camp.** My father turned the attic into a storage room. Now it's filled with dusty boxes of old clothes and shoes and old furniture.

40 I still have the drawing of my Korean name. My mother had it **framed** for me, and it hangs in my room right now. I wonder what my grandfather used to tell me those afternoons when he spoke in Korean, going on and on in this strange language that I never learned. Maybe he was telling me stories. Maybe he was telling me about his life in Korea.

41 Sometimes, if I go up into the attic and listen very carefully, I can almost hear his voice rising and falling, telling me stories I don't understand. I can almost see him in the corner, **hunched** over, listening to his radio and fanning himself. I can see him swishing his brush over the rice paper, and then pointing to me, telling me my own name.

---

nursing home place where people who are old or very sick are cared for

camp a program, usually in the country, where activities are provided for children during the summer months

framed put in a frame

hunched bent over

● Apply the Reading Strategy

Visualize

Now complete the Reading Strategy chart.

1. Review the **Reading Strategy** on page 7.
2. Copy the chart.
3. Look back at the reading. Find words that helped you **visualize** the reading.
4. Write the words in the correct column of the chart.

see	hear	taste	smell	feel
			mothballs and fish	

● Academic Vocabulary

Vocabulary for the Reading Comprehension Questions

Word	Explanation	Sample Sentence	Visual Cue
conclusion *noun*	a judgment or an opinion that you make from information you know	When Tina saw water dripping from Ana's coat, she came to the **conclusion** that it was raining.	
recognize *verb*	to remember someone or something when you see or hear that person or thing	I **recognized** an old friend on the street. We were **surprised** to see each other after so many years.	

Draw a picture and write a sentence for each word.

✓Checkpoint

What do **conclusion** and **recognize** mean? Explain in your own words.

Vocabulary Log

● Reading Comprehension Questions

Think and Discuss

1. **Recall facts** Why was Won Chul's grandfather famous in Korea?
2. **Describe** Describe Won Chul's grandfather.
3. **Draw conclusions** Why do you think Won Chul's grandfather gave Won Chul the drawing of his name?
4. **Recognize character change** Do Won Chul's feelings about his grandfather change by the end of the story? How do you know? Use Key Vocabulary words.
5. **Relate your own experience to the reading** Do you have a family member who speaks another language? How does this make you feel?
6. **Revisit the Reading Focus Questions** Go back to page 8 and discuss the questions.

Workbook
page 32

Independent Practice
CD-ROM/Online

● Literary Element

Characterization

Characters are the people in a story. **Characterization** is the way an author creates a character. Authors:

a. describe what the character looks like.

b. describe the character's words, thoughts, and actions.

c. show what others think about the character.

Through characterization, an author shows a character's **traits** (qualities) and explains a character's **motives** (why a character acts the way he or she does).

1. Read the sentences about the grandfather from "My Korean Name." Match each sentence to the way it helps you understand the character.

1. He wore **traditional** Korean clothes.	a. This sentence shows what someone thinks about the character.
2. He waved his finger at me and said, "Korean important. Yes?"	b. This sentence describes what the character looks like.
3. He **scared** me.	c. This sentence describes the character's words, thoughts, or actions.

✓Checkpoint

1. What is **characterization**?

2. How does an author help a reader understand a character?

2. Look at the reading again with a partner. Find and write more sentences that help you understand the characters.

Workbook
page 33

Independent Practice
CD-ROM/Online

HOME LIFE IN ANCIENT GREECE

● About the Reading

You read "My Korean Name," a short story about a Korean-American boy and his grandfather. Now you will read an informational text about family members in ancient Greece.

● Build Background

Ancient Greece

About 2,500 years ago, there was a great civilization in ancient Greece. This civilization started about 800 BCE. It lasted until about 146 BCE. The ancient Greeks developed many new ideas in science, math, art, and literature. Many of these ideas are still important today.

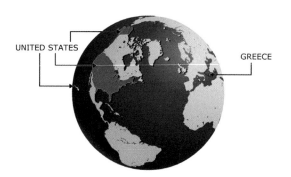

UNITED STATES

GREECE

Key Vocabulary

belong

role

tradition

● Vocabulary From the Reading

Use Context Clues to Determine Meaning

Use the context of the sentences to determine the meaning of the **highlighted** words. Discuss the meanings with a small group.

1. Last year, I **belonged** to the drama club. This year, I **belong** to the Spanish club.

2. When Juan got married, he took on the **role** of a husband.

3. We follow many Chinese New Year **traditions.** We wear the color red and buy flowers.

Vocabulary
Log

Workbook
page 34

Independent Practice
CD-ROM/Online

● Reading Strategy

Ask Questions

Good readers **ask questions** while they read. You focus on a reading and understand it better when you ask questions.

1. Read "Home Life in Ancient Greece." Stop reading after every paragraph.
2. Ask a question or two about what you read.
3. Look for answers to your questions as you continue reading.

● Text Genre

Informational Text

"Home Life in Ancient Greece" is an **informational text.** An informational text is a form of **nonfiction**—a text about something that is true. The purpose of an informational text is to give the reader information about a topic.

An informational text has the features below.

Informational Text	
headings	titles of sections
facts	statements that are true
example	something that shows or explains a fact

● Meet the Author

Melanie Ann Apel was born in Chicago. As a child, she loved to read and write. She has written more than 40 nonfiction books.

● Reading Focus Questions

As you read, think about these questions.

1. How does this reading relate to the theme of "family connections"?
2. What do you think was the author's purpose in writing "Home Life in Ancient Greece"?
3. Was life in ancient Greece very different from life today? If so, how?

✓Checkpoint

How does **asking questions** help you understand what you read?

HOME LIFE IN ANCIENT GREECE

by Melanie Ann Apel

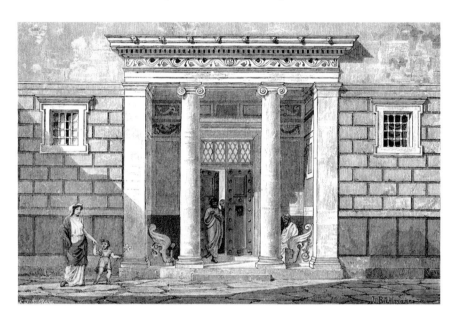

The Family

1   Family was the center of ancient Greek life. Every family provided food and **shelter** for its members. Each member of the family had a **role** in the family and felt that they **belonged.** The older members taught the younger members about the **traditions** of the family. Greeks used the word *oikos* to describe the family **unit.** This unit included relatives, slaves, and the family house. (*Oikos* was also the word for the hearth. A hearth is where cooking was done.) The family's land was passed down from father to son.

Children in Ancient Greece

2   There was great excitement each time a child was born. The birth of a boy was particularly special. Children played with toys like clay, dolls, and balls. By the age of 12 or 13, children were thought of as adults. At this age, they brought their toys to the temple and offered them to the gods.

---

shelter a building or covering that gives protection
unit group

Greek Marriage

[3] Marriage was an important part of ancient Greek culture. Men usually got married in their late twenties or early thirties. Women were usually in their middle to late **teens.** The father chose the people his children married. This was an important job for the father. The future of his family depended on male **heirs.** Once a woman was married, people expected her to have children. It was especially important for her to have boys. Only boys could work and take over their father's land.

Reading Strategy

Ask Questions Why was it important for women in ancient Greece to have boys? Look for the answer in the reading.
  Then ask a question of your own.

Reading Check

1. **Recall facts** When did men usually get married?

2. **Recall facts** Who chose the people that ancient Greeks married?

3. **Compare and contrast** Do you think the **roles** of men and women are different today? Explain.

_____

teens the ages from 13 to 19

heirs people who will inherit property

Women's Role in the Home

4   Men **ruled** ancient Greek society. They were **citizens** and could take part in the government. Women could not. The woman's job was to marry, have children, and take care of the house. Although men ruled life in general, women ruled home life. The women raised the children, made the family's clothing, and managed the household.

Communities

5   Ancient Greeks had a strong sense of community. People viewed their community as an extended family. Within the community people lived in single-family houses or apartment buildings. The ancient Greeks built their homes, public buildings, and temples around the *agora,* or town center. Every day people met in the *agora* and shopped for food or other goods there.

---

ruled controlled

citizens residents of a city or country, especially those with the right to vote

● Reading Comprehension Questions

Think and Discuss

1. **Recall facts** What toys did ancient Greek children play with?

2. **Describe** Describe the **role** of men in ancient Greek society.

3. **Analyze** How were the **roles** of men and women different?

4. **Relate your own experience to the reading** What are the **roles** in your family?

5. **Revisit the Reading Focus Questions** Go back to page 17 and discuss the questions.

Workbook page 37   Independent Practice CD-ROM/Online

Spelling

Words with the Same Sound but Different Spellings

Workbook page 38   Independent Practice CD-ROM/Online

Writing Conventions

Spelling: Contractions; Punctuation: Parentheses

Workbook page 39   Independent Practice CD-ROM/Online

⟳ Connect Readings 1 and 2

You read two stories with the theme of family connections. These activities will help you make connections between the readings.

1. With a partner, use this chart to compare the two readings.

Reading title	What is the text genre?	Who is the reading about?	What is the purpose: to entertain or to inform?
My Korean Name			
Home Life in Ancient Greece			

2. Work with a partner. Answer these questions. Share your answers with the class.

   a. What **traditions** are passed on to younger people in each reading?

   b. What is one **image** you remember from "My Korean Name"? What is one fact you remember from "Home Life in Ancient Greece"?

   c. Do you have more in common with Won Chul or the children of ancient Greece? Explain.

3. **Revisit the Chapter Focus Question** How do families teach us about ourselves? Use examples from "My Korean Name" and "Home Life in Ancient Greece" to answer this question.

Listening and Speaking

Role-play an Interview

You read about different family members in Readings 1 and 2. Role-play an interview with a character from "My Korean Name" or a member of an ancient Greek family.

1. Work with a partner.
   a. Choose a character or person from Reading 1 or Reading 2.
   b. Decide which partner will be the INTERVIEWER. The other partner will be the CHARACTER or PERSON.

2. Prepare for the interview.
   a. INTERVIEWER: Write at least five questions to ask. Look at the **Phrases for Conversation** for help.
   b. CHARACTER/PERSON: Look for information about the character or person in the reading. Look for facts and examples that help you understand him or her.

3. Perform the interview for your class.
   a. INTERVIEWER: Remember to look at your partner as you ask questions. Make sure your partner understands your questions.
   b. CHARACTER/PERSON: Answer each question the way the character or person in the reading might answer it. Use information from the reading, or create an answer based on what you know.

4. Discuss the interviews with your class.
   a. Did the interview help you understand the character or person better?
   b. Did the interviewer ask interesting questions?
   c. Did the character or person seem real?

Phrases for Conversation

Asking Questions

Who (are the people in your family)?
Where (do you live)?
When (do you study)?
What (do you like to do after school)?
Why (do you like to do this)?
How (do you learn new words)?

Reading Fluency

Choral Reading

When you listen to someone read fluently, you learn how to be a more fluent reader.

1. Your teacher will read a paragraph from a reading in this chapter. Follow along silently as your teacher reads. Pay attention to your teacher's pacing (speed), expression, and intonation (level and sound of voice).
2. Your teacher will read the paragraph again.
   a. Read aloud with your teacher and the class.
   b. Try to use your teacher's pacing, expression, and intonation.

Vocabulary Development

Suffixes: -y, -ful, -al

A **suffix** is a letter or a group of letters added to the end of a root word. A suffix changes the meaning of the root word.

Some suffixes make nouns into adjectives. A **noun** is a word that names a person, place, or thing. An **adjective** is a word that describes a noun.

Root Word (Noun)	+ Suffix	Adjective
dust	**-y**	dust**y**
color	**-ful**	color**ful**
tradition	**-al**	tradition**al**

1. Copy the chart. Look at each adjective. Write its root word. Then write the suffix.

Adjective	Root Word	Suffix
1. rainy	rain	-y
2. leaky		
3. care**ful**		
4. help**ful**		
5. music**al**		
6. education**al**		

2. Write a sentence for each word in the chart. Read your sentences to a partner.

   I always carry an umbrella on <u>rainy</u> days.

Vocabulary Log

Workbook page 40

Independent Practice CD-ROM/Online

✓Checkpoint

1. What is a **suffix**?
2. Give an example of a word ending with the suffix **-ful**.

● Grammar

The Simple Present Tense of *be*

Use the simple present tense of **be** to:

1. identify something or someone   She **is** a teacher.
2. describe   The trees **are** tall.
3. talk about location   I **am** in the library.
4. talk about origin   You **are** from Haiti.
5. talk about age   I **am** 17 years old.

Contractions

I am = I'm
he is = he's
she is = she's
it is = it's
you are = you're
we are = we're
they are = they're

The Simple Present Tense of *be*		
subject	***be***	
I	**am**	
He / She / It	**is**	in class now.
You / We / They	**are**	

Practice the Grammar Copy the paragraph. Fill in each space with the correct form of the simple present tense of **be**.

   "My Korean Name" **(1)**_____ an interesting story. It **(2)**_____ about a boy and his grandfather. The boy **(3)**_____ Korean-American. His grandfather **(4)**_____ from Korea. They **(5)**_____ very different. However, they **(6)**_____ part of the same culture.

   My grandmother and I **(7)**_____ very different, too. I **(8)**_____ Mexican-American. My grandmother **(9)**_____ from Mexico. I **(10)**_____ 16 years old. She **(11)**_____ 70. However, we **(12)**_____ good friends.

Build Your Knowledge

For information about complete sentences and sentence types, see pages 408–409.

Use the Grammar Independently

1. Answer these questions with complete sentences.
   - **a.** How old are you?
   - **b.** Where are you from?
   - **c.** Where are you now?

2. Share your sentences with a partner. Tell the class about you and your partner.

   I am 14 years old. Matine is 13 years old.

✓ Checkpoint

1. When do you use the simple present tense of **be**?
2. Give an example of a sentence with the simple present tense of **be**.

Workbook
page 41

Independent Practice
CD-ROM/Online

Grammar

The Present Progressive Tense

Use the **present progressive tense** to talk about something that is happening right now.

Present Progressive Tense		
subject	*be*	**verb +** *ing*
I	**am**	
He / She / It	**is**	eat**ing.**
You / We / They	**are**	

Notes

1. The present progressive is formed with the simple present tense of **be** and a verb with an **-ing** ending.

2. See page 400 to find spelling rules for present progressive verbs.

3. Some verbs are not usually used in the present progressive tense. These verbs include: *hear, know, like, need, remember, see, taste,* and *want.*

Practice the Grammar Copy the paragraph. Fill in each space with the correct form of the present progressive.

   In this unit, we (learn) *are learning* about families. We (**1.** read) _____ stories and informational texts. We (**2.** learn) _____ to **visualize**, too. Right now, I (**3.** think) _____ about the story "My Korean Name." I (**4.** imagine) _____ the first scene between Won Chul and his grandfather. This is what I see in my mind: Won Chul (**5.** bring) _____ tea to his grandfather. His grandfather (**6.** draw) _____ . The grandfather (**7.** take) _____ the tea from Won Chul. Now they (**8.** talk) _____ .

Use the Grammar Independently Write five sentences about things happening in your classroom right now. Read your sentences to a partner.

   My teacher is writing on the board.

Grammar Expansion

Yes/No Questions; Negative Statements

Workbook pages 43–44

Independent Practice CD-ROM/Online

✓Checkpoint

1. When do you use the **present progressive tense**?

2. Give an example of a sentence in the present progressive.

Writing Assignment

Descriptive Writing: Write a Paragraph About a Place

Descriptive writing gives a detailed picture of a person, place, or thing.

Writing Suggestion

See **Milestones Handbook.** pages 393–433

Writing Prompt

Think of your favorite place or a place you visited recently. **Visualize** yourself there. Write a descriptive paragraph about the place. Use adjectives and details to help readers imagine it. Use the present progressive tense to talk about what is happening there right now.

Write Your Descriptive Paragraph

1. **Read the student model.** It will help you understand the assignment.

Student Model

Martin Ortega

A Day at the Beach

I am imagining myself on a sunny beach. The weather is beautiful and warm. I am relaxing and listening to the big waves. Birds are flying over my head. Children are making castles in the sand. Happy families are playing in the ocean. My best friend and I are sitting on our beach towels. We are hungry. We are eating sandwiches and fruit. My friend is taking a bite of a cheese sandwich. Now he is making a face. There is sand in his sandwich! I am laughing! I am having fun at the beach.

Workbook page 45

2. **Prewrite.**

a. Choose a place to write about. You can write about:
  - the beach
  - the market
  - a room in your home
  - a sporting event
  - another place

b. Organize your ideas. Think about these questions and take notes.
  - What do you see in this place?
  - What is happening in this place?
  - What sounds do you hear in this place?

3. **Write your paragraph.** Name the place you are writing about in the first sentence of the paragraph. Include as much information and detail about the place as possible.

4. **Revise.** Reread your paragraph. Revise any ideas that are not clear or complete. Use the **editing and proofreading symbols** on page 419 to help you mark the changes you want to make.

5. **Edit.** Use the **Writing Checklist** to help you find problems and errors.

6. **Read your paragraph to the class.** Don't read the first sentence. See if your classmates can guess the place.

Writing Checklist
1. I used adjectives and details.
2. I indented my paragraph.
3. I capitalized the first word of each sentence.
4. I used the present tense of **be** correctly.
5. I used the present progressive tense correctly.

Writing Support

Spelling
Singular and Plural Nouns

Singular nouns name one person, place, or thing.

Plural nouns name two or more people, places, or things.

- Put an -*s* at the end of most singular nouns to make them plural.
    seagull / seagull**s**
- For nouns that end in *s, x, ch,* or *sh,* add -*es*.
    sandwich / sandwich**es**
- For nouns that end in a consonant + *y,* change *y* to *i* and add -*es*.
    family / famil**ies**
- For nouns that end in *f* or *fe,* change the *f* or *fe* to -*ves*.
    loaf / loa**ves**

Apply Check the plural nouns in your descriptive paragraph. Are they all spelled correctly?

Workbook
pages 46–48

Independent Practice
CD-ROM/Online

Progress Check

How well did you understand this chapter? Try to answer the questions. If necessary, go back to the pages listed for a review.

Skills	Skills Assessment Questions	Pages to Review
Vocabulary From the Readings	What do these words mean? • **annoyed, scared, surprised, traditional, wise** • **belong, role, tradition**	6 16
Academic Vocabulary	What do these academic vocabulary words mean? • **image, visualize** • **conclusion, recognize**	7 14
Reading Strategies	How can **visualizing** help you understand a reading?	7
	Why is it good to **ask questions** when you read?	16
Text Genres	What is the text genre of "My Korean Name"?	8
	What is the text genre of "Home Life in Ancient Greece"?	17
Reading Comprehension	What is "My Korean Name" about?	15
	What is "Home Life in Ancient Greece" about?	21
Literary Element	What is **characterization**? How does an author help readers understand a character?	15
Spelling	Write a sentence for each word: **to, too, two.**	21
Writing Conventions	Give the contractions for the following: **they are, I am, he is.**	21
Listening and Speaking	**Phrases for Conversation** What words can you use for asking questions?	22
Vocabulary Development	What is a **suffix**? Give an example of a word with each of the following suffixes: **-y, -ful, -al.**	23
Grammar	When is the **simple present tense** of **be** used? Give an example of a simple present sentence with **be**.	24
	When is the **present progressive tense** used? Give an example of a present progressive sentence.	25
Writing Support: Spelling	Spell the **plural** form of these words: **book, bus, city, knife.**	27

Assessment Practice

Read this descriptive passage. Then answer Questions 1 through 4.

A Summer Visit

1   Every summer, my cousins come to visit us. Before they arrive, my sister and I have to clean our room. At first, I am always annoyed that I have to clean. Then my mother reminds me that my cousins are staying for two weeks. I imagine the fun we always have. I can see us in the park. We are playing soccer. At home, we are watching movies.

2   This year, my cousins arrive in the afternoon on the train. When Maya gets off the train, I am surprised to see how tall she is. She is one year younger than I am, but now she is a lot taller. I feel short and a little shy as we walk home. When we arrive at our apartment, we first start cooking tamales, a traditional Mexican food. The heat from the stove curls our hair and makes our cheeks red. The chili peppers and onions burn our eyes. Maya and I cry and laugh at the same time. I feel warm inside. Is it the hot stove or the chili peppers? Maybe, but I think it is the warmth of family connections.

1 Read this sentence from paragraph 1.

> At first, I am always annoyed that I have to clean.

What does <u>annoyed</u> mean?

A happy

B surprised

C not happy

D cold

2 Which question can you ask for paragraph 2?

A Who cleans the room?

B What do the cousins do first?

C Where do they go to school?

D When do they play soccer?

3 What words help you visualize the heat in the kitchen?

A short and a little shy

B curls our hair and makes our cheeks red

C cry and laugh

D warmth of family connections

4 What is the main setting of this passage?

A train station

B kitchen

C school

D park

Writing on Demand: Descriptive Paragraph

Write a brief description about a special event or occasion. Give general information about the setting. Include specific information that describes how things look, sound, feel, taste, and smell. Give details about what people are doing. **(20 minutes)**

> **Writing Tip**
>
> Take your time! Read the writing prompt carefully. Take notes on important words in the prompt to help you understand it better.

CHAPTER 2

Objectives

Reading Strategies
Paraphrase; Draw conclusions

Listening and Speaking
Identify, infer, and discuss family traits

Grammar
Learn the simple present tense

Writing
Descriptive writing: Write a paragraph about yourself

Academic Vocabulary

complex	purpose
simplify	inform
	entertain

Academic Content

Traits and genes
Puerto Rico

● **Chapter Focus Question**
What do parents pass on to their children?

Reading 1 **Content:** Science
Informational text: Internet article
Genes: A Family Inheritance

Reading 2 **Literature**
Biography (excerpt)
PRIDE OF PUERTO RICO
by Paul Robert Walker

Genes: A Family Inheritance

● **About the Reading**

You are going to read a science article from an Internet Web site. The article explains how our parents pass on traits, or qualities, to us.

● Build Background

Traits and Genes

Why do you and your mother have the same color eyes? Why does your sister have the same curly hair as your father? Why is everyone in your friend's family tall? Science has the answer. Eye color, hair texture, and height are all **traits.** Traits are special qualities that parents pass on, or give, to their children through genes. Genes are the parts of a cell that determine traits.

Can you curl your tongue into a U-shape? Try it! Tongue-curling is a trait passed on through genes. You can only be a tongue-curler if one or both of your parents are tongue-curlers.

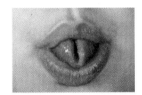

● Use Prior Knowledge

Identify Traits From Parents or Grandparents

Look at Isabela's chart below. What traits did her parents pass on to her?

Isabela	mother	father
short	✓	
blue eyes		✓
brown hair	✓	✓

1. What traits do you share with your parents or grandparents? Make a chart like Isabela's chart. You can list different traits.

2. Discuss your chart with a partner. Look at what Isabela says.

I am short like my mother. I have blue eyes like my father. I have brown hair like my mother and my father.

Key Vocabulary

- ancestor
- environment
- generation
- inheritance
- lifestyle
- personality

● Vocabulary From the Reading

Learn, Practice, and Use Independently

Learn Vocabulary Read each sentence. Look at the **highlighted** word. Think about the context (the words around the highlighted word). Use the context to determine the meaning of the word.

1. My **ancestors** came to America from Russia one hundred years ago.
2. There is too much garbage on our land and in our water. We need to clean up our **environment.**
3. This picture shows three different **generations** in a family. It shows the children, their parents, and their grandparents.
4. John's grandmother died last year. She left him a large **inheritance**, including all of her money and her house.
5. Felicia has a healthy **lifestyle.** She eats well, gets plenty of sleep, and exercises every day.
6. Grace is a nice person. She has a warm, friendly **personality.**

Practice Vocabulary Copy the chart. Work with a partner. Write the vocabulary word for each definition.

Word	Definition
inheritance	something (often money or land) passed down to someone by a relative
1. _____	the air, land, and water that people, plants, and animals live in; surroundings
2. _____	a family member from long ago (older than a person's grandparents)
3. _____	the way a person thinks, feels, and acts
4. _____	the way in which a person lives
5. _____	groups of people born during the same time period

Use Vocabulary Independently Work with a partner. Take turns giving the meaning of three Key Vocabulary words in your own words.

Ancestors are people in your family from a long time ago. My ancestors were from the north of Spain.

Checkpoint

Write a sentence for each Key Vocabulary word.

Vocabulary Log

Workbook page 49

Independent Practice CD-ROM/Online

● Academic Vocabulary

Vocabulary for the Reading Strategy

Word	Explanation	Sample Sentence	Visual Cue
complex *adjective*	having many parts or details that make something hard to understand or work with	This is a **complex** maze, and the mouse can't find the cheese.	
simplify *verb*	to make something less **complex** or less difficult to understand	Let's **simplify** the maze by taking out some of the turns.	

Draw a picture and write a sentence for each word.

● Reading Strategy

Paraphrase

When you **paraphrase**, you put part of a reading in your own words. You take **complex** ideas and **simplify** them. This helps you better understand difficult parts of a reading. Paraphrasing can also help you remember information.

1. Copy the chart.
2. As you read, stop when you come to a difficult sentence. Write the sentence in the "Sentence" column in the chart.
3. You will complete the chart after the reading.

Sentence	My Paraphrase

> **✓Checkpoint**
>
> What does it mean to **paraphrase**? How can you paraphrase while you read?

Vocabulary Log

Workbook page 50

Independent Practice CD-ROM/Online

● Text Genre

Informational Text: Internet Article

"Genes: A Family **Inheritance**" is an **informational text** from an Internet **Web site.** You must be careful when you get information from a Web site. The Web site must be a trusted source. You can usually trust information on Web sites run by museums, universities, and government agencies.

Web Site	
Web address	the location of the Web site on the Internet; for example: www.ca.gov
link	connection to another part of the Web site or another Web address; the words in these links are usually in blue type

Web address —
link —

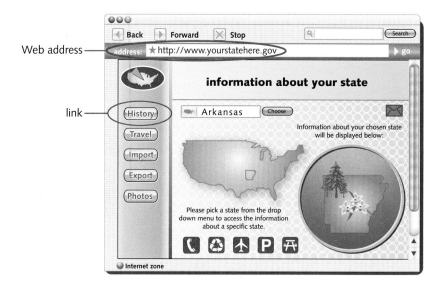

● Reading Focus Questions

As you read, think about these questions.

1. How does this reading connect to the theme of "family connections"?

2. What do you think was the author's purpose for writing "Genes: A Family **Inheritance**"?

3. What kinds of things can a parent pass on to a child?

✓Checkpoint

What is a Web page link?

Workbook
page 51

Independent Practice
CD-ROM/Online

Genes: A Family Inheritance

Your Genes

1   Who are you? The answer has a lot to do with your genes. Genes are the things that **determine** your physical traits—how you look. They also affect your health and the way your body works. Genes are your body's **instruction manual.** Each cell in your body contains about 25,000 to 35,000 genes.

Genes and Inheritance

2   You are the only person with your genes—unless you have an identical twin. (Identical twins have exactly the same genes. That's why they look alike!) Half of your genes are from your mother. The other half are from your father. Your genes were passed down from past **generations** of your family. Your parents received their genes from their parents and so on, right back to your earliest **ancestors.**

identical twins

Genes and Families

3   The people in your family share many genes. Some family traits are easy to see. Maybe you have your mother's eyes or your grandfather's nose. Some traits may skip a **generation.** Some only show up in the men in a family. Genes can be partly responsible for some illnesses such as heart disease and diabetes. These illnesses can run in families.

Reading Strategy

Paraphrase
Paraphrase this sentence. Say what the sentence means in your own words.

Reading Check

1. **Recall facts** What determines the way you look?
2. **Recall facts** Who do your genes come from?
3. **Relate to your own experience** Who do you resemble more, your father or your mother? What traits do you share?

---

determine decide
instruction manual booklet that explains how things work

Family Features

4   You inherit the genes for each of your traits from your parents. You have two copies of each gene. You inherit one copy of each gene from your mother and one from your father. The different versions you receive from your parents are called alleles.

Dominant and Recessive Genes

Reading Strategy

Paraphrase
Paraphrase paragraph 5.

5   Some alleles are stronger than others. Stronger alleles can hide weaker alleles. An allele that hides another is called *dominant*. An allele that is hidden is called *recessive*. For example, the brown-eye allele is dominant. The blue-eye allele is recessive. Someone with brown eyes may also have the allele for blue eyes. However, the brown-eye gene hides the blue-eye gene.

EYE COLOR

brown eyes: dominant

blue eyes: recessive

HAIR TEXTURE

curly hair: dominant

straight hair: recessive

FACIAL FEATURES

dimples: dominant

no dimples: recessive

Hair

6   Some hair color genes are stronger than others. For example, brown-hair genes are usually dominant. Red-hair genes are usually recessive. However, it is possible for two brown-haired parents to have red-haired children. A child who gets two red-hair genes and no brown-hair genes will have red hair.

Height

7   Your height depends partly on your genes. Tall parents usually have tall children. Short parents **tend to** have short children. This is usually true, but not always. Height can also depend on other things, such as whether you have a healthy diet.

Reading Strategy

Paraphrase
Paraphrase paragraph 6.

This is a **Punnett square.** It shows how dominant and recessive traits can be passed on.

Father

		A	a
Mother	A	AA	Aa
	a	Aa	aa

- The letter A stands for a dominant gene. The letter **a** stands for a recessive gene.
- The letters AA mean that a dominant trait is passed on.
- The letters **aa** mean that a recessive trait is passed on.
- The letters Aa stand for a dominant gene and a recessive gene. When a dominant gene and a recessive gene are together, the dominant trait is passed on.

Reading Check

1. **Recall facts** Are brown-hair genes usually dominant or recessive?
2. **Recall facts** Does your height depend only on your genes?
3. **Relate to your own experience** What traits do you think are dominant in your family?

tend to are likely to

Punnett square chart that shows what traits parents might pass down to their children

You Are a Unique Person

8   Your genes have the instructions that made you grow into the person you are. You share particular alleles with many other people. However, no one in the world has exactly the same combination of alleles as you—unless you have an identical twin.

Health, Illness, and Genes

Reading Strategy

Paraphrase
Paraphrase paragraph 9.

9   Genes affect our chances of having some common illnesses, like heart disease, asthma, and diabetes. Genes tell your body how to make all the different **proteins** it needs to survive and grow. A change in a gene may cause a change in a protein. This can affect the way it works in your body. Some genes can be partly responsible for common illnesses. Others can cause **rare** genetic conditions. However there are other factors, such as diet and **lifestyle.** Many genetic and non-genetic factors affect our health. Injury, infection or an unhealthy **lifestyle** can all make you ill.

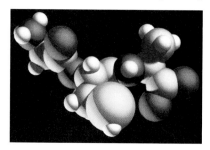

protein

---

proteins molecules in cells that make living things work correctly
rare not common

Genes and Personality

10   Are you **outgoing** or shy? Are you usually happy or unhappy? Are you relaxed or easily stressed? How much of your **personality** is determined by your genes? How much by your **environment**? Scientists believe that both your genes and your **environment** **influence** the person you become.

11   Your genes may affect how **anxious** you are, or how easily you become depressed. In turn, this may affect how you react to certain situations. But genes are far from the whole story. Although identical twins share identical genetic information, they often have very different **personalities.** Your experiences, **upbringing,** and **circumstances** are probably the most important influences on your **personality.**

Reading Strategy

Paraphrase
Paraphrase paragraph 10.

Reading Check

1. **Recall facts** Are genes the only things that influence your **personality**?

2. **Recall facts** What are probably the most important influences on your **personality**?

3. **Make inferences** The writer mentions anxiety and happiness as **personality** traits that are influenced by genes. What other **personality** traits might come from genes?

---

outgoing friendly, active in seeking the company of others

influence change or affect

anxious worried, nervously fearful

upbringing the way that a young person is raised and educated

circumstances conditions that affect someone or something

Apply the Reading Strategy

Paraphrase

Now complete the Reading Strategy chart.

1. Review the **Reading Strategy** on page 33.
2. Look at the different sentences you wrote in the "Sentence" column.
3. Paraphrase each sentence in the "My Paraphrase" column.
4. Share your chart with a partner. Did you get the idea of the sentence right? If not, revise your chart.

Sentence	My Paraphrase
You inherit the genes for each of your traits from your parents.	You get the genes for the way you look from your mother and father.

Academic Vocabulary

Vocabulary for the Reading Comprehension Questions

Word	Explanation	Sample Sentence	Visual Cue
purpose *noun*	a goal, a reason for doing something	The **purpose** of going to school is to learn.	
inform *verb*	to give information about something	Newspapers **inform** people about important events.	
entertain *verb*	to amuse, to give enjoyment	The new TV show will **entertain** you.	

Draw a picture and write a sentence for each word.

Checkpoint

What do the words **purpose, inform,** and **entertain** mean?

Vocabulary
Log

Reading Comprehension Questions

Think and Discuss

1. **Recall facts** How many of your genes are from your mother? How many are from your father?
2. **Recall facts** What are some of the things genes can influence?
3. **Explain** What is the difference between a dominant allele and a recessive allele?
4. **Discuss main ideas** Work with a partner to state the main ideas of this article. Use Key Vocabulary words.
5. **Understand author's purpose** Did the author write the article to inform or entertain readers? Explain.
6. **Discuss your ideas** Do you think your **personality** has been determined more by your genes or your **environment**? Why?
7. **Revisit the Reading Focus Questions** Go back to page 34 and discuss the questions.

Workbook
page 52

Independent Practice
CD-ROM/Online

Text Elements

Visuals and Captions

Many informational readings include **visuals,** such as photographs, illustrations, and charts. Visuals give readers more information about the text.

Visuals usually include **captions.** Captions are words that explain the information in the visuals.

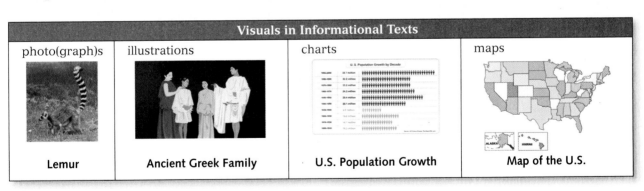

Visuals in Informational Texts			
photo(graph)s	illustrations	charts	maps
Lemur	**Ancient Greek Family**	**U.S. Population Growth**	**Map of the U.S.**

Look at the visuals in "Genes: A Family **Inheritance.**" Find a photo, an illustration, and a chart. Explain how each visual helps you understand the text better.

Checkpoint

1. What are four examples of **visuals**?
2. What is a **caption**?

Workbook
page 53

Independent Practice
CD-ROM/Online

PRIDE OF PUERTO RICO

Roberto Clemente

● About the Reading

You read an informational reading about traits that parents pass on to children in "Genes: A Family **Inheritance**." Now you will read an excerpt from a novel about the lessons a father passed on to his son, Roberto Clemente.

● Build Background

Puerto Rico

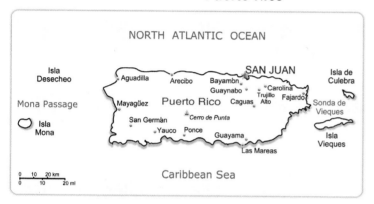

Roberto Clemente was a famous baseball player. He was born in Puerto Rico, an island in the Caribbean Sea. The island is 100 miles long and 35 miles wide. The **ancestors** of Roberto and his father are the Jíbaro people of Puerto Rico. The Jíbaro people were farmers.

Key Vocabulary

hero

honest

proud

serious

truth

● Vocabulary From the Reading

Use Context Clues to Determine Meaning

Read the paragraph. Use the context to determine the meaning of the **highlighted** words. Discuss the meanings with a partner.

My Mother

My mother is the person I admire the most. I have a lot of respect for her. She is my **hero**. She works two day jobs and goes to college at night. My mother is a **serious** person. However, she also knows how to laugh and have fun. My mother is also very **honest**. She never lies. She always tells the **truth**. I am **proud** to be her daughter.

Vocabulary Log

Workbook page 54

Independent Practice CD-ROM/Online

Reading Strategy

Draw Conclusions

Writers do not always tell you everything about the characters and events in a story. Instead, they give you clues or hints. You can use these clues to **draw** (or come to) **conclusions** about details in the story.

1. As you read *Pride of Puerto Rico,* use clues in the text to draw conclusions about the characters.
2. Compare your conclusions with a partner.

Text Genre

Biography

A **biography** is the story of a person's life. It is written by another person. Look for the following features as you read *Pride of Puerto Rico.*

Biography	
events	important things that happened in the person's life
other people	people who were important in the person's life
descriptions	details about the times and places in the person's life

Meet the Author

Paul Robert Walker has been a high school English teacher, a journalist, and a rock musician. Walker says, "We tell stories every day—you and I and everyone we know—stories true, not true, and everywhere in between. Telling stories is part of what makes us human."

Reading Focus Questions

As you read, think about these questions:

1. How does this reading relate to the theme of "family connections"?
2. What do you think was the author's **purpose** for writing *Pride of Puerto Rico?*
3. What kinds of lessons can a parent pass on to a child?

> **✓ Checkpoint**
>
> What does it mean to **draw conclusions**? How can a reader do this?

Workbook
pages 55–56

Independent Practice
CD-ROM/Online

PRIDE OF PUERTO RICO

by Paul Robert Walker

1   "Papá! Papá! Wait for me!"

2   Roberto ran through the cane field to where his father was riding. Don Melchor reached down and helped Roberto climb into the **saddle** behind him. Don Melchor Clemente was very **proud** to own such a fine horse. And Roberto was **proud** to ride behind his father.

3   "So, **Momen**," Don Melchor said as they rode home through the fields, "you come at last. I thought you had forgotten."

4   "Forgive me, Papá," said Roberto. "I was playing baseball."

5   "Ah, and how was the baseball?"

6   Roberto was silent for a moment. He thought again of the weak ground ball that ended the game for Barrio San Antón. He did not want to tell his father of his **failure,** but he knew that Don Melchor Clemente was a man who accepted only the **truth.** Finally he took a deep breath and spoke. "I lost the game, Papá."

Reading Strategy

Draw Conclusions
Is Roberto worried that his father will be disappointed in him? What clues in the text help you draw this conclusion?

---

saddle leather seat used for riding animals, usually horses

Momen Roberto's nickname used by his family

failure effort that does not succeed

7   "Hmmm," Don Melchor said. "That is very interesting." Father and son continued to ride in silence. Then Don Melchor spoke again. "I do not know very much about this baseball," he said. "But I know that there are many players on a team. I do not understand how one small boy can lose the game."

8   "But Papá," said Roberto, "I was our only hope. I could have been the **hero.** Instead I was **the last man out.** The other boys will never ask me to play again."

9   They were out of the sugar fields now and riding slowly down the red dirt road that ran through Barrio San Antón. Don Melchor looked straight ahead as he guided his horse toward home. His words were strong and clear in the evening air.

10   "Momen," he said, "I want you to listen very carefully. Perhaps the other boys will ask you again, perhaps they will not. It does not matter. There are other boys and other teams, but there is only one life. I want you to be a good man. I want you to work hard. And I want you to be a **serious** person."

> **Reading Strategy**

Draw Conclusions
Does Don Melchor think winning a baseball game is important? Does he think it can make someone a good person? What clues in the text help you draw this conclusion?

✔️ **Reading Check**

1. **Recall facts** Was Roberto the hero of the baseball game? Why or why not?

2. **Recall facts** What does Don Melchor want?

3. **Relate to your own experience** Have you ever lost at something important to you? How did you feel?

---

the last man out the baseball player who makes the out that ends a game

11   Don Melchor stopped his horse in the road. They were only a few hundred yards from home now, and Roberto could clearly see the wood and concrete house set in a grove of banana trees. Barrio San Antón lay on the **outskirts** of the city of Carolina. To the west was the capital city of San Juan. To the east were the cloud-covered slopes of El Yunque, barely **visible** in the fading light.

12   "Remember who you are," Don Melchor said. "Remember where you come from. You are Jíbaro. Like me. Like my father and my father's father. We are **proud** people. Hundreds of years ago, we went into the mountains because we refused to serve the Spanish noblemen. In the wilderness, we learned to live off the land. Now, even in the sugar fields, we do not forget what we have learned."

13   "A man must be **honest.** He must work for what he needs. He must share with his brothers who have less. This is the way of the Jíbaro. This is the way of **dignity.**" Don Melchor paused for a moment. It was dark now, and supper was waiting. "Do you understand, my son?" he asked.

Reading Strategy

Draw Conclusions
Do you think Roberto respects his father? What clues in the text help you draw this conclusion?

14   Roberto thought carefully about his father's words. Then he spoke, quietly but **firmly.** "Yes Papá," he said, "I understand."

---

outskirts outlying parts of a city or town away from the center
visible capable of being seen
dignity quality or state of being worthy of respect
firmly in a firm way, with determination

After Reading 2

● Reading Comprehension Questions

Think and Discuss

1. **Recall facts** Why was Roberto late meeting his father?

2. **Explain** Why do you think Roberto was worried about telling his father about the baseball game?

3. **Paraphrase** What kind of man does Don Melchor tell Roberto to be? Use Key Vocabulary words.

4. **Make connections between readings** What does the father in *Pride of Puerto Rico* pass on to his son? How is this like what the grandfather in "My Korean Name" (Chapter 1) passes on to his grandson? How is it different?

5. **Revisit the Reading Focus Questions** Go back to page 43 and discuss the questions.

 Workbook page 57
 Independent Practice CD-ROM/Online

Spelling

Irregular Noun Plurals

Workbook page 58
Independent Practice CD-ROM/Online

Writing Conventions

Punctuation: Identifying Titles of Documents

Workbook page 59
Independent Practice CD-ROM/Online

◔ Connect Readings 1 and 2

You read two readings on the theme of family connections. Use these activities to make connections between the readings.

1. With a partner, use this chart to compare the two readings.

Reading title	What is the text genre?	What is a feature of the text genre?	What visuals does the reading include?	What is the purpose: to entertain or to inform?
Genes: A Family Inheritance				
PRIDE OF PUERTO RICO				

2. Work with a partner. Answer these questions. Share your answers with the class.

   a. According to "Genes: A Family **Inheritance**," what kinds of things are passed on from parents to children?

   b. What do you think Don Melchor passes on to his son in *Pride of Puerto Rico*?

   c. In what ways does Roberto seem like his father? Do you think this is because he has his father's genes or because of Roberto's upbringing?

3. Revisit the Chapter Focus Question What do parents pass on to their children? Use examples from "Genes: A Family **Inheritance**" and *Pride of Puerto Rico* to answer this question.

Listening and Speaking

Identify, Infer, and Discuss Family Traits

Families help make us who we are. Use the ideas in Readings 1 and 2 to discuss the traits of the family members in this photo.

Phrases for Conversation

Giving Opinions

I think . . .
In my opinion . . .
The way I see things . . .
If you ask me . . .
I'm sure that . . .
I (really) feel that . . .

1. Think about these questions.
    a. What physical traits does each person in the photo have?
    b. Do any of the family members have the same traits?
    c. What **personality** traits do you think each person has?
    d. Do you think any of the family members have the same **personality** traits?

2. Discuss your opinions with a partner. Use the **Phrases for Conversation.**

Reading Fluency

Reading Silently

Reading silently helps you learn to read faster. Reading faster helps you become a better reader.

1. Listen to the audio recording of "Genes: A Family **Inheritance.**"

2. Silently reread paragraphs 1–7 on pages 35–37. Read them within four minutes. You will be reading 98 words per minute. Your partner will time your readings.

3. Reread the pages two more times. Each time you reread, try to increase your reading rate.

● Vocabulary Development

Word Origins: Greek Roots

Many English words and word parts come from other languages and cultures. Word parts are often called "roots." Many English words have Greek roots.

Greek Root	Meaning
bio	life
graph	write
ology	study of

English Word	Meaning
biography	the written story of a life
biology	the study of life

Look at these Greek roots and their meanings. Use the roots to figure out the meaning of the words below. Then match the words to the correct picture.

Greek Root	Meaning	Greek Root	Meaning
meter	measure	cent	hundred
cycle	wheel	phone	sound
micro	small	scope	see
tele	far	thermo	heat

1. centimeter
2. thermometer
3. telephone
4. telescope
5. microscope
6. microphone
7. motorcycle

Vocabulary Log

Workbook page 60

Independent Practice CD-ROM/Online

✓ **Checkpoint**

1. What is a **root word**?

2. Give an example of a word that contains one or more roots.

● **Grammar**

The Simple Present Tense

Use the **simple present tense** to:

1. talk about things that happen often.　I **eat** breakfast every morning.

2. talk about things that are true.　I **live** in Florida.

Simple Present Tense	
subject	**verb**
I	**work.**
He / She / It	**works.**
You / We / They	**work.**

Notes

1. When the subject of the sentence is the third person singular *(he, she,* or *it),* add an *-s* to the verb.

2. When the verb ends in *ss, sh, ch, x,* or *z,* add *-es.*

He wash**es** the dishes every night.

3. When the verb ends in a consonant + *y*: Change *y* to *i* and add *-es.*

The bird **flies** south in the winter.

Practice the Grammar

1. Copy the sentences. Choose the correct form of the simple present tense.

　a. Carla and Marcos **live / lives** with their family.

　b. She **learn / learns** about her culture from her family.

　c. Her grandfather **teach / teaches** her about Mexican traditions.

　d. You **cook / cooks** traditional foods.

　e. My mother and father **tell / tells** stories about relatives.

2. Look at the painting on page 51. It shows the artist's family vacation. What kinds of things happen during a typical family vacation for this artist? Complete the sentences below the painting with the simple present tense of the verb given.

Hammerhead Shark on Padre Island
by Carmen Lomas Garza

a. (visit)   The family _____ the beach.
b. (relax)   They _____ in the sun.
c. (bring)   Her mother _____ a cooler of juice drinks.
d. (play)   The children _____ in the water.
e. (run)   The dog _____ on the beach.
f. (catch)   Her uncle _____ fish.
g. (enjoy)   They _____ the day!

Grammar Expansion

Yes/No Questions in the Simple Present Tense; Negative Statements in the Simple Present Tense

Workbook   Independent Practice
pages 63–64   CD-ROM/Online

Use the Grammar Independently

1. Write three sentences about things you do every day.

   I practice the piano every day.

2. Write three sentences about what a family member or a friend does every day.

   My sister rides her bike every day.

✓**Checkpoint**

1. When do you use the **simple present tense**?

2. Give an example of a simple present tense sentence.

Workbook   Independent Practice
pages 61–62   CD-ROM/Online

● Writing Assignment

Descriptive Writing: Write a Paragraph About Yourself

Writing Suggestion

See **Milestones Handbook.** pages 393–433

Writing Prompt

Write a paragraph about yourself. Use descriptive words and details to paint a picture of yourself for the reader. Use the simple present tense.

Write Your Descriptive Paragraph

1. **Read the student model.** It will help you understand the assignment.

Student Model

Marie Pierre

About Me

People often think I am quiet and shy. Then they get to know me. They are surprised. They discover I am not quiet and shy. I have long, brown hair. I have brown eyes. I usually wear blue jeans and a black, white, or brown T-shirt. I wear a comfortable, old pair of white sneakers almost every day. I like to wear hats. However, while my clothes are quiet, my personality is not. I talk a lot, and I talk loudly! I love to laugh and have fun with my friends. My mother says I bring life to any room I walk into. The next time you hear someone shouting or laughing in class, don't be surprised. It's probably me!

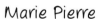
Workbook
page 65

2. **Brainstorm.** Copy the chart. Brainstorm ideas about your appearance (what you look like) and your **personality.**

My Appearance	My Personality
long, red hair	happy

3. **Write your paragraph.**

   a. Start your paragraph with an interesting sentence to get your reader's attention.

   b. Use the information from your chart.

   c. Include as many details and descriptive words as possible. If you need help, use a thesaurus to find descriptive words.

4. **Revise.** Reread your paragraph. Add, delete, or rearrange words or sentences to make your paragraph clearer. Use the **editing and proofreading symbols** on page 419 to help you mark the changes you want to make.

5. **Edit.** Use the **Writing Checklist** to help you find problems and errors.

> **Writing Checklist**
>
> 1. I used many descriptive words and details.
>
> 2. I indented my paragraph.
>
> 3. I capitalized the first word of each sentence.
>
> 4. I used the simple present tense correctly.

 Writing Support

Grammar: Adjectives
Use and Placement

Adjectives are words that describe nouns. Adjectives make your writing more interesting. Look at the difference between a sentence with and without adjectives.

Without adjectives: I like my father's face.

With adjectives: I like my father's **handsome** and **kind** face.

Be careful to put adjectives in the right place in a sentence.

- Adjectives can come before nouns.   I have a **loud** voice.
- Adjectives can also come after the verb **be.**   My voice is **loud.**

Apply Reread your descriptive paragraph. Are the adjectives in the correct place? Can you add more adjectives to make your writing more interesting?

Progress Check

MILESTONES TRACKER

How well did you understand this chapter? Try to answer the questions. If necessary, go back to the pages listed for a review.

Skills	Skills Assessment Questions	Pages to Review
Vocabulary From the Readings	What do these words mean?	
	• ancestor, environment, generation, inheritance, lifestyle, personality	32
	• hero, honest, proud, serious, truth	42
Academic Vocabulary	What do these academic vocabulary words mean?	
	• complex, simplify	33
	• entertain, inform, purpose	40
Reading Strategies	What does **paraphrase** mean?	33
	What does **draw conclusions** mean?	43
Text Genres	What is the text genre of "Genes: A Family **Inheritance**"?	34
	What is the text genre of *Pride of Puerto Rico*?	43
Reading Comprehension	What is "Genes: A Family **Inheritance**" about?	41
	What is *Pride of Puerto Rico* about?	47
Text Elements	How can using **visuals** and **captions** help you understand a reading?	41
Spelling	Give the plural of these nouns: **child, mouse, fish, foot.**	47
Writing Conventions	When do you use quotation marks around the title of a document? When do you use underlining or italics?	47
Listening and Speaking	**Phrases for Conversation** What phrases can you use to give an opinion?	48
Vocabulary Development	How can recognizing roots help you understand unfamiliar words? Give a word with a Greek root.	49
Grammar	When is the **simple present tense** used? Give a sentence with a verb in the simple present tense.	50
Writing Support: Grammar	What is an **adjective**? Where can adjectives be placed in a sentence?	53

Assessment Practice

Read this informational text. Then answer Questions 1 through 4.

Identical Twins

1   Identical twins are two people who share the same parents and the same birthday. They have exactly the same genes. Scientists study identical twins to learn about genes and inheritance.

2   Scientists have studied identical twins' personalities. They have found that most identical twins do not share the same personalities. This shows that people's personalities develop from their environment more than from their genes. However, scientists have also studied identical twins who did not grow up together. Some of these studies show that twins who never knew each other often choose the same jobs, clothes, and hairstyles. So some parts of personality may come from genes.

1 Read this sentence from paragraph 2.

> This shows that people's personalities develop from their environment more than from their genes.

What does <u>environment</u> mean?

A   your body's instruction manual

B   the world around you

C   inheritance

D   lifestyle

2 According to the passage, what is one reason scientists study identical twins?

A   to learn about their jobs

B   to learn about their looks

C   to learn about their ancestors

D   to learn about their personalities

3 What conclusion can you draw from this passage?

A   Identical twins always share personality traits.

B   Identical twins never share personality traits.

C   Identical twins sometimes share personality traits.

D   Scientists do not know if identical twins share personality traits.

4 What was the author's purpose for writing this article?

A   to write about personal feelings

B   to give information to readers

C   to show visuals about twins

D   to entertain readers

Writing on Demand: Descriptive Paragraph

Write a descriptive paragraph about you and a family member. Write about how you are similar to and different from this person. Include descriptions of your looks and your personalities. **(20 minutes)**

Writing Tip

Remember to brainstorm a list of ideas before you begin writing. Then look at your list and circle words and ideas you want to include in your paragraph.

Apply & Extend

Objectives

Listening and Speaking
Deliver a response to literature presentation

Media
Analyze families in television programs

Writing
Write a descriptive essay

Projects

Independent Reading

● Listening and Speaking Workshop
Deliver a Response to Literature Presentation

Topic

Give a response to literature presentation. In a response to literature presentation, you give your ideas about aspects of a reading. In this response to literature presentation, you will tell about the traits and characteristics of two characters you read about in this unit.

1. **Choose Characters to Examine**
   Choose the grandfather and grandson from "My Korean Name" (pages 9–13) or the father and son from *Pride of Puerto Rico* (pages 44–46).

2. **Brainstorm**
   Think about these focus questions and take notes on your ideas. You will answer these questions in your presentation.
   a. What physical and personality traits does each character have?
   b. What adjectives would you use to describe each character? Why?
   c. What family traits do you think these two characters share?

3. **Organize Your Presentation**
   Write your ideas on note cards. Use one note card for each focus question. Use your note cards when you give your presentation.

4. **Plan**
   Find visuals, facts, and examples from the readings to support your ideas. Also include sensory details—what you see, hear, feel, smell.

5. **Practice, Present, and Evaluate**
   a. Practice your presentation.
   b. Present it to the class.
   c. Ask the class for feedback. Use the **Speaking Self-Evaluation** to evaluate your presentation. Use the **Active Listening Evaluation** to evaluate and discuss your classmates' presentations.

Speaking Self-Evaluation

1. My presentation answered the focus questions.

2. I used examples and visuals to answer the questions.

3. I included concrete sensory details.

4. I spoke clearly and loudly enough for people to hear me.

5. I looked at the audience while I spoke.

Active Listening Evaluation

1. You spoke at the right speed—not too slowly and not too quickly.

2. I learned more about the characters from your presentation.

3. I think _____ was the most interesting part of your presentation.

4. I think your presentation needed more information about _____ .

● Media Workshop

Analyze Families on Television

Many television programs focus on families. The families and characters on some of these programs are more realistic than others.

1. With your class, list four or five television programs that focus on families.

2. Choose and watch two of the programs. Think about the following questions as you watch each program. Write down your answers.
   a. What kind of program is it? Is it a comedy? A drama?
   b. Who are the members of the family?
   c. Where does the family live?
   d. Do the characters seem real? Do the things they say seem real? Why or why not?

3. Tell your class which programs you watched. Share your answers to the questions with the class. Talk about other things you noticed about the families on the program.

4. Discuss with your class: Do these television programs show realistic or unrealistic families?

UNIT 1
Apply & Extend

Writing Suggestion

See **Milestones Handbook.**
pages 393–433

Writing Suggestion

Close your eyes and imagine the person. What do you see? Hear? Smell? Touch? Add these ideas to your essay. Use adjectives to describe the person. Sensory details and **images** will help the reader **visualize** the person you are writing about.

● Writing Workshop
Descriptive Essay

In a **descriptive essay**, you describe a person, place, or thing. You use words and details that help readers visualize what you are describing.

Writing Prompt

Write a descriptive essay about someone important to you. This could be a family member, a friend, a teacher, or a neighbor. Describe the person. What makes this person special? Use descriptive words (adjectives) and details that will help readers "see" the person in their mind.

PREWRITE

1. Read the student model on the next page. It will help you understand how to write a descriptive essay.
2. Think about these questions. Take notes on your ideas.
   a. Who will you write about?
   b. What are some of this person's physical traits?
   c. What are some of the person's personality traits?
   d. Why is this person special?

WRITE A DRAFT

1. The first paragraph of the essay is the **introduction.** It tells what the essay is about. In the first sentence, tell who the person is and why he or she is important to you. This is the **topic sentence** of the paragraph. It tells the most important idea of the paragraph.
2. Next, write the **body** of the essay. The body should have one or two paragraphs. In this part of the essay, write about the person's physical and personality traits. Be sure to use adjectives and details to help readers "see" the person.
3. Write the **conclusion.** The **conclusion** is the last paragraph. Use different words to restate why this person is important to you.

Student Model

Title

Introduction

Include descriptive words.

Include sensory details.

Body

Conclusion

Diego Lopez

My Grandmother

My grandmother is the most important person in my life. She always gives me advice, love, and support. I look up to her because she is a very gentle person, but she is also very strong.

I love my grandmother's face. She has many deep wrinkles on her kind face. I think she is beautiful, especially when she smiles. She has a big, bright, happy smile. When she smiles, her soft, brown eyes light up. I also love how my grandmother smells. She uses lotion on her hands. The lotion smells like roses. Every time I smell roses, I think of my grandmother. I think of her warm, loving hugs. Although she is small, she gives big, strong hugs. Whenever I come to her house, she gives me one of these hugs. Then she makes me sweet, delicious hot chocolate. This is our tradition.

My grandmother is also a very strong person. My grandfather died many years ago. She lives alone and takes care of herself. When I have a problem, I always go to her. She is very wise and gives good advice. My grandmother can also be very strict. She wants me to get good grades and to be responsible. I always try my best because I want her to be proud of me.

My grandmother is a very important person to me. I can't imagine life without her. Sometimes I worry that one day she will not be here. However, I know that my grandmother's beautiful smile and her loving hugs will always be in my heart.

REVISE

1. Review your essay. Make sure you used descriptive words and details. You may want to use a thesaurus to find words that will help readers **visualize** the text.

2. Exchange your essay with a partner. Ask your partner to use the **Peer Review Checklist** to review your essay. Your partner will point out errors and give suggestions for making your draft better.

3. Revise your draft. You may want to add or delete sentences. You may want to rearrange sentences to make your ideas clearer.

4. Use the **editing and proofreading symbols** on page 419 to help you mark the changes you want to make.

EDIT

1. Use the **Revising and Editing Checklist** to evaluate your essay.

2. Fix any errors in grammar, spelling, and punctuation.

Peer Review Checklist

1. There is a title.

2. The first paragraph says who the essay is about.

3. There are many details and descriptions in the essay.

4. The essay helps me "see" the person.

5. The essay would be better if _____ .

Revising and Editing Checklist

1. My topic sentence states the main idea.

2. I included details and examples from the reading in the body.

3. I used different words to restate the main idea, or **purpose,** in the **conclusion.**

4. I used capital letters and punctuation correctly.

5. I used the verb **be** correctly.

6. I used the simple present tense correctly.

Build Your Knowledge

See page 428 for information about using a word processing program on a computer. Read and follow the steps for creating a document.

PUBLISH

1. Write your essay in your best handwriting. Be sure it is clear and easy to read. You can also use a computer. If you do, use the spell check and the grammar check.

2. Read your essay to the class. Read clearly and slowly enough so that everyone can understand you. Change the tone and expression of your voice to express the important ideas.

● Projects

Choose one or more of the following projects to explore the theme of family connections further.

PROJECT 1
Write a Paragraph About a "Person of the Year"

1. Choose a member of your family or a friend to win a "Person of the Year" award. For example, you might choose your grandmother for "Grandmother of the Year."
2. Write a paragraph about why this person deserves the award. Give examples of things the person does.
3. Read your paragraph to the class. Answer any questions your classmates may have about the person.

PROJECT 2
Interview a Family Member About Your Family History

1. Interview a member of your family to find out about your family's history. Ask questions like:
   - Where are you from?
   - What is that place like?
   - Are there traits shared by many members of our family?
   - Can you tell me any interesting family stories?
2. Take notes on important information.
3. Report back to your class on the interview.

PROJECT 3
Use the Internet to Learn About a Famous Family

1. Choose a famous family such as the American Kennedy family or the Japanese royal family.
2. Type the family name into an Internet search engine.
3. Take notes on important information you learn.
4. Share your findings with a classmate.

PROJECT 4
Make a Presentation About a Family

1. Choose and read one of the books from the Independent Reading list on page 62.
2. Give a brief summary presentation to the class. Include information on the characters, setting, and plot.
3. Describe one memorable incident from the story in detail.

President John F. Kennedy and his family

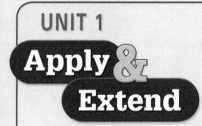

UNIT 1
Apply & Extend

Heinle Reading Library

Pollyanna by Eleanor H. Porter

In a specially adapted version by Mariana Leighton

Pollyanna is all alone in the world, except for her Aunt Polly. But Aunt Polly doesn't understand children. Will she ever understand her niece?

● Independent Reading

Explore the theme of family connections further by reading one or more of these books.

Pride of Puerto Rico: The Life of Roberto Clemente by Robert Paul Walker, Odyssey Classics, 1991.

This is the story of Roberto Clemente, an all-time great baseball player. The story begins with Clemente's childhood in Puerto Rico. Then it tells about Clemente's years in the major leagues, the prejudices he faced, and the ways he helped young people in his native Puerto Rico.

In My Family/En mi familia by Carmen Lomas Garza, Children's Book Press, 2000.

Lomas uses colorful paintings and brief narratives to share her childhood memories of growing up in a loving family within a traditional Mexican-American community.

Under the Royal Palms: A Childhood Growing Up in Cuba by Alma Flor Ada, Atheneum, 1998.

In these ten stories, the author tells of growing up in Cuba in the 1940s. The author's family lived with aunts, uncles, and cousins in a large, shared family home. The stories focus on the importance of extended family and are filled with humor and wisdom. The book has black-and-white photographs of the author and her family.

Kira-Kira by Cynthia Kadohata, Aladdin, 2006.

The Takeshima family moves to Georgia in the 1950s. This Japanese-American family faces many problems there, including poverty, sickness, and prejudice. Despite their struggles, the Takeshimas find a way to create a loving home.

Child of the Owl by Laurence Yep, Laurel Leaf, 1978.

This story is set in 1960 in San Francisco's Chinatown. It focuses on Casey, a Chinese-American teen. From her grandmother, Casey learns about her Chinese heritage and the mother she never knew. She slowly begins to understand and value her Chinese heritage.

Milestones to Achievement

Writing: Revise and Edit

Read this rough draft of a student's descriptive paragraph, which may contain errors.

An Afternoon with My Brother

(1) My friends are going to the mall. (2) I want to go with them. (3) Instead I am watching my brother run around the house. (4) He is yelling loudly. (5) He is pretending to be a fire engine. (6) I decide to play with him. (7) I say, "Help! My cat is stuck in a tree." (8) My brother rushes over. (9) I point to the sofa. (10) He climbs on the sofa. (11) He saves my toy cat. (12) I clap my hand. (13) "Thank you, Mr. Firefighter," I say. (14) My brother looks proud. (15) He also looks hot and thirsty. (16) I suggest we get a snack. (17) I pour us some apple juice. (18) Then I cut sandwiches in the shape of fire engines. (19) My brother is happy. (20) He jumps up and down. (21) I smile. (22) I am happy, too. (23) Today was nice after all.

1 Which topic sentence should you insert before sentence 1?

A Today, I babysit my little brother.

B Today, I babysits my little brother.

C Today, I am babysitting my little brother.

D Today, I am babysit my little brother.

2 How can you change sentence 12 to correct it?

A I clap my handz.

B I clap my hands.

C I clap my handes.

D I clap my handves.

3 Which sentence can you add before sentence 14?

A "You are my proud!"

B "You are my ancestor!"

C "You are my wise!"

D "You are my hero!"

4 Which change will make sentence 23 more interesting?

A Today was great after all.

B Today was rainy after all.

C Today was sunny after all.

D Today was terrible after all.

Writing on Demand: Descriptive Paragraph

Write a descriptive paragraph about spending time with someone younger than you. Describe the setting, people, and events that are happening. Use details in your descriptions. **(20 minutes)**

> **Writing Tip**
> Begin your paragraph with an interesting topic sentence. You should get the reader's attention and tell the reader what the paragraph is going to be about.

● Reading

Read this description of a famous family. Then answer Questions 1 through 8.

A Family of Leaders

1   The Kennedy family is one of the most famous families in the United States. The leader of the Kennedy family was Rose Fitzgerald Kennedy. Rose was a mother and grandmother of leaders, and she was a powerful leader herself.

2   Rose Fitzgerald Kennedy was born in 1890 in Boston, Massachusetts. She was very musical and studied piano. She also went to college. Unlike most young women her age, Rose organized groups to talk about leaders and problems in the world. At age 24, she married Joseph P. Kennedy. He became the U.S. ambassador to Great Britain. Rose helped her husband with this job. Then they began a family. They had nine children. Many of them were strong leaders.

3   Joseph P. Kennedy Jr. was Rose's oldest son. He was a leader in the army. He died during World War II. John F. Kennedy, Rose's second son, was a U.S. senator from Massachusetts. Then he became the president of the United States. He was very popular. Sadly, after a few years as president, he was shot and killed. Robert F. Kennedy, John's younger brother, became the U.S. attorney general, the main lawyer for the whole country. He fought for all people to have the same rights. Robert wanted to be president, too. Unfortunately, he was shot and killed before the election. Eunice Kennedy Shriver, Rose's daughter, is a leader who works to improve the lives of people with intellectual disabilities. Her work led to the establishment of the Special Olympics. Edward Kennedy is Rose's youngest child. He is a U.S. senator from Massachusetts.

4   Rose's grandchildren continue her tradition of proud leadership. Caroline Kennedy Schlossberg, John Kennedy's daughter, writes about leadership. She also fights for people's rights. Maria Shriver, daughter of Eunice Kennedy Shriver, also writes about leaders. She is married to Arnold Schwarzenegger, the famous actor who became California's governor. Now she helps her husband lead California.

5   From parents to children to grandchildren, each generation of the Kennedy family has strong leaders. Why is this family so powerful? Is it in their genes? Is leadership part of a family's inheritance? If you look at the Kennedy family, maybe it is.

1 Read this sentence from paragraph 2.

> Rose organized groups to talk about leaders and problems in the world.

What does <u>organized</u> mean?

A   told

B   put together, arranged

C   inherited

D   informed

2 Who was Rose's second son?

A   Arnold Schwarzenegger

B   Robert Kennedy

C   Joseph Kennedy Jr.

D   John F. Kennedy

3 Based on the details in paragraph 2, what conclusion can you draw about Rose?

A   She was a silly young woman.

B   She was a serious, kind, and wise young woman.

C   She was not very intelligent, but she was kind.

D   She was a scared young woman.

4 What is a question you can ask about paragraph 3?

A   What kind of leaders are Rose's children?

B   What kind of leader was Rose's husband?

C   What kind of leaders are Rose's grandchildren?

D   What kind of leader was Rose?

5 How can you paraphrase this sentence?

> Rose's grandchildren continue her tradition of proud leadership.

A   Rose's grandchildren have children.

B   Rose's grandchildren celebrate family traditions.

C   Rose's grandchildren are also leaders.

D   Rose has many grandchildren.

6 What examples does the author give to support this sentence?

> Rose's grandchildren continue her tradition of proud leadership.

A   Rose organized groups, taught poor children, and helped her husband lead.

B   Joseph, John, Robert, Eunice, and Edward were strong leaders.

C   Eunice Kennedy Shriver leads the Special Olympics.

D   Caroline Kennedy Schlossberg and Maria Shriver write about leadership and work as leaders in their communities.

7 In the word <u>musical</u>, what do you call the letters <u>al</u>?

A   a Greek root

B   a suffix

C   a prefix

D   the simple present

8 What is the author's purpose for this passage?

A   to inform

B   to entertain

C   to tell readers that they should do something

D   to write about the author's personal feelings and thoughts

Discovery

Explore the Theme

1. What does the word **discovery** mean?
2. Describe the kinds of discoveries you see in the pictures.

Theme Activity

   Work with a small group. Make a list of famous discoveries. Do you know who made each discovery? If so, include this information on your list. If not, look up the information on the Internet or in your library.

Discovery	Who discovered it?
fire	cavemen

CHAPTER 1

Objectives

Reading Strategies

Make predictions; Talk through a problem

Listening and Speaking

Discover what you have in common with a classmate

Grammar

Learn to use subject and object pronouns; Learn to use imperatives

Writing

Creative writing: Write a scene from a play

Academic Vocabulary

revise	perspective
confirm	reflect

Academic Content

Native Americans
Circumference

● **Chapter Focus Question**

How can discoveries teach us about ourselves and the world around us?

Reading 1 **Literature**

Play

THE STRONGEST ONE

by Joseph Bruchac

Reading 2 **Content: Math**

Textbook

Circles and Circumference

THE STRONGEST ONE

● **About the Reading**

You are going to read a traditional Native American story. At the end of the story, the main character makes a discovery about himself.

● Build Background

Native Americans and Oral Tradition

Native Americans are the first people of America. They were living in America when Christopher Columbus arrived in 1492.

The Strongest One is a Native American story. Native American stories were originally passed down from generation to generation through oral tradition. "Oral" means "spoken." Oral tradition helps other generations learn about the world and themselves.

Look at the picture and describe what you see happening between the generations.

● Use Prior Knowledge

Think About a Self-Discovery of Your Own

Think about a time when you made a discovery about yourself. For example, did you discover that you have a talent, ability, or quality? With a partner, answer these questions.

1. What was the self-discovery?
2. How did you make the self-discovery?
   a. Did you speak to someone? If so, whom? How did this help you make the discovery?
   b. Did you go somewhere? If so, where? How did this help you make the discovery?
   c. Did you do something? If so, what? How did this help you make the discovery?
3. How did the self-discovery change the way you think about yourself?

Key Vocabulary
burn
ceremony (singular) / ceremonies (plural)
freeze
located
melt
relative
wonder

✓ **Checkpoint**

1. Name three kinds of **ceremonies**.
2. Name three kinds of **relatives**.

● **Vocabulary From the Reading**
Learn, Practice, and Use Independently

Learn Vocabulary Read the paragraph. Use the context to determine the meanings of the **highlighted** words. Discuss the meanings with a partner.

   Last month, my sister got married. She had a small party at our house after the wedding **ceremony.** She invited only a few friends and our family members. I wanted to do something special for our **relatives,** so I made the cake. However, I put the cake in the oven and forgot about it. My mother walked into the kitchen and said, "Did you **burn** something?" I had to make the cake all over again. The second time, the cake came out great. However, it was a really hot day. The cake started to **melt** in the heat. So I put it in the freezer to keep it cold. I didn't think it would **freeze** so quickly, but an hour later it was frozen! Fortunately, there is a good bakery **located** near our house. I picked up a cake on the way to the wedding. I **wonder** if I will ever bake a cake again!

Practice Vocabulary Work with a partner. Answer the questions.

1. What was the last **ceremony** you went to?
2. Who is your favorite **relative**?
3. What is something you can **burn**?
4. What is something you can **freeze**?
5. What is something that **melts** in hot weather?
6. Where is your school **located**?
7. What is something you **wonder** about?

Use Vocabulary Independently Write one sentence for each Key Vocabulary word. Read your sentences to a partner.

Vocabulary Log

Workbook page 69

Independent Practice CD-ROM/Online

● Academic Vocabulary

Vocabulary for the Reading Strategy

Word	Explanation	Sample Sentence	Visual Cue
revise *verb*	to change something already written in order to make corrections or to improve it	When I write an essay, I **revise** it until the essay is perfect.	
confirm *verb*	to make sure something is right by checking it	I think I spelled this word correctly. But I will look in the dictionary to **confirm** it.	

Draw a picture and write a sentence for each word.

● Reading Strategy

Make Predictions

When you **make predictions,** you try to guess what will happen next. Try to make predictions as you read a story or play. Making predictions helps you to be a more active reader.

1. As you read each scene of *The Strongest One,* imagine what will happen next. Look for clues to help you make and **revise** predictions.

2. Copy the chart. Write your predictions in the "My Predictions" column of the chart.

3. After you read the play, you will reread each scene and your predictions. You will **confirm** your predictions.

	My Predictions	What Actually Happened
Scene 1		
Scene 2		
Scene 3		

√Checkpoint

1. What is a **prediction**?
2. How do you make a prediction?

Vocabulary Log

Workbook page 70

Independent Practice CD-ROM/Online

● **Text Genre**

Play

The Strongest One is a **play.** Plays are written to be presented to an audience by a group of actors. Each actor pretends to be one of the characters in the play. Look for these features of a play as you read *The Strongest One.*

Play	
scene	a part of a play that happens in one place and at one time
act	one or more scenes that make up a major part of the play; short plays sometimes have only scenes and no acts
narrator	the character who describes the scene and gives background information
stage directions	notes within the play that tell characters how to speak and move

● **Meet the Author**

Joseph Bruchac is a Native American writer and storyteller. He has written many books of traditional Native American stories. Bruchac says he writes down these stories so that they will not be forgotten. He loves being a storyteller and says, "The special skills necessary for being a storyteller are really very simple. Those basic skills are to listen, to observe, to remember, and to share."

✓ **Checkpoint**

1. Who is the **narrator** of a play?

2. What do you call the notes within the play that tell characters how to speak and move?

● **Reading Focus Questions**

As you read, think about these questions.

1. How does the reading relate to the theme of "discovery"?

2. What do you think was the author's purpose for writing *The Strongest One*?

3. What kinds of discoveries can people make about themselves?

Workbook
page 71

Independent Practice
CD-ROM/Online

THE STRONGEST ONE

by Joseph Bruchac

Prologue

1   *The Strongest One* is a play based on a Zuni folktale. The Zunis are Native Americans of the Southwest who live in pueblos. Pueblos are compact villages made up of **multistoried** buildings of **adobe brick** and **beams**. The Zunis' pueblo, which is also called Zuni, is **located** in present-day New Mexico. The Zunis and the other pueblo people developed a way to grow their crops in the dry lands of the Southwest and are regarded as very **sophisticated** farmers.

Zuni pueblo

2   The Zuni people are famous for their **ceremonies,** which are designed to give thanks to all living things.

Scene 1: Inside the Ants' Hole

*On a darkened stage, the ants **crouch** together.*

3   **Narrator:** Little Red Ant lived in a hole under the Big Rock with all of its **relatives.** It often **wondered** about the world outside: Who in the world was the strongest one of all? One day in late spring Little Red Ant decided to find out.

4   **Little Red Ant:** I am going to find out who is strongest. I am going to go outside and walk around.

5   **Second Ant:** Be careful! We ants are very small. Something might step on you.

6   **Third Ant:** Yes, we are the smallest and weakest ones of all.

7   **Fourth Ant:** Be careful, it is dangerous out there!

8   **Little Red Ant:** I will be careful. I will find out who is strongest. Maybe the strongest one can teach us how to be stronger.

Reading Strategy

Make Predictions
Who do you think Little Red Ant will find out is strongest? Why do you think this?

✓
Reading Check

1. **Recall facts** What is this play based on?

2. **Compare and contrast** How is Little Red Ant different from the other ants?

---

multistoried having many floors or levels

adobe building material made of clay and straw hardened in the sunlight

brick block of hard clay used as building material

beams long, thick pieces of wood used to make buildings

sophisticated ahead in development, complex

crouch bend down at the knees

Scene 2: The Mesa

Ant walks back and forth onstage.

9   **Narrator:** So Little Red Ant went outside and began to walk around. But as Little Red Ant walked, the snow began to fall.

Snow walks onstage.

10   **Little Red Ant:** Ah, my feet are cold. This snow makes everything **freeze.** Snow must be the strongest. I will ask. Snow, are you the strongest of all?

11   **Snow:** No, I am not the strongest.

Reading Strategy

Make Predictions Do you think Sun is the strongest one? Why or why not?

12   **Little Red Ant:** Who is stronger than you?

13   **Snow:** Sun is stronger. When Sun shines on me, I **melt** away. Here it comes!

As Sun walks onstage, Snow hurries offstage.

14   **Little Red Ant:** Ah, Sun must be the strongest. I will ask. Sun, are you the strongest of all?

15   **Sun:** No, I am not the strongest.

16   **Little Red Ant:** Who is stronger than you?

17   **Sun:** Wind is stronger. Wind blows the clouds across the sky and covers my face. Here it comes!

As Wind comes onstage, Sun hurries offstage with face covered in hands.

18   **Little Red Ant:** Wind must be the strongest. I will ask. Wind, are you the strongest of all?

19   **Wind:** No, I am not the strongest.

20   **Little Red Ant:** Who is stronger than you?

21   **Wind:** House is stronger. When I come to House, I cannot move it. I must go **elsewhere.** Here it comes!

As House walks onstage, Wind hurries offstage.

---

mesa flat-topped hill with steeply sloping sides

elsewhere some other place

22   **Little Red Ant:** House must be the strongest. I will ask. House, are you the strongest of all?

23   **House:** No, I am not the strongest.

24   **Little Red Ant:** Who is stronger than you?

25   **House:** Mouse is stronger. Mouse comes and **gnaws** holes in me. Here it comes!

As Mouse walks onstage, House hurries offstage.

26   **Little Red Ant:** Mouse must be the strongest. I will ask. Mouse, are you the strongest of all?

27   **Mouse:** No, I am not the strongest.

28   **Little Red Ant:** Who is stronger than you?

29   **Mouse:** Cat is stronger. Cat chases me, and if Cat catches me, Cat will eat me. Here it comes!

*As Cat walks onstage, Mouse hurries offstage, **squeaking**.*

30   **Little Red Ant:** Cat must be the strongest. I will ask. Cat, are you the strongest of all?

31   **Cat:** No, I am not the strongest.

32   **Little Red Ant:** Who is stronger than you?

33   **Cat:** Stick is stronger. When Stick hits me, I run away. Here it comes!

As Stick walks onstage, Cat hurries offstage, meowing.

34   **Little Red Ant:** Stick must be the strongest. I will ask. Stick, are you the strongest of all?

35   **Stick:** No, I am not the strongest.

Reading Strategy

Make Predictions
Who do you think Stick will say is the strongest?

✔
Reading Check

1. **Recall facts** Who does House say is the strongest?

2. **Recall facts** What does Mouse do when Cat walks on stage?

3. **Understand cause and effect** Why does Cat say that Stick is stronger?

---

gnaws bites at something over a period of time
squeaking making a sharp, high-pitched sound that is not very loud

Little Red Ant: Who is stronger than you?

Stick: Fire is stronger. When I am put into Fire, Fire **burns** me up! Here it comes!

As Fire walks onstage, Stick hurries offstage.

Little Red Ant: Fire must be the strongest. I will ask. Fire, are you the strongest of all?

Fire: No, I am not the strongest.

Little Red Ant: Who is stronger than you?

Fire: Water is stronger. When Water is poured on me, it kills me. Here it comes!

Reading Strategy

Make Predictions Do you think Fire will say it is the strongest? If not, who do you think Fire will say is the strongest?

As Water walks onstage, Fire hurries offstage.

42   **Little Red Ant:** Water must be the strongest. I will ask. Water, are you the strongest of all?

43   **Water:** No, I am not the strongest.

44   **Little Red Ant:** Who is stronger than you?

45   **Water:** Deer is stronger. When Deer comes, Deer drinks me. Here it comes!

As Deer walks onstage, Water hurries offstage.

46   **Little Red Ant:** Deer must be the strongest. I will ask. Deer, are you the strongest of all?

47   **Deer:** No, I am not the strongest.

48   **Little Red Ant:** Who is stronger than you?

49   **Deer: Arrow** is stronger. When **Arrow** strikes me, it can kill me. Here it comes!

---

arrow long thin piece of wood, metal, or plastic with a point at one end and feathers at the other

*As Arrow walks onstage, Deer runs offstage with **leaping bounds.***

50   **Little Red Ant:** Arrow must be the strongest. I will ask. Arrow, are you the strongest of all?

51   **Arrow:** No, I am not the strongest.

52   **Little Red Ant:** Who is stronger than you?

53   **Arrow:** Big Rock is stronger. When I am shot from the bow and I hit Big Rock, Big Rock breaks me.

54   **Little Red Ant:** Do you mean the same Big Rock where the Red Ants live?

55   **Arrow:** Yes, that is Big Rock. Here it comes!

As Big Rock walks onstage, Arrow runs offstage.

56   **Little Red Ant:** Big Rock must be the strongest. I will ask. Big Rock, are you the strongest of all?

57   **Big Rock:** No, I am not the strongest.

58   **Little Red Ant:** Who is stronger than you?

59   **Big Rock:** You are stronger. Every day you and the other Red Ants come and carry little pieces of me away. Someday I will be all gone.

Scene 3: The Ants' Hole

60   **Narrator:** So Little Red Ant went back home and spoke to the ant people.

The ants crouch together on the darkened stage.

61   **Second Ant:** Little Red Ant has returned.

62   **Third Ant:** He has come back alive!

63   **Fourth Ant:** Tell us about what you have learned. Who is the strongest of all?

64   **Little Red Ant:** I have learned that everything is stronger than something else. And even though we ants are small, in some ways we are the strongest of all.

---

leaping jumping in the air
bounds long jumps

Reading Strategy

Make Predictions
What do you think Little Red Ant will say he has learned?

Reading Check

1. **Recall facts** What do the Red Ants do to Big Rock?
2. **Recall facts** Where does the final scene take place?
3. **Paraphrase** What has Little Red Ant learned?

● Apply the Reading Strategy

Make Predictions

Now complete the Reading Strategy chart.

1. Review the **Reading Strategy** on page 71.
2. Review the predictions you made for each scene.
3. Reread each scene. **Confirm** whether or not each prediction was correct.
4. Complete the "What Actually Happened" column.

	My Predictions	What Actually Happened
Scene 1	The other ants are going to convince him not to go.	The other ants warned him not to go but didn't try to stop him. Little Red Ant left the ant hole.
Scene 2		
Scene 3		

● Academic Vocabulary

Vocabulary for the Reading Comprehension Questions

Word	Explanation	Sample Sentence	Visual Cue
perspective *noun*	a way of seeing things	Some people see two faces in the picture. Others see a vase. It depends on your **perspective**.	
reflect *verb*	to think deeply about	The old man liked to **reflect** on the things he had done in his life.	

Draw a picture and write a sentence for each word.

✓ Checkpoint

1. Tell a partner your **perspective** of the picture.
2. What do you **reflect** on before you fall asleep?

Vocabulary
Log

Reading Comprehension Questions

Think and Discuss

1. **Recall facts** Name at least six of the animals and things Little Red Ant speaks to.

2. **Identify** What is the setting of both the first and the last scenes of the play?

3. **Retell** Retell the plot of the story in your own words. Use at least three Key Vocabulary words.

4. **Recognize author's use of language** What are some phrases the different characters repeat throughout the play? Why do you think the author repeats these phrases so often?

5. **Understand perspective** Why does each character have a different idea about who is the strongest one?

6. **Reflect** At the end of the play, Little Red Ant makes a discovery about himself. Tell about a discovery you have made about yourself.

7. **Revisit the Reading Focus Questions** Go back to page 72 and discuss the questions.

Workbook
page 72

Independent Practice
CD-ROM/Online

Literary Element

Dialogue

All plays have **dialogue.** Dialogue is the words characters say to each other. In a play, the dialogue appears next to the name of the character. Dialogue gives important information about the characters and the events of the play.

1. Look at items **a** and **b**. Which is a dialogue?

    a. Maria asked Bill for his dictionary. He gave it to her.

    b. Maria: Can I borrow your dictionary?

    Bill: Sure. Here you go.

2. Read the paragraph. With a partner, write a dialogue based on the paragraph. Then act out your dialogue.

    Marta really wanted Sara to go to the party. Sara didn't want to go to the party. She was tired and wanted to stay home. Marta tried to convince Sara to go. She gave many reasons why Sara should go. Nothing worked. Finally Marta reminded Sara that her best friend would be at the party. Then Sara agreed to go.

> ✓ **Checkpoint**
>
> What is **dialogue**? Explain in your own words.

Workbook
page 73

Independent Practice
CD-ROM/Online

Circles and Circumference

● About the Reading

In *The Strongest One*, you read a play about self-discovery. Now you will read a section from a textbook. It is about an important math discovery about circles.

● Build Background

Math Symbols

A **symbol** is something that represents something else. There are many math symbols. In this reading you will read about one of them. The symbol is called *pi*. It looks like this: π

Can you identify the following math symbols?

Symbol	What the Symbol Means
+	plus
−	
=	
×	
÷	

● Vocabulary From the Reading

Use Context Clues to Determine Meaning

Use the context of each sentence to determine the meaning of the **highlighted** word. Discuss the meanings with a small group.

1. Wheels, CDs, oranges, and the sun all have a **circular** shape.
2. Pizza **consists** of dough with tomato sauce and cheese on top.
3. The **distance** between Boston and New York City is about 250 miles.
4. The **ratio** of teachers to students in my school is 1 to 20. There is one teacher for every 20 students.

Checkpoint

Draw pictures of two **circular** objects. Your partner will guess what they are.

Vocabulary Log

Workbook page 74

Independent Practice CD-ROM/Online

● Reading Strategy
Talk Through a Problem

When you do math, **talk through the problem.** Putting the problem in your own words helps break down the information. This helps you understand the problem. Use this strategy for the problems in "Circles and Circumference."

1. Describe the problem in your own words to a partner.
2. Describe how to solve the problem.
3. Try to solve the problem out loud.

● Text Genre
Textbook

"Circles and Circumference" is from a math **textbook.** The purpose of a textbook is to teach students about a specific school subject. As you read, look for these common features of math textbooks.

Math Textbook	
chapter headings	names of chapters; they tell you what the chapter is about; they also help you find information in the book
words in bold	heavy, dark type for important words; sometimes these words are also in color
examples	problems with answers given to help students understand how to solve the problem
exercises	problems for students to solve by themselves

● Reading Focus Questions

As you read, think about these questions.

1. How does this reading relate to the theme of "discovery"?
2. What do you think was the author's purpose for writing "Circles and Circumference"?
3. What discoveries have been made about circles and circumference? Why are these important discoveries?

> **√Checkpoint**
> 1. How do you **talk through a problem**?
> 2. How do **examples** in math textbooks help you?

Vocabulary Log

Workbook pages 75–76

Independent Practice CD-ROM/Online

Content
Math

Circles and Circumference

Prologue

The ancient Greeks discovered many of the mathematical **principles** and **formulas** that we use today. For example, they made an important discovery about circles. They discovered that the circumference—the **distance** around any circle—is about 3.14 (or $\frac{22}{7}$) times longer than the **distance** across the circle. They named this number *pi*. The symbol for *pi* is π.

What You'll Learn:
1. To identify parts of a circle
2. To find circumference

. . . And Why
To find the circumference of an archery target, as in Example 3.

New Vocabulary ● circle ● radius ● chord ● diameter ● circumference

 Identifying Parts of a Circle

A circle is a shape with points that are all the same **distance** from the center. A circle is named after its center point.

Reading Math
Radii (RAY dee eye) is the plural of *radius*.

A **radius** is a **segment** that connects the center to the circle.

A **chord** is a segment that has both endpoints on the circle.

A **diameter** is a chord that passes through the center of a circle.

Center

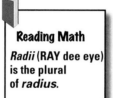

Reading Strategy

Talk through a problem Rephrase question **1a** in your own words. Explain out loud what you need to do to solve the problem. Try to solve it out loud.

1 | **Example** Identifying Parts of a Circle

a. List the radii shown in circle P.
Answer: The radii are $\overline{PA}$, $\overline{PB}$, $\overline{PC}$, and $\overline{PD}$.

b. List the chords shown in circle P.
Answer: The chords are $\overline{AB}$, $\overline{BC}$, $\overline{CD}$, $\overline{DA}$, $\overline{AC}$, and $\overline{BD}$.

 List the diameters shown in circle P.

In Example 1, the diameter $\overline{AC}$ **consists** of two radii $\overline{PA}$ and $\overline{PC}$. So, the length of a diameter of a circle is twice the length of a radius. Of course, this means that the radius is half the length of a diameter!

---

principles basic truths or assumptions
formulas rules expressed in symbols
segment piece

Ferris wheel

▷ **Reading Strategy**

2 **Example** Finding Radius and Diameter

Amusement Parks The diameter of a **Ferris wheel** is 250 feet. How long is its radius?

$r = \frac{1}{2} \times 250$ ← **The radius is half the diameter.**

$\quad = 125$ ← **Simplify.**

Answer: The radius of the Ferris wheel is 125 feet.

✓ **Check Understanding** ❷ Find the unknown length for a circle with the given **dimension**.

Reading Strategy

Talk Through a Problem Rephrase the problem in your own words. Explain out loud what you need to do to solve the problem. Try to solve the problem out loud.

Objective 2 Finding Circumference

The **distance** around a circle is its **circumference**. The **ratio** of the circumference C of a circle to its diameter d is the same for *every* circle. The symbol π (read "pi") represents this **ratio**. So, $\pi = \frac{C}{d}$.

Two ways of expressing π are 3.14 and $\frac{22}{7}$. Use $\frac{22}{7}$ when measurements are a multiple of 7 or use fractions. You can also use the π key on a calculator.

Key Concepts **Circumference of a Circle**

$C = \pi d$

$C = 2\pi r$

---

3 **Example** Finding the Circumference of a Circle

Archery An archery target has a circle with a 48-inch diameter. Find the circumference of a target to the nearest inch.

$C = \pi d$ ← **Use the formula for the circumference of a circle.**

$\quad = 3.14 \times 48$ ← **Substitute 48 for d and 3.14 for π.**

$\quad = 150.72$ ← **Multiply.**

Answer: The circumference of a target is about 151 inches.

✓ **Check Understanding** ❸ Find the circumference of a circle with a diameter of 5.8 centimeters. **Round** to the nearest centimeter.

✓ **Reading Check**

1. **Recall facts** What is the **distance** around a circle called?

2. **Recall facts** What are two ways of expressing *pi*?

3. **Paraphrase** Explain the first paragraph of "Objective 2: Finding Circumference" in your own words.

Ferris wheel amusement park ride **consisting** of a large wheel with chairs rising to the top as the wheel goes around

dimension measurement of something in one direction

round lower or raise a figure to the nearest whole number

List each of the following for circle Q.

Example 1   **1.** three radii   **2.** one diameter   **3.** two chords

Example 2   Find the unknown length for a circle with the given dimension.

4. $r = 35$ mi, $d = $ ▨   **5.** $d = 6.8$ yd, $r = $ ▨

6. $r = 18$ ft, $d = $ ▨   **7.** $d = 0.25$ km, $r = $ ▨

Find the circumference of each circle. Round to the nearest unit. Exercise 8 has been started for you.

Example 3

8. 12 m

$C = \pi d$
$C = 3.14(12)$

9. 5 in.

10. 23 ft

11. 9 cm

12. 30 m

13. 14 mi

14. Tanks A **circular** water tank has a radius of 3.9 meters. What is the circumference of the tank?

15. Writing in Math A pebble got stuck in a bicycle's tire and left a mark in the track made by the tire every 69 inches. Explain how you would find the circumference of the tire.

16. Bicycles The diameter of a bicycle wheel is 3 feet. How far will the bicycle travel when the wheel makes one full turn?

Test Prep

17. What is the radius of a circle with a diameter of 8.46 kilometers? Round to the nearest hundredth kilometer.

18. The diameter of a circle is 2.24 centimeters. What is the circumference? Use 3.14 for pi and round to the nearest hundredth.

19. The circumference of a circle is 11 meters. What is the diameter of the circle to the nearest tenth meter?

20. The circumference of a circle is 48 inches. Suppose the radius of the circle is doubled. What is the new circumference to the nearest inch?

Talk Through a Problem Rephrase question **14** in your own words. Explain out loud what you need to do to solve the problem. Try to solve it out loud.

● Reading Comprehension Questions

Think and Discuss

1. **Recall facts** Who discovered *pi*?

2. **Identify** What is the relationship between a radius and a diameter?

3. **Explain** How do you find the circumference of a circle?

4. **Identify text features** What are some of the text features that helped you understand the reading?

5. **Apply** Find a **circular** object in your classroom. Measure the diameter of the object and find its circumference.

6. **Revisit the Reading Focus Questions** Go back to page 81 and discuss the questions.

Workbook
page 77

Independent Practice
CD-ROM/Online

Spelling

Apostrophes with Possessive Nouns

Workbook
page 78

Independent Practice
CD-ROM/Online

Writing Conventions

Punctuation: Colons in Plays, Speeches, and Interviews

Workbook
page 79

Independent Practice
CD-ROM/Online

↺ Connect Readings 1 and 2

You read two readings on the theme of discovery. Use these activities to make connections between the readings.

1. With a partner, use this chart to compare the readings.

Reading title	What is the text genre?	What are two features of the text genre?	What is the purpose of the reading?	Which reading was more difficult for you? Why?
THE STRONGEST ONE				
Circles and Circumference				

2. Work with a partner and answer these questions. Share your answers with the class.

   a. What number did the Greeks discover? What did Little Red Ant discover?

   b. Which do you think is more important: personal discoveries or scientific discoveries? Why?

3. **Revisit the Chapter Focus Question** How can discoveries teach us about ourselves and the world around us? Use examples from *The Strongest One* and "Circles and Circumference" to answer this question.

● Listening and Speaking

Discover What You Have in Common with a Classmate

Phrases for Conversation

Asking for Repetition

What?
Pardon me?
Excuse me?
What did you say?
Can you repeat that, please?
I'm sorry. Could you repeat that?

There are many kinds of discoveries. Some discoveries are mathematical or scientific, like the ancient Greeks' discovery of π. Other discoveries are personal, like Little Red Ant's discovery in *The Strongest One*.

It can be exciting to make discoveries about yourself and others. In this activity, you will discover things you have in common with a classmate.

1. Work with a partner. Ask and answer questions to find out more about each other. Take turns. Here are some topics you can ask about, with sample questions.

    a. likes / dislikes (Do you like Italian food?)

    b. sports (Do you play baseball?)

    c. leisure time activities (Do you go to the movies often?)

    d. school (Are you good at math?)

    e. languages (What languages do you speak?)

2. Take notes on your partner's answers. If you don't understand something your partner tells you, use one of the phrases from the **Phrases for Conversation** box.

3. Continue talking until you find five things you have in common.

4. Report back to your class on what you discovered.

● Reading Fluency

Readers' Theater

Participating in Readers' Theater can help you build fluency and learn to read aloud with expression.

1. With a group, choose a scene from *The Strongest One*. Assign characters to each student in the group.

2. Rehearse your scene several times.

3. Perform the scene for your class. Be sure to read your part with appropriate expression and intonation.

● Vocabulary Development

Word Origins: Latin Root Words

Many English words contain **root words** from other languages, such as Latin. (Latin was the language of ancient Rome.) Recognizing root words can help you improve your vocabulary. When you recognize a root word in an unfamiliar word, you can often figure out the meaning of the word.

Look at the Latin root words and their meaning. Then look for these root words in the words from this chapter.

Latin Root Word	Meaning	English Words from This Chapter
circ	round, around	**circle**, **circumference**, **circular**
dict	speak	**prediction**
form	form, shape	**formula**
frac	break	**fraction**
loc	place	located

Each word in the list below includes one of the Latin roots from the chart above. Write the word. Underline the root in each word. Then use the root to match the word to the correct definition.

Words

1. uniform
2. fracture
3. dictation
4. local
5. circus

Definitions

a. to crack or break

b. having always the same form

c. a traveling show of performers and trained animals who usually perform in a round tent surrounded by seats

d. relating to a city or town but not to a larger area

e. the act of one person speaking while another person writes down exactly what is said

✓Checkpoint

1. How can recognizing **root words** help you understand unfamiliar vocabulary?

2. Give an example of a **Latin root word.** What is an English word that is based on this root?

Vocabulary Log   Workbook page 80   Independent Practice CD-ROM/Online

● **Grammar**

Subject and Object Pronouns

The subject of a sentence can be a noun. A **subject pronoun** takes the place of a noun in the subject position.

(subject noun)   (subject pronoun)

Mike had lunch with Jessica. = He had lunch with Jessica.

The object of a sentence can be a noun. An **object pronoun** takes the place of a noun in the object position.

(object noun)   (object pronoun)

Mike had lunch with Jessica. = Mike had lunch with her.

Subject Pronouns		Object Pronouns	
I	**I** know him.	**me**	He knows **me**.
you	**You** need her.	**you**	She needs **you**.
he	**He** asks you.	**him**	You ask **him**.
she	**She** visits us.	**her**	We visit **her**.
it	**It** likes her.	**it**	She likes **it**.
we	**We** see them.	**us**	They see **us**.
they	**They** help you.	**them**	You help **them**.

Grammar Expansion

Compound Subjects and Objects

Workbook pages 82   Independent Practice CD-ROM/Online

Practice the Grammar Rewrite the sentences. Replace the underlined words with a subject or object pronoun.

1. <u>Mrs. Munez</u> read the play *The Strongest One* out loud today.
2. I liked listening to <u>Mrs. Munez</u> read.
3. The play is by <u>Joseph Bruchac</u>.
4. <u>The play</u> is about a character named Little Red Ant.
5. <u>His **relatives**</u> are worried about him.
6. He learns a lesson from <u>a mouse, a cat, and a deer</u>.

Use the Grammar Independently

Think of a story from a book or movie. Write a few sentences about the story. Use subject and object pronouns.

✓ Checkpoint

1. What can a **subject pronoun** take the place of? What can an **object pronoun** take the place of?

2. Write a sentence that has a subject noun and object noun. Rewrite the sentence with a subject pronoun and an object pronoun.

Workbook page 81   Independent Practice CD-ROM/Online

Grammar

Imperatives

Use imperatives to:

1. give instructions.	**Turn** right at the corner.
2. give warnings.	**Be** careful!
3. give advice.	**Eat** lots of vegetables.
4. give orders.	**Sit** down now.
5. make requests.	Please **open** the window.

Imperatives		
affirmative	**negative**	
base form of verb	*don't*	base form of verb
Open the door.	Don't open the door.	

Notes

1. The implied subject of imperative statements is always "you," but the subject is not included in the statement.

2. Add "please" to the beginning or the end of an imperative to make a request sound more polite.

   Please shut the door.   Shut the door, please.

3. Strong warnings or orders end with an exclamation point (!).

   Watch out!   Shut the door!

Practice the Grammar Use the words provided to give advice to Little Red Ant. Use affirmative or negative imperatives.

   go / far from the ant hole.   Don't go far from the ant hole.

1. talk / to dangerous animals	4. forget / us
2. stay away / for a long time	5. be / brave
3. tell / us about your adventure	6. come / home soon

Use the Grammar Independently Give imperatives for each situation.

1. I want to get a good grade in this class.

   Take good notes every day in class.

2. I want to make a lot of friends.

3. Tomorrow is my mother's birthday.

Grammar Expansion

Polite Imperatives

Workbook pages 84   Independent Practice CD-ROM/Online

✓**Checkpoint**

1. Give three examples of when to use **imperatives**.

2. Explain the steps for cooking a simple recipe. Use imperatives for each step.

Workbook page 83

Independent Practice CD-ROM/Online

● **Writing Assignment**

Creative Writing: Write a Scene from a Play

Writing Suggestion

See **Milestones Handbook.** pages 393–433

Writing Prompt

Reread the play *The Strongest One*. Imagine what other animals or things Little Red Ant could speak with. Write a scene to add to the play. Include pronouns and imperatives in your dialogue.

Write Your Scene from a Play

1. **Read the student model.** It will help you understand how to write your scene.

Student Model

Little Red Ant: Look! There's a whale. Whales are big and strong. Whales must be the strongest. I will ask. Come here please, whale. Are you the strongest of all?

Whale: No, I am not the strongest.

Little Red Ant: Who is stronger than you?

Whale: Fisherman is stronger. When he comes out to sea in his boat, he catches me. Here he comes!

As Fisherman walks onstage, Whale swims offstage.

Little Red Ant: Ah, fisherman must be the strongest. Fisherman, please answer this question. Are you the strongest of all?

Fisherman: No, I am not the strongest.

Little Red Ant: Who is stronger than you?

Fisherman: Storm is stronger than I am. When it comes, it tips my boat over.

Workbook
page 85

2. **Brainstorm.** Think of at least three new characters for Little Red Ant to speak with. Think of reasons why each character might think the next character is stronger.

3. **Write your scene from a play.**

   a. Write each character's name before the line the character speaks.

   b. Follow the general pattern of the dialogue from *The Strongest One.*

   c. Remember to include pronouns and imperatives.

4. **Revise.** Reread your scene and dialogue. **Revise** your dialogue if you see any problems in it.

   Use the **editing and proofreading symbols** on page 419 to help you mark the changes you want to make.

5. **Edit.** Use the **Writing Checklist** to help you find problems and errors.

6. **Perform your scene from a play.**

   a. Choose a role to play. Ask classmates to play the other roles.

   b. Practice the scene a few times.

   c. Perform the scene for your class. Be sure to speak clearly and use appropriate pace, intonation, and expression as you perform your part.

> ## Writing Checklist
>
> **1.** I wrote each character's name before the words he or she speaks.
>
> **2.** I followed the general style of the dialogue in *The Strongest One.*
>
> **3.** I included pronouns and imperatives in my dialogue.
>
> **4.** I used correct capitalization in my scene.

Writing Support

Mechanics

Capitalization

Make sure to use correct **capitalization** in your writing.

1. Use a capital letter for the first letter of the first word of a sentence.

   Good writers capitalize words correctly.

2. Use a capital letter for the pronoun **I**.

   My mother and **I** went shopping yesterday.

3. Use capital letters for proper nouns. These include names of people, holidays, days of the week, and months.

   We celebrate **T**hanksgiving the third **T**hursday of every **N**ovember.

4. Use capital letters for the first word and all important words in the titles of books, stories, poems, articles, and plays.

   The Strongest One   *A Wrinkle in Time*

Apply Read your scene from a play. Be sure you used capital letters correctly.

Workbook
pages 86–88

Independent Practice
CD-ROM/Online

UNIT 2 • CHAPTER 1

Progress Check

How well did you understand this chapter? Try to answer the questions. If necessary, go back to the pages listed for a review.

Skills	Skills Assessment Questions	Pages to Review
Vocabulary From the Readings	What do these words mean?	
	• burn, ceremony, freeze, located, melt, relative, wonder	70
	• circular, consist, distance, ratio	80
Academic Vocabulary	What do these academic vocabulary words mean?	
	• revise, confirm	71
	• perspective, reflect	78
Reading Strategies	How can you make predictions while reading?	71
	How can you talk through a problem?	81
Text Genres	What is the text genre of *The Strongest One*?	72
	What is the text genre of "Circles and Circumference"?	81
Reading Comprehension	What is *The Strongest One* about?	79
	What is "Circles and Circumference" about?	85
Literary Element	What is **dialogue?**	79
Spelling	Give the **possessive form** of these words: ants, storyteller, Joseph, authors.	85
Writing Conventions	In a play, when is a **colon** used?	85
Listening and Speaking	**Phrases for Conversation** What phrases can you use to ask for repetition?	86
Vocabulary Development	Give an example of a word with a **Latin root word.**	87
Grammar	Give an example of a sentence with both a **subject pronoun** and an **object pronoun.**	88
	Give an example of an **imperative** sentence.	89
Writing Support: Mechanics	Give three examples of when to use capital letters in writing.	91

Assessment Practice

Read this scene from a play. Then answer Questions 1 through 4.

The Ants and the Cricket

cricket

1   **Narrator:** One hot summer, a cricket sat in a tree. He sang happily. Below him, a long line of ants worked hard. They carried food to their home.

2   **Cricket:** Hello, Ants! Why are you working? Why don't you rest?

3   **Ant One:** We can't rest. We must get food for the long winter.

4   **Cricket:** But winter is far away. We can get food later. I want to sing!

5   **Narrator:** The ants worked all summer. Then winter came. The cricket started to freeze. He was hungry. He went to the ant's hill.

6   **Cricket:** *(knocking)* Please let me in! I'm freezing and I'm hungry!

7   **Ant One:** Oh, Cricket! We wondered when you would come.

8   **Ant Two:** What were you doing all summer while we worked?

9   **Cricket:** I was singing. I was making the world happy with my singing.

10   **Ants:** Singing? Well, now try dancing!

---

1 What does <u>freeze</u> mean in line 5?

> **The cricket started to freeze.**

A get hungry
B get tired from work
C cry
D get very cold

2 Which lines show a dialogue?

A 1–3
B 2–4
C 3–5
D 5–7

3 What do you predict will happen at the end of this text?

A The cricket will warm up.
B The cricket will keep singing.
C The ants will take the cricket in.
D The ants will close their door.

4 What is the genre of this text?

A descriptive paragraph
B informational text
C play
D short story

Writing on Demand: Scene from a Play

Write the next scene for this play. What does the cricket say and do? What do the ants say and do? **(20 minutes)**

> **Writing Tip**
> Reread your draft. Circle or underline parts that don't make sense or that you want to change.

CHAPTER 2

Objectives

Reading Strategies

Understand sequence of events; Recognize mood in poetry

Listening and Speaking

Give a news report about a discovery

Grammar

Learn the simple past tense of **be**; Learn the simple past tense

Writing

Creative writing: Write a historical fiction paragraph

Academic Vocabulary

locate	evaluate
focus	speculate

Academic Content

Scientific discoveries
Libraries

● Chapter Focus Question

How do discoveries change us and change our world?

Reading 1 **Content:** Science

Informational text
Eureka!
by Richard Platt

Reading 2 **Literature**

Poetry
The First Book
by Rita Dove
Unfolding Bud
by Naoshi Koriyama
Application
A Library Card Application

Eureka!

● About the Reading

You are going to read an informational text. It is about great scientific discoveries.

● Build Background

Words from Other Languages

The title of Reading 1 is "Eureka!" "Eureka" is an English word that comes from the Greek word *heureka*. It means "I have found it!" "Eureka" is the official motto of the State of California. It refers to the discovery of gold in California.

Many common words in English come from Greek. For example: *airplane, athlete, history, microscope, music,* and *oxygen*.

Other common words come from Latin. For example: *item, agenda, solar, lunar,* and *justice*.

What words do you know in English that come from other languages?

● Use Prior Knowledge

Discover What You Know About Science

"Eureka!" gives information about different science topics. What do you know about these topics?

1. Make a **KWL** (**K**now, **W**ant to Know, **L**earned) chart like the one below.
2. In the first column, write what you know about the topics.
3. In the second column, write what you want to know.
4. After you read "Eureka!" write what you learned about these topics in your KWL chart.

KWL CHART		
	What I *Know*	**What I *Want* to Know**	**What I *Learned***
gravity		Who discovered it?	
germs			
penicillin			

Key Vocabulary

- equal
- germ
- mixture
- pure
- realize
- remind

● Vocabulary From the Reading

Learn, Practice, and Use Independently

Learn Vocabulary Read each sentence. Look at the **highlighted** word. Use the context (the words around the highlighted word) to determine the meaning of the word.

1. Two plus two is **equal** to three plus one.
2. Doctors wash their hands with soap and water before surgery to kill **germs.**
3. The sauce is a **mixture** of cream, flour, and chicken broth.
4. I don't like meat in my rice. I like **pure** rice.
5. Your music is too loud. Do you **realize** that it's keeping me awake?
6. I sometimes forget my sister's birthday, but my mother always **reminds** me.

Practice Vocabulary Complete each sentence with a Key Vocabulary word.

1. The stones are _____ in weight.

4. He cleans his house to get rid of _____ .

2. He leaves notes to _____ himself to do things.

5. She likes cooking with a _____ of spices.

3. Does he _____ that he has a problem?

6. His shirt is made of _____ cotton.

✓ Checkpoint

Write a sentence for each Key Vocabulary word.

Use Vocabulary Independently Explain three Key Vocabulary words to your partner. Your partner guesses the words.

Vocabulary
Log

Workbook
page 89

Independent Practice
CD-ROM/Online

Academic Vocabulary

Vocabulary for the Reading Strategy

Word	Explanation	Sample Sentence	Visual Cue
locate *verb*	to find by searching	Using a map, the man **located** the buried treasure.	
focus *verb*	to center one's attention	Good tennis players always **focus** on the ball.	

Draw a picture and write a sentence for each word.

Reading Strategy

Understand Sequence of Events

   The **sequence of events** is the order in which events happen. Understanding the sequence of events can help you remember what you read. It can also help you **locate** and **focus** on the most important information.

1. As you read each section of "Eureka!," identify the sequence of events.

2. Look at the graphic organizer. After the reading, you will write the events for each section in the correct sequence.

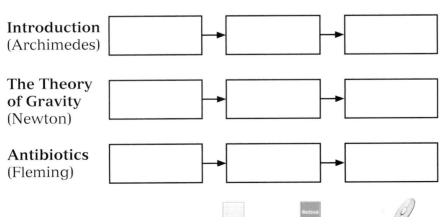

Introduction (Archimedes)

The Theory of Gravity (Newton)

Antibiotics (Fleming)

Vocabulary Log

Workbook page 90

Independent Practice CD-ROM/Online

> ✓**Checkpoint**
>
> 1. What is a **sequence of events**?
> 2. Explain the sequence of events in a story you know.

● Text Genre

Informational Text

"Eureka!" is an **informational text.** The purpose of an informational text is to give the reader information about a topic. The chart below shows features of informational texts. Look for these features as you read "Eureka!"

Informational Text	
facts	true information about the topic
problems	the author presents a problem
solutions	the author explains how a problem was solved
actual events	things that really happened
dates	when important events happened

● Meet the Author

Richard Platt was born in England in 1953. His father was an engineer and his mother was a pharmacist. He studied both engineering and art in college. Platt has worked as a photographer, a teacher, and a writer. He is the author of more than 50 books for young readers.

● Reading Focus Questions

As you read, think about these questions.

1. How does this reading relate to the theme of "discovery"?
2. What do you think was the author's purpose for writing "Eureka!"?
3. What kinds of things happen before moments of discovery?

✓Checkpoint

1. What is the purpose of an **informational text**?
2. Name two features of an informational text.

Workbook
page 91

Independent Practice
CD-ROM/Online

Eureka!
by Richard Platt

Introduction

1   Nothing is as exciting as a sudden scientific discovery. Sometimes engineers and inventors solve a difficult problem with one smart idea. We call these sudden **leaps** of **knowledge** "eureka moments" after the shout of Archimedes (287–212 BCE). Archimedes was a Greek **genius.** He made a discovery while taking a bath. The discovery made him jump up from his bath. He then ran through his city, shouting "Eureka!" Eureka is Greek for "I've got it!"

2   Archimedes had been thinking over a difficult problem. The king gave a **craftsman** a block of gold to make a crown. When it was finished, the crown weighed the same as the block. However, the king believed the craftsman switched some gold for cheaper silver. The king told Archimedes to prove this or die!

Archimedes

3   Archimedes was thinking about the problem as he stepped into his bathtub. The bath **overflowed.** This made him **realize** something. The amount of water flowing out was **equal** to the space his body took up.

---

leaps jumps forward

knowledge understanding of something and the ability to use that understanding through study and experience

genius person of great intelligence and ability

craftsman worker who makes something with great skill

overflowed spilled over or beyond the edges of something

Reading Strategy

Understand Sequence of Events Which event happened first?

- Archimedes jumped up from his bath and yelled "Eureka!"
- The king told Archimedes to prove that some of the gold had been replaced with silver.

✓ Reading Check

1. **Recall facts** What did the King want Archimedes to prove?

2. **Cause and effect** What caused Archimedes to jump up from his bath and shout "Eureka"?

Describe Archimedes and his surroundings.

4   Archimedes could use the same idea to test the crown. Was the crown **pure** gold? If it was, it would take up the same space as a gold block of **equal** weight. But silver is lighter than gold. So a block of silver the same weight as the **pure** gold block would be twice as big. So a crown of mixed **metals** would take up more room than a **pure** gold one. To test the crown, he lowered a block of **pure** gold that was the same weight as the crown into a bowl of water. Next he changed the block for the crown. If it was **pure** gold, the water would fill the bowl exactly as before. But as he lowered in the crown, some water overflowed.

5   This proved that the crown was a **mixture** of gold and silver. The clever test saved Archimedes' life!

6   Most scientists do not have so much **at stake.** However, they still feel great excitement when they find what they have been searching for.

7   The following stories are memorable because they make science and technology interesting and help **remind** us of great discoveries.

Reading Strategy

Understand Sequence of Events Explain how Archimedes tested the crown. Tell the steps in sequence.

---

metals basic metallic elements, usually hard, shiny substances that can be melted, shaped, and cut to make things

at stake being risked

The Theory of Gravity

8   When we drop something, why does it always fall down? Why does it never fall in another direction? English scientist Isaac Newton (1642–1727) was the first to explain this. He discovered gravity. Gravity is the **force** that gives objects weight and keeps our feet on the ground. Newton's discovery of gravity is the most famous eureka moment of all time.

Newton's Eureka Moment

9   One summer day in 1665, Newton was deep in thought. Suddenly he saw an apple fall from a tree. He wondered, "Why does the apple never fall up or to the side?" He guessed that some **invisible** force must be pulling the apple toward the center of the Earth.

Reading Strategy

Understand Sequence of Events Explain the events that happened to Newton on a summer day in 1665.

EUREKA! Newton **realized** that this force does not just draw together apples and Earth but all objects. It could even explain why Earth **orbits** the Sun instead of flying off into **outer space**. He called this force "gravity."

Taking It Further

10   Newton thought more about gravity and explained its characteristics in his universal theory of gravity. This showed that the force of gravity pulls all objects together. Its strength is **determined** by the mass and distance of the object. Objects that have more mass have greater gravitational pull. Objects that are further apart have less gravitational pull.

Reading Check

1. **Recall facts** In what year did Newton discover gravity?

2. **Explain** What is gravity?

3. **Distinguish fact from opinion** In paragraph 8, the author says "Newton's discovery of gravity is the most famous eureka moment of all time." Is this a fact or an opinion? Explain.

---

theory mathematical or logical explanation for something, especially one that has been repeatedly tested and is widely accepted
force source of power or energy
invisible not able to be seen
orbits goes around
outer space area of space immediately outside of Earth's atmosphere
determined decided

Antibiotics

11   Alexander Fleming (1881–1955) was a Scottish doctor. He worked as an army doctor in World War I. He saw many soldiers die from common infections. After the war, Fleming searched for new drugs to kill **germs** and stop **infections.** A lucky accident in 1928 led him to a great medical discovery. He discovered one of medicine's most powerful **weapons** in the fight against **germs:** penicillin.

Fleming's Eureka Moment

12   Alexander Fleming was a brilliant scientist. However, he was messy in the laboratory. In 1928 he went away on vacation. He left behind a pile of failed experiments. These experiments were jelly-filled glass dishes. He grew **bacteria** in these dishes. When Fleming returned, he went to wash the dishes. He noticed that one dish was different from the others. A **patch** of **mold** had grown on it. A circle of jelly around the mold was free of bacteria.

Reading Strategy

Understand Sequence of Events Describe the sequence of events in 1928 that led to Fleming's discovery.

> **EUREKA!** Fleming **realized** that the mold was killing the bacteria. He thought that it might be a way of curing the diseases that bacteria cause.

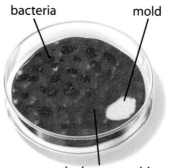

bacteria   mold

no growth close to mold

A glass dish in which bacteria are growing. The dish includes a patch of *penicillium* mold. No bacteria are growing around the mold.

----

antibiotics types of medicines that are effective in killing bacteria

infections diseases or sicknesses caused by germs or viruses

weapons tools used to harm or kill

bacteria tiny living things, **germs**

patch small area or piece of something that stands out from the rest

mold fungus that grows on materials

From Mold to Drug

13   Fleming studied the mold (which he called *penicillium*) for a while. However, he did not turn it into a drug. Instead, he simply wrote about his discovery in the *British Journal of Experimental Pathology*.

14   In 1939, an English professor named Howard Florey (1898–1968) and his assistant, Ernst Chain (1906–1979), read the article. They tested the mold on eight mice. Each of the mice was infected with a **deadly** disease. Only the four treated with the *penicillium* survived.

Nobel Prize Winners

15   Florey and Chain's lab became a penicillin factory. Soon the United States government started to **manufacture** large quantities of penicillin. Penicillin was the first of a group of drugs called antibiotics. It proved to be a lifesaver. For this discovery Fleming, Florey, and Chain shared the Nobel Prize in Medicine in 1945.

Reading Strategy

Understand Sequence of Events List these events in the sequence that they happened.

- Florey and Chain tested the mold on mice.

- Fleming, Florey, and Chain won the Nobel Prize in Medicine.

- Fleming wrote about his discovery in a journal.

Reading Check

1. **Recall facts** What is the name of the group of drugs penicillin belongs to?

2. **Make an inference** Why did the four mice Florey and Chain treated with penicillin survive?

deadly likely to cause death

manufacture make something for sale using machinery

● Apply the Reading Strategy
Understand Sequence of Events

Now complete the Reading Strategy graphic organizer.

1. Review the **Reading Strategy** on page 97.
2. Copy the graphic organizer.
3. Reread each section of the reading. Identify the sequence of events in each section.
4. Write the events in sequence in the boxes. Add as many boxes as you need.

Introduction (Archimedes)

| The King told Archimedes to prove that the crown wasn't pure gold. | → | Archimedes thought about the problem as he was stepping into a bath. | → | |

The Theory of Gravity (Newton)

| | → | | → | |

Antibiotics (Fleming)

| | → | | → | |

● Academic Vocabulary
Vocabulary for the Reading Comprehension Questions

Word	Explanation	Sample Sentence	Visual Cue
evaluate *verb*	to study and make a judgment about	The teacher will use a form to **evaluate** the student presentations.	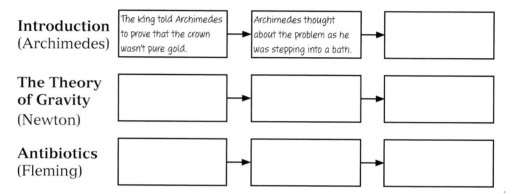
speculate *verb*	to think about and make a guess	I don't know what career I will have after college. However, I like to **speculate** about it.	

Draw a picture and write a sentence for each word.

✓Checkpoint

Explain **evaluate** and **speculate** in your own words.

Reading Comprehension Questions

Think and Discuss

1. **Recall facts** What phrase does the author use to describe sudden leaps of knowledge?
2. **Identify cause and effect** What experience caused Alexander Fleming to search for drugs to stop infections?
3. **Explain** What is gravity? Explain it in your own words.
4. **Use visual elements** How did looking at the picture on page 102 help you understand Fleming's discovery?
5. **Evaluate** Which of the discoveries in this reading do you think is the most important? Why?
6. **Speculate** What discoveries do you think people will make in the next 10 years? In the next 100 years?
7. **Revisit the Reading Focus Questions** Go back to page 98 and discuss the questions.

Workbook
page 92

Independent Practice
CD-ROM/Online

Text Elements

Writing Style and Tone

    Writing style is the author's way of using language. This includes word choice, grammar, sentence length, and punctuation.

    Tone is the author's attitude toward his or her subject and audience. Some examples of tone are formal, informal, serious, sad, and funny. Authors create tone through their writing style.

Examples from the Reading	Style	Tone
The King told Archimedes to prove this or die! The clever test saved Archimedes' life!	use of exclamation points	creates a tone of danger, excitement, and enthusiasm
But silver is lighter than gold. **So** a block of silver the same weight as the **pure** gold block would be twice as big.	beginning sentences with *But* and *So*	creates an informal tone

1. Choose and skim a reading from Unit 1 or 2.
2. Identify the tone. Find the elements of the writer's style that create this tone.
3. Read a paragraph of the reading out loud. Be sure to use the correct expression to match the tone of the reading.

✓Checkpoint

What is **writing style**? What is **tone**? Explain in your own words.

Workbook
page 93

Independent Practice
CD-ROM/Online

The First Book
Unfolding Bud
A Library Card Application

● About the Readings

In "Eureka!" you read an informational text about moments of great scientific discovery. Now you will read two poems about the discovery of literature. Then you will fill out an application for a library card so that you can discover some new literature yourself.

● Build Background
Libraries

You can make discoveries of your own every day through books. With books you can discover new worlds and ideas. The best place to find books on every subject is the library. The only thing you need to borrow books from your public library is a library card. Library cards are free. You can fill out an application for a library card at your local library or on the Internet.

● Vocabulary From the Reading
Use Context Clues to Determine Meaning

Use the context of the sentences to determine the meanings of the **highlighted** words. Discuss the meanings with a partner.

1. The child is only two years old. I'm **amazed** that she can already speak!
2. I stepped on some gum. It is on the **bottom** of my shoe.
3. Look at that **bud**. Soon it will become a beautiful flower.
4. I learned Spanish **gradually.** It took me four or five years to speak it very well.

Key Vocabulary

amazed

bottom

bud

gradually

✓Checkpoint

1. Name two things that make you feel **amazed.**
2. What is at the **bottom** of your backpack?

Vocabulary Log

Workbook page 94

Independent Practice CD-ROM/Online

Reading Strategy

Recognize Mood in Poetry

Mood is the feeling the writer wants the reader to get from a reading. When you read a poem, think about the words the poet chose and the mood these words create. Recognizing the mood of a poem will help you understand it better.

Text Genre

Poetry

You are going to read two poems. A poem is a piece of **poetry.** Look for one or more of these features in the poems.

Poetry	
stanzas	groups of lines
images	words and phrases that help readers create pictures in their minds
figurative language	writing that expresses ideas in imaginative ways, such as comparing two things that are not alike

Meet the Authors

Rita Dove was born in Akron, Ohio, in 1952. She received the 1987 Pulitzer Prize for a book of poems based on her grandparents' life. In 1993, Rita Dove became the Poet Laureate (the national poet) of the United States. She was the youngest person and the first African American to receive this honor.

Naoshi Koriyama was born in Japan in 1926. He studied English in Japan and then came to the United States for college. After returning to Japan in 1967, he taught American poetry at Tokyo University.

Reading Focus Questions

As you read, think about these questions.

1. How do these poems relate to the theme of "discovery"?
2. What do you think each poet's purpose was for writing each poem?
3. How do you think the poets feel about books and poetry? Explain your answer.

Workbook
pages 95–96

Independent Practice
CD-ROM/Online

✓**Checkpoint**

1. What is **mood**? How does an author create mood?
2. What are **stanzas**?

The First Book
by Rita Dove

Open it.

Go ahead, it won't bite.

Well . . . maybe a little.

More a **nip,** like. A **tingle.**

It's **pleasurable,** really.

You see, it keeps opening.

You may fall in.

Sure, it's hard to get started;

remember learning to use

knife and fork? Dig in:

you'll never reach **bottom.**

It's not like it's the end of the world —

just the world as you think

you know it.

nip quick, small bite

tingle prickly feeling

pleasurable pleasant, enjoyable

Unfolding Bud

by Naoshi Koriyama

1   One is **amazed**
By a water-lily **bud**
Unfolding
With each passing day,
Taking on a richer color
And new **dimensions.**

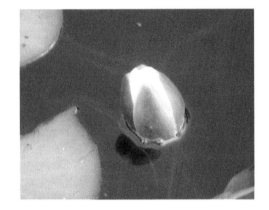

2   One is not **amazed**,
At a first **glance**,
By a poem,
Which is as tight-closed
As a tiny **bud.**

◄ **Reading Strategy**

Recognize Mood in Poetry What do you think is the mood of this poem? Give examples of words and phrases from the poem that create this mood.

3   Yet one is surprised
To see the poem
Gradually unfolding,
Revealing its rich inner self,
As one reads it
Again
And over again.

Reading Check

1. **Recall facts** What is the poet of "The First Book" encouraging the reader to do?

2. **Paraphrase text** Explain the poem "Unfolding **Bud**" in your own words.

---

dimensions measurements of width, height, and length
glance quick, short look
revealing uncovering, showing something hidden

A Library Card Application

You have read two poems about discovering literature. "The First Book" is about discovering books. "Unfolding **Bud**" is about discovering poetry.

The best place to discover new literature is at your public library. All you need is a library card. Look at the sample library card application form. Here is what you do to complete it.

1. Copy the application.
2. Fill in the application with a pen. Print carefully.
3. If there are any questions that do not apply to you, write "n/a" ("not applicable").
4. Before you hand in the application:
   a. Check that all the information is correct.
   b. Check your spelling.
5. Sign and date your application.

Anytown Public Library

123 Main Street
Anytown, PA 12003

(215) 555-1234

www.anytownlibrary.org

Library Card Application

Name _____
    First   Middle   Last

Address _____
    Street   City   State   Zip

Phone number _____

E-mail address _____

Date of birth _____ Gender: Male ☐   Female ☐

School name _____

Driver's license number _____

Signature _____ Date _____

After Reading 2

● Reading Comprehension Questions

Think and Discuss

1. **Recall facts** Name two or three pieces of information asked for on the application form on page 110.
2. **Identify imagery** In each poem the poet includes an image of the book or poem opening up. Find these lines in each poem.
3. **Identify figurative language** What does the poet compare a book to in "The First Book"? What does the poet compare a poem to in "Unfolding **Bud**"?
4. **Compare and contrast** In what ways are the poems similar? In what ways are they different?
5. **Relate to your experience** The last lines of "Unfolding **Bud**" describe how a reader understands and finds more and more meaning in a poem with each reading. Have you ever felt you understood a reading better after you read it again? What was the reading?
6. **Revisit the Reading Focus Questions** Go back to page 107 and discuss the questions.

Workbook page 97   Independent Practice CD-ROM/Online

Spelling

I Before e Except After c

Workbook page 98   Independent Practice CD-ROM/Online

Writing Conventions

Punctuation: Quotation Marks with Dialogue; Interjections

Workbook page 99   Independent Practice CD-ROM/Online

⟳ Connect Readings 1 and 2

You read two readings on the theme of discovery. Use these activities to make connections between the readings.

1. With a partner, use this chart to compare the two readings.

Reading title	What is the text genre?	Which reading includes facts?	Which reading includes figurative language?	What is the purpose: to entertain? to inform? Both?
Eureka!				
The First Book / Unfolding Bud				

2. Answer the questions about the readings. Then compare and discuss your answers with a partner.

   a. Do you think the poets of "The First Book" and "Unfolding **Bud**" believe readers of literature can have "eureka" moments? How might these moments be similar to the moments of scientific discovery? How might they be different?

   b. Which of the readings was your favorite? Why?

3. **Revisit the Chapter Focus Question** How do discoveries change us and change our world? Use examples from the readings to answer the question.

Listening and Speaking

Give a News Report About a Discovery

Imagine that your group is a news team reporting on an important new discovery. Together you will choose a discovery to report on, write a script, and perform the news report for your class.

1. Work in groups of three or four.
2. Brainstorm a list of discoveries—ones you read about in this chapter or other famous discoveries.
3. Each member of the group should suggest at least one discovery to report on. To make suggestions, use phrases from the **Phrases for Conversation** box.
4. Vote on a discovery to report on.
5. Work as a group to create a script to read.
6. Think about your audience. What information will be interesting to them?
7. Deliver the news report as a group. Use your words, voice, facial expressions, and gestures to keep the interest of your audience.

Phrases for Conversation

Making Suggestions

Let's . . .
We should . . .
Why don't we . . .?
How about . . .?
What about . . .?
I suggest that we . . .
I recommend that
 we . . .

Reading Fluency

Repeated Reading

Repeated reading helps you build fluency, accuracy, and comprehension.

1. With a partner, read the poem "Unfolding **Bud**" (page 109). Your partner will listen for errors. Your partner will also time your reading.
2. When you finish, your partner will give you feedback on your errors and your reading time.
3. Read the poem three times. Each time you reread it, try to reduce your errors and improve your reading speed. As your reading fluency improves, **focus** on adding more intonation and expressiveness to the reading.
4. Switch roles with your partner.

● Vocabulary Development

Understand Synonyms and Use a Thesaurus

Synonyms are words that have similar meanings. You can use synonyms to make your writing more interesting. For example, instead of using the same word again and again, the author of "Eureka!"uses synonyms like *smart* and *clever*, and *same* and **equal.**

A **thesaurus** is a reference book or online resource that lists synonyms for words. To find a synonym in a thesaurus:

a. Identify the word you want a synonym for. For example, imagine you are writing about a discovery. However, you do not want to use the word *discovery* again and again.

b. Look up the word in a thesaurus. In a thesaurus, the words are in alphabetical order. The synonyms will be listed after the word you looked up. The entry for the word *discovery* might look like this.

> **discovery** exploration, finding, invention, learning, revelation, sighting, uncovering, unearthing

c. Choose the synonym that works best for your writing.

You can also find thesauruses online. To use an online thesaurus, type the word "thesaurus" into a search engine. Then type in the word you want a synonym for.

1. Read this paragraph from "Eureka!"

   Nothing is as exciting as a **sudden** scientific discovery. Sometimes engineers and inventors **solve** a **difficult** problem with one smart idea. We call these sudden leaps of **knowledge** "eureka moments" after the shout of Archimedes (287–212 BCE).

2. Copy the chart below.

3. Use a thesaurus. Find synonyms for each **bold** word in the paragraph. Write the synonyms in the chart.

Word	Synonyms
1. sudden	
2. solve	
3. difficult	
4. knowledge	

> **Build Your Knowledge**
>
> Many thesauruses also include **antonyms**—words that have opposite meanings. For example, antonyms for *discovery* are: *hiding, covering up.*
>
> Knowing a synonym or antonym of an unknown word can help you determine the unknown word's meaning.

> **✓ Checkpoint**
>
> 1. What is a **synonym**? What is a **thesaurus**?
>
> 2. Use a thesaurus to find synonyms for these Key Vocabulary words: **mixture, remind, gradually.**

Vocabulary Log

Workbook page 100

Independent Practice CD-ROM/Online

● **Grammar**

The Simple Past Tense of *be*

Use the simple past tense of the verb **be** to talk about something that was true in the past.

She **was** a teacher. (Now she is a writer.)

They **were** at home last night. (Now they are in the library.)

The Simple Past Tense of *be*		
subject	***be***	
I	**was**	born in 1983.
You	**were**	at home last night.
He / She / I	**was**	cold yesterday.
You / We / They	**were**	in Texas last week.

Note

To form the negative of the simple past tense of **be**, add **not** after **was** or **were**.

I **was not** in class yesterday.

My friends **were not** at the mall.

Practice the Grammar Complete each sentence with the correct form of the simple past tense of **be**.

1. Alexander Fleming _____ a great scientist.

2. He _____ an army doctor in World War I.

3. Florey and Chain _____ interested in Fleming's ideas.

4. Their experiments with penicillin _____ successful.

5. Penicillin _____ a very important discovery.

6. It _____ the first of a group of drugs called antibiotics.

Use the Grammar Independently

1. Write four sentences about yourself and your life now. Use the simple present tense of **be**. Then write four sentences about your life five years ago. Use the simple past tense of **be**.

2. Share your sentences with a partner.

I am in the United States now. I was in Haiti five years ago.

Grammar Expansion

Simple Past of
be: Negative

Workbook
page 102

Independent Practice
CD-ROM/Online

Workbook
page 101

Independent Practice
CD-ROM/Online

● Grammar

The Simple Past Tense

The simple past tense describes an action that began and ended in the past. Regular past tense verbs end in **-d** or **-ed**.

The Simple Past Tense: Affirmative Statements		
subject	**base form of verb + -d / -ed**	
I You He / She / It We They	work**ed** danc**ed** wait**ed**	last night.

The Simple Past Tense: Negative Statements			
subject	*did + not*	**base form of verb**	
I You He / She / It We They	**did not**	work dance wait	last night.

Note

Irregular verbs do not have the **-d / -ed** ending in the simple past tense. For a list of irregular verbs, see page 402.

Practice the Grammar Complete each sentence with the correct simple past tense form of the verb in parentheses.

1. Archimedes (live) _____ in ancient Greece.
2. He (solve) _____ a difficult problem while in the bathtub.
3. He (not wait) _____ to tell people about his idea.
4. He (jump) _____ out of his bathtub.
5. He (not walk) _____ into town. He ran.
6. He (shout) _____ "Eureka!"
7. Archimedes (discover) _____ an important idea that day.
8. However, he still (need) _____ a bath!

Use the Grammar Independently Write simple past tense sentences about yourself and people you know. Use the verbs in the box.

visit	play	cook	clean	call	open	watch

My parents visited my grandmother last weekend.

Workbook
pages 103–104

Independent Practice
CD-ROM/Online

> ✓ **Checkpoint**
> 1. When should you use the **simple past tense**?
> 2. Give an example of a simple past tense sentence.

Writing Assignment

Creative Writing: Write a Historical Fiction Paragraph

Historical fiction is a story that is set in a real time in history. Some features, such as characters and setting, may be real. Others, such as dialogue, may be made up or imagined.

Writing Suggestion

See **Milestones Handbook.** pages 393–433

Writing Prompt

Write a historical fiction paragraph about a famous "eureka" moment in history. Use the simple past tense.

Write Your Historical Fiction Paragraph

1. **Read the student model.** It will help you understand how to write your historical fiction paragraph.

Student Model

The Discovery of Tutankhamen's Tomb

Prologue: In 1922, a British archeologist named Howard Carter made a great discovery. He discovered the tomb of King Tutankhamen. This ancient Egyptian tomb was over 3,000 years old.

Carter and his team were in Egypt. They dug and dug. Finally they found a stairway of 16 steps. Carter walked down the steps. He walked through a door. On the other side, there was a tunnel filled with rocks and dirt. His team dug out the rocks and dirt. Then Carter walked through the tunnel. Finally, he arrived at a second door. He was excited and nervous. He opened the door. His heart stopped for a moment. He was completely quiet. Carter was amazed. Everywhere he looked, he saw gold. He also saw ancient objects and statues. Finally, Carter yelled out, "I found it! I searched for ten years. Now here it is. We found King Tutankhamen's tomb!"

Workbook
page 105

2. **Prewrite**
   a. Choose a "eureka" moment from history. You can write about one of the "eureka" moments you read about in this unit, or a different famous moment of discovery.
   b. Gather information about the moment. Find information on the Internet, in an encyclopedia, and/or in library books. Take notes on important information.

3. **Write your paragraph of historical fiction.**
   a. Include a short prologue before the paragraph. The prologue should give the reader basic information about the discovery.
   b. Write a paragraph about the moment of discovery. The paragraph should be about a real moment in history. However, remember that you can be creative with historical fiction! Use your imagination to add your own ideas and to create your own dialogue for your characters to speak.

4. **Revise.** Reread your paragraph. Revise your paragraph if any ideas are not clear or complete.
   Use the **editing and proofreading symbols** on page 419 to help you mark the changes you want to make.

5. **Edit.** Use the **Writing Checklist** to help you find problems and errors.

> **Writing Checklist**
>
> 1. I included a prologue before my paragraph.
>
> 2. I indented my paragraph.
>
> 3. I capitalized the first word of each sentence.
>
> 4. I used the past tense of **be** and the simple past tense correctly.

Writing Support

Mechanics
Punctuation Marks at the End of Sentences

- **Period (.):** Use a period at the end of a statement.

  Howard Carter discovered King Tutankhamen's tomb.

- **Question mark (?):** Use a question mark at the end of a question.

  When did he discover the tomb?

- **Exclamation point (!):** Use an exclamation point at the end of a sentence to show strong feeling.

  At last, I found the tomb!

Apply Read your paragraph of historical fiction. Check to make sure that you used the correct punctuation mark at the end of each sentence.

Workbook
pages 106–108

Independent Practice
CD-ROM/Online

Progress Check

MILESTONESTRACKER

How well did you understand this chapter? Try to answer the questions. If necessary, go back to the pages listed for a review.

Skills	Skills Assessment Questions	Pages to Review
Vocabulary From the Readings	What do these words mean?	
	• equal, germ, mixture, pure, realize, remind	96
	• amazed, bottom, bud, gradually	106
Academic Vocabulary	What do these academic vocabulary words mean?	
	• locate, focus	97
	• evaluate, speculate	104
Reading Strategies	What is a **sequence of events**? How can understanding the sequence of events help you understand a reading?	97
	What is **mood**? How can recognizing mood help you understand poetry?	107
Text Genre	What is the text genre of "Eureka!"?	98
	What is the text genre of "The First Book" and "Unfolding **Bud**"?	107
Reading Comprehension	What is "Eureka!" about?	105
	What are "The First Book" and "Unfolding **Bud**" about?	111
Text Elements	What are **writing style** and **tone**?	105
Spelling	Give two words that are spelled with **i** before **e**.	111
Writing Conventions	Where do you put the **quotation marks** when writing a person's exact words? What is an **interjection**?	111
Listening and Speaking	**Phrases for Conversation** What phrases can you use for making suggestions?	112
Vocabulary Development	What is a **synonym**? Give an example of a pair of synonyms. How do you find a synonym in a **thesaurus**?	113
Grammar	Give an example of a sentence with the **past tense** of **be**.	114
	Give an example of a **simple past tense** sentence.	115
Writing Support: Mechanics	What kinds of punctuation marks can come at the end of a sentence? Explain when to use each mark.	117

Assessment Practice

Read this poem. Then answer Questions 1 through 4.

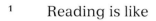

bee

Like Being a Bee

1   Reading is like

2   being a bee

3   buzzing in a field,

4   sometimes stopping

5   and

6   tasting

7   sometimes flying quickly on to the next bud,

8   but always landing,

9   at the end,

10 in a home full of honey.

1 Read line 7.

> sometimes flying quickly on to the next bud,

What does bud mean?

A bottom

B focus

C young flower

D field

2 What mood does line 7 create?

A excitement

B danger

C fear

D sadness

3 What is this text about?

A how reading is similar to being a bee

B how a bee makes honey

C how a bee flies

D how you can learn a lot about reading by watching a bee

4 What is the genre of this text?

A play

B poetry

C letter

D informational text

Writing on Demand: Poem/Descriptive Paragraph

Write a poem or a descriptive paragraph about reading. You can compare reading to another activity. You can write about your favorite book. You can write about how you feel about reading and why. **(20 minutes)**

Writing Tip
Use sensory details (what you see, hear, feel) in your descriptions of people, places, things, or experiences.

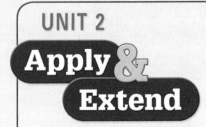
Apply & Extend

Objectives

Listening and Speaking
Deliver a "how-to" presentation

Media
Discover persuasive techniques in advertising

Writing
Write a persuasive letter

Projects

Independent Reading

● Listening and Speaking Workshop
Deliver a "How-To" Presentation

> **Topic**
>
> Deliver a "how-to" presentation to help your classmates discover a new skill.

1. Plan

  a. Choose a topic for your "how-to" presentation. Here are some ideas for skills you may want to teach.

- how to cook something
- how to play a sport
- how to build or make something

  b. Think about these questions. Take notes on your ideas.

- Why is this a good skill to learn?
- What materials or equipment does a person need?
- What are the steps involved in doing it?

2. Organize Your Presentation

  a. Write each step of the activity on a timeline.

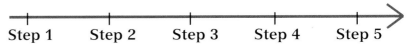

Step 1   Step 2   Step 3   Step 4   Step 5

  b. Use **transition words** to make the chronological order of the steps clear. Transition words include:

first	second	next	after	then	finally

  c. Include graphics to clarify the steps.

3. Practice

Use your timeline when you practice. Think about each part of the **Speaking Self-Evaluation** before you practice.

4. Present and Evaluate

Give your presentation. Ask your class for feedback. Use the **Speaking Self-Evaluation** to evaluate your presentation. Use the **Active Listening Evaluation** to discuss your classmates' presentations.

5. Follow Multiple-Step Instructions

Take notes on your classmates' presentations. Choose one presentation and try to perform the skill. Follow the steps presented. Then report on your experience to the class.

Speaking Self-Evaluation	Active Listening Evaluation
1. I used a timeline to order the steps.	**1.** I thought the topic was interesting.
2. I included transition words to make the chronological order clear.	**2.** The steps were presented clearly and were easy to understand.
3. I included graphics to support my presentation.	**3.** I think I could do this activity myself now.
4. I spoke clearly and loudly enough for the audience to hear me.	**4.** The graphics helped me understand the process involved.

● Media Workshop

Discover Persuasive Techniques in Advertising

The purpose of advertisements is to get you to buy things. Advertisers use **persuasive techniques** to try to get you to buy their product. Persuasive techniques often include false or misleading information. These are some persuasive techniques.

a. **Celebrity endorsements:** This is when a celebrity, such as a movie star or a sports figure, gets paid to sell a product.

   Hi. I'm Leon Woodson, and I wear Liko sneakers.

b. **Emotional appeals:** These are statements that try to create strong feelings instead of using facts and evidence.

   Tell your mother you love her with a Tallbank card.

c. **Hyperbole:** This is exaggeration.

   Get Kresp toothpaste for the whitest teeth, the freshest breath, and the happiest mouth.

d. **Scientific or statistical claims:** This is when an advertisement seems to make scientific claims.

   Our studies show that Nova cream reduces wrinkles by 71%.

1. Pay attention to advertisements on TV, in newspapers, and in magazines. Take notes on each advertisement.

2. Identify at least one advertisement that uses each of these techniques.

3. In a small group, discuss the persuasive techniques you found.

4. Work in groups to make up your own advertisement for a product. Use persuasive techniques.

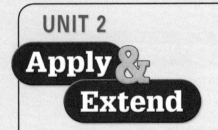

Apply & Extend

Writing
Suggestion

See **Milestones Handbook**.
pages 393–433

● Writing Workshop

Persuasive Letter

In **persuasive** writing, you try to convince the reader to agree with your position, or opinion, on something.

Writing Prompt

The richest woman in the world will give one billion dollars for the discovery of one of these things:
- a cure for cancer
- life on another planet

Which discovery do you think she should give the money to? Write a persuasive letter to her to convince her of your position.

PREWRITE

1. Read the student model on the next page. It will help you understand how to write a persuasive letter.
2. Decide which discovery you think the money should go to.
3. Make a list of reasons for and against this choice.

Arguments For My Position	Arguments Against My Position

4. Look up information on the topic in sources such as library books, the Internet, and electronic encyclopedias. Take notes and add important facts and details to your list.

WRITE A DRAFT

1. Write the opening paragraph. This paragraph should state the issue and your position.
2. Write the body.
   a. In one paragraph, summarize arguments others might make against your position. Respond to these points, and explain why your position is strongest.
   b. In the next one or two paragraphs, give at least two strong reasons to support your position. Support each of your reasons with facts, examples, or evidence.
3. Write the conclusion. It should restate your position. It should strongly encourage the reader to take the action you suggest.

Student Model

In this persuasive letter, the student suggests a different use for the money—discovering new forms of energy.

December 19, 2008

Dear Ms. Richey,

Opening Paragraph

You are giving one billion dollars to research an important discovery. This is very generous! I am writing to you with an idea. The world is running out of fossil fuel. I think you should give the money to research new forms of energy.

Summary of opposing arguments

Some people think there are better ways to spend money. For example, some think it is more important to find a cure for cancer. Some even feel that we do not need new forms of energy. They feel that there is still a lot of fossil fuel left in the world. I think these are not good arguments.

Body

Right now we really depend on fossil fuels. We use them for over 75% of our energy needs. Someday we will run out of fossil fuels. This will be a disaster. Energy is so important to our lives. People need energy to drive to work, to heat their homes, to cook their food. No one knows how much fossil fuel is left in the world. However, everyone agrees that there is a limited amount. When it runs out, we will be in trouble. We cannot make fossil fuels.

Writer's position (with facts)

Some people want your money to go to finding a cure for cancer. However, discovering a new form of energy may help fewer people get cancer! Fossil fuels are dangerous for our environment and for our health. Tiny pieces of fossil fuels can go into our lungs. If we find new forms of energy, our environment will be healthier. If our environment is healthier, we will be healthier.

Conclusion

These are some of the reasons why I urge you to give your money to research new forms of energy. I think new forms of energy will lead to a healthier world and healthier people. What could be more important than that?

Yours truly,
Choi Soon Yong

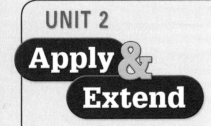

REVISE

1. **Review** your draft. Make sure your opening paragraph states your position. Make sure the body supports this position with facts and examples.

2. Exchange your persuasive letter with a partner. Ask your partner to use the **Peer Review Checklist** to review your letter. Your partner will point out errors and give suggestions for making your draft better.

3. Revise your draft. You may need to add or delete sentences. You may need to rearrange sentences to make your ideas clearer.

4. Use the **editing and proofreading symbols** on page 419 to help you mark the changes you want to make.

EDIT

1. Use the **Revising and Editing Checklist** to evaluate your essay.

2. Fix any errors in grammar, spelling, and punctuation.

Peer Review Checklist

1. The writer's position is stated in the opening paragraph.

2. The writer included facts and examples to support his/her position.

3. The ideas in the letter are clear.

4. The letter persuaded me to agree with the writer.

Revising and Editing Checklist

1. I stated my position clearly.

2. I summarized the opposing position.

3. I supported my position with facts, examples, and evidence.

4. I checked for errors in punctuation.

5. I checked for misspelled words.

PUBLISH

1. Write your letter in your best handwriting or use a computer.

2. Read your letter to the class. Read clearly and slowly enough so that everyone can understand you. Change the level of your voice to express the important ideas in your letter.

3. Discuss the strengths and weakness of each student's letter.

4. Display your letters in the classroom.

● Projects

Choose one or more of the following projects to explore the theme of discovery further.

PROJECT 1
Discover Your Local Library

Go to your local library and do the following.

1. If you do not have a library card, fill out an application.
2. Explore the different sections of the library. Make a list of these different sections.
3. Explore and list the resources available at the library.
4. Find and check out a book of poetry.
5. Find a poem you like and read it to your class.

PROJECT 2
Explore a Possible Career

1. Learn about a career you are interested in.
   a. Find articles about the career on the Internet.
   b. Find books about it at the library.
   c. Try to find and interview someone who has this career.
2. Report back to the class. Now that you know more about this career, are you still interested in it? Why or why not?

PROJECT 3
Discover Another Culture

1. Find a person from a culture you are interested in.
2. Interview the person about his or her culture. Ask about things such as customs, foods, and holidays.
3. Report back to your class on what you learned.

PROJECT 4
Discover Literature from Around the World

You read a Native American folktale. Go to your library and discover other literature.

1. Find a folktale, fable, legend, myth, or fairy tale from three different cultures.
2. Take notes for each story. Include information about the culture, genre, characters, setting, and plot.
3. Report back to your class. Retell each story. Talk about what you discovered about the three cultures.

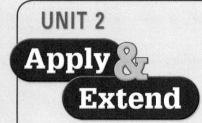

Apply & Extend

● **Independent Reading**

Explore the theme of discovery further by reading one or more of these books.

Eureka!: Great Inventions and How They Happened by Richard Platt, Kingfisher, 2003.

This book tells the stories of 29 of the world's greatest discoveries and inventions. Each story **focuses** on the events leading up to the moment of discovery and inspiration. The stories also include brief biographies of the scientists and inventors.

Mystery of the Hieroglyphs: The Story of the Rosetta Stone and the Race to Decipher Egyptian Hieroglyphs by Carol Donoughue, Oxford University Press, 2002.

Hieroglyphs are the shapes and symbols used in an ancient Egyptian writing system. For hundreds of years, no one understood hieroglyphs. Then in 1799, French soldiers in Egypt discovered the Rosetta Stone. This book tells about the discovery of the stone, and how it held the key to unlocking the mystery of hieroglyphs.

Things Not Seen by Andrew Clements, Philomel, 2002.

Fifteen-year-old Bobby Phillips wakes up one morning and finds that he is invisible. This changes everything in his life and causes many problems. Then Bobby meets Alicia, a friend who accepts him as he is. Alicia is blind and does not care about Bobby's invisibility. This award-winning science fiction story explores the themes of friendship and self-discovery.

Girl of the Shining Mountains: Sacagawea's Story by Peter Roop and Connie Roop, Hyperion Press, 1999.

In this historical novel, 16-year-old Sacagawea tells her thoughts and feelings as she takes part in the historic journey of discovery led by Lewis and Clark. For Sacagawea, the expedition also offers the chance to find her family and friends from whom she was stolen years ago. Through Sacagawea's voice, we learn about her journey of discovery.

Milestones to Achievement

Writing: Revise and Edit

MILESTONES TRACKER

Read this rough draft of a student's nonfiction paragraph, which may contain errors. Then answer Questions 1 through 4.

Discovering Mathematics

(**1**) During elementary school, math was not my favorite subject. (**2**) Every night, I couldn't do my math homework. (**3**) My mother tried to help me. (**4**) My older brother tried to help me. (**5**) I became more annoyed every night. (**6**) Finally, I gave up. (**7**) I said, "I'm not good at math." (**8**) I stopped trying to learn math. (**9**) I focused on my other subjects. (**10**) I thought, "If I am great in those subjects, my teachers won't notice that I'm not good in math." (**11**) That plan worked until this year. (**12**) Ms. Nuñez, my sixth grade math teacher, saw I am not learning. (**13**) She asked me to stay after school every day. (**14**) She was patient. (**15**) She explained everything once, twice, even three times. (**16**) I began to understand math. (**17**) I also began to enjoy math. (**18**) I learned that I can do math? (**19**) More importantly, I learned not to stop trying when something is difficult. (**20**) Now I know that if I ask for help and try hard, I can learn anything.

1 What synonym can you use for **learned** in sentence 18?

A scared   C discovered

B reminded   D located

2 What is the BEST way to revise sentence 8?

A I stopped trying to learn him.

B I stopped trying to learn it.

C I stopped trying to learn her.

D I stopped trying to learn them.

3 How can you improve sentence 12?

A Change *am* to *was*.

C Change *am* to *were*.

B Change *am* to *is*.

D Change *am* to *are*.

4 What punctuation should be used at the end of sentence 18?

A "   C Leave as is.

B ,   D !

Writing on Demand: Expository Writing

What is the most important thing you learned this year? You can write about something you learned to do, something you discovered about yourself, or an important lesson you learned. Explain what you learned or discovered. Give at least three reasons why this lesson or discovery was important. Use interesting adjectives and descriptive words. (**20 minutes**)

> ### Writing Tip
> Use specific details to support your reasons. Include a short personal story to help explain one of your reasons why what you learned was so important.

● Reading

Read this informational text. Then answer Questions 1 through 8.

Doctor Adventure

1   Carlos Juan Finlay is famous because he discovered the cause of malaria, a serious disease. However, you could also call him "Doctor Adventure" because of all of his travels and adventures. Finlay was born on December 3, 1833, in Puerto Principe, Cuba. When he was a baby, his travels began. His family moved to Havana, the capital of Cuba. For a few years, he lived a quiet life with his relatives. At age 11, his adventures really began. He traveled alone, across the ocean, to France to begin school. However, disease and war interrupted his schooling. In 1846, he got cholera, a serious stomach virus. He returned to Cuba for two years. In 1848, he tried to return to France to finish school, but a revolutionary war stopped him. He traveled and studied in other cities in Europe. Then he went to the United States to study medicine. Finally, in 1857, he returned home to study in Havana. There he finished his schooling and became a doctor.

2   Even though Finlay's formal schooling was over, his adventures were not. After he became a doctor, he went to Peru in South America. He began to study malaria. There he realized that mosquitoes carried the disease. In 1860, he went back to France and continued to study and test his ideas about malaria. He also invented a vaccine made from mosquitoes. In 1865, Finlay married Adela Shine, who was from Trinidad, an island in the Caribbean Sea. Together the Finlays traveled to Trinidad and New York City. Then they settled in Havana, Cuba. At the age of 65, Finlay returned to the United States to advise the government about malaria.

3   Late in his life, Finlay became the head doctor in Cuba, a job he had for eight years. Then Finlay's adventures and travels ended. He died on August 20, 1915. A monument honoring Dr. Finlay is located in Havana, Cuba. He is remembered as a dedicated physician. His discovery about malaria saved millions of lives.

1 Read this line from paragraph 1.

> For a few years, he lived a quiet life with his relatives.

What does <u>relatives</u> mean?

A family

B friends

C long distances

D relationships

2 Read this line from paragraph 2.

> There he realized that mosquitoes carried the disease.

What does <u>realized</u> mean?

A remembered

B was surprised

C understood

D slowly

3 Why didn't Finlay finish his studies in France?

A He didn't like the university there.

B He didn't have enough money.

C He found a better university in Cuba.

D There was a war in France.

4 How do people catch malaria?

A from germs in the air

B from drinking dirty water

C from gravity

D from mosquitoes

5 From whose perspective is this text written?

A Carlos J. Finlay's

B the reader

C the author

D Finlay's wife

6 What is the tone of this text?

A formal

B sad

C informal

D humorous

7 In paragraph 2, to whom does the subject pronoun in this sentence refer?

> Then they settled in Havana, Cuba.

A Carlos

B Carlos and Adela

C Adela

D Trinidad and New York City

8 What is the best synonym for the word <u>discovery</u> in this line from paragraph 3?

> His discovery about malaria saved millions of lives.

A finding

B invention

C perspective

D germ

Dreams

Explore the Theme

1. What is a dream?
2. What dreams do you see in the pictures?

Theme Activity

    What do you dream about? Draw a picture of your dream, or cut out a picture from a magazine. Explain your dream to a partner. Display your pictures on the bulletin board to make a dream wall.

Objectives

Reading Strategies

Compare and contrast; Relate your own experiences to a reading

Listening and Speaking

Deliver an oral response to literature

Grammar

Use the conjunctions **and** and **but**

Writing

Expository writing: Write a compare and contrast paragraph

Academic Vocabulary

compare	inference
contrast	predict
similar	

Academic Content

The Wright brothers
Leonardo da Vinci

● Chapter Focus Question

How can dreams lead to new inventions and new ideas?

Reading 1 **Literature**
Play (excerpt)
Dragonwings
by Laurence Yep

Reading 2 **Content:** Social Studies
Magazine article
DA VINCI'S DREAMS
by Nick D'Alto

Dragonwings

● About the Reading

You are going to read a play that takes place in San Francisco, California, in 1909. It is about a Chinese boy and his father. The father has a dream to build and fly an airplane. His son shares this dream.

● Build Background

The First Airplane

Before the 1900s, there were no airplanes. In 1903, two brothers from the United States built and flew the first airplane. Orville and Wilbur Wright named their airplane *Flyer*. They flew it from a hill in Kitty Hawk, North Carolina, on December 17, 1903.

Look at the picture of the Wright brothers' airplane. How is it similar to airplanes today? How is it different?

● Use Prior Knowledge

Think About a Time You Helped Someone

In *Dragonwings*, a boy and his father need help to make their dream come true. Have you ever helped someone?

1. Copy the chart.
2. Fill in the boxes with the name of the person who needed help, the problem, how you helped, and the result.

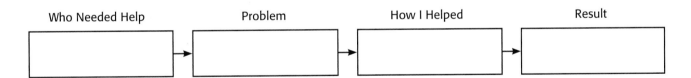

Who Needed Help	Problem	How I Helped	Result

Key Vocabulary

- design
- disappear
- machine
- merchant
- rhythm
- serious
- steep

● Vocabulary From the Reading

Learn, Practice, and Use Independently

Learn Vocabulary Read each sentence. Look at the **highlighted** word. Use the context (the words around the highlighted word) to determine its meaning.

1. Esme makes her own dresses. She knows how to **design** and then sew clothes.
2. One minute I could see the lady. The next minute, she was gone. She **disappeared.**
3. We have a lot of work to do. A **machine** will make the work go faster.
4. Clothing **merchants** often have their stores in shopping malls.
5. The children clapped to the **rhythm** of the music.
6. Juan does not laugh often. He is very **serious.**
7. Kwan climbed a mountain. It was so **steep** that he almost fell off it.

Practice Vocabulary Copy the chart. Work with a partner. Write the Key Vocabulary word for each definition.

Word	Definition
merchant	a person or business that buys and sells goods
1.	to go out of sight
2.	to draw sketches or plans
3.	piece of equipment that uses power to do work
4.	thoughtful and quiet
5.	at an angle at which one could easily fall
6.	a regular beat, especially in music or movement

Use Vocabulary Independently Write one sentence for each Key Vocabulary word. Read your sentences to a partner.

✓Checkpoint

1. Give an example of a **machine**. What does this **machine** do?
2. Describe a **serious** person you know.
3. Explain what a **merchant** does.

Vocabulary Log

Workbook page 109

Independent Practice CD-ROM/Online

● Academic Vocabulary

Vocabulary for the Reading Strategy

Word	Explanation	Sample Sentence	Visual Cue
compare *verb*	to look for ways that things are the same	People often **compare** my brother and me because we look alike.	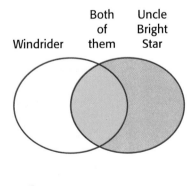
contrast *verb*	to look for ways that things are different	In school today, we had to **contrast** the population of the United States with the population of Mexico.	
similar *adjective*	almost the same	My dress is **similar** to yours.	

Draw a picture and write a sentence for each word.

● Reading Strategy

Compare and Contrast

   When you **compare** two or more things, you see how they are **similar**. When you **contrast**, you see how they are different. You can **compare** and **contrast** things in a story to help you understand characters and events better.

1. As you read *Dragonwings,* think about the characters.
   a. Who is Windrider? What is he like?
   b. Who is Uncle Bright Star? What is he like?
2. **Compare** and **contrast** Windrider and Uncle Bright Star. How are they **similar**? How are they different?
3. Look at the Venn Diagram. As you read, think about how to use it to **compare** Windrider to Uncle Bright Star. You will complete the Venn Diagram after the reading.

Windrider | Both of them | Uncle Bright Star

✓ Checkpoint
Compare and **contrast** an apple and a banana. How are they **similar**? How are they different?

Vocabulary Log

Workbook page 110

Independent Practice CD-ROM/Online

● **Text Genre**

Play

Dragonwings is a **play.** A play is written to be performed for an audience. The purpose is to entertain. Look at the features of a play in the chart below. Identify these features in *Dragonwings* as you read.

Play	
cast of characters	the people in a play
dialogue	words characters say to one another
stage directions	words that tell the actors how to move and speak; these words are usually set in parentheses. For example: *(WINDRIDER enters from upstage.)*
scene	part of a play

● **Meet the Author**

Laurence Yep is a Chinese-American writer. He was born in San Francisco. He began writing stories when he was a child. His first story was published when he was 18. *Dragonwings* is one of his most famous novels. It won many awards. He turned the novel into the play you are going to read.

● **Reading Focus Questions**

As you read, think about these questions.

1. How does the reading relate to the theme of "dreams"?

2. What do you think was the author's purpose in writing *Dragonwings*?

3. How does it feel when a dream comes true?

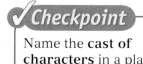

Checkpoint

Name the **cast of characters** in a play you know.

Workbook
page 111

Independent Practice
CD-ROM/Online

Dragonwings

by Laurence Yep

Prologue

Moon Shadow, a teenager from China, lives in San Francisco with his father, Windrider. Windrider works for a **laundry**. He dreams of saving money to bring his whole family to the United States. He also dreams of flying *Dragonwings*, the flying **machine** that he has built. However, someone steals their money. At the beginning of this scene, Moon Shadow is writing to his mother in China.

Cast of Characters

MOON SHADOW a Chinese teenager; the narrator of the story
WINDRIDER Moon Shadow's father
MISS WHITLAW owner of a **stable** in San Francisco where the narrator and his father live
UNCLE BRIGHT STAR a laundry owner
RED RABBIT the horse that pulls the laundry **wagon**

Scene 9

1   **MOON SHADOW:** September twenty-second, Nineteen-**ought**-nine. Dear Mother. I have bad news. We are going to lose *Dragonwings* before father can fly it. Black Dog[1] stole all we have. So we'll have to move and leave *Dragonwings* behind. We have asked Miss Whitlaw for help, but her new house has taken up all her money. And even if Uncle would speak to us, he has probably spent all he has on rebuilding his laundry.

(UNCLE BRIGHT STAR and MISS WHITLAW enter from left.)

---

laundry place where clothes are washed
stable building like a small barn for keeping horses, cows, etc.
wagon four-wheeled vehicle usually pulled by horses
ought zero

[1] Uncle Bright Star's son

Reading Strategy

Compare and Contrast Who do you think is richer: Uncle Bright Star or Moon Shadow's father? How do you know?

Reading Check

1. **Recall facts** Who arrives in the wagon?
2. **Make a prediction** Do you think Moon Shadow and his father will fly *Dragonwings*?

2   **MOON SHADOW:** Uncle, Miss Whitlaw!

3   **MISS WHITLAW:** How are you?

(Shaking MOON SHADOW'S hand. WINDRIDER enters from upstage. He is wearing a cap.)

4   **WINDRIDER:** Come to laugh, Uncle?

5   **UNCLE BRIGHT STAR:** I came to help you fly your **contraption.**

Reading Strategy

Compare and Contrast
What words does Uncle Bright Star use to **compare and contrast** himself with Moon Shadow?

6   **MOON SHADOW:** But you don't believe in flying **machines.**

7   **UNCLE BRIGHT STAR:** And I'll take that thing back down when it doesn't fly. Red Rabbit and me were getting fat anyway. But look at how tall you've grown. And how thin. And **ragged.** *(Pause.)* But you haven't broken your neck which was more than I ever expected.

8   **MISS WHITLAW:** As soon as I told your uncle, we **hatched** the **plot** together. You **ought to** get a chance to fly your airplane.

9   **WINDRIDER:** We need to pull *Dragonwings* to the very top.

10   **UNCLE BRIGHT STAR:** That hill is a very **steep** hill.

11   **WINDRIDER:** It has to be that one. The winds are right.

---

contraption item, usually a **machine,** put together in a strange way
ragged torn and old
hatched created
plot secret plan
ought to should

¹² **WINDRIDER:** Take the ropes. Got a good grip?

*(MOON SHADOW **stumbles** but gets right up. Stamping his feet to get better footing, he keeps tugging.)*

¹³ **MOON SHADOW:** *(Giving up.)* It's no good.

¹⁴ **UNCLE BRIGHT STAR:** Pull in **rhythm.** As we did on the railroad.

*(UNCLE BRIGHT STAR stamps his feet in a slow **rhythm** to set the beat and the others repeat. The **rhythm** picks up as they move.)* **Ngúng, ngúng. Dew gùng.**

¹⁵ **OTHERS:** *Ngúng, ngúng. Dew gùng.*

¹⁶ **UNCLE BRIGHT STAR:** *(Imitating the intonation of the Cantonese.)* Púsh, púsh. Wòrk, wòrk.

¹⁷ **MOON SHADOW:** We made it. **Tramp** the grass down in front.

(WINDRIDER stands center as the others stamp the grass. They can't help smiling and laughing a little.)

¹⁸ **WINDRIDER:** That's enough.

¹⁹ **MOON SHADOW:** *(To MISS WHITLAW)* Take that **propeller.**

Reading Strategy

Compare and Contrast Think about these questions: Who pulls *Dragonwings* up the hill? Who supervises, but does not pull? What does this show about this character?

Reading Check

1. **Recall facts** Why did Uncle Bright Star come?
2. **Recall facts** What do they use to move *Dragonwings?*
3. **Relate your experience** Have you ever worked with someone to reach a goal? Tell about the experience.

---

stumbles almost falls
Ngúng, ngúng. Dew gùng a Cantonese chant
tramp step hard on to make a surface flat
propeller blade in front of a plane that helps it move

20   **MISS WHITLAW:** Listen to the wind on the wings.

21   **UNCLE BRIGHT STAR:** It's alive.

22   **WINDRIDER:** All right.

(MOON SHADOW and MISS WHITLAW pull down on the propellers and back away quickly. Propellers begin to turn with a roar.)

23   **UNCLE BRIGHT STAR:** *(Slowly turning.)* What's wrong? Is it just going to roll down the hill?

(MISS WHITLAW crosses her fingers as they all turn to watch the airplane.)

24   **MISS WHITLAW:** He's up!

25   **MOON SHADOW:** *(Pointing.)* He's turning.

26   **UNCLE BRIGHT STAR:** He's really flying.

27   **MISS WHITLAW:** I never thought I'd see the day. A human up in the sky. Off the ground.

*(They turn and **tilt** their heads back.)*

Reading Strategy

Compare and Contrast
What does Miss Whitlaw **compare** Windrider to? What does Uncle Bright Star **compare** him to? How are these two descriptions of Windrider different?

28   **MISS WHITLAW:** Free as an **eagle.**

29   **UNCLE BRIGHT STAR:** *(Correcting her.)* Like **dragon.**

30   **MOON SHADOW:** Father, you did it. You did it.

---

tilt make one side higher than another
eagle large bird from North America
dragon large, fierce, imaginary reptile usually able to fly and to breathe fire

(MOON SHADOW steps forward and addresses the audience.)

31   **MOON SHADOW:** I thought he'd fly forever and ever. But then some of the **guy wires** broke, and the right wings separated. *Dragonwings* came crashing to earth. Father had a few broken bones, but it was nothing **serious.** Only the airplane was wrecked. Uncle took him back to the laundry to recover. Father didn't say much, but thought a lot—I figured he was busy **designing** the next airplane. But when Father was nearly well, he made me sit down next to him.

32   **WINDRIDER:** Uncle says he'll make me a partner if I stay. So the western officials would have to change my **immigration class.** I'd be a **merchant,** and **merchants** can bring their wives here. Would you like to send for Mother?

33   **MOON SHADOW:** But *Dragonwings*?

34   **WINDRIDER:** When I was up in the air, I tried to find you. You were so small. And getting smaller. Just **disappearing** from sight. *(Handing the cap to MOON SHADOW.)* Like you were **disappearing** from my life. I knew it wasn't the time.

(MOON SHADOW turns to the audience.)

35   **MOON SHADOW:** We always talked about flying again. Only we never did. *(Putting on cap.)* But dreams stay with you, and we never forgot.

Reading Strategy

Compare and Contrast
Compare and contrast Windrider's feelings about flying before he flew the airplane and after he flew the airplane.

✓
Reading Check

1. **Recall facts** What happens to *Dragonwings*?

2. **Recall facts** What will Windrider become if Uncle makes him a partner?

3. **Analyze characters** How does the fall change Windrider?

---

guy wires thin ropes that keep an object in place
immigration class foreign person's official position in another country

● Apply the Reading Strategy
Compare and Contrast

Now that you have read *Dragonwings,* complete the Venn Diagram.

Both of them

Windrider · Uncle Bright Star

poor | Chinese | rich

1. Review the **Reading Strategy** on page 135.
2. Copy the Venn Diagram.
3. Look back at the reading. **Compare** and **contrast** Windrider and Uncle Bright Star.
4. Write your ideas about the characters in the diagram. When something about them is **similar,** write it where the circles overlap.

● Academic Vocabulary
Vocabulary for the Reading Comprehension Questions

Word	Explanation	Sample Sentence	Visual Cue
inference *noun*	a guess based on some information	What **inference** can you make from seeing his clothing?	He must be a painter
predict *verb*	to say what will happen in the future	I **predict** that the Chicago Bears will win the football game.	I predict that the Chicago Bears will win this game.

Draw a picture and write a sentence for each word.

✓Checkpoint

1. Make an **inference** about something.
2. What can you **predict** will happen in school tomorrow?

Vocabulary Log

Reading Comprehension Questions

Think and Discuss

1. **Recall facts** Who comes to see Moon Shadow and his father at the beginning of the play?

2. **Make inferences** Does Uncle Bright Star believe that *Dragonwings* will fly? Why do you think this?

3. **Describe** How does Windrider make the airplane fly?

4. **Explain** Using Key Vocabulary words, explain why Windrider decides not to fly *Dragonwings* again.

5. **Predict** What do you think will happen to the family after the end of the play?

6. **Use your own knowledge to compare** What parts of *Dragonwings* can you still find on modern airplanes?

7. **Revisit the Reading Focus Questions** Go back to page 136 and discuss the questions.

Workbook
page 112

Independent Practice
CD-ROM/Online

Literary Element

Theme

A **theme** is an idea explored in literature. A piece of literature can have more than one theme. The author usually does not state the theme directly. The reader figures out the theme (or themes) while reading.

Some of the themes in *Dragonwings* are dreams, determination, and teamwork.

1. With a partner, choose another piece of literature you have read in this book.

2. Use the Table of Contents at the beginning of your book to find this reading. Skim (read quickly through) the reading.

3. Discuss the theme or themes of the reading with a partner.

4. **Compare** the theme(s) in this reading with the themes in *Dragonwings*. How are they **similar**? How are they different?

✓ Checkpoint

1. What is a **theme**?

2. What is one of the themes of *Dragonwings*? Explain.

Vocabulary
Log

Workbook
page 113

Independent Practice
CD-ROM/Online

DA VINCI'S DREAMS

● **About the Reading**

You read about the dreams of fictional characters in *Dragonwings*. Now you will read a magazine article about the dreams of a real person who lived long ago.

● **Build Background**

Leonardo da Vinci

Leonardo da Vinci was a great artist and inventor. He was born in Italy in 1452. Da Vinci had many interests and was curious about everything. Some people think he was the most intelligent person who ever lived.

Key Vocabulary

engineer

experiment

invention

modern

● **Vocabulary From the Reading**

Use Context Clues to Determine Meaning

Use the context of each sentence to determine the meaning of the **highlighted** word. Discuss the meanings in a small group.

1. An **engineer** plans and builds things like computers, cars, bridges, and tall buildings.

2. The scientist performed an **experiment** to test her ideas.

3. The airplane was an important **invention.** It allowed people to travel long distances in less time.

4. E-mail is the **modern** way of writing messages. Many people do not write letters anymore.

✓Checkpoint

What do you think are three important **modern inventions?**

Vocabulary Log

Workbook page 114

Independent Practice CD-ROM/Online

● Reading Strategy

Relate Your Own Experiences to a Reading

As you read "Da Vinci's Dreams," try to relate the reading to your personal experiences. Think about how you are **similar** to Leonardo da Vinci. This will help you understand the character and the story better.

● Text Genre

Informational Text: Magazine Article

A **magazine article** is a short work of **nonfiction.** People usually read magazine articles for information and enjoyment. Look for these characteristics of magazine articles as you read "Da Vinci's Dreams."

Magazine Article	
illustrations	art or photos that help the reader understand something described in the article
captions	short explanations of the illustrations

● Meet the Author

Nick D'Alto was born in New York City. When he was a child, his parents took him to a museum. At the museum, D'Alto saw one of Leonardo da Vinci's notebooks. This inspired him to become an inventor, too. Today, D'Alto **designs machines** that help airplanes fly. He also writes stories about great inventors.

● Reading Focus Questions

As you read, think about these questions.

1. How does this reading connect to the theme of "dreams"?
2. What do you think was the author's purpose for writing "Da Vinci's Dreams"?
3. What were da Vinci's dreams? How are they **similar** to and different from Windrider's dream in *Dragonwings*?

✓**Checkpoint**

Name two magazines. What kinds of **articles** does each one have?

Workbook
pages 115–116

Independent Practice
CD-ROM/Online

DA VINCI'S DREAMS

by Nick D'Alto

Reading Strategy

Relate Your Own Experiences to a Reading Do you use any of da Vinci's **inventions**? Are they important **inventions**? Why or why not?

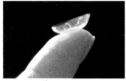

contact lens

monkey wrench

diving snorkel

modern parachute

1   Every new **invention** starts with a dream. One of the greatest dreamers and inventors in history was Leonardo da Vinci.

2   The **chain** and **gears** of your bicycle were **designed** in 1490. By whom? Of course…Leonardo da Vinci! Leonardo also invented the first contact lenses, the monkey wrench, the diving snorkel, and the first parachute. He even developed an early form of **air conditioning**—five hundred years ago!

3   Most of Leonardo da Vinci's **inventions** were never made during his life. But he still may be the greatest inventor in history. In his notebooks, he **designed inventions** that were hundreds of years ahead of their time. Some of his ideas still look **modern** today.

4   How did Leonardo dream up so many great ideas? Da Vinci was interested in everything. He saw each idea as connected to another. Drawing the **petals** of a flower might give him the idea to create a new type of gear. You could try connecting ideas this way yourself.

5   Leonardo filled notebooks with thousands of drawings for his **inventions.** He often put many ideas on the same page, jumping from one idea to another.

6   Today, he is remembered as one of the first **modern engineers.** He did **experiments** and made **models** to test his ideas. His drawings are so good that **modern engineers** can build his amazing **machines** and watch them work.

7   The next time you see a bicycle, or a monkey wrench, or a parachute, remember: It all started with a dream in Leonardo's notebooks.

---

chain set of metal rings or loops that are connected
gears parts of a **machine** that make other parts of the **machine** turn
air conditioning way of cooling air
petals colored parts of a flower
models small versions of things

After Reading 2

● **Reading Comprehension Questions**

Think and Discuss

1. **Identify** Name three of da Vinci's **inventions**.

2. **Recall facts** Were most of da Vinci's **inventions** made when he was alive?

3. **Determine the main idea** What is the main idea of this magazine article?

4. **Describe** Describe how da Vinci's ideas are important today, using at least two Key Vocabulary words.

5. **Relate to your own experiences** Do you have an idea for a great **invention**? What is it? What other **inventions** would you draw in a notebook?

6. **Revisit the Reading Focus Questions** Go back to page 145 and discuss the questions.

Workbook
page 117

Independent Practice
CD-ROM/Online

Spelling

Titles Used with Names

Workbook
page 118

Independent Practice
CD-ROM/Online

Writing Conventions

Punctuation: Commas in a Series

Workbook
page 119

Independent Practice
CD-ROM/Online

Connect Readings 1 and 2

You read two readings on the theme of dreams. Use these activities to make connections between the readings.

1. With a partner, use this chart to **compare** the two readings.

Reading title	What is the text genre?	Is it fiction or nonfiction?	Who is the reading about?	Which reading is the most interesting to you? Why?
Dragonwings				
DA VINCI'S DREAMS				

2. Think about the dreams that each reading talks about.
   a. What dream did Windrider have? What dreams did da Vinci have?
   b. Did anyone share the dreams of Windrider and da Vinci? Explain.
   c. How were Windrider and da Vinci **similar**? How were they different?

3. **Revisit the Chapter Focus Question** How can dreams lead to new **inventions** and ideas? Use examples from *Dragonwings* and "Da Vinci's Dreams" to answer this question.

Phrases for Conversation

Showing Interest

That's interesting.
Good point.
Tell me more.
I see what you mean.
I never thought of it
   that way.
That's an interesting
   way to look at it.

● Listening and Speaking

Respond Orally to Literature

Dreams are an important theme in *Dragonwings* and "Da Vinci's Dreams." Use the readings to explore and discuss your ideas about dreams.

1. Think about these questions.
   a. What dream does Windrider have in *Dragonwings*? What dreams did Leonardo da Vinci have?
   b. How are the dreams of Windrider and da Vinci **similar**? How are they different?

2. Scan (look quickly for) details from the readings to support your ideas. Take notes on these ideas for your discussion.

3. Discuss your ideas with a small group. Use the **Phrases for Conversation** to show interest in your classmates' ideas.

4. Finally, discuss what you know about dreams.
   a. What kinds of dreams do people have today?
   b. What are your dreams? How are they similar to and different from Windrider's dreams and da Vinci's dreams?

● Reading Fluency

Reading Words in Chunks

Good readers do not read word by word. They read words in "chunks." Chunks are groups of words that you read together. Reading words in chunks will help you read faster. It will also help you understand what you read.

1. Read the paragraph aloud. Do not read word by word. Read the chunks separated with a slash (/). Adjust your reading rate (read more slowly) if the text is difficult.

> The chain and gears of your bicycle / were **designed** in 1490. / By whom? / Of course… / Leonardo da Vinci! / Leonardo also invented / the first contact lenses, / the monkey wrench, / the diving snorkel, / and the first parachute. / He even developed / an early form of air conditioning / five hundred years ago!

2. Now read the paragraph aloud again. Focus on your pace, intonation, and expression. Try to read at a medium pace (not too slow and not too fast). Change your intonation (level of your voice) for sentences with an exclamation mark (!). Read these sentences with more feeling.

3. Discuss this question: Would the paragraph be easier or harder to read if you read it word by word? Why?

● Vocabulary Development

Use a Dictionary

When you read, you sometimes see a word you do not know. First, try to determine the meaning from the context of the sentence. If you still do not understand the word, look it up in a print dictionary or an online dictionary.

Look at this sentence from "Da Vinci's Dreams." Then look at the dictionary entry for the **highlighted** word.

• He did experiments and made **models** to test his ideas.

> **model** / mŏdl / *n.*
> **1** a small version of something. **2** a person who poses for artists or with products for sale. *adj.* showing a good example.
> < French modèle, from Latin modus *measure, standard* >

  a. Word: You find the word in alphabetical order.

  b. Pronunciation of the word: Your teacher will help you say the word correctly.

  c. Part of speech: for example: *n.* = noun, *adj.* = adjective

  d. Definitions: There may be more than one definition for a word. Decide which definition makes the most sense in the context of the sentence.

  e. Word origin: This is the language the word comes from.

1. Work with a partner. Read each sentence below.

2. Look up the highlighted word in a dictionary.

3. Copy the chart. Fill it out for each sentence.

   a. Moon Shadow's father wants to become a **merchant.**

   b. They pulled *Dragonwings* up a **steep** hill.

   c. Each of da Vinci's **inventions** started with a sketch.

   d. Da Vinci's ideas still look **modern** today.

Word	Definition	Part of Speech	Origin
a. merchant			
b.			
c.			
d.			

✓**Checkpoint**

1. In what order are words listed in the **dictionary**?

2. What are **parts of speech**?

Vocabulary Log

Workbook page 120

Independent Practice CD-ROM/Online

● Grammar

Conjunctions: and, but

A **conjunction** is a word that combines parts of a sentence. Conjunctions can connect words, phrases (groups of words), or independent clauses (parts of a sentence that can stand alone as a sentence).

When conjunctions connect independent clauses, they create **compound sentences.**

Word Origins

The word **conjunction** comes from the Latin word *conjunction: to join with.*

The conjunction **and** connects two **similar** ideas. It can connect:

words	He is wearing a <u>hat</u> **and** <u>gloves</u>.
phrases	Marta <u>ate a sandwich</u> **and** <u>drank a glass of juice</u> for lunch.
independent clauses	Leonardo **designed inventions**, **and** he made models to test his ideas.*

The conjunction **but** connects two **contrasting** ideas. It can connect:

words	It is <u>cold</u> **but** <u>sunny</u> today.
independent clauses	<u>Father had a few broken bones</u>, **but** <u>it was nothing **serious**</u>.*

*When **and** or **but** are used to connect two independent clauses, put a comma before the conjunction.

Practice the Grammar

A. Fill in the correct conjunction: **and** or **but**.

   1. Today we learned to **compare** _____ **contrast**.

   2. My father is **serious** _____ funny.

   3. I **predict** you will live a long _____ happy life.

   4. My parents are **similar** in some ways _____ different in others.

   5. We climbed up the **steep** hill, _____ we had a picnic at the top.

B. Connect the sentences with **and** or **but** to form one compound sentence.

   Leonardo was an inventor. He was a dreamer.
   Leonardo was an inventor, and he was a dreamer.

   1. Leonardo **designed** many **inventions.** Many of the **inventions** were not built during his life.

   2. Moon Shadow writes a letter to his mother. He tells her the bad news.

   3. *Dragonwings* rolled down the hill. It lifted in the air.

   4. Uncle does not think the airplane will work. He will help them anyway.

   5. Leonardo and Windrider are **similar** in some ways. They are different in others.

Use the Grammar Independently Complete each compound sentence with **and** or **but** and an idea of your own.

   The book is long, *but it is not difficult.*

1. Maria works in a hospital, _____.

2. My father is a teacher, _____.

3. She lives in an apartment, _____.

4. I study every night, _____.

Grammar Expansion

Conjunction: or

Workbook   Independent Practice
pages 123–124   CD-ROM/Online

✓Checkpoint

  1. What **conjunction** joins together two **contrasting** ideas?

  2. What conjunction joins together two **similar** ideas?

● **Writing Assignment**

Expository Writing: Write a Compare and Contrast Paragraph

Writing Suggestion

See **Milestones Handbook.** pages 393–433

> **Writing Prompt**
>
> **Compare** and **contrast** Windrider's dream with a dream you have. Write a compare and contrast paragraph. How are the dreams **similar**, and how are they different? Give examples. Use the conjunctions **and** and **but**.

Write Your Compare and Contrast Paragraph

1. **Read the student model.** Read the model of a **compare** and **contrast** paragraph. In this model, a student **compares** and **contrasts** herself to the character of Won Chul from "My Korean Name" in Unit 1.

Student Model

Won Chul and I

In some ways, Won Chul and I are very different, but in many ways we are very similar. Won Chul is from Korea, but I am from Mexico. Won Chul is a boy. I am a girl. However, in other ways, we are not very different. Won Chul's grandfather lived with his family, and my grandmother lives with my family. Both Won Chul and I learned about our culture from our grandparents. Won Chul's grandfather gave him a traditional drawing of his name. My grandmother teaches me about my culture all the time. She tells me stories about her life in Mexico, and she gave me a beautiful serape, a traditional Mexican shawl. I keep my grandmother's gift in my bedroom. I use it as a blanket. Every day I see it on my bed and it reminds me of my heritage.

Workbook
page 125

2. **Prewrite.** Make a list of ways in which Windrider's dream and your dream are **similar** and different.

3. **Write your paragraph.**

   a. **Write a topic sentence.** A **topic sentence** is a sentence that states your main idea. The topic sentence tells readers what you will be writing about.

   • Look at the student model. Find the topic sentence.

   b. **Write the rest of your paragraph.** All the sentences in your paragraph should **compare** the ways that Windrider's dream and your dream are alike and **contrast** the ways they are different. They should also support your topic sentence. Be sure to give examples from *Dragonwings* to support your topic sentence.

   • Look at the student model. Find examples from the reading and from the writer's life that support the topic sentence.

4. **Revise.** Reread your paragraph. Revise your paragraph if any ideas are not clear or complete.
   Use the **editing and proofreading symbols** on page 419 to help you mark the changes you want to make.

5. **Edit.** Use the **Writing Checklist** to help you find problems and errors.

6. **Read your paragraph to the class.** Read words in "chunks." Focus on your pace, intonation, and expression.

> ### Writing Checklist
>
> 1. I **compared** and **contrasted** my dream with Windrider's dream.
>
> 2. I combined some of my sentences with the conjunctions **and** and **but.**
>
> 3. I left margins on both sides of my paragraph.
>
> 4. I indented my paragraph.
>
> 5. I capitalized the first word of each sentence.

Writing Support

Grammar
Pronoun Referents

   A **pronoun** is a word that takes the place of a noun. A **pronoun referent** is a pronoun that refers to a noun that came before. Using pronoun referents makes your writing sound more natural.

In a few ways **Won Chul and I** are very different, but in more ways ~~Won Chul and I~~ *we* are very similar.

Apply Read your **compare** and **contrast** paragraph aloud. Can you make your writing sound more natural by using some pronoun referents?

Workbook
pages 126–128

Independent Practice
CD-ROM/Online

Progress Check

How well did you understand this chapter? Try to answer the questions. If necessary, go back to the pages listed for a review.

Skills	Skills Assessment Questions	Pages to Review
Vocabulary From the Readings	What do these words mean? • **design, disappear, machine, merchant, rhythm, serious, steep**	134
	• **engineer, experiment, invention, modern**	144
Academic Vocabulary	What do these academic vocabulary words mean? • **compare, contrast, similar**	135
	• **inference, predict**	142
Reading Strategies	How can you **compare** and **contrast** elements in a reading?	135
	How can you relate your own experiences to a reading?	145
Text Genres	What is the text genre of *Dragonwings*?	136
	What is the text genre of "Da Vinci's Dreams"?	145
Reading Comprehension	What is *Dragonwings* about?	143
	What is "Da Vinci's Dreams" about?	147
Literary Element	What is a **theme**? Name one of the themes in *Dragonwings*.	143
Spelling	Spell the **title** and name of three teachers in your school.	147
Writing Conventions	Where do you place **commas in a series** of items?	147
Listening and Speaking	**Phrases for Conversation** What phrases can you use to show interest in your classmates' ideas?	148
Vocabulary Development	What information can you find in a **dictionary**?	149
Grammar	What are **conjunctions**?	150–151
	Give an example of a sentence with the conjunction **and**.	
	Give an example of a sentence with the conjunction **but**.	
Writing Support: Grammar	Give an example of a sentence with a **pronoun referent**.	153

Assessment Practice

Read this passage. Then answer Questions 1 through 4.

The Wright Brothers

1   Before 1900, many people dreamed about flying and designed flying machines. However, they were not successful. Wilbur and Orville Wright also dreamed of flying. In 1899, they built a glider, a flying machine without an engine. They took it to a place where the wind was good. Their glider flew. They showed the world that a machine that was heavier than air could fly.

2   Four years later, they built and flew the first airplane. On December 17, 1903, Orville Wright flew 12 seconds in their airplane. In that moment on December 17, the Wright brothers achieved their dream and the dream of many others: flying.

1 Read this sentence from paragraph 1.

> They built a glider, a flying machine without an engine.

What does <u>machine</u> mean?

A glider

B engine

C piece of equipment that uses power to work

D glider that uses an engine to fly

2 How is a glider similar to an airplane?

A They both have motors.

B One has a motor; one does not.

C One has wings; one does not.

D They both fly.

3 Make an inference. How did the Wright brothers feel after their first flight?

A very excited

B frightened

C disappointed

D worried

4 What is the text genre of this passage?

A a play

B an informational text

C a poem

D a persuasive essay

Writing on Demand:
Compare and Contrast Paragraph

Compare and contrast the Wright brothers' dream with one of your dreams. How are they similar? How are they different? Give examples to support your point. **(20 minutes)**

> **Writing Tip**
> When writing a **compare** and **contrast** paragraph, make a Venn diagram to help you determine similarities and differences.

Objectives

Reading Strategies

Distinguish fact from opinion; Identify repetition in poetry

Listening and Speaking

Write and perform a short play

Grammar

Learn modals

Writing

Persuasive essay: Nominate a person to honor

Academic Vocabulary

distinguish	affect
evidence	support

Academic Content

Martin Luther King Jr.
Segregation

● **Chapter Focus Question**

How do dreams help people make changes in their lives and the lives of others?

Reading 1 **Content:** Social Studies

Informational text
Martin Luther King Jr. Day
by Mir Tamim Ansary

Reading 2 **Literature**

Poetry
Dreams
by Langston Hughes
The Dream on My Wall
The Student Teacher
by Jane Medina

Martin Luther King Jr. Day

● **About the Reading**

You are going to read an informational text about the holiday named after Martin Luther King Jr. You will learn about Martin Luther King Jr.'s dream, and the people and events that helped make the dream come true. You are also going to read excerpts from a famous Martin Luther King Jr. speech.

● Build Background

Segregation

Before the 1950s, the United States was a very different place from the country that we know today. Some people were treated unfairly because of their skin color. For example, in many places, African Americans could not eat in the same restaurants or go to the same schools as white people. This separation of African American and white people was called **segregation.** Leaders like Martin Luther King Jr. worked hard to end segregation. Their work helped to change unfair laws and to bring equal rights to all Americans.

Describe what you see in these pictures. Which pictures were taken before segregation ended? Which were taken after segregation ended?

● Use Prior Knowledge

Think About Equal Rights

Martin Luther King Jr. helped bring equal rights to African Americans. A "right" is something that the law allows you to do or have. What rights should all people have? Work with a small group to brainstorm ideas.

1. On a piece of paper, write this phrase: *All people have the right to…*
2. Work with your group to write three sentences that begin with the phrase.
3. Share your group's sentences with the class.

> All people have the right to . . .
>
> 1. All people have the right to an education.
> 2.
> 3.

Key Vocabulary

honor

peace

segregation

slave

violence

wisdom

● Vocabulary From the Reading
Learn, Practice, and Use Independently

Learn Vocabulary Read each sentence. Look at the **highlighted** word. Use the context to determine the meaning of the word.

1. The soldier was very brave. The town will **honor** him with a statue.
2. After the war, the country returned to **peace.**
3. For many years, **segregation** kept African Americans and whites apart.
4. Many years ago, African Americans in the United States were **slaves.** They had to do anything their owners told them to do.
5. There is too much **violence** on television. Many programs show people using guns and knives.
6. That old woman has a lot of **wisdom.** She has learned many things in her long life.

Practice Vocabulary Match each Key Vocabulary word to its definition.

Word	Definition
1. honor	a. knowledge usually gained from experience
2. segregation	b. strong force that hurts someone or something
3. peace	c. separation of a group from a larger group
4. slave	d. a time of quiet and cooperation
5. wisdom	e. to show respect or to give recognition
6. violence	f. a person who is owned by someone else

Use Vocabulary Independently Write one sentence for each Key Vocabulary word. Read your sentences to a partner.

✓Checkpoint

1. What are some ways to **honor** a person?
2. Name someone who has a lot of **wisdom.**

Vocabulary Log

Workbook page 129

Independent Practice CD-ROM/Online

● Academic Vocabulary

Vocabulary for the Reading Strategy

Word	Explanation	Sample Sentence	Visual Cue
distinguish *verb*	to see or understand how things are different	It is difficult to **distinguish** between Ella and her twin sister.	She is Ella. Bella Ella
evidence *noun*	words or things that show something is true	The police have **evidence** that he stole the watch. They found his fingerprints on the watch.	

Draw a picture and write a sentence for each word.

● Reading Strategy

Distinguish **Fact** from **Opinion**

It is important to **distinguish fact** from **opinion.** A fact is a piece of information that is true. A fact can be proven with **evidence.** An opinion is something that someone thinks or believes. An opinion cannot be proven to be true or false.

Fact: There are 12 months in a year.

Opinion: May is the most beautiful month of the year.

As you read, look for examples of facts and opinions. You will complete the chart after you finish reading.

Fact	Opinion

> ✓ **Checkpoint**
> 1. Give an example of a **fact.**
> 2. Give your **opinion** about something.

● **Text Genre**

Informational Text

Martin Luther King Jr. Day is an **informational text.** Look for these features of informational text in the reading.

Informational Text	
facts	information that can be proven
headings	titles used for separate sections of the text, usually in large bold type
captions	words that explain a picture

● **Meet the Author**

Mir Tamim Ansary was born in 1948 in Kabul, the capital of Afghanistan. His father taught science and literature at Kabul University. His American mother taught English at the first girls' school in Afghanistan. In 1964, Ansary came to the United States to attend high school. He has written novels, books about American history, and a memoir about being both Afghani and American.

● **Reading Focus Questions**

As you read, think about these questions.

1. How does this reading relate to the theme of "dreams"?
2. What do you think was the author's purpose for writing *Martin Luther King Jr. Day*?
3. Why did Martin Luther King Jr. call equality his "dream"?

Look at one of your textbooks. Identify two **headings** and two **captions**.

Workbook
page 131

Independent Practice
CD-ROM/Online

Martin Luther King Jr. Day

by Mir Tamim Ansary

Dr. Martin Luther King Jr.

1   Dr. Martin Luther King Jr. was not a president or a **general.** He didn't start a new religion. But he gave our country something wonderful. He gave us a dream. To understand this dream you have to know about things that happened in our country long ago.

Slavery and the Civil War

2   Long ago, African Americans were **slaves. The Civil War** set them free. But they did not get equal rights. They were not allowed to vote in many places. They could not get good jobs. Many people disliked them because they had darker skin.

New Laws

3   Some states passed laws to keep African Americans apart from other people. This was called **segregation.** African American people could not eat in the same restaurants as white people. African American people could not marry white people. They could not sit in the same parts of a bus as white people. They even had to go to separate schools.

An early African American classroom (1900)

---

general military officer of the highest level

the Civil War in the United States, the war between the North and the South that lasted from 1861 to 1865

Reading Strategy

Distinguish Fact from Opinion
Which sentence in this paragraph is an opinion?

✔ **Reading Check**

1. **Recall facts** What did Martin Luther King Jr. give our country?

2. **Recall facts** After the Civil War, did African Americans have equal rights?

3. **Describe** How were African Americans treated? Give examples from the reading.

From Boy to Man

Reading Strategy

Distinguish Fact from Opinion
Name two facts in this paragraph.

4   Martin Luther King Jr. grew up with **segregation**. He was born in Atlanta, Georgia, in 1929. He wanted to change many things. But he didn't want to hurt anyone. He had deep religious feelings. After college, he became a **minister** in Montgomery, Alabama. He also began studying the **wisdom** of Mohandas Gandhi.

The Wisdom of Gandhi

5   Gandhi was an Indian teacher and leader. He believed the world could be changed without **violence**. He told his followers to meet hate with love. Gandhi said people should not obey unfair laws. But they should not fight either. Dr. King wanted to try this **peaceful** way of pushing for change.

Mohandas Gandhi

---

minister Protestant clergyman or clergywoman

Rosa Parks Says No

6   In Alabama, the law said African American people had to sit in the back of the bus. One day in 1955, a woman named Rosa Parks said no to this. The police arrested her. Dr. King said the law was wrong. He asked people to stop riding buses. The bus company started losing money. Sure enough, the law was changed.

The Lunch Counter Sit-In

7   Then four African American students sat at a white people's lunch counter in Greensboro, North Carolina. No one served them. Some people called them names. But they kept sitting there for four days! Some people sat with the students to show their support. Dr. King led a march to cheer for these students. Soon, African Americans stopped **obeying segregation** laws in many cities. Dr. King was arrested for giving them the idea.

Reading Strategy

Distinguish Fact from Opinion Are there any opinions in this paragraph?

Rosa Parks sitting in the front of the bus in 1956

Reading Check

1. **Recall facts** Where was Martin Luther King Jr. born?

2. **Recall facts** Whose **wisdom** did Martin Luther King Jr. study?

3. **Make an inference** Why did Rosa Parks refuse to sit in the back of the bus?

---

obeying doing what is asked or ordered

A Letter from Jail

8   Dr. King wrote to newspapers. He explained why he was leading marches against **segregation.** He said all Americans should have the same rights. Thousands of people agreed with him. They too began to march. Even children joined these marches. Alabama sheriff Bull Connors put many of these children in jail.

Dr. King's Dream

Reading Strategy

Distinguish Fact from Opinion Find one fact and one opinion in this paragraph.

9   In 1963, Dr. King led a march to Washington, D.C. There he gave his greatest speech. He spoke to people about his dream. He said he dreamed of a world that was fair. People of all colors lived together in **peace.** A crowd of 250 thousand people heard him and began to dream, too.

Martin Luther King Jr. delivers his "I Have a Dream" speech in front of the Lincoln Memorial in Washington, D.C.

From Martin Luther King Jr.'s "I Have a Dream" Speech

I have a dream that one day . . . the sons of former **slaves** and the sons of former **slave** owners will be able to sit down together at the table of brotherhood . . .

I have a dream that one day . . . little black boys and black girls will be able to join hands with little white boys and white girls as sisters and brothers . . .

And if America is to be a great nation, this must become true . . .

Let freedom ring. And when this happens . . . we will be able to join hands and sing . . . "Free at last! Free at last! Thank God Almighty, we are free at last!"

Meeting Hate with Love

10   The dream spread across America. Millions of people began working for equal rights. Sometimes police beat them up, but they never fought back. They followed Dr. King's rule—meet hate with love. It worked. Slowly, **segregation** ended. In 1964, new laws were passed. They promised equal rights to all Americans.

The Death of Dr. King

11   Four years later, in 1968, a man shot Dr. King. Millions of people cried. What would happen to Dr. King's dream? Had the bullet killed that, too? Dr. King was buried. Four days later, Congressman John Conyers of Michigan had an idea: America should have a holiday to **honor** Martin Luther King Jr.

Remembering the Dream

12   Martin Luther King Jr. Day began in 1983. It is on the third Monday of January. People across the country get together to remember Dr. King's dream. It's a good day to start living the dream, too. It's a good day to reach out and make new friends.

Reading Strategy

Distinguish **Fact from Opinion** Find one fact and one opinion in this paragraph.

Statue **honoring** Martin Luther King Jr.

✓

Reading Check

1. **Recall facts** Where did Martin Luther King Jr. give his greatest speech?

2. **Recall facts** How many people heard this speech?

3. **Draw conclusions** Why do you think a man shot Martin Luther King Jr.?

● Apply the Reading Strategy

Distinguish Fact from Opinion

Now complete the Fact and Opinion chart.

1. Review the **Reading Strategy** on page 159.
2. Copy the chart.
3. Write facts and opinions from the reading in the chart.
4. Share your chart with a partner. Read aloud the facts and opinions in your chart. Check your partner's chart.

Fact	Opinion
He was born in Atlanta, Georgia, in 1929.	

● Academic Vocabulary

Vocabulary for the Reading Comprehension Questions

Word	Explanation	Sample Sentence	Visual Cue
affect *verb*	to change, to have an impact on	The weather **affects** my mood.	
support *verb*	to hold up, to keep from falling or slipping	My grandfather uses a cane to **support** himself when he walks.	

Draw a picture and write a sentence for each word.

✓Checkpoint

How do funny movies **affect** you? How do scary movies **affect** you?

Vocabulary
Log

Reading Comprehension Questions

Think and Discuss

1. **Recall facts** When was Martin Luther King Jr. born?
2. **Explain** How did Gandhi's **wisdom affect** Martin Luther King Jr.'s ideas?
3. **Analyze photos** Why do you think photos are used with the reading instead of illustrations? How do the photos help you understand the reading better?
4. **Describe character traits** What three words describe Martin Luther King Jr. best?
5. **Paraphrase** Reread the excerpt of Martin Luther King Jr.'s "I Have a Dream" speech. In your own words, explain his dream.
6. **Discuss** Why is Martin Luther King Jr. Day an important holiday? Use information from the reading as **evidence** to **support** your opinion.
7. **Revisit the Reading Focus Questions** Go back to page 160 and discuss the questions.

Workbook
page 132

Independent Practice
CD-ROM/Online

Text Element

Chronological Order

The author describes many historical events in *Martin Luther King Jr. Day*. He writes about these events in the order in which they happened. This is called **chronological order.**

Many informational texts present information in chronological order. These texts include dates and **signal words.** Signal words give the reader information about the order of events. Some signal words are:

before   during   after   then

1. Reread *Martin Luther King Jr. Day.* Look for dates and signal words that help you understand the order of events.
2. As you read, take notes on the dates and signal words.
3. After you read, create a chart of the chronological order of events in the reading.

✓Checkpoint

1. What does **chronological order** mean?
2. Describe something that happened yesterday. Use three **signal words.**

Vocabulary
Log

Workbook
page 133

Independent Practice
CD-ROM/Online

Dreams
The Dream on My Wall
The Student Teacher

● About the Reading

You read *Martin Luther King Jr. Day,* an informational text about the dream of a great American leader. Now you will read three poems about the importance of dreams.

● Build Background

Rhyming Poems and Free Verse Poems

You will read a rhyming poem and two free verse poems. The sound of these two kinds of poems is different.

Kind of Poem	Explanation	Example
rhyming poem	lines end with rhyming words (words with the same ending sounds)	I'm Nobody! Who are **you**? Are you—Nobody—**Too**? from "I'm Nobody! Who are you?" by Emily Dickinson
free verse poem	lines do not end with rhyming words; more like a conversation	Ink runs from the corners of my mouth. There is no happiness like mine. I have been eating poetry. from "Eating Poetry" by Mark Strand

Key Vocabulary

frozen

hope

stuck

● Vocabulary From the Reading

Use Context Clues to Determine Meaning

1. Read the definition of each word.
   a. **frozen:** changed into a solid state by low temperatures
   b. **hope:** to want something to happen
   c. **stuck:** attached with glue, tape, or a pointed object
2. Answer the questions.
   a. Can a person **hope?** Can a book **hope?** Can a tree?
   b. Can water be **frozen?** Can fire be **frozen?** Can juice?
   c. Can a picture be **stuck** on a refrigerator? Can a nail be **stuck** in a wall? Can a tree be **stuck** to a house?

✓Checkpoint

1. Give an example of something **frozen**.
2. Give an example of something **stuck**.
3. What do you **hope** for?

Vocabulary Log

Workbook page 134

Independent Practice CD-ROM/Online

Reading Strategy

Identify Repetition in Poetry

Repetition is saying or writing something more than once. A poem can include repetition of a sound, a word, a phrase, or a line. Poets often use repetition to draw the reader's attention to an important idea or to create a mood.

Text Genre

Poetry

You are going to read three **poems**. Poems usually contain some or all of these features.

Poem	
stanzas	groups of lines
rhyme	words having the same ending sound
sensory language	words that help you see, hear, smell, touch, and taste what the poet is describing
rhythm	a regular beat

Meet the Authors

Langston Hughes was born in 1902 and died in 1967. He was one of the first successful African American authors. His characters and poems often deal with issues and problems important to African American culture.

Jane Medina is a teacher and poet. She teaches English language learners and has a special interest in multicultural education. Medina and her family speak both English and Spanish. They celebrate both American and Mexican traditions.

Reading Focus Questions

As you read, think about these questions:

1. How does this reading relate to the theme of "dreams"?
2. What do you think each poet's purpose was for writing his/her poem?
3. Do you think the poets believe it is important to have dreams?

✓**Checkpoint**

1. Give an example of a song that includes **repetition**.
2. Give an example of two words that **rhyme**.

Workbook
pages 135–136

Independent Practice
CD-ROM/Online

Dreams

by Langston Hughes

Reading Strategy

Identify Repetition in Poetry Which line is repeated in the poem? Why do you think the poet repeats this line?

1   Hold **fast** to dreams
For if dreams die
Life is a broken-winged bird
That cannot fly.

2   Hold fast to dreams
For when dreams go
Life is a **barren** field
Frozen with snow.

The Frost
by Claude Monet (1840–1926)
What is the artist trying to show in this painting?
How does the painting relate to the poem?

---

fast firmly, tightly

barren not able to produce anything

The Dream on My Wall

by Jane Medina

1 I have a dream on my wall.
I drew it in the second grade.
The teacher said,
"Draw your dreams, boys and girls.
Draw the dreams that only you can see."
Most kids drew
rooms full of dollar bills,
or pretty houses with flowers and **chimneys**,
or toys or candy or Disneyland.
But I drew a dream
of a class full of kids
and a pretty brown teacher
who looked just like me.

2 I have a dream on my wall.
I **stuck** it there with yellow tape.

3 Now the tape is **curling** at the ends.

Reading Strategy

Identify Repetition in Poetry Find a line repeated in this poem. Why do you think the poet repeats this line?

✔ Reading Check

1. **Recall facts** What did the teacher tell the boys and girls to draw?
2. **Recall facts** What dreams did most of the kids draw?
3. **Compare and contrast** How were the poet's dreams different from the dreams of her classmates?

---

chimneys structures for passing smoke from a stove or fireplace into the open air
curling twisting or bending

The Student Teacher

by Jane Medina

Reading Strategy

Identify Repetition in Poetry Which words and phrases are repeated in this poem? Why do you think the poet repeats them?

1 "Esperanza Moreno,"
        the chalkboard says.
Mr. North is smiling so big,
        his mouth hardly fits on his face.
"Tell us about yourself," he says
        to the dark young lady
        standing in front of her name.

2 So Miss Moreno begins to talk to us
        with a chocolate-sweet voice.

3 She tells us
        how hungry she was
        when she came from El Salvador as a girl.
She tells us
        how hungry she was to learn,
        how hungry she was to speak,
        how hungry she was to **hope.**
She tells us
        of college,
        of books,
        and of money.
Then she tells us of a dream she has,
a dream, she says,
        that is coming true.

4 And I think of the
        dream on my wall:
        the dream
        of a class full of kids
        and a pretty brown teacher
        who looks just like me:
        the dream with the yellow tape
        that's curling
        at the ends.

Reading Comprehension Questions

Think and Discuss

1. **Identify literary characteristics** Which poem is a rhyming poem? Which poems are free verse poems?

2. **Understand figurative language** In "Dreams," the poet compares life without dreams to a "broken-winged bird." Why does he make this comparison?

3. **Explain** How do you know that "The Student Teacher" and "The Dream on My Wall" are narrated by the same character?

4. **Make connections between readings** How is the Langston Hughes poem similar to the Jane Medina poems? How is it different?

5. **Revisit the Reading Focus Questions** Go back to page 169 and discuss the questions.

Workbook
page 137

Independent Practice
CD-ROM/Online

Spelling

Abbreviations in Names

Workbook
page 138

Independent Practice
CD-ROM/Online

Writing Conventions

Punctuation: Commas in Addresses

Workbook
page 139

Independent Practice
CD-ROM/Online

Connect Readings 1 and 2

You have read several readings on the theme of dreams. Use these activities to make connections between the readings.

1. With a partner, use this chart to compare the readings.

Reading title	What is the text genre?	Which reading includes facts?	Which readings have stanzas?	What is the purpose of the reading?
Martin Luther King Jr. Day				
Dreams, The Dream on My Wall, The Student Teacher				

2. Answer the questions about the readings. Then compare and discuss your answers with a partner.

   a. Look at the Langston Hughes poem "Dreams." Imagine Martin Luther King Jr. reading the poem. Explain each stanza of the poem through his eyes.

   b. Which of the readings was your favorite? Why?

3. **Revisit the Chapter Focus Question** How do dreams help people make changes in their lives and the lives of others? Use examples from *Martin Luther King Jr. Day*, "Dreams," "The Dream on My Wall," and "The Student Teacher" to answer this question.

● Listening and Speaking

Write and Perform a Short Play

Write and perform a short play. Base it on one of the events described in *Martin Luther King Jr. Day,* or on the poems "The Dream on My Wall" and "The Student Teacher."

1. Work in a small group.

2. Think of an event or a scene you would like to base the play on. Use the **Phrases for Conversation** to express your preference to your group. As a group, decide which event or scene to use.

3. Work with your group to write a short play based on the event or scene.

4. Review the features of a play on page 136.

5. Choose group members to play each character. Be sure the dialogue is appropriate for the characters.

6. Rehearse, or practice, the play several times. Do not speak too fast. Do not speak too softly or too loudly.

7. Perform the play for your class. Be sure to use appropriate expression, body language, and gestures.

Phrases for Conversation

Expressing Preferences

I like (the scene with Rosa Parks).

I prefer (the scene with Rosa Parks).

I think we should (do the scene with Rosa Parks).

I would choose (the scene with Rosa Parks).

● Reading Fluency

Echo Read Aloud

Good readers do not just read words. They read the words with expression, or feeling. Echo reading helps you read with expression. To echo means to repeat something in the same way it was said the first time.

1. Turn to the Langston Hughes poem "Dreams" on page 170. Listen to your teacher recite one line of the poem.

2. Recite the same line aloud with the same expression your teacher used. Adjust your reading rate (speed) and intonation (level of your voice) to help you read with expression.

3. Continue listening and reciting.

● Vocabulary Development

Multiple-Meaning Words

Multiple-meaning words are two or more words that are pronounced the same and often spelled the same. However, the words have different meanings.

For example, the word **change** is a multiple-meaning word. It can mean:

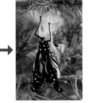

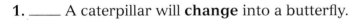

change: coins   **change:** to make something different

Work with a partner. Read each sentence. Match the word to the correct picture.

1. _____ A caterpillar will **change** into a butterfly.

2. _____ I have a pocket full of **change**.

3. _____ African Americans had to sit in the **back** of the bus.

4. _____ My **back** hurts from lifting heavy boxes.

5. _____ The Civil War set the **slaves free**.

6. _____ I didn't pay for this sweater. It was **free**.

7. _____ In 1963, Dr. King led a **march** to Washington, D.C.

8. _____ My birthday is in **March**.

9. _____ Birds **fly** north in the spring.

10. _____ A **fly** landed on the leaf.

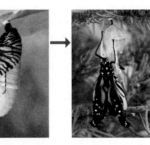

✓ Checkpoint

1. What is a **multiple-meaning word**?

2. Give three examples of multiple-meaning words.

Vocabulary Log

Workbook page 140

Independent Practice CD-ROM/Online

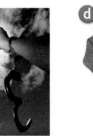

● **Grammar**

Modals: can, could, should, must

A **modal** is a special "helping" verb. It is used with another verb to express an idea.

Modal	Use to ...	Example
can	talk about ability in the present	I am 18. I **can** vote this year.
could	talk about ability in the past	I was 17 last year. I **could** not vote last year.
should	give advice and suggestions	You look sick. You **should** go to the doctor.
must	talk about something that is necessary or required	Cars **must** stop at red lights.

Note: Modals do not end in -s in the third person.

Modals: Affirmative			
subject	**modal**	**base form of verb**	**(object)**
John	**should**	do	his homework.

Modals: Negative				
subject	**modal**	*not*	**base form of verb**	**(object)**
John	**should**	**not**	forget	his book.

Note: The negative of **can** is **cannot** or **can't**.

Practice the Grammar

A. Complete each sentence with the right modal.

1. You _____ stop.

2. You _____ cover your mouth when you cough.

3. You _____ have green beans, tomatoes, or carrots.

4. Ten years ago I _____ touch my toes, but now I _____ .

B. Complete the paragraph with the right modals.

Before the civil rights movement, most African Americans (1) _____ not vote. They (2) _____ not get good jobs. African American children (3) _____ go to school. However, they (4) _____ not go to school with white children. Today African Americans (5) _____ do anything white Americans can do. We (6) _____ remember the leaders of the civil rights movement. They taught our country an important lesson: We (7) _____ respect every citizen of this country.

Grammar Expansion

Positive and Negative Modals;
Question Modals;
Modal: **must**

Workbook   Independent Practice
pages 142–144   CD-ROM/Online

Use the Grammar Independently Discuss these questions with a partner.

1. What are three things you could not do five years ago? What are three things you can do now?

I could not swim five years ago. Now I can swim.

2. What is your dream? What are some things you can, should, or must do to make your dream come true?

I want to be a doctor. I must get good grades.

✓**Checkpoint**

1. Tell two things that you **can** do.

2. Tell two things that you **should** do.

3. Tell two things that you **must** do.

● Writing Assignment

Persuasive Essay: Nominate a Person to Honor

Writing Suggestion

See **Milestones Handbook.**
pages 393–433

Writing Prompt

Martin Luther King Jr. was a great American. He was **honored** with a holiday in his name. Nominate another person to **honor.** Write a **persuasive essay.** A persuasive essay convinces the reader about something. Explain why this person deserves a holiday in his or her name. Use modals in your essay.

Write Your Persuasive Essay

1. Read the student model.

Student Model

Davi Amaral

Pelé Day

It is a great honor to have a holiday named after you. Only very special people deserve this honor. Only people who accomplish a lot should receive this honor. People who are heroes to others should receive it. I know someone who deserves to be honored: Pelé.

Pelé is a very famous soccer player from my country, Brazil. Pelé doesn't play soccer now, but he is still very famous. Pelé accomplished a lot. He was a great soccer player. Pelé played soccer for over 20 years. He scored a goal in almost every international game he played. He helped win three World Cup titles. Pelé is a hero in Brazil. Other soccer teams wanted him, but Pelé was loyal. He did not leave his team. Pelé is a good person, too. He helped the poor people of Brazil.

Pelé is a very special person. He did a lot for Brazil and for the sport of soccer. For these reasons, he must have a holiday named after him.

2. **Brainstorm.** Choose a person to nominate. Brainstorm reasons why this person should have a holiday in his or her name. You may wish to find more information about the person on the Internet or in the library.

3. **Write your essay.**

   a. Give your essay a title.

   b. Leave margins on each side.

   c. In the first paragraph, describe the kind of person who deserves to be **honored.** Then state the person you are nominating.

   d. In the second paragraph, provide **evidence.** Include facts, details, and examples to **support** your opinion. The information in this paragraph should convince the reader.

   e. In the third paragraph, re-state your nomination and the reasons for your nomination.

4. **Revise.** Reread your essay. Revise it if any ideas are not clear or complete. Use the **editing and proofreading symbols** on page 419 to help you mark the changes you want to make.

5. **Edit.** Use the **Writing Checklist** to help you find problems and errors.

> ### Writing Checklist
>
> **1.** I used modals.
>
> **2.** I combined sentences with conjunctions.
>
> **3.** I persuaded my audience.
>
> **4.** I indented my paragraphs.
>
> **5.** I capitalized the first word of each sentence.

Writing Support

Spelling
Commonly Confused Words

Some words sound the same but have different meanings and different spellings. When a writer uses the wrong word, readers can become confused. It is important to learn about **commonly confused words.**

their = *possessive pronoun*	They wrote **their** essays.
there = a place	My class is **there.**
they're = *contraction for* **they are**	**They're** working together.

Apply Check your persuasive essay for these commonly confused words. Make sure they are spelled correctly.

UNIT 3 • CHAPTER 2

Progress Check

How well did you understand this chapter? Try to answer the questions. If necessary, go back to the pages listed for a review.

Skills	Skills Assessment Questions	Pages to Review
Vocabulary From the Readings	What do these words mean? Can you use each of them in a sentence?	
	• **honor, peace, segregation, slave, violence, wisdom**	**158**
	• **frozen, hope, stuck**	**168**
Academic Vocabulary	What do these academic vocabulary words mean?	
	• **distinguish, evidence**	**159**
	• **affect, support**	**166**
Reading Strategies	What is the difference between a **fact** and an **opinion**? How can you **distinguish** between them?	**159**
	How can identifying **repetition** in a poem help you understand the poem?	**169**
Text Genre	What is the text genre of *Martin Luther King Jr. Day*?	**160**
	What is the text genre of "Dreams," "The Dream on My Wall," and "The Student Teacher"?	**169**
Reading Comprehension	What is *Martin Luther King Jr. Day* about?	**167**
	What are "Dreams," "The Dream on My Wall," and "The Student Teacher" about?	**173**
Text Element	What is **chronological order**? What are some words that signal chronological order?	**167**
Spelling	Give three examples of **abbreviations with names.**	**173**
Writing Conventions	Rewrite this **address using commas:** 11 Maple Lane Newton Texas 75966	**173**
Listening and Speaking	**Phrases for Conversation** What expressions can you use for expressing preferences?	**174**
Vocabulary Development	Give three examples of **multiple-meaning words.**	**175**
Grammar	Name four **modals.** Use a modal in a sentence.	**176**
Writing Support: Spelling	What are **commonly confused words**? Give an example of two commonly confused words.	**179**

Assessment Practice

Read this text. Then answer Questions 1 through 4.

Girl Dancing

1   I dreamed of dancing,
2   put on the music,
3   then I was prancing.
4   My brothers laughed.
5   My body moved
6   and turned about.

7   I dreamed of dancing,
8   stretched and whirled,
9   without glancing
10   back at others who
11   smiled and said,
12   dancing is not for you.

13   I dreamed of dancing,
14   I worked and hoped,
15   took a leap, chancing
16   that I might make it.
17   My dream is on stage.
18   I'll dance on and take it.

1   Read line 14.

> I worked and hoped,

What does <u>hoped</u> mean?

A   believed
B   jumped
C   leaped
D   played

2   Which lines are an example of repetition?

A   the even ones (2, 4, 6, 8, etc.)
B   the odd ones (1, 3, 5, 7, etc.)
C   1, 3, 4, and 6
D   1, 7, and 13

3   Which line begins with a chronological order signal word?

A   1
B   3
C   5
D   7

4   What is the text genre of this passage?

A   play
B   informational text
C   poetry
D   persuasive essay

Writing on Demand: Persuasive Essay

The poet dreams of becoming a dancer, but others laugh at her. Write a short persuasive essay to convince her to continue her dreams. Give her at least three reasons why she should continue dancing. **(20 minutes)**

> **Writing Tip**
> Using the modals **should**, **must**, and **can** will help you write a persuasive essay.

Apply & Extend

Objectives

Listening and Speaking
Deliver an informative presentation

Media
Analyze advertisements that "sell" dreams

Writing
Response to literature: essay

Projects

Independent Reading

Build Your Knowledge

Try giving your presentation using technology. Read and follow the steps for giving a technology presentation on page 429.

● Listening and Speaking Workshop

Deliver an Informative Presentation

Topic

An **informative presentation** gives facts and examples about a topic. Deliver an informative presentation about a famous person who made a dream come true.

1. **Brainstorm**

   With a small group, talk about people who had a dream. This can include inventors, scientists, astronauts, artists, and politicians. Together, choose one of these people for your group's presentation.

2. **Plan**

   Your group's presentation will focus on three questions.

   a. What dream did this person follow?

   b. How did the person make the dream come true?

   c. Why was this dream important?

   Find facts, details, and examples to answer the questions. Use two or more sources such as books, magazines, or online encyclopedias. Ask your teacher or school librarian for help. Take notes on the information.

3. **Outline**

   Work with your group to write an outline for the presentation. Include visuals to make the presentation more interesting. This can include a timeline, a chart, or a graph. You may also include pictures from magazines or the Internet.

4. **Practice**

   Decide which members of your group will present each part of the presentation. Think about each part of the **Speaking Self-Evaluation** before you practice.

5. **Present**

   Give the presentation. Use the level of your voice to emphasize (stress) important points. This will help listeners follow main ideas. Use your voice and gestures to show that you are excited about the topic. Speak slowly and loudly enough for listeners to hear you.

6. Evaluate

Ask your group members for feedback. Use the **Speaking Self-Evaluation** to evaluate your part of the presentation. Use the **Active Listening Evaluation** to evaluate and discuss your classmates' presentations.

Speaking Self-Evaluation
1. I answered the focus questions with facts, details, and examples.
2. I spoke slowly and loudly enough for people to hear me.
3. I looked at the audience while I spoke.
4. I used intonation to emphasize main ideas.

Active Listening Evaluation
1. The opening of your presentation was interesting.
2. Your presentation was well organized.
3. I understood the main ideas of your presentation.
4. I think your presentation needed more information about ____.

● Media Workshop

Analyze Advertisements that Sell Dreams

Advertisements often show pictures of "dream" situations. The people look happy and beautiful. They are in wonderful places. Advertisements show people in dream situations to sell products. The advertisements seem to say: *Buy this product and your dreams will come true!*

1. Find an advertisement that sells a dream.
2. Work with a partner. Discuss your advertisements.
   a. What product is advertised?
   b. Describe the advertisement. What words and pictures does it use to sell the dream?
   c. Do you think this product can make this dream come true? Why or why not?

Imagine Yourself in a Zero 3000 . . . .

3. With your partner, create an advertisement that sells a dream.
   a. Decide on a product and a "dream" situation to help you sell it.
   b. Draw a picture of the dream situation.
   c. Write a few words or a sentence for the advertisement.
4. Present your advertisement to the class.

Writing
Suggestion

See **Milestones Handbook**.
pages 393–433

● **Writing Workshop**

Response to Literature: Essay

In a **response to literature** essay, you write about how the events in a story change the main character. Writing a response to literature essay helps you understand more about the characters and themes of a story.

> **Writing Prompt**
>
> How do the events in *Dragonwings* change the character of Windrider?

PREWRITE

1. Read the student model on the next page. It will help you understand how to write a response to literature essay.
2. Think about these questions. Take notes on your ideas.
   a. What is important to Windrider at the beginning of *Dragonwings*?
   b. What is important to him by the end of the play?
   c. What events help create this change?
3. Reread *Dragonwings*. Look for details and examples in the reading to support your answers. Take notes.

WRITE A DRAFT

1. Write the **introduction.** The introduction should include the title, the author, and the main character of the reading. It should also include a **topic sentence.** A topic sentence states the main idea and purpose of your essay. In this essay, the topic sentence should give a short answer to the writing prompt.
2. Next, write the **body** of the essay. The body should be one or two paragraphs. All the sentences in the body should support your topic sentence. Use the details and examples you found in the reading. This will support your topic sentence.
3. Write the **conclusion.** The conclusion is the last paragraph. It summarizes the important points in the essay. It should also restate your topic sentence in different words.

Student Model

In this response to literature essay, the student responds to the following **Writing Prompt:** *"How do the events in "My Korean Name" change the character of Won Chul?"*

Diego Perez

Title

What Won Chul Learns

Introduction

"My Korean Name" is a story about Won Chul. Won Chul is a Korean American boy. He lives with his parents and his grandfather. At the beginning of the story, Won Chul is not interested in his grandfather, and he is not interested in his culture. However, during the story, his grandfather teaches Won Chul many things. By the end of the story, Won Chul's feelings change. He is interested in his name and in his culture.

> Your essay must include a topic sentence.

At the beginning of the story Won Chul is scared of his grandfather. He and his grandfather speak different languages. His grandfather seems strange and different to Won Chul, but one day this starts to change. His grandfather speaks Korean to Won Chul. He tells Won Chul that Korean is important. Then he paints Won Chul's name. Won Chul says, "That looks neat." Later his mother tells him about this painting. It is a special Korean way of writing. He learns that his grandfather was a famous artist in Korea.

Body

> Include details and examples from the reading.

After his grandfather dies, Won Chul hangs up the painting in his room. He thinks about his grandfather in a new way. He does not think about how different they are anymore. Won Chul remembers his grandfather speaking Korean, and now he is curious. What was his grandfather telling him? Was he talking about his life in Korea?

> Use different words to restate the main idea in your topic sentence.

By the end of the story, Won Chul is interested in his grandfather's life. He is also interested in his own culture. Won Chul's grandfather opened Won Chul's eyes. Won Chul used to think his culture was not important, but now he knows that it is.

Conclusion

Apply & Extend

Writing Suggestion

If possible, combine some of your sentences with the conjunctions **and** and **but**.

REVISE

1. Review your draft. Make sure your topic sentence is clear. Make sure you included examples from the reading to support your topic sentence.

2. Exchange your essay with a partner. Ask your partner to use the **Peer Review Checklist** to review your essay. Your partner will point out errors and give suggestions for making your draft better.

3. Revise your draft. You may need to add or delete sentences. You may need to rearrange sentences to make your ideas clearer.

4. Use the **editing and proofreading symbols** on page 419 to help you mark the changes you want to make.

EDIT

1. Use the **Revising and Editing Checklist** to evaluate your essay.

2. Fix any errors in grammar, spelling, and punctuation.

Peer Review Checklist

1. There is a topic sentence.

2. There are examples from the reading to support the topic sentence.

3. The essay helped me understand how the character changed.

4. The conclusion summarizes the main points.

5. The essay would be better if _____ .

Revising and Editing Checklist

1. My topic sentence is clear and states the main idea.

2. I included details and examples from the reading in the body.

3. I used different words to restate the main idea in the conclusion.

4. I used capital letters and punctuation correctly.

5. I used the conjunctions **and** and **but** correctly.

PUBLISH

1. Write your essay in your best handwriting or use a computer. Use correct spacing between letters and words. If you use a computer, use a spell check and a grammar check.

2. Read your essay to the class. Read clearly and slowly enough so that everyone can understand you. Change the level of your voice to express the important ideas in your essay.

● Projects

Choose one or more of the following projects to explore the theme of dreams further.

PROJECT 1
Present Your Dream House

1. Draw a picture of your dream house.
2. Write a paragraph about what is inside the house.
3. Share your drawing and paragraph with your class.

PROJECT 2
Interview Your Classmates About Their Hopes and Dreams

1. Write a list of questions to ask your classmates about their hopes and dreams.
2. Take notes on their responses.
3. Report your findings to the class. Did many students have similar hopes and dreams? Which were the most interesting dreams?

PROJECT 3
Literature About Dreams From Around the World

1. Go to your library and find folktales, fables, legends, myths, and fairy tales with the theme of dreams.
2. Choose three from different cultures.
3. For each story, take notes about the plot, the characters, and their dreams.
4. Report back to the class. Retell the plot of each story. Talk about the characters' dreams.

PROJECT 4
Learn About the Science of Dreams

1. Find information in the library or on the Internet to answer these questions.
   a. Does everyone dream when they sleep?
   b. What happens when people dream?
2. Report back to your class on what you learned.

UNIT 3

Apply & Extend

Heinle Reading Library

The Adventures of Huckleberry Finn
by Mark Twain

In a specially adapted version by Deidre S. Laiken

Huckleberry Finn hopes to find a better life. He becomes friends with Jim, a runaway slave. Together, they float on a raft down the Mississippi River and dream of a new life.

Build Your Knowledge

Read several poems from *The Collected Poems of Langston Hughes*. Write a review that compares the poems. Include information about the features of the poems (rhyme, rhythm, sensory language) as well as the mood the poems create.

● Independent Reading

Explore the theme of dreams further by reading one or more of these books.

Dragonwings by Laurence Yep, Dramatists Play Service, Inc., 1993.

A Chinese boy travels to America to join his father. The father dreams of building and flying his own airplane. As the son helps his father achieve his dream, they build a strong relationship.

Martin Luther King Jr. Day by Mir Tamim Ansary, Heinemann, 2006.

Martin Luther King Jr. had a dream that brought great changes to the United States. Today he is honored with a special holiday in his name.

The Collected Poems of Langston Hughes by Langston Hughes, Alfred A. Knopf/Vintage, 1994.

This arrangement of poems written by Langston Hughes throughout his lifetime shows Hughes's humor and insight into the world.

Dezbah and the Dancing Tumbleweeds by Margaret Garaway, Treasure Chest Publishing, 1990.

The story of a Navajo girl who gives up her dream of becoming an Olympic runner when an accident occurs. The support of a teacher inspires her to find a new dream.

A Peddler's Dream by Janice Shefelman, Illustrated by Tom Shefelman, Houghton Mifflin, 1992.

The story of a Lebanese immigrant who comes to America at the turn of the century. Solomon Joseph Azar brings nothing to America but his dream of making his fortune and bringing his wife to America. His intelligence, hard work, and good luck help him realize his dream.

The Contender by Robert Lipsyte, HarperCollins Children's Books, 1987.

Alfred Brooks is a 17-year-old African American torn between the street life of his Harlem neighborhood and his dream of becoming a champion boxer. He struggles through difficult training to prove himself.

Writing: Revise and Edit

MILESTONES TRACKER

Read this rough draft of a student's persuasive essay, which may contain errors. Then answer Questions 1 through 4.

Fun Play, Important Lesson

(**1**) You should read the play *The Strongest One* by Joseph Bruchac. (**2**) I think it is fun to read. (**3**) It is about a small red ant who leaves his anthill. (**4**) He wants to find out who is the strongest in the world. (**5**) You will enjoy the play and you will also learn an important lesson. (**6**) Little Red Ant's relatives ask who is strongest. (**7**) When Little Red Ant returns to the anthill, he is wiser. (**8**) Little Red Ant says, "Everything is stronger than something else. (**9**) And even though we ants are small, in some ways we are the strongest of all." (**10**) This important lesson is true about people, too. (**11**) Bruchac teaches us in his play that everyone is strong in some way. (**12**) I think that if you like easy and exciting stories, you should read Bruchac's play. (**13**) Their is an important lesson to learn.

1 How can you edit sentence 5?
  A Add a period after *play*.
  B Add a period after *and*.
  C Add a comma after *play*.
  D Add a comma after *and*.

2 Where should you move sentence 7?
  A After sentence 5.
  B After sentence 1.
  C After sentence 8.
  D After sentence 2.

3 How can you improve sentence 8?
  A Change *Little Red Ant* to *I*.
  B Change *Little Red Ant* to *We*.
  C Change *Little Red Ant* to *He*.
  D Change *Little Red Ant* to *She*.

4 How can you correct sentence 13?
  A Change *Their* to *They're*.
  B Change *Their* to *Here*.
  C Change *Their* to *The're*.
  D Change *Their* to *There*.

Writing on Demand: Magazine Article

Write a short magazine article (one paragraph) about an invention. It can be a modern machine, something electronic, or anything else you know about. Draw an illustration with a caption to accompany your article. (**20 minutes**)

> **Writing Tip**
> Give several facts and at least one opinion about the invention. For opinions, use statements like *I believe* or *I think*.

Read this play. Then answer Questions 1 through 8.

Rosa Refuses to Get Up

Characters: Narrator, Rosa Parks, her Friend, Bus Driver, Police

1   **Rosa:** *(warming her hands)* Oh, here's my bus. I hope I get a seat today.

2   **Friend:** *(warming her ears)* Well, don't refuse to go to the back door like you did before. You know that the bus driver will get mad.

3   **Rosa:** *(getting on the bus from the back door)* It's going to change someday soon, you'll see.

4   **Bus Driver:** Move to the back seat.

5   **Narrator:** Rosa sat in the last seat—the one for African Americans. At the next stop, six white people got on. Five found seats. One did not. He didn't mind standing. However, the law said that an African American must give up a seat for a white person.

6   **Bus Driver:** *(looking over his shoulder at Rosa)* Get up. Give up your seat.

7   **Rosa:** *(quietly)* Why? I've paid my money. I have a right to sit.

8   **Bus Driver:** *(standing over Rosa)* You get up now!

9   **Rosa:** No.

10 **Bus Driver:** *(yelling)* You get up or I'll call the police! I'm serious!

11 **Rosa:** *(calmly)* Do it.

12 **Bus Driver:** *(on his radio)* I need some help here! A black woman is not giving up her seat. Get her out of here!

13 **Police:** *(arresting Rosa)* Too tired to stand up? Well you can rest all night in jail.

14 **Narrator:** *(to the audience)* Rosa's refusal to get up started the Montgomery Bus Boycott. African Americans refused to ride the buses. The bus company lost money. The company began to listen to the African Americans' argument that segregation was wrong. Rosa said later...

15 **Rosa:** *(sitting alone on the bus)* People always say that I didn't give up my seat because I was tired, but that isn't true. I was not tired physically...I was tired of giving in to segregation.

1 What does the word <u>serious</u> mean in this sentence?

> You get up or I'll call the police! I'm serious!

A angry

B not telling a joke

C violent

D not peaceful

2 What does the word <u>segregation</u> mean in this sentence?

> The company began to listen to the African Americans' argument that segregation was wrong.

A separating people because of their race

B hurting people by physical force

C making people work without paying them

D convincing someone by giving them reasons

3 What is the most important difference between Rosa and her friend?

A Rosa is cold.

B Rosa is African American.

C Rosa stands up for her rights.

D Rosa gets on the bus.

4 At the time of this play, what were the laws about bus riding in Alabama?

A African Americans must enter through the back door.

B African Americans must sit in the back.

C African Americans must give up their seats for white people.

D All of the above.

5 What happens last in this play?

A Rosa gets on the bus.

B The bus driver tells Rosa to give up her seat for a white man.

C Rosa gets arrested.

D Rosa explains to the audience why she didn't give up her seat.

6 What is one theme of this play?

A being strong in the face of injustice

B honor for your country

C peace in a time of violence

D love for everyone

7 Rosa has to sit at the back of the bus. What is the meaning of the word <u>back</u>?

A a part of the body

B to move backwards

C not the front

D to review

8 What is the conjunction in this sentence?

> People always say that I didn't give up my seat because I was tired, but that isn't true.

A always

B give up

C tired

D but

Conflict and Resolution

Explore the Theme

1. What does **conflict** mean? What does **resolution** mean?
2. Describe the conflicts and resolutions you see in the pictures.

Theme Activity

Work with a small group. Create a chart about conflicts.

- Who has conflicts?
- What are the conflicts often about?

Conflicts	
Who has conflicts?	What are the conflicts often about?
parents and children	clothes, schoolwork

Objectives

Reading Strategy
Identify cause and effect

Listening and Speaking
Create and evaluate a conflict/resolution scene

Grammar
Learn to use the future tense with **will** and with **be going to**

Writing
Personal narrative: Write a diary entry

Academic Vocabulary

cause	**examine**
effect	**develop**

Academic Content

World War II
Map of Europe
Conflict resolution strategies

● **Chapter Focus Question**

How can people work out conflicts they have with each other?

Reading 1 **Literature**

Historical Fiction
Suzy and Leah
by Jane Yolen

Reading 2 **Content:** Science / Health

Informational text
The Kids' Guide to Working Out Conflicts
by Naomi Drew

Suzy and Leah

● **About the Reading**

You are going to read a short story about a girl named Leah. She comes to the United States from Germany during World War II.

Leah has conflicts with Suzy, an American classmate. Little by little, Suzy and Leah learn to understand each other. The author tells this story in diary entries. A diary is a book in which people write about their thoughts and experiences.

Build Background

Concentration Camps

During World War II (1939–1945), a group called the Nazis ruled Germany. The Nazis hated many groups of people. The Nazis put these people in concentration camps. Concentration camps were like jails. However, the people in concentration camps did not commit any crimes. Concentration camps were terrible places. Some people died of hunger and disease. The Nazis killed many others. Most people in the concentration camps were Jewish. About six million Jewish people died in concentration camps during World War II.

Find Germany on the map of Europe.

Use Prior Knowledge

Gather Ideas About World War II

The story "Suzy and Leah" takes place during World War II. Work with a group. Make a list of information you know about World War II.

1. Write the words **World War II** at the top of the list.
2. Work with your group to write any information you know about World War II. Use these question words to help you: Who? What? When? Where? Why?
3. Share your information with the class.

World War II
started in the 1930s

Key Vocabulary

- apology
- comfort
- grateful
- refugee
- safe
- trust

● Vocabulary From the Reading
Learn, Practice, and Use Independently

Learn Vocabulary Read each sentence. Look at the **highlighted** word. Use the context (the words around the highlighted word) to determine its meaning. Use a dictionary if you need help.

1. I'm sorry. I didn't mean to hurt your feelings. Please accept my **apology.**

2. Mothers **comfort** their sick children with kisses and sweet songs.

3. My teacher always gives me extra help. I feel very **grateful.**

4. During the war, the **refugee** went to a nearby country. He was looking for safety and a better life.

5. There is a lot of crime in John's neighborhood. He does not feel **safe** there.

6. I know you never lie. I **trust** you completely.

Practice Vocabulary Look at the pictures. Complete each sentence with a Key Vocabulary word.

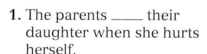

1. The parents _____ their daughter when she hurts herself.

2. The woman is _____ for his help.

3. They _____ their daughter to drive carefully.

4. The man is giving an _____ for stepping on her foot.

5. The woman is a _____ . She does not feel _____ .

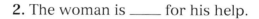

✓ Checkpoint

1. What is something you are **grateful** for?

2. Who is someone you **trust**?

Use Vocabulary Independently Write one sentence for each Key Vocabulary word. Read your sentences to a partner.

Vocabulary Log   Workbook page 149   Independent Practice CD-ROM/Online

Academic Vocabulary

Vocabulary for the Reading Strategy

Word	Explanation	Sample Sentence	Visual Cue
cause *noun*	a reason why something happens	The burning candle was the **cause** of the fire.	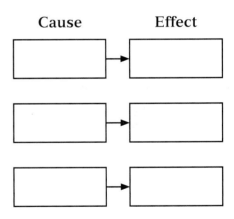
effect *noun*	a result	The candle fell over. The **effect** was a fire.	

Draw a picture and write a sentence for each word.

Reading Strategy

Identify Cause and Effect

Sometimes one event makes another one happen. The event that happens first is the **cause**. The one that follows it is the **effect**. Look at this example:

cause: You eat a large meal.

effect: You feel full.

Understanding the connection between a **cause** and an **effect** helps you understand a reading better.

1. As you read "Suzy and Leah," look for **cause** and **effect** events in the story.

2. Look at the chart. After you read, you will look back at the reading. You will find and write **causes** and **effects** from the story to complete the chart.

Cause   **Effect**

✓Checkpoint

1. What is a **cause**? What is an **effect**?

2. Give an example of a **cause** and an **effect** from your life.

Vocabulary Log

Workbook page 150

Independent Practice CD-ROM/Online

● **Text Genre**

Historical Fiction

"Suzy and Leah" is **historical fiction.** Historical fiction is a story that is set in a real time in history. Some features in historical fiction may be real. Others are fictional (made-up or imagined). Look at the features of historical fiction in the chart. Then look for these features as you read.

Historical Fiction	
setting	the story is set in a real place and time in the past
characters	the characters may be made-up or imaginary; some may also be real people
plot	the plot is a combination of fictional events and events that really happened

● **Meet the Author**

Jane Yolen was born in New York City in 1939. This was the year that World War II began. Yolen always loved to write. She and her brother created a newspaper for their apartment building. They interviewed neighbors and wrote articles. After college, Yolen began writing books for children and young adults. Yolen has written over 280 books!

● **Reading Focus Questions**

As you read, think about these questions.

1. How does the reading relate to the theme of "conflict and resolution"?

2. What do you think was the author's purpose for writing "Suzy and Leah"?

3. What kinds of things can **cause** conflict between people from different cultures?

✓ **Checkpoint**

Name a book, story, show, or movie that is **historical fiction.** Briefly describe the setting, characters, and plot.

Workbook
page 151

Independent Practice
CD-ROM/Online

Suzy and Leah

by Jane Yolen

August 5, 1944

Dear Diary,

1   Today I walked past that place, the one that was in the newspaper, the one all the kids have been talking about. Gosh, is it ugly! A line of **rickety** wooden buildings just like in the army. And a fence lots higher than my head. With **barbed wire** on top. How can anyone—even a **refugee**—live there?

2   I took two candy bars along, just like everyone said I should. When I held them up, all those kids just **swarmed** over to the fence, grabbing. Like in a zoo. Except for this one girl, with two dark braids and bangs nearly covering her eyes. She was just standing to one side, staring at me. It was so **creepy**. After a minute I looked away. When I looked back, she was gone. I mean gone. Disappeared as if she'd never been.
    Suzy

August 5, 1944

My dear Mutti,

3   I have but a single piece of paper to write on. And a broken pencil. But I will write small so I can tell all. I address it to you, Mutti, though you are gone from me forever. I write in English, to learn better, because I want to make myself be understood.

4   Today another girl came. With more sweets. A girl with yellow hair and a **false** smile. Yonni and Zipporah and Ruth, my friends, all grabbed for the sweets. Like wild animals. Like . . . like prisoners. But we are not wild animals. And we are no longer prisoners. Even though we are still **penned in.**

5   I stared at the yellow-haired girl until she was forced to look down. Then I walked away. When I turned to look back, she was gone. Disappeared. As if she had never been.
    Leah

Reading Check

1. **Recall facts** Where does Suzy meet Leah?
2. **Recall facts** Does Leah grab the candy Suzy holds up?
3. **Make inferences** Why do you think Leah stared at Suzy?

---

rickety unstable, weak, and likely to fall
barbed wire wire with sharp points on it used as a fence
swarmed moved in a crowd, like a group of insects
creepy causing fear and disgust, scary
false fake, not honest
penned in trapped, as in a cage

September 5, 1944

Dear Diary,

⁶ So how are those **refugee** kids going to learn? Our teachers teach in English. This is America, after all.

⁷ I wouldn't want to be one of them. Imagine going to school and not being able to speak English or understand anything that's going on. I can't imagine anything worse.
Suzy

September 5, 1944

My dear Mutti,

⁸ The adults of the Americans say we are **safe** now. And so we must go to their school. But I say no place is **safe** for us. Did not the Germans say that we were **safe** in their camps? And there you and baby Natan were killed.

Reading Strategy

Identify Cause and Effect What **caused** Leah to feel that no place is **safe** for her and the other **refugees**?

⁹ And how could we learn in this American school anyway? I have a little English. But Ruth and Zipporah and the others, though they speak Yiddish and Russian and German, they have no English at all. None beyond *thank you* and *please* and *more sweets*. And then there is little Avi. How could he go to this school? He will speak nothing at all. He stopped speaking, they say, when he was hidden away in a **cupboard**

by his grandmother who was taken by the Nazis after she swore there was no child in the house. And he was almost three days in that cupboard without food, without water, without words to **comfort** him. Is English a **safer** language than German?

There is barbed wire still between us and the world.
Leah

---

cupboard piece of furniture where things are kept inside

September 14, 1944

Dear Diary,

10   At least the **refugee** kids are wearing better clothes now. And they all have shoes. Some of them still had those stripy pajamas when they arrived in America.

11   The girls all wore dresses to their first day at school, though. They even had hair bows, gifts from the teachers. Of course I recognized my old blue **pinafore.** The girl with the dark braids had it on, and Mom hadn't even told me she was giving it away. I wouldn't have minded so much if she had only asked. It doesn't fit me anymore, anyway.

12   The girl in my old pinafore was the only one without a name tag, so all day long no one knew her name.
        Suzy

September 14, 1944

My dear Mutti,

13   I put on the blue dress for our first day. It fit me well. The color reminded me of your eyes and the blue skies over our farm before the smoke from the burning darkened it. Zipporah braided my hair, but I had no mirror until we got to the school and they showed us the toilets. They call it a bathroom, but there is no bath in it at all, which is strange. I have never been in a school with boys before.

14   They have placed us all in low grades. Because of our English. I do not care. This way I do not have to see the girl with the yellow hair who smiles so falsely at me.

15   But they made us wear tags with our names printed on them. That made me afraid. What next? Yellow stars? I tore mine off and threw it behind a bush before we went in.
        Leah

Reading Strategy

Identify Cause and Effect Leah threw her name tag away. What **effect** did this have in class?

Reading Check

1. **Recall facts** Whose pinafore does Leah wear on the first day of school?

2. **Recall facts** Who did the dress remind Leah of? Why?

3. **Draw conclusions** Why do you think the name tags made Leah afraid?

---

pinafore dress with no sleeves, sometimes worn like an apron over another dress

September 16, 1944

Dear Diary,

¹⁶   Mr. Forest has assigned each of us to a **refugee** to help them with their English. He gave me the girl with the dark braids, the one without the name tag, the one in my pinafore. Gee, she's as **prickly** as a **porcupine.** I asked if I could have a different kid. He said I was the best English student and she already spoke the best English. He wants her to learn as fast as possible so she can help others. As if she would, Miss Porcupine.

¹⁷   Her name is Leah. I wish she would wear another dress.
Suzy

Reading Strategy

Identify Cause and Effect What caused Mr. Forest to put Suzy and Leah together?

September 16, 1944

My dear Mutti,

¹⁸   Now I have a real notebook and a pen. I am writing to you at school now. I cannot take the notebook back to the **shelter.** Someone there will surely borrow it. I will instead keep it here. In the little cupboard each one of us has been given.

¹⁹   I wish I had another dress. I wish I had a different student helping me and not the yellow-haired girl.
Leah

September 20, 1944

Dear Diary,

²⁰   Can't she ever smile, that Leah? I've brought her candy bars and apples from home. She wouldn't take any of them.

²¹   Her whole name is Leah Shoshana Hershkowitz. At least, that's the way she writes it. When she says it, it sounds all different, low and growly.

²²   Mom says I should invite her home for dinner soon. We'll have to get her a special **pass** for that. But I don't know if I want her to come. It's not like she's any fun at all. I wish Mr. Forest would let me trade.
Suzy

---

prickly having thorns, difficult
porcupine animal with sharp spines

shelter place where homeless people can sleep and eat
pass permission note

September 20, 1944

My dear Mutti,

23   The girl with the yellow hair is called Suzy Ann McCarthy. It is a silly name. It means nothing. I asked her who she was named for, and she said, "For a book my mom liked." A book! I am named after my great-grandmother on my mother's side, who was an important woman in our village. I am proud to carry on her name.

24   This Suzy brings many sweets. But I must call them candies now. And a handkerchief. She expects me to be **grateful.** But how can I be **grateful**? She treats me like a pet, a pet she does not really like or **trust.** She wants to feed me like an animal behind bars.

25   If I write all this down, I will not hold so much anger. I have much anger. And **terror** besides. *Terror.* It is a new word for me, but an old feeling. One day soon this Suzy and her people will stop being nice to us. They will remember that we are not just **refugees** but Jews, and they will turn on us. Just as the Germans did. Of this I am sure.

        Leah

September 30, 1944

Dear Diary,

26   Leah's English is very good now. But she still never smiles. Especially she never smiles at me. It's like she has a **permanent frown** and permanent frown lines between her eyes. It makes her look much older than anyone in our class. Like a little old lady.

27   I wonder if she eats enough. She won't take the candy bars. And she saves the school lunch in her napkin, hiding it away in her pocket. She thinks no one sees her do it, but I do. Does she eat it later? I'm sure they get dinner at the shelter. Mom says they do. Mom also says we have to eat everything on our plates. Sometimes when we're having dinner I think of Leah Shoshana Hershkowitz.

        Suzy

> ### Reading Strategy
>
> **Identify Cause and Effect** Leah writes her thoughts in her diary. What **effect** does she hope this will have?

> ## Reading Check
>
> 1. **Recall facts** Who was Leah named for?
> 2. **Make predictions** What do you think Leah will do with the school lunch she hides in her pocket?

---

terror great fear

permanent lasting, or meant to last, forever or for a long time

frown look of disapproval made by pulling the eyebrows down and tightening the mouth

September 30, 1944

My dear Mutti,

28   Avi loves the food I bring home from school. What does he know? It's not even **kosher.** Sometimes they serve ham. But I do not tell Avi. He needs all the food he can get. He is a growing boy.

29   I, too, am growing fast. Soon I will not fit into the blue dress. I have no other.
        Leah

October 9, 1944

Dear Diary,

Reading Strategy

Identify Cause and Effect What caused Leah to be skipped up to Suzy's grade?

30   They skipped Leah up to our grade, her English has gotten so good. Except for some words, like **victory,** which she pronounces "wick-toe-ree." I try not to laugh, but sometimes I just can't help it!

31   Leah knows a lot about the world and nothing about America. She thinks New York is right next to Chicago, for goodness sakes! She can't dance at all. She doesn't know the words to any of the top songs. And she's so stuck up, she only talks in class to answer questions. The other **refugees** aren't like that at all. Why is it only my **refugee** who's so mean?
        Suzy

---

kosher meeting certain rules about food in Jewish law
victory triumph, success

October 9, 1944

My dear Mutti,

32   I think of you all the time. I went
to Suzy's house because Mr. Forest
said they had gone to a great deal of
trouble to get a pass for me. I did not
want to go so much, my stomach hurt
the whole time I was there.

33   Suzy's *Mutti* was nice, all pink and
gold. She wore a dress with pink roses
all over it and it reminded me of your
dress, the blue one with the asters. You
were wearing it when we were put on
the train. And the last time I saw you at
the camp with Natan. Oh, *Mutti.* I had to **steel** my heart against
Suzy's mother. If I love her, I will forget you. And that I must
never do.

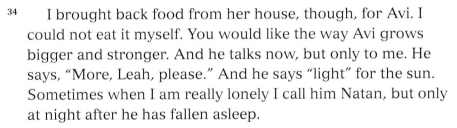

Reading Strategy

Identify Cause and Effect • What effect did meeting Suzy's mother have on Leah?

34   I brought back food from her house, though, for Avi. I
could not eat it myself. You would like the way Avi grows
bigger and stronger. And he talks now, but only to me. He
says, "More, Leah, please." And he says "light" for the sun.
Sometimes when I am really lonely I call him Natan, but only
at night after he has fallen asleep.

    Leah

October 10, 1944

Dear Diary,

35   Leah was not in school today. When I asked her friend
Zipporah, she **shrugged.** "She is ill in her stomach," she said.
"What did she eat at your house?"

36   I didn't answer "Nothing," though that would have been
true. She hid it all in a handkerchief Mom gave her. Mom
said, "She eats like a bird. How does she stay alive?"

    Suzy

Reading Check

1. **Recall facts** Why did Leah go to Suzy's house?
2. **Recall facts** Why isn't Leah in school on October 10th?
3. **Draw conclusions** Who do you think *Mutti* and Natan are? Why do you think this?

---

steel harden to prepare for something bad
shrugged lifted shoulders upward, as a sign of not caring or not knowing

October 11, 1944

Dear Diary,

37   They've asked me to gather Leah's things from school and bring them to the hospital. She had to have her **appendix** out and nearly died. She almost didn't tell them she was sick until too late. Why did she do that? I would have been screaming my head off with the pain.

38   Mom says we have to visit, that I'm Leah's American best friend. Hah! We're going to bring several of my old dresses, but not my green one with the white trim. I don't want her to have it. Even if it doesn't fit me anymore.
      Suzy

October 12, 1944

Dear Diary,

39   I did a terrible thing. I read Leah's diary! I'd kill anyone who did that to me. At first it made no sense. Who were *Mutti* and Natan, and why were they killed? What were the yellow stars? What does kosher mean? And the way she talked about me made me **furious.** Who did she think she was, little Miss Porcupine? All I did was bring her candy and fruit and try to make those poor **refugee** kids feel at home.

Reading Strategy

Identify Cause and Effect What **caused** Suzy to ask her mother so many questions?

40   Then, when I asked Mom some questions, carefully, so she wouldn't guess I had read Leah's diary, she explained. She said the Nazis killed people, mothers and children as well as men. In places called concentration camps. And that all the Jews—people who weren't Christians like us—had to wear yellow stars on their clothes so they could be **spotted** blocks and blocks away. It was so awful I could hardly believe it, but Mom said it was true.

41   How was I supposed to know all that? How can Leah stand any of us? How could she live with all that pain?
      Suzy

---

appendix body organ located on the right side of the abdomen
furious very angry
spotted seen

October 12, 1944

My dear Mutti,

42   Suzy and her mother came to see me in the hospital. They brought me my notebook so now I can write again.

43   I was so frightened about being sick. I did not tell anyone for a long time, even though it hurt so much. In the German camp, if you were sick and could not do your work, they did not let you live.

44   But in the middle of the night, I had so much fever, a doctor was sent for me. Little Avi found me. He ran to one of the guards. He spoke out loud for the first time. He said, "Please, for Leah. Do not let her go into the dark."

45   The doctor tells me I nearly died, but they saved me. They have given me much medicines and soon I will eat the food and they will be sure it is kosher, too. And I am alive. This I can hardly believe. *Alive!*

46   Then Suzy came with her *Mutti,* saying, "I am sorry. I am so sorry. I did not know. I did not understand." Suzy did a bad thing. She read my notebook. But it helped her understand. And then, instead of making an **apology,** she did a strange thing. She took a red book with a lock out of her pocket and gave it to me. "Read this," she said. "And when you are out of the hospital, I have a green dress with white **trim** I want you to have. It will be just perfect with your eyes."

47   I do not know what this trim may be. But I like the idea of a green dress. And I have a new word now, as well. It is this: *diary.*

48   A new word. A new land. And—it is just possible—a new friend.
     Leah

---

trim decoration

Reading Strategy

Identify Cause and Effect What effect did reading Leah's diary have on Suzy?

✓
Reading Check

1. **Recall facts** Why didn't Leah tell anyone she was sick?

2. **Explain** Why did Suzy give Leah her own diary instead of an **apology**?

● **Apply the Reading Strategy**

Identify Cause and Effect

Now complete the Reading Strategy chart.

1. Review the **Reading Strategy** on page 197.
2. Copy the chart.
3. Look back at the reading. Find **causes** and **effects**. Write the **causes** and **effects** in the chart. Add boxes as necessary.
4. Share your chart with your classmates.

Cause	Effect
Suzy brought candy bars to the **refugee** camp.	→ The kids swarmed to the fence to grab them.
	→

● **Academic Vocabulary**

Vocabulary for the Reading Comprehension Questions

Word	Explanation	Sample Sentence	Visual Cue
examine *verb*	to look at closely	Doctors **examine** their patients carefully to make sure they are healthy.	
develop *verb*	to turn into something more complete, greater, better, or bigger	A tadpole **develops** into a frog.	frog, egg, tadpole

Draw a picture and write a sentence for each word.

✓**Checkpoint**

1. What can you **examine** with a microscope?
2. How can you **develop** your math skills?

Vocabulary Log

● Reading Comprehension Questions

Think and Discuss

Workbook
page 152

Independent Practice
CD-ROM/Online

1. **Recall details** What languages do the refugees speak before they learn English?

2. **Compare and contrast** How are Suzy and Leah similar? How are they different? Give examples of each character's thoughts and actions to support your description. Use at least three Key Vocabulary words in your description.

3. **Understand the author's choices** Why does the author tell the story in diary entries? How does this help you understand the characters better?

4. **Analyze character development** How do Suzy and Leah change and **develop** as characters by the end of the reading?

5. **Revisit the Reading Focus Questions** Go back to page 198 and discuss the questions.

● Literary Elements

Plot, Conflict, Climax, and Resolution

> **plot**
> The sequence of events in a story is called the **plot**. A plot usually has a beginning, a middle, and an end. It also usually includes a conflict and a resolution.

> **conflict and climax**
> Most plots include a **conflict**. A conflict is a problem or struggle at the center of the story.
> The conflict often grows to an exciting or high point when things start to change. This is called the **climax**.

> **resolution**
> The end of a story usually shows the **resolution** of the conflict. The resolution is how the conflict is resolved.

Work with a partner to discuss and answer the following questions.

1. What is the plot of "Suzy and Leah"?
2. What is the conflict in "Suzy and Leah"?
3. What is the climax of the story?
4. How is the conflict resolved?

✓ **Checkpoint**

Explain the **plot**, **conflict**, **climax**, and **resolution** in your favorite book or movie.

Vocabulary
Log

Workbook
page 153

Independent Practice
CD-ROM/Online

The Kids' Guide to Working Out Conflicts

● About the Reading

You read about fictional characters who resolved their conflicts in "Suzy and Leah." Now you will read an informational text that teaches real people how to resolve conflicts.

● Build Background

Guide Books and Self-Help Books

The Kids' Guide to Working Out Conflicts is a guide book, or self-help book. These kinds of books help

people learn new skills and improve their lives. For example, there are guide books and self-help books about making new friends, getting accepted to college, and staying healthy.

Are there any new skills you want to learn? Find a self-help book or guide book on the subject. You can find a book at the library. Ask your librarian for help. Or, you can type the skill and the words "self-help book" or "guide" into an Internet search engine. Tell a partner about the guide(s) you find.

● Vocabulary From the Reading

Use Context Clues to Determine Meaning

Use context to determine the meaning of the **highlighted** words in the paragraph. Discuss the meanings with a small group.

> Even best friends sometimes have **misunderstandings.** These disagreements can be small or large. You may have a friend who sometimes says something that **annoys** you. Maybe it doesn't just bother you a little. Maybe it **upsets** you and makes you feel angry or hurt. What should you do? Take my **advice:** do not **blame** your friend. Talk to your friend instead. Think about the part each of you plays in the **misunderstanding.** You can't have everything your own way. It's important to **compromise.**

Key Vocabulary

advice

annoy

blame

compromise

misunderstanding

upset

✓Checkpoint

Tell about a **misunderstanding** you had with a friend.

Vocabulary Log

Workbook page 154

Independent Practice CD-ROM/Online

● Reading Strategy

Identify Cause and Effect

Sometimes one event makes another one happen. The event that happens first is the **cause**. The one that follows it is the **effect**. As you read *The Kids' Guide to Working Out Conflicts,* try to identify **causes** and **effects**.

● Text Genre

Informational Text

Informational text gives information and facts about a topic. *The Kids' Guide to Working Out Conflicts* gives information about how to deal with conflict. As you read, look for these features of an informational text.

Informational Text	
subject	what the text is about
headings	titles that tell you what a part of the text is about
definitions	meanings of new words

● Meet the Author

Naomi Drew was born in New Jersey. She was a teacher for over 20 years. As a teacher, she wished she had a book to teach kids how to handle conflict. Because she could not find one, she wrote one herself.

● Reading Focus Questions

As you read, think about these questions.

1. How does this reading relate to the theme of "conflict and resolution"?
2. What do you think was the author's purpose for writing *The Kids' Guide to Working Out Conflicts*?
3. How can you prevent or help resolve conflicts?

√Checkpoint

Think of a conflict you had with a friend. What was the **cause** of the conflict?

Workbook
pages 155–156

Independent Practice
CD-ROM/Online

The Kids' Guide to Working Out Conflicts

by Naomi Drew

1   A conflict is a fight, disagreement, or **misunderstanding.** Conflicts happen between people of all ages everywhere: in homes and schools, neighborhoods and communities, workplaces and playing fields. They happen between individuals, groups, and countries.

What Starts a Conflict? What Makes It Grow?

2   Although there are lots of different **causes** for conflicts, they usually stem from people's needs and wants.

Reading Strategy

Identify Cause and Effect Name four **causes** of conflicts.

3   Hurt feelings are another major **cause** of conflict. You've probably been in situations where someone says or does something that hurts your feelings. So you respond by saying something hurtful in return or talking behind the person's back. What happens next? The person reacts to what you do, and then . . . ? Conflict.

4   Bad moods can lead to conflict, too.

Conflict Triggers

5   Needs and wants, hurt feelings, bad moods—all of these can trigger (set off) a conflict. One way you can help yourself handle conflicts better is to understand what **annoys** or **upsets** you. That's your trigger. Once you understand your trigger, you can be **aware** of it. Then you can stop yourself before you do something to create more conflict.

Decide to Become a Conflict Solver

6   You can decide to be a conflict solver rather than a conflict maker. If you do this, your whole life could improve. When there's conflict, the choices *you* make each moment can determine the **outcome.**

---

aware having knowledge about, understanding of

outcome result, consequence

Where Do You Stand?

7   How good of a conflict solver are you right now? Take this quick self-test to find out. **Respond** *yes* or *no* to each statement:

When I have a conflict . . .

✓ I try to **calm down** before I react.

✓ I do my best to **avoid** physical fighting.

✓ I believe I have more to **gain** by working things out.

✓ I listen to what the other person has to say.

✓ I try to see how I'm **responsible** instead of just **blaming** the other person.

✓ I look for ways to solve the problem rather than win the argument.

✓ I'm willing to **compromise**.

✓ I avoid using **put-downs**.

✓ I say what I think, but I do it **respectfully**.

✓ I try to put myself in the other person's place.

8   How many times did you answer yes?

• Five or more? If so, you're already a conflict solver a good part of the time. Keep at it!

• Fewer than five? You're not there yet . . . but you can get there. Choose one new idea to try and do it until it starts to come more easily. Then choose another. Also continue doing whatever you said *yes* to.

---

respond answer

calm down relax

avoid stay away from

gain get, acquire

responsible at fault, guilty

put-downs remarks that embarrass a person

respectfully with proper politeness toward someone

> **Reading Strategy**
>
> **Identify Cause and Effect** Why is it good to avoid put-downs? What do you think the **effect** of a put-down will usually be?

> ✓ **Reading Check**
>
> 1. **Recall facts** What do conflict solvers do before they react?
> 2. **Recall facts** Do conflict solvers **blame** others?
> 3. **Evaluate** Take the self-test. How well did you do?

What to Do When Your Friends Have Conflicts

9   Maybe you're someone who wants to make things better for your friends, but you don't know how. Here are some things you can do:

10   **Try not to take sides.** This is especially important if you feel caught between two people who are both close friends of yours. One or both friends may ask you for **advice,** or feel they really need your help. Be willing to listen, but let them know you care about both of them and need to stay **neutral** rather than take sides.

11   **Don't get involved in gossip.** If one friend starts talking about the other to you or to different people, don't join in. You should always avoid discussing your friends' problems with other kids. Even though you might **mean well,** this can still be seen as gossiping.

Reading Strategy

Identify Cause and Effect What might be the **effect** of discussing your friends' problems with other kids?

12   **Put yourself in their place.** Imagine you were the one involved in the conflict and think about what would help you resolve it. Then, if your friends ask for **advice,** tell them your idea. Do this *only* if they ask for your opinion, though. Otherwise, don't try to fix the problem yourself.

Are You Ready to Become a Conflict Solver?

13   By becoming a conflict solver, you'll change your life. You'll also **affect** the lives of the people around you. Are you willing to become a conflict solver? I hope so, because you will improve your own life and help our world move a little closer toward peace. Be patient with yourself and **congratulate** yourself for each step you take.

---

take sides defend one position or person against another

neutral not on either side in a disagreement

gossip talk about other people's lives, sometimes in an untruthful way

mean well want good for others

affect influence

congratulate give praise for something well done

● Reading Comprehension Questions

Think and Discuss

1. **Recall information** Name three things you should do when your friends have conflicts.

2. **Explain** What is a conflict "trigger"?

3. **Determine the main idea** What is the main idea of this reading?

4. **Relate to your own experience** What are your "triggers"? What are some things you need to do to become a conflict solver? Use at least three Key Vocabulary words.

5. **Revisit the Reading Focus Questions** Go back to page 211 and discuss the questions.

Workbook
page 157

Independent Practice
CD-ROM/Online

⟳ Connect Readings 1 and 2

You read two readings with the theme of conflict and resolution. Use these activities to make connections between the readings.

1. Read these passages (sections of text) from *The Kids' Guide to Working Out Conflicts*. Think about how the passages relate to "Suzy and Leah," and then answer the questions.

   a. Conflicts happen between people of all ages everywhere: in homes and schools, neighborhoods and communities, workplaces and playing fields. They happen between individuals, groups, and countries.

      Why does conflict happen between Suzy and Leah? Where does it happen?

   b. Although there are lots of different **causes** for conflicts, they usually stem from people's needs and wants.

      What does Suzy need or want? What does Leah need or want? How does this lead to conflict?

   c. One way you can help yourself handle conflicts better is to understand what **annoys** or **upsets** you. That's your trigger.

      What is Leah's trigger? What is Suzy's trigger?

   d. When I have a conflict, I believe I have more to gain by working things out.

      What do Suzy and Leah have to gain by working things out?

   e. I try to put myself in the other person's place.

      Does Suzy try to put herself in Leah's place? Find examples in the reading to support your answer.

2. **Revisit the Chapter Focus Question** How can people work out conflicts they have with each other?

Spelling

Full Forms and Abbreviations of Days and Months

Workbook
page 158

Independent Practice
CD-ROM/Online

Writing Conventions

Punctuation: Cited Sources

Workbook
page 159

Independent Practice
CD-ROM/Online

Phrases for Conversation

Giving Positive Feedback

I liked when . . .

I thought it was good when . . .

You did a great job with . . .

Identifying a Problem

I got confused when . . .

I wasn't sure about . . .

Maybe it would be better if . . .

● Listening and Speaking

Create and Evaluate a Conflict/Resolution Scene

You read about a fictional conflict in "Suzy and Leah." You learned about ways of dealing with conflicts in the informational text *The Kids' Guide to Working Out Conflicts.* Keep these readings in mind as you create your own conflict/resolution scene.

1. With your partner, decide who the people in your conflict/resolution scene will be. Are they parent and child? Friends? Neighbors? Next, decide on the situation that is the **cause** of the conflict.

2. Write dialogue for a scene about these people and their conflict. Include a resolution.

3. Perform your scene for the class. Be sure to use appropriate expressions, body language, and gestures. If possible, videotape the scene.

4. After the scene, the class will evaluate it. If there is a videotape of the scene, the class may want to review it. As a class, discuss the following questions. You may want to use some of the phrases for giving positive feedback and for identifying a problem during the discussion.

   a. Summarize the conflict and the resolution.

   b. Was the conflict realistic? Why or why not?

   c. Did the nonverbal messages relate to the verbal communication? (Were the facial expressions, body language, and gestures of each character appropriate?)

   d. How well did each character handle the conflict? Were there ways the characters could have handled it better?

● Reading Fluency

Rapid Word Recognition

Good readers recognize words quickly. This helps them read fluently. You can practice recognizing words quickly to increase your reading speed.

On the next page, there is a list of several key words from the readings. After the key word is a line followed by other words. As quickly as possible, point to the word that matches the key word. See how many correct words you can point to in 12 seconds or less. Your partner will time you.

1.	green	name	speak	dress	green	smile
2.	speak	green	dress	smile	name	speak
3.	dress	dress	speak	green	smile	name
4.	smile	name	speak	green	smile	dress
5.	name	speak	dress	name	smile	green
6.	smile	green	smile	speak	green	name
7.	green	name	smile	green	speak	dress
8.	speak	speak	dress	smile	green	name
9.	name	smile	speak	green	dress	name
10.	smile	name	speak	dress	green	smile
11.	green	green	dress	smile	name	speak
12.	name	dress	speak	green	smile	name
13.	smile	speak	dress	name	smile	green
14.	dress	speak	dress	name	smile	green
15.	name	smile	speak	green	dress	name

Now, as a class, practice the pronunciation of the words.

Finally, with your partner, read the words aloud. Your partner will time you. Count how many words you read correctly in 20 seconds.

Vocabulary Development

Use Figurative Language

Figurative language describes something by comparing it to something else. Authors use figurative language to give the reader a new way of looking at something.

Look at this sentence from "Suzy and Leah."

> When I held them up, all those kids just swarmed over to the fence, grabbing. Like in a zoo.

Of course, Leah and her friends don't live in a zoo. However, this comparison helps readers form images.

In this example, the author compares two things with the word "like." This kind of figurative language is called a **simile**. Finish these sentences to create your own similes.

1. It is like . . . outside today.

It is like an oven outside today.

2. My room is like . . .

3. School is like . . .

4. Life is like . . .

Build Your Knowledge

Here are two more examples of figurative language that make writing more interesting.

- A **metaphor** states how something is like something else, without using *like* or *as*.
  Examples: I am ice cold. My memory is foggy.
- **Hyperbole** is exaggeration.
  Examples: I died laughing. I called a million times.

✓ Checkpoint

Create a **simile** comparing yourself to something.

Vocabulary Log

Workbook page 160

Independent Practice CD-ROM/Online

● Grammar

The Future Tense: *will*

Use **will**:

1. to make predictions about the future.

> One day soon this Suzy and her people **will stop** being nice to us.

2. when the speaker decides to do something at the moment of speaking.

> **I will write** small so I can tell all.

3. for promises.

> **I will become** a conflict solver.

The Future Tense with *will*			
subject	*will*	*(not)*	base verb
I He / She / It You / We / They	will	(not)	try.

Notes:

- Form the contraction with the subject pronoun + **will**:
  I + will = I'll   **he + will = he'll**   **you + will = you'll**
- The contraction for **will not** is **won't.**
- Contractions are used in informal language. Do not use them in formal writing.

Practice the Grammar Make predictions about Suzy and Leah's future. Complete the sentences with **will** or **will not.**

1. Suzy and Leah _____ become best friends.
2. Leah _____ teach English to the other **refugees.**
3. Suzy _____ read Leah's diary again.
4. Leah _____ begin to feel **safe** in the United States.
5. Leah _____ live in the **refugee** camp for a long time.
6. Leah and her brother _____ live with Suzy's family.
7. Suzy _____ learn Leah's first language.
8. Leah and Suzy _____ go to college.

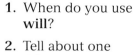

✓ Checkpoint

1. When do you use **will**?
2. Tell about one thing you will do today and one thing you will not do today.

Workbook
page 161

Independent Practice
CD-ROM/Online

Use the Grammar Independently You learned many things about conflict resolution in this chapter. Write five sentences about how you will handle conflict better in the future.

I will compromise more often.

The Future Tense: *be going to*

Use **be going to**:

1. to make predictions about the future based on evidence.

Look at the clouds in the sky. It **is going to rain** soon.

2. to talk about plans for the future.

My brother **is going to move** to a new apartment next week.

The Future Tense with *be going to*				
subject	*be*	*(not)*	*going to*	base verb
I	am			
He / She / It	is	(not)	going to	leave.
You / We / They	are			

Practice the Grammar Complete the sentences with the correct form of **be going to**.

1. I have a test tomorrow. I _____ study tonight.
2. Our television broke. We _____ buy a new one today.
3. Kenji wants to eat healthy foods. He _____ have dessert.
4. Magda bought a new dress today. She _____ wear it to a party this weekend.
5. They are sick today. They _____ go to school.

Use the Grammar Independently Write four sentences about your plans for the future using **be going to**.

Grammar Expansion

Future Tense Questions with **will** and **be going to**; Future Perfect Tense

Workbook pages 163–164   Independent Practice CD-ROM/Online

✓Checkpoint

1. When do you use **be going to**?
2. Tell about three things you plan to do this weekend using **be going to**.

● Writing Assignment

Personal Narrative: Write a Diary Entry

Writing Suggestion

See **Milestones Handbook.** pages 393–433

> **Writing Prompt**
>
> Write a diary entry about a conflict going on in your life right now. Write your ideas for how you will resolve the conflict. Use conflict resolution ideas from the readings. Use the future tense with **will** and **be going to.**

Write Your Diary Entry

1. **Read the student model.** It will help you write your diary entry. Discuss these questions with a partner.

   a. Who is the conflict between?

   b. What is the conflict?

   c. How will Gabrielle resolve the conflict?

Student Model

December 12, 2008

Dear Diary,

    I am having a conflict with my best friend, Marta. We always used to meet after school. Then I became friends with Alba. Marta is angry about this. We haven't spoken for three days.

    I want to resolve this conflict with Marta so we can stay friends. I think I will speak with her about it. I'm going to stay calm. I'll tell her that I understand how she feels. I'll suggest that we compromise. We should make sure we get together a few times each week after school. I'm going to also suggest that we all get together some time. I think Marta and Alba will like each other!

Gabrielle

Workbook
page 165

2. **Prewrite.** Who are you having a conflict with in your life right now? What is the conflict about? How will you resolve it? Use a problem-solution chart to organize your ideas.

| Problem
(What is the conflict?) | Solution
(How will you resolve it?) |
|---|---|
| | |
| | |

3. **Write your diary entry.** Use the ideas from your chart to write your diary entry. Write one paragraph about the conflict. Write another paragraph about how you will try to resolve it.

4. **Revise.** Reread your paragraphs. Revise your paragraphs if any ideas are not clear or complete.
   Use the **editing and proofreading symbols** on page 419 to help you mark any changes you want to make.

5. **Edit.** Use the **Writing Checklist** to help you find problems and errors.

Writing Checklist

1. I included the date at the top right-hand corner of my diary entry.

2. I signed my name at the end.

3. I included a conflict and a resolution to the conflict.

4. I capitalized the first word of each sentence.

5. I used **will** and **be going to** in my diary entry.

Writing Support

Grammar
Adverbs of Frequency

Adverbs of frequency tell how often something happens. They include:

never   rarely   sometimes   often   usually   always

0% of the time   100% of the time

Put adverbs of frequency:
- after the verb **be.**   She is **often** late.
- before all other verbs.   We **usually** study together.

Apply Read your diary entry. Are there any adverbs of frequency? If so, make sure you used them correctly.

Workbook
pages 166–168

Independent Practice
CD-ROM/Online

Progress Check

How well did you understand this chapter? Try to answer the
questions. If necessary, go back to the pages listed for a review.

Skills	Skills Assessment Questions	Pages to Review
Vocabulary From the Readings	What do these words mean? • **apology, comfort, grateful, refugee, safe, trust** • **advice, annoy, blame, compromise, misunderstanding, upset**	196 210
Academic Vocabulary	What do these academic vocabulary words mean? • **cause, effect** • **examine, develop**	197 208
Reading Strategy	How can identifying **causes** and **effects** help you understand a reading?	197, 211
Text Genres	What is the text genre of "Suzy and Leah"?	198
	What is the text genre of *The Kids' Guide to Working Out Conflicts*?	211
Reading Comprehension	What is "Suzy and Leah" about?	209
	What is *The Kids' Guide to Working Out Conflicts* about?	215
Literary Elements	Explain these literary elements: **plot, conflict, climax, resolution**	209
Spelling	Write the days and months using abbreviations.	215
Writing Conventions	Add punctuation to this source: World War I Globe Encyclopedia 2006	215
Listening and Speaking	**Phrases for Conversation** What phrases can you use to give positive feedback? What phrases can you use for identifying a problem?	216
Vocabulary Development	What does **figurative language** mean? Give an example of a **simile**.	217
Grammar	Give an example of a sentence with **will**.	218
	Give an example of a sentence with **be going to**.	219
Writing Support: Grammar	Give a sentence with an **adverb of frequency**.	221

Assessment Practice

Read this passage. Then answer Questions 1 through 4.

How to Be a Mediator

Conflicts happen in many personal and professional situations. The conflicts may be large or small. Whatever the size of the conflict, sometimes people in conflict need help. A *mediator* is a person who helps resolve, or end, conflicts. Some mediators are professionals. They have gone to school to study how to best resolve conflicts. Other people become mediators because their friends and family trust them. You can become a mediator by learning and practicing a few simple steps. The steps include: offer to help; listen to each person; find a compromise to resolve the conflict.

1 Read this sentence.

> **Other people become mediators because their friends and family trust them.**

What does <u>trust</u> mean?

A have confidence in

B compromise

C misunderstand

D suggest

2 **What causes some people to become mediators?**

A They like conflict.

B They have a conflict.

C They are professionals.

D Their friends and family trust them.

3 **How do mediators find a resolution to a conflict?**

A They need help.

B They become a mediator.

C They find a compromise.

D They get angry.

4 **What is the text genre of this passage?**

A historical fiction

B biography

C informational text

D descriptive essay

Writing on Demand: Diary Entry

Write a diary entry about a time when you mediated, or helped resolve, a conflict. Describe the conflict and the people involved. Then tell how you resolved it. Also tell how you and the others felt after the resolution. **(20 minutes)**

> **Writing Tip**
> Remember to tell your thoughts and feelings as well as information that you think is important.

Objectives

Reading Strategies

Put text information in an outline; Identify cause and effect

Listening and Speaking

Create an oral fable about a conflict

Grammar

Learn to use **some** and **any**

Writing

Persuasive writing: Write a newspaper editorial

Academic Vocabulary

outline	summarize
numeral	text

Academic Content

The U.S. Civil War and its causes

Native American folktales

● Chapter Focus Question

What kinds of things cause conflicts?

Reading 1 **Content:** Social Studies

Textbook
The Civil War: Background to the Conflict

Reading 2 **Literature**

Fable
THE QUARREL BETWEEN WIND AND THUNDER
retold by Jane Louise Curry

The Civil War: Background to the Conflict

● About the Reading

You are going to read an informational reading from a textbook. This reading is about the differences between the North and the South of the United States in the mid-1800s. These differences led to a war.

Build Background
The U.S. Civil War

A civil war is a war between two groups in one country. The U.S. Civil War was a war between the Northern and Southern states between 1861 and 1865. During the mid-1800s, the Northern states wanted slavery to end. Slavery is when a person is owned by another person and has to work for no money. The Southern states wanted slavery to continue. They

Free States and Slave States Before the Civil War

■ Free states and territories ■ Slave states ■ Territories open to slavery

also wanted to have their own nation and make their own laws. However, the North did not want the country to be divided. This disagreement led to the Civil War. Three million soldiers fought in this war and over 600,000 soldiers died.

Look at the map of the United States before the Civil War. How many states and territories (areas that were not yet states) had slavery? How many did not have slavery? How many territories were open to slavery?

Use Prior Knowledge
Brainstorm Ideas Related to Slavery

What do you know about slavery in the United States?

1. Work with a group. Make a word web.
2. Write the word **slavery** in the center circle. Write other words and ideas related to slavery in the other circles.
3. Share your word web with the class.

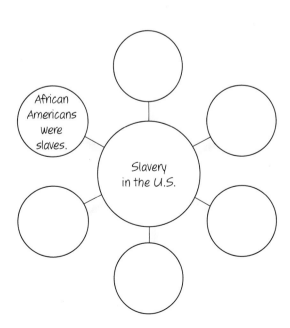

Key Vocabulary

crop

factory
(singular)/
factories
(plural)

manufacture

product

region

technology

factory

● ## Vocabulary From the Reading
Learn, Practice, and Use Independently

Learn Vocabulary Look at the pictures, captions, and sentences. Use them to determine the meaning of the **highlighted** words.

1. Farmers had a good **crop** of wheat this year.
2. The workers **manufacture** that **product** in a **factory**.
3. The Northeast is a **region** of the United States.
4. **Technology** makes life easier.

crop

manufacture

products

technology

regions

Practice Vocabulary Complete each sentence with your own idea.

Corn is an example of a **crop**.

1. ____ is another example of a **crop**.
2. Workers **manufacture** ____ in a **factory**.
3. ____ is an example of a **product** for sale in stores.
4. ____ is a **region** of the United States.
5. ____ and ____ are examples of kinds of **technology**.

Use Vocabulary Independently Use your own words to write a definition for each Key Vocabulary word.

factory: a special place where workers make things with machines

✓Checkpoint

What kinds of **products** are **manufactured** in **factories**?

Vocabulary Log

Workbook page 169

Independent Practice CD-ROM/Online

● Academic Vocabulary

Vocabulary for the Reading Strategy

Word	Explanation	Sample Sentence	Visual Cue
outline *noun*	a list of the main ideas of something	She made an **outline** of the ideas she wanted to include in her essay.	
numeral *noun*	a symbol that represents (stands for) a number	The Roman **numeral** IX stands for **9**.	IX=9

Draw a picture and write a sentence for each word.

● Reading Strategy

Put Text Information in an Outline

After you read a textbook reading, put the important information in an **outline**. This will help you understand and remember the information in the text. Look at the steps for making an **outline**. You will use these steps after you read "The Civil War: Background to the Conflict."

1. Use the subheadings in the text as the main topics. Use Roman **numerals** (I, II, III) for these main topics.

2. Under each main topic, list the important facts about the topic. Use capital letters (A, B, C) for these important facts.

3. Below is the start of an **outline** for this reading. You will copy it and complete it after you finish the reading.

The Civil War: Background to the Conflict

I. Differences in the **Regions**
   A. In the North: people moved to cities.
   B.

II.

> **✓Checkpoint**
>
> 1. Write your age in Roman **numerals**.
>
> 2. Explain what an **outline** is in your own words.

Vocabulary Log

Workbook page 170

Independent Practice CD-ROM/Online

● **Text Genre**

Informational Text: Textbook

"The Civil War: Background to the Conflict" is a reading from a social studies **textbook**. The purpose of textbooks is to teach students about a specific content area. Textbooks include many features to help students understand the information in the text. As you read, look for these textbook features.

Textbook	
headings	titles of major sections; the letters of a heading are usually larger and sometimes in a different color than the rest of the text
subheadings	titles that divide major sections into smaller sections; the letters of a subheading are usually larger and sometimes in a different color than the rest of the text (but smaller than headings)
graphics	visual features, such as pictures, maps, graphs, and charts
captions	words that explain graphics

● **Reading Focus Questions**

As you read, think about these questions.

1. How does this reading relate to the theme of "conflict and resolution"?

2. What do you think was the purpose for writing "The Civil War: Background to the Conflict"?

3. How do the graphics help you understand the conflict described in the text?

Checkpoint

Using one of your **textbooks**, point out an example of each textbook feature.

Workbook
page 171

Independent Practice
CD-ROM/Online

The Civil War: Background to the Conflict

Differences in the Regions

1 Differences among Americans make the United States strong. Sometimes, however, differences come between people. In the mid-1800s differences became disagreements between Americans in the North and the South. These disagreements led to a conflict. The conflict was the Civil War. This war almost tore the country apart.

2 Differences between the North and the South developed over time. People in each of the **regions** had different ways of living. In the mid-1800s, most Americans lived and worked on farms. For many, however, life was changing.

3 In the North, **factories** were built. They made many kinds of **products**. Many people moved from farms to cities. In the cities, they worked in the **factories**. Some people came from other countries to find jobs in the North.

4 In the South, life did not change as quickly. **Factories** were built and cities grew. However, farming was the most common way to make money. The biggest farms were large **plantations** near the Mississippi River. Here the **soil** was good and the weather was warm. The plantation owners raised many **crops**, such as cotton, rice, tobacco, and sugarcane.

Reading Strategy

Put Text Information in an Outline What is the name of the subheading for this section? What Roman **numeral** will you use for it?

Many people in the North moved to the city to find work. This painting shows a busy street scene in New York City.

In the South, farming continued to be the center of life. This scene shows a cotton plantation along the Mississippi River.

Reading Check

1. **Recall facts** When did the differences between the North and the South lead to a conflict?

2. **Recall facts** What kinds of **crops** did the plantation owners grow?

3. **Describe** How was life in the North different from life in the South in the mid-1800s?

---

plantations large farms in a warm climate where one thing is grown

soil earth or dirt

5   Many white Southerners dreamed of owning their own plantations. Yet few ever did. Most Southerners lived on small farms. They **raised cattle**, cut wood, and grew only enough food to feed their families.

6   Partly because of the differences in work opportunities between the two **regions**, more people lived in the North than in the South. By 1860, the population of the North was about 19 million. Only 11 million people lived in the South. Of those 11 million people, about 4 million were African slaves.

REVIEW *How was the North different from the South?*

The Slave Economy

7   Slavery had been a part of American life since **colonial days**. In many places, however, slavery did not continue. Some people thought that slavery was wrong and unfair. Others could not make money using slaves. The cost of feeding, clothing, and housing slaves was too great.

8   Yet slavery continued in the South. Plantation owners needed the slaves. Slaves were forced to work as **miners, carpenters, factory** workers, and house **servants**. Most, however, were taken to large plantations. They worked in the fields and raised **crops**.

9   Not every white Southerner had slaves. In fact, most did not. By 1860, only one-quarter of white Southern families owned slaves. Many of these families lived on small farms with one or two slaves. Only a few rich farmers lived on large plantations with many slaves. These planters together owned more than half of the population of slaves in the South.

REVIEW *Why was slavery important in the Southern states?*

Reading Strategy

Put Text Information in an Outline What important facts from this section will you put in your **outline**?

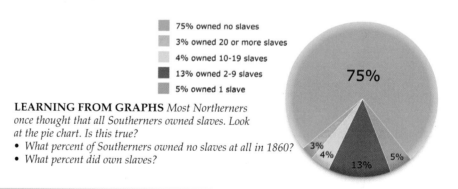

- 75% owned no slaves
- 3% owned 20 or more slaves
- 4% owned 10-19 slaves
- 13% owned 2-9 slaves
- 5% owned 1 slave

75%

3%
4%
13%
5%

LEARNING FROM GRAPHS *Most Northerners once thought that all Southerners owned slaves. Look at the pie chart. Is this true?*
- *What percent of Southerners owned no slaves at all in 1860?*
- *What percent did own slaves?*

---

raised brought up and cared for

cattle cows, bulls, and oxen as a group

colonial days the time when the United States was made up of 13 colonies

miners workers who dig underground for minerals

carpenters workers who make things with wood

servants workers who do household jobs

230   Unit 4 • Chapter 2

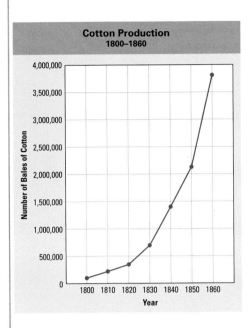

Cotton Production
1800–1860

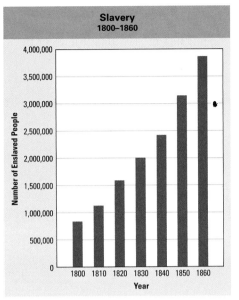

Slavery
1800–1860

"King Cotton"

10   In the early years of the South, few farmers grew cotton. Cotton is the plant from which cotton **cloth** is made. But before cotton could be sold, workers had to separate the small seeds from the white cotton **fibers**. This was a slow, hard job that took many people a lot of time. Inventor Eli Whitney changed this.

11   In 1793, Whitney invented a machine called the cotton gin. The cotton gin removed the seeds from the cotton fibers faster than workers could. This change in **technology** led to other changes.

12   With the cotton gin, cotton was cleaned and prepared for market in less time. Farmers then sold more cotton and made more money. They sold the cotton to **textile mills** in the North and in Europe.

Demand for cotton made both Southern cotton planters and Northern textile-mill owners rich. It also created a demand for more slaves. Planters needed slaves to plant the seeds, weed the fields, pick the cotton, and run the cotton gins.

REVIEW   *How did the cotton gin help cotton production?*

Reading Strategy

Put Text Information in an Outline What important facts from this section should you put in your **outline**?

Reading Check

1. **Recall facts** In the early years of the South, did many farmers grow cotton? Why or why not?

2. **Recall facts** When did Eli Whitney invent the cotton gin?

3. **Cause and effect** What did the cotton gin create more of a demand for? Why?

---

cloth materials woven from threads

fibers threads from a source used for making cloth or rope

textile cloth, fabric made by weaving

mills factories

North and South Disagree

14   The biggest disagreement between the North and the South was over states' **rights** and slavery. Northerners and Southerners had argued about slavery for many years. By the mid-1800s, some Southerners didn't like the way **industry** was growing in the North. Taxes on **imports** caused Southerners to buy most of the **manufactured goods** they needed from the North.

15   As a writer for one Alabama newspaper described it,

> *The North fattens and grows rich upon the South. We depend upon it for our entire supplies…. The **slaveholder** dresses in Northern goods, rides in a Northern saddle…. His floor is swept by a Northern broom, and is covered with a Northern carpet… and he is furnished with Northern inventions.*

16   The disagreement over slavery worsened because of the **rapid settlement** of the western **frontier.** Over the years, American **pioneers** and soldiers had pushed many of the Native American peoples off their lands. This made it possible for more settlers to move west into areas such as Illinois, Iowa, Missouri, and Arkansas. The settlers took with them their ways of life. For settlers from the North, this meant a way of life without slaves. For some settlers from the South, however, this meant taking their enslaved workers with them.

REVIEW *Why did the settlement of the western frontier cause disagreements?*

Settlers come to the western frontier.

Reading Strategy

Put Text Information in an Outline Should you put a long quote like this in your outline?

---

rights what someone can legally have

industry the making and selling of **products**

imports products that are brought from one place or country into another

goods items that can be bought or sold

slaveholder someone who owns slaves

rapid quick

settlement establishment of people in an area

frontier edge of settled land

pioneers first people to enter new land to work and live there

17   Soon the question of slavery in the frontier lands became one of the biggest disagreements in the country. Most white Northerners thought that slavery should stay in the South. Most white Southerners believed that slave owners had the right to take their slaves wherever they wanted.

18   The disagreement over slavery led to arguments. Even so, the number of people held as slaves in the South continued to grow. So did the number of enslaved people who were taken west.

Disagreements Lead to Conflict

19   In the next years, the disagreements between the North and the South grew worse. The Southern states **seceded** from the United States. On April 12, 1861, a Civil War between the North and the South began. The war continued for four years. Over 600,000 Americans died. Most of the South was **destroyed**. Finally, on April 9, 1865, the South surrendered.

The Battle of Gettysburg in Pennsylvania (reenactment)

Reading Strategy

Put Text Information in an Outline What will be the name of the last subheading of your **outline**? What Roman **numeral** will you use for it?

Reading Check

1. **Recall facts** What were the biggest issues the North and South disagreed about?

2. **Recall facts** When did the Civil War begin?

3. **Explain** Why did the South secede from the United States?

---

seceded withdrew from
destroyed broken down

● **Apply the Reading Strategy**

Put Text Information in an Outline

Now complete the Reading Strategy **outline**.

1. Review the **Reading Strategy** on page 227.
2. Copy the beginning of the **outline**.
3. Look back at the reading for the information you need and complete your **outline**.

The Civil War: Background to the Conflict

I. Differences in the **Regions**
   A. In the North: people moved to cities.
   B.

II.

● **Academic Vocabulary**

Vocabulary for the Reading Comprehension Questions

Word	Explanation	Sample Sentence	Visual Cue
summarize *verb*	to give a brief statement of the most important features of something	We **summarize** a long report by giving its main ideas.	They won the game in overtime.
text *noun*	written material	The student looked through many **texts** to find the information he needed.	

Draw a picture and write a sentence for each word.

✓Checkpoint

1. **Summarize** the last movie you saw.
2. What **texts** do you use in your classes?

Vocabulary Log

● Reading Comprehension Questions

Think and Discuss

1. **Recall facts** In the mid-1800s, where did most Americans live and work?

2. **Compare and contrast** How were the North and the South similar in the mid-1800s? How were they different?

3. **Analyze cause and effect** What effect did the invention of the cotton gin have on slavery?

4. **Summarize** Summarize the main conflicts between the North and the South that led to the Civil War.

5. **Find similarities and differences across texts** Look up "Genes: A Family Inheritance" and "Martin Luther King Jr. Day" in the table of contents of this book. Look back at these readings. What **text** features do all of these readings share? Why do you think they all have this **text** feature?

6. **Revisit the Reading Focus Questions** Go back to page 228 and discuss the questions.

Workbook
page 172

Independent Practice
CD-ROM/Online

● Text Element

Graphs

Informational **texts** often include **graphs**. Graphs illustrate information from the **text** visually. Different kinds of graphs show different kinds of information.

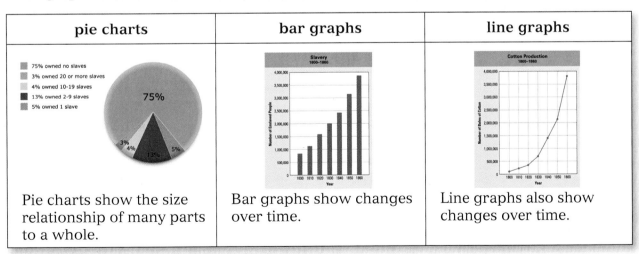

pie charts	bar graphs	line graphs
Pie charts show the size relationship of many parts to a whole.	Bar graphs show changes over time.	Line graphs also show changes over time.

1. What information does each graph show?

2. Survey the students in your class about their interests. Create a pie chart that shows the results of your survey.

✓ Checkpoint

Name and describe three kinds of **graphs**.

Workbook
page 173

Independent Practice
CD-ROM/Online

THE QUARREL BETWEEN WIND AND THUNDER

● About the Reading

You read a textbook reading about the conflicts that divided a country in "The Civil War: Background to the Conflict." Now you will read an Apache story about a conflict between two elements of nature: wind and thunder. The Apache are one of many Native American groups.

● Build Background

Personification

"The Quarrel Between Wind and Thunder" is a fable. Fables often use **personification.** This is when a writer gives human qualities to something that is not human, such as an animal or an object. In "The Quarrel Between Wind and Thunder," wind and thunder are personified.

Preview the illustrations on pages 238–240. Discuss these questions with a partner.

1. How do the faces and bodies of Wind and Thunder seem human?

2. What human emotions do Wind and Thunder seem to have?

Key Vocabulary

bragging

heal

proud

shrink

● Vocabulary From the Reading

Use Context Clues to Determine Meaning

Use the context of each sentence to determine the meaning of the **highlighted** word. Discuss the meanings with a small group.

1. Mrs. Diaz tells everyone about her son's perfect scores. Her friends are tired of her **bragging.**

2. Dr. Patel likes her job. She likes to **heal** people and make them better.

3. Mr. Brown is very **proud** of his daughter. She always gets 100% on her exams.

4. My clothes often **shrink** in the wash. Then they are too small to wear.

✓Checkpoint

1. Explain **personification** in your own words.

2. What is something that you are **proud** of?

Vocabulary Log

Workbook page 174

Independent Practice CD-ROM/Online

Reading Strategy

Identify Cause and Effect

Sometimes one event makes another one happen. The first event is the **cause.** The second is the **effect.** As you read "The Quarrel Between Wind and Thunder," look for cause and effect events in the story.

Text Genre

Fable

"The Quarrel Between Wind and Thunder" is a **fable.** Fables are stories that people have passed down from one generation to the next. Originally these stories were told orally. Now they are also written. Look for these features as you read "The Quarrel Between Wind and Thunder."

Fable	
lesson or moral	fables usually teach something or show how to behave
simplicity	the stories are simple; the conflicts are clear
animal or object characters	the characters are often not human
personification	the non-human characters often have human qualities such as goodness

Meet the Author

Jane Louise Curry wrote and performed plays for friends and neighbors when she was a child. In high school, she wrote articles for the school paper. Curry has been interested in Native American stories for many years.

Reading Focus Questions

As you read, think about these questions.

1. How does this reading relate to "conflict and resolution"?
2. What do you think was the author's purpose for writing "The Quarrel Between Wind and Thunder"?
3. What is the cause of Wind and Thunder's conflict? How do they resolve the conflict?

✓Checkpoint

1. Explain a weather-related **cause** and **effect.**
2. Describe one of the characteristics of a **fable.**

Workbook
pages 175–176

Independent Practice
CD-ROM/Online

THE QUARREL BETWEEN WIND AND THUNDER

an Apache fable retold by Jane Louise Curry

1   At sunrise, Wind and Thunder looked over the bright, new earth and saw that it was a good place to live.

2   Wind **puffed out** his chest. "My earth! How **proud** of it I am!" After all, I am the one who works to keep it **trim** and beautiful. I should be **proud!**"

Reading Strategy

Identify Cause and Effect What is the cause of Thunder's fury?

3   "You?" Thunder **rumbled** in **fury.** "I am the one who should be **proud.** I am the one who keeps the earth as it should be. I, not you, you . . . you **sack** of wind!"

---

puffed out made bigger, by breathing in air
trim slender, in good physical condition
rumbled made a low, powerful rolling noise
fury violent anger
sack bag

4   Thunder was so angry that he could not listen to any more of Wind's **bragging** or even **bear** the sight of him. He **stomped** away, **crashing** and **booming** all the way up the sky.

5   Once Thunder was out of hearing, Wind said to himself, "Poh! The earth does not need that **bad-tempered fellow.** I don't need him. I shall keep this beautiful earth neat and green by myself. I shall make the grass greener, the **blooms** brighter, the trees taller. Let him watch and see!"

6   So Wind began to blow. "Grow, grow!" he sang as he blew. He blew and he blew and he BLEW! But no grass or flowers or trees grew. Every day the earth was more brown and **parched.** The lakes and creeks began to **shrink.** Wind grew frightened at last and knew that he would have to search the sky to find Thunder.

Reading Strategy

Identify Cause and Effect What is the effect of all of Wind's blowing?

Reading Check

1. **Recall facts** Why does Thunder leave?

2. **Recall facts** Does Wind think he needs Thunder?

3. **Recognize character development** How does Wind's failure change him?

---

bear stand

stomped stepped down strongly with the foot

crashing violently hitting against something, creating a loud sound

booming making a deep, loud noise

bad-tempered angry, having a bad emotional nature

fellow informal word for a man or boy

blooms flowers

parched very hot and dry

7

When he found him, he said, "I was wrong, Thunder. I cannot take care of the earth alone. We must be brothers again, and work together. Without you, I have worked hard, but everywhere I have made the earth dry and brown. Will you come down with me so that we may **heal** it?"

Thunder was pleased, and he hurried back down the sky with Wind. He **growled** and **grumbled** and **roared** as he went, so that the clouds grew dark, and the rain rained down. Here, the grass grew high. There, the **yucca** plants bloomed. Along the **streambeds, cottonwood** trees **sprouted** new green leaves. Wind followed Thunder and his rain across the earth, and was happy again as he blew through the high grass.

9 So it was that the two became brothers again, and work together still.

Reading Strategy

Identify Cause and Effect What is the effect of Wind's apology?

---

growled made a low, angry sound

grumbled complained in a quiet, unhappy manner

roared made a loud, scary sound like a lion

yucca kind of plant with stiff leaves

streambeds paths of small rivers

cottonwood kind of tree that grows cottony hairs

sprouted started to grow

● Reading Comprehension Questions

Think and Discuss

1. **Recall facts** Why does Wind think he should be proud? Why does Thunder?

2. **Identify narrator** Is this fable a first- or third-person narrative? Explain to a partner and support your answer with evidence.

3. **Retell** Tell the story in your own words. Use Key Vocabulary words.

4. **Analyze character traits** Describe the character of Wind. Describe the character of Thunder. How do their character traits lead to the conflict?

5. **Recognize literary devices** The author describes Thunder's actions with words that sound like sounds (for example: **rumble, stomped,** and **crashing**). Can you find more of these words? Why do you think the author uses these kinds of words?

6. **Analyze theme** What is the theme of this fable? Explain your answer.

7. **Revisit the Reading Focus Questions** Go back to page 237 and discuss the questions.

Workbook page 177

Independent Practice CD-ROM/Online

Spelling

Abbreviations of State Names

Workbook page 178

Independent Practice CD-ROM/Online

Writing Conventions

Capitalization: Using Capital Letters

Workbook page 179

Independent Practice CD-ROM/Online

Connect Readings 1 and 2

You have read two **texts** on the theme of conflict and resolution. Use these activities to make connections between the readings.

1. With a partner, use this chart to compare the two readings.

Reading title	What is the genre?	Are there characters in the reading?	Does the reading include facts?	Is the reading interesting to you? Why?
The Civil War: Background to the Conflict				
THE QUARREL BETWEEN WIND AND THUNDER				

2. Discuss these questions with a partner.
   a. Who are the conflicts between in each reading?
   b. What is the cause of the conflict in each reading?
   c. What bad things follow the conflict in each reading?
   d. How is the conflict resolved in each reading?

3. **Revisit the Chapter Focus Question** What kinds of things cause conflicts?

Phrases for Conversation

Inviting Group Members to Give Ideas

What do you think?
Are there any more
   suggestions?
Does anyone else
   have any more ideas?
We haven't heard
   from you yet, (name
   of student).
Would you like to add
   anything, (name of
   student)?

● Listening and Speaking

Create an Oral Fable About a Conflict

Review the features of a fable on page 237. Work with a small group to create your own oral fable.

1. In a small group, discuss these questions.
   a. What will the title of the fable be?
   b. Who will the characters in your fable be?
   c. What will the conflict be?
   d. What will the events of the story be?
   e. What will the climax of the story be?
   f. What will the moral be?

2. All students in your group should participate in the discussion. You can use the **Phrases for Conversation** to ask group members to give their ideas.

3. Work together to create an **outline** of the fable.

4. Use your **outline** to tell your fable to the class. Each student in your group should tell a part of the fable.

● Reading Fluency

CD-Assisted Reading Practice

Listening to a reading on a CD as you read can help you become a more fluent reader. Use the CD recording of "The Quarrel Between Wind and Thunder" to practice this activity.

1. Listen to the CD of this fable without looking at the book.

2. Listen to the CD again, this time following along in your book as you listen.

3. Listen to the fable again. This time read aloud along with the recording.

4. How successful were you at each of these tasks?

Listening only	1	2	3	4	5	6
	not very good				very good	
Listening and following along silently	1	2	3	4	5	6
	not very good				very good	
Listening and reading aloud	1	2	3	4	5	6
	not very good				very good	

5. In preparation for the next CD-Assisted Reading Practice, what do you need to do to make improvements?

Vocabulary Development

Prefixes: un-, dis-

A **prefix** is a letter or a group of letters added to the beginning of a root word. A prefix changes the meaning of the root word. The prefixes **un-** and **dis-** both mean *not* or *the opposite of.*

Look at the words in the first column below. Each is formed with a prefix and a root word. Notice how the prefixes change the meaning of the root words.

Word	Prefix	Root Word	Word in Context
unfair	**un-**	**fair**	Some people thought that slavery was wrong and **un**fair.
disagreement	**dis-**	**agreement**	The **dis**agreement over slavery led to arguments.

Complete each sentence with a word made of a prefix and a root from the chart.

dis-	un-
agree	fair
like	happy
honest	healthy

Build Your Knowledge

Notice that the prefixes **un-** and **dis-** create **antonyms**—words that have opposite meanings. Knowing these prefixes can help you determine the meanings of words.

I never had a pet because I *dislike* most animals.

1. My brother and I always have different opinions. We ____ about everything.

2. You eat too much junk food. It's ____ .

3. John failed the exam. He was ____ about it.

4. The child did not tell the truth. He was ____ .

5. You did not help us with the team project. That's ____ !

✓**Checkpoint**

1. What is a **prefix**? Explain in your own words.

2. What prefixes mean *not* or *the opposite of*?

● **Grammar**

Some, Any

Some and **any** are words that talk about the quantity (amount) of something. **Some** and **any** do not tell the exact number. Use **some** and **any** when:

- you talk about more than one thing.
- you do not know the exact number or the exact number is not important.

Some, Any		
	When to Use	**Example**
some	Use **some** in affirmative statements.	The North and South disagreed about **some** important issues.
any	Use **any** in negative statements.	The North didn't want **any** slavery.
	Use **any** in questions.	Was there **any** slavery in the North?

Notes:

- **Some** and **any** are used with both count and noncount nouns. Count nouns are nouns you can count.

    I have one **egg.** I have 12 **carrots.**

    Noncount nouns can't be counted.

    I like **milk.** I eat **cheese.**

- Indefinite pronouns with **some-** (such as **someone, something,** and **somewhere**) and **any-** (such as **anyone, anything,** and **anywhere**) are used in the same way as **some** and **any.**

    I am looking for **someone.**

    I don't have **anything** to give you.

___

Practice the Grammar

A. Look at the pictures. Complete the sentences.

1. She has ____ money.
2. He doesn't have ____ money.
3. She doesn't want ____ grapes.
4. He wants ____ grapes.

5. There aren't ___ buses on the street.
6. There are ___ cars.

B. Look at the picture. With a partner, take turns asking and answering questions about what is in the refrigerator. Use **some** and **any** and the words provided.

Do we have any eggs?

Yes. We have some eggs.

1. eggs	3. milk	5. apples	7. butter
2. cheese	4. tomatoes	6. juice	8. yogurt

Grammar Expansion

Indefinite Pronouns;
A lot of and **Many** in Affirmative Sentences;
A lot of, **Much**, and **Many** in Negative Sentences

Workbook   Independent Practice
pages 182–184   CD-ROM/Online

Use the Grammar Independently

1. Write three sentences about things you have with you today. Use **some**.

2. Write three sentences about things you do not have with you today. Use **any**.

3. Share your sentences with a partner.

I have some books.
I don't have any pencils.

✓*Checkpoint*

1. Explain when to use **some** and **any**.

2. Give a sample sentence for each.

● Writing Assignment

Persuasive Writing: Write a Newspaper Editorial

Newspaper editorials are letters or articles in newspapers. Editorials give the writer's opinion about events or issues important at the moment.

Writing Suggestion

See **Milestones Handbook.**
pages 393–433

> ### Writing Prompt
>
> Imagine you live in either the North or the South during the Civil War. Write a short newspaper editorial about your **region's** view of the conflict. Use the information from the reading "The Civil War: Background to the Conflict" in your editorial.

Write Your Newspaper Editorial

1. **Read the student model.** It shows the first paragraph of an editorial.
2. **Choose a side.** Decide whether you will write from the perspective of the North or the South.

Student Model

> ### The North-South Conflict
>
> A few years ago our country was peaceful. However, in the last few years, there have been big changes in the North. These changes created differences in the way people in the North and South live. They also created differences in our opinions. Now the South wants to withdraw from the Union. I think this is wrong. These are some reasons why I disagree.
>
> First of all, . . .

Workbook
page 185

3. **Find information.** Scan (look quickly through) "The Civil War: Background to the Conflict" to find information for your editorial. Take notes. Put the information in an **outline.**

4. **Write your editorial.**
   a. The first paragraph of your editorial should include a statement of the opinion you will present.
   b. The body of your editorial should be one or two paragraphs. It should support the opinion you are presenting.
   c. Finish your editorial with a final paragraph. This paragraph should restate the opinion presented in the introduction.

5. **Revise.** Reread your editorial. Revise it if any ideas are not clear or complete.
   Use the **editing and proofreading symbols** on page 419 to help you mark any changes you want to make.

6. **Edit.** Use the **Writing Checklist** to help you find problems and errors.

Writing Checklist

1. I found information from the reading and used it in my editorial.

2. The first paragraph of my editorial included an introduction stating an opinion.

3. I used words with the prefixes **un-** and **dis-**.

4. I used **some** and **any** in my editorial.

Writing Support

Grammar
Definite Article: the

Use the definite article **the** correctly in your writing. Follow these rules. Use **the** before:

1. geographical areas: **the** North, **the** Middle East
2. names of rivers, oceans, seas: **the** Nile, **the** Pacific, **the** Black Sea
3. points on the globe: **the** Equator, **the** North Pole

Do *not* use **the** before:

- names of countries (Mexico, China) except countries like: **the** Netherlands, **the** United States, **the** United Kingdom.
- names of cities or states (Seoul, Florida)
- names of streets (Main Street, Austin Road)
- names of lakes (Lake Titicaca, Lake Erie)
- names of mountains (Mount Everest, Mount Fuji)

Apply Read your newspaper editorial aloud. Did you use the definite article **the** correctly? Correct any mistakes.

Progress Check

How well did you understand this chapter? Try to answer the questions. If necessary, go back to the pages listed for a review.

Skills	Skills Assessment Questions	Pages to Review
Vocabulary From the Readings	What do these words mean?	
	• **crop, factory, manufacture, product, region, technology**	226
	• **bragging, heal, proud, shrink**	236
Academic Vocabulary	What do these academic vocabulary words mean?	
	• **numeral, outline**	227
	• **summarize, text**	234
Reading Strategies	How can you put **text** information in an **outline**?	227
	What is a **cause**? What is an **effect**?	237
Text Genres	What is the **text** genre of "The Civil War: Background to the Conflict"?	228
	What is the **text** genre of "The Quarrel Between Wind and Thunder"?	237
Reading Comprehension	What is "The Civil War: Background to the Conflict" about?	235
	What is "The Quarrel Between Wind and Thunder" about?	241
Text Elements	What are **pie charts, bar graphs,** and **line graphs**?	235
Spelling	Give the state names for these abbreviations: NY, FL, IL, PA.	241
Writing Conventions	Rewrite these sentences using capital letters: mrs. ellen vargas teaches history I. She is from the southwest. Her favorite store is cindy's fashions.	241
Listening and Speaking	**Phrases for Conversation**	
	What phrases can you use to ask people to give ideas?	242
Vocabulary Development	What is a **prefix**? Name a word that begins with the prefix **un-**. Name a word that begins with the prefix **dis-**.	243
Grammar	When is the word **some** used? When is **any** used?	244
Writing Support: Grammar	What is a definite article? Give three examples of when it should be used.	247

Assessment Practice

Read this passage. Then answer Questions 1 through 4.

Aesop's Fable of the North Wind and the Sun

1   The Sun and the North Wind were having an argument. "Every living thing needs the power of my light and heat. That's why I am more powerful than you," said the Sun. He was proud of himself.

2   "No! I am stronger! I can start powerful storms that last for days. I blow trees down. Humans fear me!" bragged the North Wind.

3   "We will have a contest," said the Sun. "Let's prove who is the most powerful." They looked down at a man traveling on the road. "Whoever can make that man take off his coat is the most powerful."

4   The North Wind tried his power first. He blew with all his strength. The more he blew, the more the man wrapped his coat around himself. Tired, the North Wind said, "I give up. Let's see what you can do." The Sun shone out with all his warmth. The man felt the Sun's rays and took off his coat.

1   **Read this sentence from paragraph 1.**

> **He was proud of himself.**

What does <u>proud</u> mean?
A   feeling surprised
B   feeling good about oneself
C   feeling weak
D   feeling bad about oneself

2   **What effect does the North Wind have on the man?**
A   The man shakes with fear.
B   The man gets tired.
C   The man takes off his coat.
D   The man wraps his coat around himself.

3   **How do the Sun and the North Wind resolve their conflict?**
A   They argue.
B   They have a contest.
C   They yell and scream.
D   They ask the man for advice.

4   **What is the genre of this text?**
A   fable
B   persuasive essay
C   play
D   diary entry

Writing on Demand:
Persuasive Newspaper Editorial

Write a persuasive newspaper editorial about this story. Imagine that you observed the argument between the Sun and the North Wind. Retell the story from your perspective. Include your own opinions and judgments about how the Sun and the North Wind act. **(20 minutes)**

> ## Writing Tip
> Include phrases that tell the reader you are stating an opinion, such as **I think, I believe, I feel,** etc.

Apply & Extend

Objectives

Listening and Speaking
Give a response to literature presentation

Media
Compare information about a conflict in an online news story and a blog

Writing
Write a research report

Projects

Independent Reading

● Listening and Speaking Workshop
Give a Response to Literature Presentation

> **Topic**
>
> Analyze a conflict in a piece of literature. Then deliver a presentation on this conflict.

1. **Plan**
   a. Look back at the literature selections you read in this book. Choose one for your presentation.
   b. Identify the conflict in this piece of literature. Include specific information about the cause(s) and effect(s).
   c. Think about these focus questions.
      • What is the conflict?
      • Is it resolved? If so, how?
      • Was the conflict handled well by the characters?
      • Could the conflict have been handled better? If so, how?
   d. Find facts, details, and examples from the reading to support your ideas.
   e. Take notes on the information you find.

2. **Outline**
   Write an outline for your presentation. Be sure that your outline covers all of the questions asked in the "Plan" step.

3. **Practice**
   Use your outline to practice your presentation. Think about each part of the **Speaking Self-Evaluation** before you practice.

4. **Present and Evaluate**
   Give the presentation. When the presentation is finished, ask your group members for feedback. Listen carefully to their feedback. Use the **Speaking Self-Evaluation** to evaluate your part of the presentation. Use the **Active Listening Evaluation** to evaluate and discuss your classmates' presentations.

Speaking Self-Evaluation	Active Listening Evaluation
1. I answered the focus questions.	**1.** Your presentation was well organized.
2. I provided facts, details, and examples.	**2.** You used your voice and gestures to emphasize important points.
3. I spoke clearly and loudly enough for my audience to hear me.	**3.** I agree with you about _____ .
4. I emphasized important points with my voice and gestures.	**4.** I disagree about _____ .

Media Workshop

Compare an Online News Story and a Blog

In this activity, you will focus on a conflict happening in the world today. You will find an online news article about the conflict and compare it to a blog article about the same conflict. A **blog** is a personal journal on the Internet. People use blogs to post, or publish, their ideas and opinions.

1. Choose a conflict happening in the world today.
2. Go on the Internet. Find and read an online news article about the conflict.
3. Find and read a blog entry on the same conflict.
4. Think about these questions.
   a. Do the news article and the blog include the same information?
   b. Is the information in the news article and the blog told in the same way?
   c. Which includes more facts? Which includes more opinions? What do you think is the reason for this?
   d. Does either the news article or the blog entry try to persuade the reader about anything? If so, how does it do this?
   e. Does either the blog or the news article contain inferences (educated guesses) with no details or evidence? Does either contain propaganda? **Propaganda** is ideas or information presented to deliberately influence opinions, emotions, and attitudes. It presents only one point of view.
5. Tell a partner about the article and the blog entry you read. Explain the differences between them.

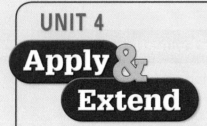

UNIT 4
Apply & Extend

Writing Suggestion

See **Milestones Handbook**.
pages 393–433
See especially pages 422–426
for The Research Process,
including information
on how to use reference
materials.

● Writing Workshop
Research Report

A **research report** gives information about a topic. To prepare a research report, a writer chooses a topic and researches information about it using different sources.

Writing Prompt

In this unit you learned about conflict and resolution. Some of the conflicts you read about were wars. Choose a war to write a research report about.

PREWRITE

1. Read the student model on the next page.
2. Choose a war to write about. Some possible choices are:
   - The American Revolution
   - The Civil War
   - World War I
   - World War II
3. Make a list of questions to research, such as:
   a. What regions or countries fought in this war?
   b. What was the **cause** of the war?
   c. What was the turning point of the war?
   d. What was the result of the war?
4. Research information that answers your focus questions. Look up information in different sources such as books, the Internet, and encyclopedias. Use titles, headings, tables of contents, glossaries, indexes, and graphic features to locate information.
5. Put your notes into an **outline** before you begin to write.

WRITE A DRAFT

1. Write the **introduction.** It should give background information the reader needs to know.
2. Write the **body.** The body should be two or three paragraphs, each focusing on one main idea.
3. Write the **conclusion.** The conclusion should restate the idea you expressed in your introduction.
4. List the **sources** you used. For books, include the title, the author, the publisher, and the year of publication. For Web sites, list the name and address of the Web site.

Jennifer Reyes

The American Revolution

Introduction

Until the American Revolution, America was not an independent country. It was 13 colonies controlled by the British. The American Revolution was a war that changed America forever. It made America an independent country.

Body

Until 1763, there was no conflict between Britain and the colonies. The British generally left the colonies alone. However, this changed in 1763. The British were at war with France. Britain needed money for the war. They suddenly put taxes on many things in the American colonies. For example, they put taxes on newspapers, tea, and sugar. The colonists thought the tax was unfair because nobody spoke for the colonists in the British government. The British made laws colonists did not agree to. This made the colonists angry. On December 16, 1773, the colonists protested against Britain. They threw British tea off ships into Boston Harbor. This protest was called the Boston Tea Party. This event led to a war between the colonists and Britain. This war was the American Revolution.

The colonists and Britain fought until 1781. After many battles, the colonists started winning the war. They had help from the French. In September of 1781, a French army won an important battle. The French and colonist soldiers outnumbered the British soldiers. The general of the British army gave up. This ended the war. The colonists won the war.

Conclusion

Because the colonists won the war, they won their independence from Britain. The colonies came together and formed the United States of America. The United States was now an independent country. From then on, America made its own decisions and created its own laws.

Sources

Scholastic Children's Encyclopedia, Scholastic Reference, 2004
Yahoo! Education: http://education.yahoo.com/reference/
encyclopedia/entry/AmerRev

Apply & Extend

REVISE

1. Review your draft. Make sure your introduction tells what the report is about. Also check that each paragraph of the body focuses on one main idea.

2. Exchange your research report with a partner. Ask your partner to use the **Peer Review Checklist** to review your essay. Your partner will point out errors and give suggestions for making your draft better.

3. Revise your draft. You may need to add or delete sentences. You may need to rearrange sentences to make your ideas clearer.

4. Use the **editing and proofreading symbols** on page 419 to help you mark the changes you want to make.

EDIT

1. Use the **Revising and Editing Checklist** to evaluate your report.

2. Fix any errors in grammar, spelling, punctuation and capitalization. See pages 416–418 for how to write the titles of your source documents and for rules for capitalization.

Writing Suggestion

When you revise your draft, try combining short, related sentences. You can use noun phrases, participial phrases, adjectives, adverbs, and prepositional phrases.

Peer Review Checklist

1. The topic of the report is clearly stated in the first paragraph.

2. The report includes a list of sources.

3. The most interesting thing I learned from this report is _____ .

4. This report would be better if _____ .

Revising and Editing Checklist

1. My introduction tells the subject of my report.

2. Each paragraph in the body of the report is about one idea.

3. I included details and examples from my sources in the body.

4. I used the definite article **the** correctly.

5. My report has a conclusion.

Build Your Knowledge

You may want to publish and present your report using technology. Read and follow the steps for giving a technology presentation on page 429.

PUBLISH

1. Write your report in your best handwriting or use a computer.

2. Read your report to the class. Read clearly and slowly so that everyone can understand you. Change the level of your voice to express your important ideas.

● Projects

Choose one or more of the following projects to explore the theme of conflict and resolution further.

PROJECT 1
Find Out About a Conflict Happening in the World or Your Community

1. Read today's newspaper. You can find one at your library.
2. Scan the newspaper for articles about conflicts happening in the world or your community right now.
3. Choose an article about one conflict. Read the article. Take notes on the important facts and information.
4. Report back to your class on what you learned.

PROJECT 2
Literature About Conflict

1. Go to your library and find a fantasy, fable, legend, myth, and fairy tale with the theme of conflict.
2. For each story, take notes about the plot, the characters, and the conflict.
3. Also take notes about the features of each form of literature.
4. Report back to the class. Describe the features of each form of literature. Retell the plot of each story. Explain the conflict.

PROJECT 3
Compare Tales from Different Cultures

1. Read the description of the book *A Worldwide Cinderella* on page 256. Look for this book in your school or local library.
2. Read the story and explain what happens to Cinderella in your own words.
3. Reread "The Quarrel Between Wind and Thunder" (page 238). Compare the two tales. Make a list of similarities and differences. Write a paragraph to compare and contrast the two.
4. Give a theory about why different cultures have similar tales.

Apply & Extend

Heinle Reading Library

The Three Musketeers
by Alexandre Dumas

In a specially adapted version by Malvina G. Vogel

Join the young soldier D'Artagnan in this fantastic adventure set in the 1600s. D'Artagnan teams up with the three musketeers as they struggle to save the Queen's honor and defeat the evil but powerful Cardinal Richelieu.

● Independent Reading

Explore the theme of conflict and resolution further by reading one or more of these books.

The Kids' Guide to Working Out Conflicts by Naomi Drew, M.A. Free Spirit Publishing, 2004.

This guide book teaches teenagers how to avoid conflicts and become problem solvers. The author gives readers tips on staying calm and making good choices.

James Printer: A Novel of Rebellion by Paul Samuel Jacobs, Scholastic, 2000.

This novel of historical fiction tells the story of James Printer. James is a Nipmuck Native American raised as an Englishman. When war breaks out between the white settlers and local Indian tribes, James is caught in the middle and forced to take sides.

Motherland: A Novel by Vineeta Vijayaraghavan, Soho Press, 2002.

Fifteen-year-old Maya's mother sends her to India for the summer. During her time in India, Maya learns about herself, her family, and her culture. This experience helps Maya heal the conflicts between herself and her mother. It also helps her come to terms with the conflicts between the Eastern and Western cultures that she is a part of.

With Every Drop of Blood: A Novel of the Civil War by James Collier & Christopher Collier, Bantam Doubleday Dell Books for Young Readers, 1997.

After his father's death in a Civil War battle, fourteen-year-old Johnny is left to take care of his family. When Johnny takes on a dangerous mission to bring food to Confederate soldiers, he is captured by a Union soldier named Cush. Cush is a former slave and is Johnny's age. At first Johnny and Cush's relationship is full of conflict, but ultimately they become friends.

A Worldwide Cinderella by Paul Fleischman, Henry Holt and Company, 2007.

The story of Cinderella is one of the most widely told tales on earth. In this retelling, the author blends together the characters, setting, plot, and conflict from 17 world cultures into one tale.

Milestones to Achievement

● Writing: Revise and Edit

MILESTONESTRACKER

Read this rough draft of a student's diary entry, which may contain errors. Then answer Questions 1 through 4.

(1) April 8, 1992

(2) Dear Diary,

(3) My teacher, Ms. Sturm, told us to keep a diary. (4) We read *The Diary of Anne Frank* in class last week. (5) Now that the war has reached our neighborhood in the Sarajevo, Ms. Sturm thinks we should begin our own diaries.

(6) My name, Andrija, means "warrior" (a fighter or soldier) in Serbian. (7) I am in the wrestling club. (8) I almost win, but I am not bragging. (9) I am proud, but I am not a warrior. (10) I don't understand why people fight wars.

(11) I heard the loud noise of any bombs last night. (12) I was scared. (13) My sister was crying. (14) I tried to comfort her. (15) I think I would like to change my name to Mir, which means "peace."

(16) Andrija/Mir

---

1 **How can you correct sentence 5?**

  A Change *the Sarajevo* to *my Sarajevo.*

  B Change *in the Sarajevo* to *to the Sarajevo.*

  C Delete *the* from *the Sarajevo.*

  D Change *our* to *of us.*

2 **How can you correct sentence 8?**

  A Add *always* after *almost.*

  B Add *usually* after *almost.*

  C Add *sometimes* after *almost.*

  D Add *often* after *almost.*

3 **How can you correct sentence 11?**

  A Change *any* to *one.*

  B Change *any* to *in.*

  C Change *any* to *some.*

  D Change *any* to *on.*

4 **What sentence can you add after sentence 15?**

  A I hope my country finds peace.

  B I hope the war continues.

  C I will board up the windows.

  D There will be school tomorrow.

Writing on Demand: Diary Entry

Write a diary entry about war. Think of wars you know or have learned about. What do you think and feel about war? Why? **(20 minutes)**

> ### Writing Tip
> Try using adverbs of frequency (**never, rarely, sometimes, often, usually, always**) to explain how you feel.

● Reading

Read this excerpt from a social studies textbook. Then answer Questions 1 through 8.

The Gettysburg Address

1   On November 19, 1863, President Abraham Lincoln gave an address (a speech) in Gettysburg, Pennsylvania. It was in the middle of the Civil War between the North and South of the United States. A big battle had been fought on the field where Lincoln was speaking. The North had won the battle. However, both the North and the South had lost many men. More than 7,500 soldiers died. The President was in Gettysburg to dedicate the Soldiers' National Cemetery on the battlefield. President Lincoln's speech became one of the most famous speeches in the history of the United States.

2   President Lincoln spoke for only a few minutes. However, his words were very powerful. He reminded Americans of their first fight for freedom—the Revolutionary War—87 years before. "Four score and seven years ago our fathers brought forth on this continent a new nation, conceived in liberty, and dedicated to the proposition that all men are created equal." Lincoln's famous words may sound complicated to us. Said more simply, he stated that 87 years ago, the founders of the United States made a new country based on freedom for all people. Then President Lincoln went on to say that the Civil War was a battle to see if this nation could survive. He also said that the men who were fighting in the Civil War were trying to keep the United States a country that is run by a "government of the people, by the people, and for the people." In other words, they were fighting to keep the country a democracy.

3   President Lincoln's speech comforted a nation that was torn apart by war. It promised healing to a region that was suffering. It said that the fight would bring a new freedom. It would bring true equality not for just some people, but for all people.

1 What does the word <u>comforted</u> mean in this sentence from paragraph 3?

President Lincoln's speech comforted a nation that was torn apart by war.

A upset

B apologized

C calmed

D took away

2 What does the word <u>region</u> mean in this sentence from paragraph 3?

It promised healing to a region that was suffering.

A area

B world

C get well

D town

3 What kind of conflict did Lincoln talk about in his speech?

A state

B war

C family

D enemy

4 What did Lincoln say the fight would bring?

A pain

B freedom

C suffering

D 87 years

5 What would be a good subhead for paragraph 2?

A The Revolutionary War

B The Civil War

C Lincoln's Words

D Battlefield to Cemetery

6 What would be another good graphic for this passage?

A a chart of all the battles of the Civil War

B a chart of all the battles of the Revolutionary War

C a map of the United States

D a picture of the Lincoln Memorial

7 Which word shows an amount in this sentence from paragraph 3?

It would bring true equality not for just some people, but for all people.

A equality

B some

C just

D people

8 Which word from the passage has a prefix?

A unhappy

B dedicate

C powerful

D founders

Survival

Explore the Theme

1. What does **survival** mean?
2. Look at the photos. How does each photo show or relate to survival?

Theme Activity

Work with your classmates to create a presentation of survival situations.

1. Choose a survival situation. Draw a picture of it, or find a picture in a magazine or on the Internet.
2. What situation does your picture show? Write a caption for it. Use a dictionary if necessary.
3. Put your picture on a wall in your classroom. Your classmates will add their pictures, too.

261

CHAPTER 1

Objectives

Reading Strategies

Recognize chronological order; Think aloud

Listening and Speaking

Create a map and give directions

Grammar

Use the present progressive tense; Use the past progressive tense

Writing

Creative writing: Write a survival journal

Academic Vocabulary

chronological	contribute
indicate	aid

Academic Content

Antarctica
Temperature: Fahrenheit and Celsius
The wilderness

● Chapter Focus Question

What do people need to survive in dangerous situations?

Reading 1 **Literature**

Graphic novel
Shackleton and the Lost Antarctic Expedition
by Blake A. Hoena

Reading 2 **Content:** Math

Informational text
Using Math to Survive in the Wild
by Hilary Koll, Steve Mills, Jonny Crockett

Shackleton and the Lost Antarctic Expedition

● About the Reading

You are going to read a story about the explorer Ernest Shackleton. Shackleton and his men sailed to Antarctica in a ship called the *Endurance*. They wanted to cross the South Pole on foot. They were not successful. However, their story of survival is famous.

● Build Background

Antarctica

Antarctica is the continent that is furthest south on the globe. It is the coldest place on Earth. It is covered in ice. Even the sea freezes in winter. Only a few animals can survive in Antarctica. These include penguins, fish, whales, and seals. The only people who live in Antarctica are scientists. They wear special clothes and use special equipment to help them survive.

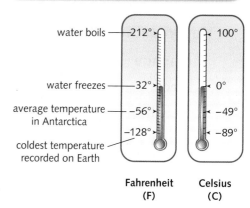

The average temperature on the Antarctic continent is –56° Fahrenheit (–49° Celsius). The lowest temperature ever recorded anywhere on Earth was measured there at –128.6°F (–89°C).

What is the temperature where you are today?

Antarctica

Penguin in Antarctica

● Use Prior Knowledge

Discuss Extreme Temperatures

Where is the coldest place you have been? Where is the hottest place? Copy and complete the chart. Then discuss the questions with a partner.

	Coldest Place: _____	Hottest Place: _____
1. How did you dress?		
2. What things did you do to keep warm or cool?		
3. Did you like being in this place?		
4. Why? Why not?		

Key Vocabulary

damage

force

freezing

injury
(singular) /
injuries
(plural)

rescue

supplies

● Vocabulary From the Reading
Learn, Practice, and Use Independently

Learn Vocabulary Read each sentence. Look at the **highlighted** word. Use the context (the words around the highlighted word) to figure out the meaning of the word. Use a dictionary if you need help.

1. Please don't kick the table. That will **damage** it.
2. Strong winds sometimes **force** boats to go onto the beach.
3. It is **freezing** outside. Don't go outside without a warm coat, hat, and gloves.
4. The basketball player has a foot **injury**. He can't play again until his foot heals.
5. Firefighters **rescue** people from burning buildings.
6. We had many camping **supplies**. We had flashlights, water bottles, and sleeping bags.

Practice Vocabulary Complete the paragraph with the correct Key Vocabulary words.

There is a terrible snowstorm in the Midwest right now. The storm will **(1)**___ many people to leave their homes. Some people will need to leave because the temperature is **(2)**____ and they have no heat in their homes. Some people don't have basic **(3)**____ like food, matches, and flashlights. Strong winds are knocking down trees and doing **(4)**___ to many houses. One family was trapped in their car. Luckily the police were able to **(5)**___ the family. One police officer suffered a serious **(6)**___.

Checkpoint

1. Did you ever **damage** anything badly? What was it?

2. Did you ever have an **injury**? What was it?

Use Vocabulary Independently Choose a Key Vocabulary word. Without saying the word, describe the meaning of the word to your partner. Your partner will guess the word. Take turns.

Vocabulary Log

Workbook page 189

Independent Practice CD-ROM/Online

● Academic Vocabulary

Vocabulary for the Reading Strategy

Word	Explanation	Sample Sentence	Visual Cue
chronological *adjective*	arranged in the order in which events happen over time	My school records list my schools in **chronological** order.	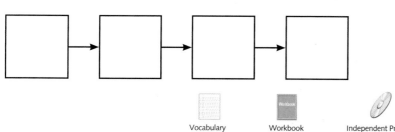
indicate *verb*	to show where or what something is	The boy **indicated** the fruit he wanted by pointing to the apple.	

Draw a picture and write a sentence for each word.

● Reading Strategy

Recognize Chronological Order

The order in which events happen in a story is called **chronological** order. Dates and time words **indicate** **chronological** order. Time words, like those in the box below, help you understand the order of events in a story.

before	after	first	next	then	finally

1. As you read, pay attention to dates and time words.

2. Ask yourself questions about what happens first, next, and last.

3. After you finish the reading, you will complete the **chronological** order chart with the events of the story in order. You will also include date and time words.

☐ → ☐ → ☐ → ☐

Vocabulary Log

Workbook page 190

Independent Practice CD-ROM/Online

✓Checkpoint

1. What schools have you gone to? Write them in **chronological** order.

2. What country (or countries) is your family from? **Indicate** it (or them) on a map.

● Text Genre

Graphic Novel

Shackleton and the Lost Antarctic Expedition is a **graphic novel.** A graphic novel is a book with text and art in comic book style. Graphic novels have these features.

Graphic Novel	
story	can be either fiction (made up) or nonfiction (true)
varied story genres	can be historical fiction, action-adventure, fantasy, or science fiction
illustrations	comic book style illustrations are on every page
dialogue	conversation between characters; the dialogue often appears in "speech bubbles"

● Meet the Author

Blake A. Hoena grew up in the midwestern United States. As a boy, he liked reading fantasy and adventure novels. These books inspired him to become a professional writer. Hoena enjoys writing about famous people, like Ernest Shackleton. He also enjoys writing his own fantasy and adventure books. He has written the text for many illustrated books.

● Reading Focus Questions

As you read, think about these questions.

1. How does this reading relate to the theme of "survival"?
2. What do you think was the author's purpose for writing *Shackleton and the Lost Antarctic Expedition*?
3. Could the crew survive without Shackleton? Why or why not?

✓Checkpoint

Describe a **graphic novel.**

Workbook
page 191

Independent Practice
CD-ROM/Online

Shackleton and the Lost Antarctic Expedition

by Blake A. Hoena

Illustrated by Dave Hoover and Charles Barnett III

Prologue

1　In July 1907, Ernest Shackleton and his **crew set out** to be the first to reach the South Pole. However, very bad weather, **injuries,** and food **shortages forced** them to give up. They were just 97 miles (156 kilometers) from the South Pole!

2　In 1911, a Norwegian explorer named Roald Amundsen was the first to reach the South Pole. Shackleton needed a different goal. He decided to be the first to cross Antarctica on foot. In 1914, Shackleton and his team **set off** on their ship, the *Endurance*. Things did not go well. The ship got stuck and then sank.

3　Shackleton and his men were **shipwrecked**. They were in one of the most difficult **environments** on Earth. They had no way to contact the outside world. There was no one to **rescue** them. Shackleton and his team had a new goal—survival.

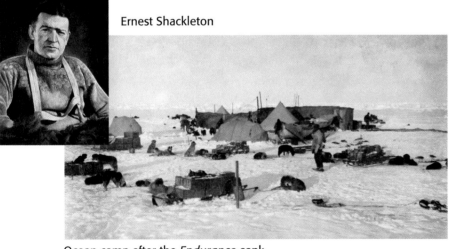

Ernest Shackleton

Ocean camp after the *Endurance* sank

---

crew workers, often on a ship, train, or airplane

set out began with a definite purpose

shortages not having enough of some things

set off began a journey

shipwrecked experiencing the loss or destruction of a ship

environments surroundings that people, plants, and animals live in

Reading Strategy

Recognize Chronological Order
When did Shackleton and his team set off on the *Endurance*?

Reading Check

1. **Recall facts** Who reached the South Pole first?

2. **Recall facts** What was the *Endurance*?

3. **Draw conclusions** Why do you think Shackleton needed a different goal?

The Fight to Survive

Shackleton and his crew **salvaged** as much food, clothing, and other **supplies** as they could from the wrecked ship. Then the crew **set up** camp about a mile from the *Endurance*.

Men, we'll sail to land when the warm weather breaks up the ice.

I WILL see my crew home safely!

But the hopelessness of their situation **sank in** on November 21. The **wreckage** of the *Endurance* finally disappeared into the Weddell Sea.

Reading Strategy

Recognize Chronological Order
On what date did the *Endurance* sink into the sea?

salvaged saved something **damaged**

set up put in readiness for an operation

sank in was absorbed or understood

wreckage remains of something that has been destroyed

Shackleton worried about how far they were from land. His crew had only three small boats to carry his 28 men through the rough, ice-filled sea.

We are now 250 miles from Paulet Island

I know there's food **stored** on the island. It was left years ago by another **expedition**.

The closer we can get the boats to the island when the ice breaks up, the better off we'll be.

A **spell** of hard work would do everybody good.

Reading Strategy

Recognize Chronological Order
Shackleton remembers that there is food on Paulet Island. When was this food stored there?

Reading Check

1. **Recall facts** Why was Shackleton worried?

2. **Analyze character traits** What does the text on this page tell you about Shackleton's character?

stored saved for use in the future

expedition group organized and equipped to make a journey for a special purpose

spell period of time

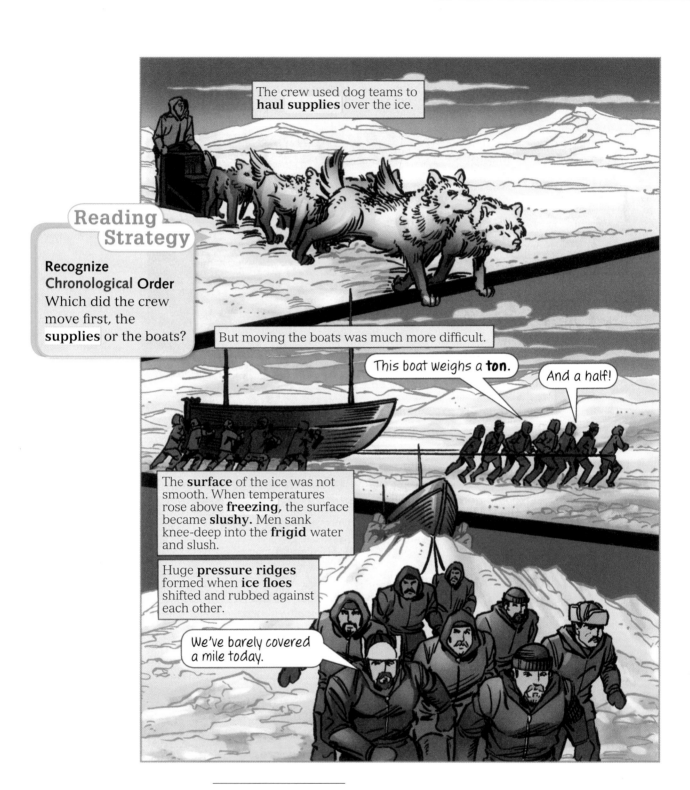

The crew used dog teams to **haul supplies** over the ice.

Reading Strategy

Recognize Chronological Order
Which did the crew move first, the **supplies** or the boats?

But moving the boats was much more difficult.

This boat weighs a **ton**.

And a half!

The **surface** of the ice was not smooth. When temperatures rose above **freezing,** the surface became **slushy.** Men sank knee-deep into the **frigid** water and slush.

Huge **pressure ridges** formed when **ice floes** shifted and rubbed against each other.

We've barely covered a mile today.

---

haul carry

ton unit of measurement of weight; in the U.S., 2,000 pounds (907 kilograms)

surface flat, top layer of something

slushy like soft melting snow mixed with dirt

frigid very cold, **freezing**

pressure ridges ice formations created when one sheet of ice pushes up against another

ice floes large sheets of floating ice

---

leads cracks that form in sea ice

hull shell of a ship, without its sails and inside rooms

insane crazy

By the beginning of 1916, the men had used up much of their food **supplies.** Breakfast consisted of powdered milk and **pemmican.** For lunch they ate biscuits and a few lumps of sugar. Dinner was their only hot meal. They ate seal and penguin meat.

By the end of March, they had killed all of the dogs to save food.

On April 9, the ice had broken up enough that Shackleton gave the order to **launch** the boats. But by this time, they had **drifted** past Paulet Island.

We'll have to head north to Elephant Island, about 50 miles away.

Reading Strategy

Recognize Chronological Order
Which happened first?
• Shackleton gave the order to launch the boats.
• The ice broke up.

Reading Check

1. **Recall facts** What was the crew's only hot meal of the day?

2. **Draw conclusions** How do you think the men feel at this point in the expedition? Why?

---

pemmican a food made of dried meat, dried berries, and fat

launch push into the water

drifted floated, carried by wind or water currents

The men rowed between large ice floes and **bergs** that could easily crush their tiny boats.

Some nights they camped on large ice floes.

Other times they **anchored** their boats to icebergs. Crewmembers **huddled** together for warmth.

I can't feel my feet.

Put them under me to keep them from **freezing**.

Reading Strategy

Recognize Chronological Order
What did the men do during the day? What did they do at night?

---

bergs large, floating bodies of ice that broke off of a glacier; short for *iceberg*

anchored used a heavy metal device to keep a boat from moving

huddled stayed close together

Reading Strategy

Recognize Chronological Order
How many days were the men at sea before they reached the island?

Reading Check

1. **Recall facts** Why must the men reach land soon?

2. **Understand mood** What is the mood of this page before the men reach land?

oars poles with a flat blade pulled by hand to row a boat

● Apply the Reading Strategy

Recognize Chronological Order

Now complete the Reading Strategy graphic organizer.

1. Review the **Reading Strategy** on page 265.
2. Draw the chart on a piece of paper.
3. Fill in the boxes with events from the story in **chronological** order. Add more boxes if you need them. Remember to include dates and time words.
4. Work with a partner to compare your charts.
5. Make a timeline from your chart.

July 1907: Shackleton sets out to be the first to reach the South Pole.

● Academic Vocabulary

Vocabulary for the Reading Comprehension Questions

Word	Explanation	Sample Sentence	Visual Cue
contribute *verb*	to give; to participate positively in something	Many people **contribute** money to the charity.	CURE CANCER!
aid *verb*	to assist or help	With his glasses, he can see more clearly. His glasses **aid** his vision.	ZSHC HSKRN CHKRVO HONSDCV OKNONRCS / ZSHC HSKRN CHKRVO HONSDCV OKNONRCS

Draw a picture and write a sentence for each word.

✓Checkpoint

1. What do you **contribute** to your class?
2. What can **aid** you in learning a language?

Vocabulary Log

Reading Comprehension Questions

Think and Discuss

1. **Recall facts** What happened to the *Endurance*?
2. **Identify cause and effect** What things caused the crew to complain? Use Key Vocabulary words in your answer.
3. **Discuss character traits** What three adjectives would you use to describe Shackleton? Give examples of his words and actions from the reading to support your answer.
4. **Using text features** How do the illustrations **aid** your understanding of the characters and the story?
5. **Understand mood** What is the mood of the reading? How do the illustrations **contribute** to the mood?
6. **Reflect** Imagine that you were a member of Shackleton's crew. Would you have survived? Why or why not?
7. **Revisit the Reading Focus Questions** Go back to page 266 and discuss the questions.

Workbook page 192   Independent Practice CD-ROM/Online

Literary Element

Setting

Every story has a **setting.** The setting of a story is the place and time in which it happens. The setting often has an effect on the characters and on the plot of the story. Setting is very important in *Shackleton and the Lost Antarctic Expedition.* The setting of this story is Antarctica in 1914–1916. Throughout the story, the characters struggle against the cold and the danger of this place. The setting creates **conflict.** Some people want to give up. Some people want to struggle on. The conflict ends when the characters escape the danger of the setting.

Look back at the stories in other units of this book. Identify the setting of each story. Explain how the setting affects the characters and plot of each story.

✓ Checkpoint

1. What is a **setting**?
2. Think of your favorite book or movie. What is the setting?

Workbook page 193   Independent Practice CD-ROM/Online

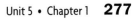

Using Math to Survive in the Wild

About the Reading

You read a graphic novel, *Shackleton and the Lost Antarctic Expedition,* about a group's struggle to survive in Antarctica. Now you will read an informational text. The text tells you to imagine being lost in the wilderness. It shows you how to use math to survive.

Build Background

The Wilderness

The wild is another word for *the wilderness.* The wilderness is land in its natural state. It is large areas that humans have not changed or spoiled. What are some things you can find in the wilderness? Look at the wilderness picture to give you ideas. Add more ideas of your own. Use a dictionary or ask your teacher for help if necessary.

Vocabulary From the Reading

Understand and Use Definitions

Read the definitions for each word. Discuss them with a partner. Then work with your partner to create a sentence for each word.

1. **attitude** *n.* feeling about or toward someone or something
2. **equipment** *n.* useful items needed for a purpose, such as work or sports
3. **knowledge** *n.* information about or familiarity with something
4. **skill** *n.* ability to do a particular thing well because of practice, talent, or special training
5. **task** *n.* assignment, job to be performed

Key Vocabulary

attitude

equipment

knowledge

skill

task

✓Checkpoint

1. What is your favorite sport? What **equipment** do you need to play this sport?
2. What **tasks** do you usually do at home?

Vocabulary Log

Workbook page 194

Independent Practice CD-ROM/Online

● Reading Strategy

Think Aloud

As you read *Using Math to Survive in the Wild,* stop after each question or problem. Try to answer the question or problem by **thinking aloud.** Thinking through your ideas aloud can help you find the answer. This is a very helpful strategy to use, especially with math texts.

● Text Genre

Informational Text

Using Math to Survive in the Wild is an **informational text.** Like other informational texts, it includes facts and information. It also includes problems to solve and activities for students to work on.

● Meet the Authors

Hilary Koll and **Steve Mills** were math teachers. They are now full-time writers and consultants in math education. They have written over 150 books together. To create *Using Math to Survive in the Wild,* Koll and Mills teamed up with **Jonny Crockett.** Crockett is an expert in survival education. He runs a survival school in England.

● Reading Focus Questions

As you read, think about these questions.

1. How does this reading relate to the theme of "survival"?
2. What do you think was the author's purpose for writing *Using Math to Survive in the Wild*?
3. Do you think you could survive in the wild? Why or why not?

✓**Checkpoint**

1. How can **thinking aloud** help you understand a reading?
2. What does an **informational text** include?

Workbook
pages 195–196

Independent Practice
CD-ROM/Online

Using Math to Survive in the Wild
by Hilary Koll, Steve Mills, Jonny Crockett

LOST IN THE FOREST

You and your friends decide to head for Wooden Bridge. But now it is late. It is getting dark. You are lost in the **forest**! You all agree. It will be best to stay where you are overnight. There are only a few hours of **daylight** left. You need a plan to survive the night. There are many things you could do. You could build a **shelter** or light a fire. Then again, maybe you should look for water. Maybe you should **hunt** for food, such as berries and nuts. Maybe you should **gather** leaves to keep you warm. You want to stay together in one group. So you will not have time to do everything. Which **tasks** should you pick? The light is **fading** fast. You must decide quickly.

Reading Strategy

Think Aloud Which **tasks** seem most important to you? Why? Discuss your thoughts aloud.

SURVIVAL FACT
When you are in a survival situation, you need to think about shelter, fire, water, and food. You have to decide which are most important for the environment you are in.

---

forest large area with many trees
daylight light from the sun during the day
shelter any building or covering (tree branches, a cave, etc.) that gives physical protection

hunt search
gather bring together, collect
fading disappearing gradually

SURVIVAL FACT

If you survive a plane crash or a car accident in the wilderness, stay with the **wreckage**. The wreckage is easier to find than a person wandering alone.

SURVIVAL FACT

To stay alive in the wild, you need to be fit. You also need to have the right **equipment**, **knowledge**, and **skills** to survive. Most importantly, you need to have a **positive mental attitude**.

Survival Work

Look at the table in the DATA BOX on page 282. The table shows how long the **various tasks** might take. The table also shows how useful each **task** is for helping you stay alive. Use this information to answer these questions.

1) Which jobs could you do in the four hours you have left before it is dark? (Make sure that the jobs do not take more than four hours altogether.)

2) **Exactly** how long will it take to do the jobs you decide on? (Give your answers in hours and minutes.)

3) After you finish the chosen **tasks**, how much of the four hours will you have left?

Look at the table in the DATA BOX on page 282.

Reading Strategy

Think Aloud Think through this question aloud.

Reading Check

1. **Recall facts** What does the table in the data box on page 282 show?
2. **Reflect** Why do you think it is important to have a positive mental **attitude** to stay alive in the wild?

---

various different, diverse

exactly accurately, precisely

wreckage remains of something that has been destroyed

positive hopeful, optimistic

mental related to the mind

Survival Tasks

This table shows about how much time each job might take to complete. The jobs are also graded from 1 to 10 on how useful they are. 10 is very useful and 0 is not useful at all.

Job	Time to Complete	Usefulness
hunt for food	210 minutes	6
build shelter	150 minutes	8
light a fire	45 minutes	9
look for water	105 minutes	7
gather leaves to keep warm	150 minutes	5

MATH CHALLENGE

Use the time **estimates** in the **DATA BOX** above to answer these questions.

1 How much time would it take to do all of the jobs
  a in minutes?   **b** in hours?
2 Doing two of the jobs takes 4 ¼ hours. Which jobs are they?

Reading Strategy

Think Aloud Think through this question aloud.

—————————————

estimates informed guesses or approximations

After Reading 2

● Reading Comprehension Questions

Think and Discuss

1. **Recall facts** What are two survival tips you learned in this reading?

2. **Identify** What are four **tasks** you need to do to survive a night in the wild? Use Key Vocabulary words in your answer.

3. **Form questions** What additional questions would you ask the authors about surviving in the wilderness?

4. **Discuss** Which math problem do you think was most difficult to answer? Why?

5. **Revisit the Reading Focus Questions** Go back to page 279 and discuss the questions.

Workbook page 197

Independent Practice CD-ROM/Online

⟳ Connect Readings 1 and 2

You have read two readings on the theme of survival. Use these activities to make connections between the readings.

1. Discuss these questions with a partner.

   a. What are some of the things Shackleton's crew did to survive in Antarctica? What are some of the things a person must do to survive in the wild? Are these things the same or different? Explain.

   b. Do you think it would be harder to survive in Antarctica or in the wild? Explain your answer.

   c. Which reading was most interesting to you? Why?

2. **Revisit the Chapter Focus Question** What do people need to survive in dangerous situations? Use examples from *Shackleton and the Lost Antarctic Expedition* and *Using Math to Survive in the Wild* to answer this question.

> **Spelling**
>
> Ordinal Numbers
>
> Workbook page 198 | Independent Practice CD-ROM/Online
>
> **Writing Conventions**
>
> Capitalization: Place Names
>
> Workbook page 199 | Independent Practice CD-ROM/Online

● Listening and Speaking

Create a Map and Give Directions

Maps are an important survival tool. For example, a map can help you if you are lost in a forest. Maps are also important in everyday life. Imagine there is a new student in your class. In this activity you will make a map of your school. You will then use it to give directions to the student.

1. With a small group, discuss these questions.
   a. What are the important places in your school? Make a list.
   b. Where is each of these places in the school? Take notes.
2. Create a map of your school, including all the important places on your list.
3. Work in pairs to role-play a scene with a new student.
   a. The new student chooses a place in the school. The student asks for directions to this place, using the phrases for "Asking for Directions" from the **Phrases for Conversation** box.
   b. The other student gives directions, using the map and the phrases for "Giving Directions."
   c. Do the role-play again. This time, switch roles.

Phrases for Conversation

Asking for Directions

Can you tell me where (the) ___ is, please?

Excuse me. How can I get to (the) ___?

Giving Directions

Walk straight.
Turn right.
Turn left.
Go up/down the stairs.
It's across from ___.
It's between ___ and ___.

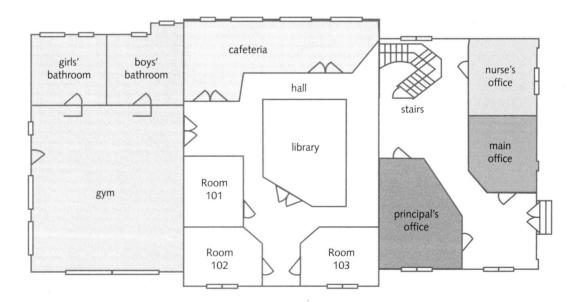

● Reading Fluency

Using Pace and Expression to Read a Dialogue

A dialogue is a conversation between two characters. When you read a dialogue out loud, you need to read the words at an appropriate pace (speed). It is also important to read naturally and with expression. Using appropriate pace and expression will make the dialogue sound natural.

1. Turn to page 272 of *Shackleton and the Lost Antarctic Expedition.* Listen to the audio for this page. Pay attention to the speaker's pace and expression.

2. With a partner, take turns reading the dialogue between Shackleton and his crew member.

3. Perform the dialogue for your class. Ask your classmates if you and your partner read with expression. Did the dialogue sound natural?

● Vocabulary Development

The Adverb Suffix -*ly*

Adverbs often describe verbs. An adverb usually tells *how* a verb is done.

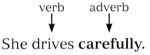

She drives **carefully.**

The suffix **-ly** changes many adjectives into adverbs. Look at these adverbs from this chapter's readings. Each is formed with an adjective and the suffix **-ly.**

Adverb	Adjective	+ -ly
quick**ly**	quick	-ly
safe**ly**	safe	-ly

Copy the sentences. <u>Underline</u> the adverb in each sentence. ⟨Circle⟩ the verb the adverb describes.

He ⟨speaks⟩ English <u>perfectly</u>.

1. I cook badly.
2. She dances beautifully.
3. Turtles move slowly.
4. You spelled my name correctly.
5. The airplane landed safely.

> **✓Checkpoint**
> 1. What is an **adverb**?
> 2. Give an example of an adverb with the **-ly** suffix. Use this adverb in a sentence.

Vocabulary Log

Workbook page 200

Independent Practice CD-ROM/Online

● Grammar

The Present Progressive Tense: Spelling and Review

Use the **present progressive tense** to talk about things happening now. Form the present progressive tense with **am/is/are** + base verb + **-ing.**

Base Form	Spelling in the Present Progressive	Rule
work	work**ing**	For most verbs: add **-ing.**
write dance	writ**ing** danc**ing**	For verbs that end in a **consonant + e:** drop the **e** and add **-ing.**
sit plan	sit**ting** plan**ning**	For one-syllable verbs that end in **one vowel + one consonant:** double the consonant and add **-ing.**
  play read listen think	 play**ing** read**ing** listen**ing** think**ing**	Do not double the last consonant before **-ing** when the verb: • ends in **w, x,** or **y** • ends in two vowels and then one consonant • has more than one syllable (when the stress is on the first syllable) • ends in two or more consonants

Spelling of Verbs Ending in *-ing*

Practice the Grammar Complete the paragraph. Put the verbs in the correct present progressive form.

There is a terrible storm outside. It (**1.** rain) ____ hard. The wind (**2.** blow) ____ branches off the trees. I (**3.** sit) ____ in my house with my family. We (**4.** listen) ____ to the news on the radio. The weather reporter (**5.** talk) ____. She (**6.** say) ____ that the storm (**7.** move) ____ over our city right now. I (**8.** get) ____ a little nervous. My mother (**9.** smile) ____ at me. She (**10.** try) ____ to make me feel better.

Use the Grammar Independently You are a weather reporter in a local park. Tell about the weather and what people in the park are doing.

I am standing in Robertson Park. The sun is shining and people are enjoying the day. Some people are having picnics in the park. Others are...

✔ Checkpoint

1. How do you form the **present progressive tense?**

2. Spell the **-ing** form of these verbs: **take, stop, cry, run, wear.**

Workbook
pages 201–202

Independent Practice
CD-ROM/Online

Grammar

The Past Progressive Tense

Use the **past progressive tense:**

1. to talk about something that was happening at a particular time in the past.

   I **was studying** at 8:00 last night.

2. to talk about something that was happening in the past when something else happened.

   We **were watching** television when you called.

The Past Progressive Tense		
subject	*was/were* (past of *be*)	base verb + *ing*
I	**was**	
He / She / It	**was**	eat**ing.**
You / We / They	**were**	

Practice the Grammar Complete each sentence. Put the verb in the correct past progressive form.

(cook) He <u>was cooking</u> when the fire alarm went off.

1. (read) I ＿＿ at 9:00 last night.
2. (snow) It ＿＿ an hour ago.
3. (sleep) John ＿＿ when the alarm rang.
4. (walk) We ＿＿ down the street when it started to rain.
5. (play) Linh ＿＿ tennis when she hurt her leg.

Use the Grammar Independently Think about the things you did yesterday. Tell a partner what you were doing at every hour of the day from 9:00 AM to 9:00 PM.

> At 10:00 I was walking into my biology class.

Workbook
pages 203–204

Independent Practice
CD-ROM/Online

✓ Checkpoint

1. When do you use the **past progressive tense**?

2. Give an example of a past progressive sentence.

● **Writing Assignment**

Creative Writing: Write a Survival Journal

Creative writing is any writing in which you use your imagination.

> **Writing Suggestion**
>
> See **Milestones Handbook.** pages 393–433

> **Writing Prompt**
>
> Choose a survival situation. Imagine being in that situation for three days. Create a journal entry for each day. Use the past progressive tense when appropriate.

Write Your Survival Journal

1. **Read the student model. It is a model for one day.** It will help you write your journal entries.

2. **Brainstorm.** Choose a survival situation. You might want to write about one of these situations:

   - being shipwrecked on an island
   - being lost in a forest
   - being lost in Antarctica
   - being lost in the desert

Student Model

June 5, 2008

This morning I was hiking in the forest with two friends. My friends wanted to rest for 10 minutes. I wanted to keep hiking. We decided to meet back at our campsite in an hour. While I was hiking, I got confused about my direction. I didn't have a map or a compass. I was lost! I was also getting hungry. So I had to find some food. I looked for some nuts and berries. But there was not much daylight left. The sun was going down and it was getting cold. I decided to find shelter until the next day. I was a little scared, but it's important to keep a positive attitude. I knew they were probably looking for me at that moment.

Workbook
page 205

3. **Prewrite.** Plan your writing. Think about these questions. Take notes on your ideas.

   a. Imagine the setting for the survival situation you chose. What does it look like? What do you hear?

   b. What problems do you face? What solutions do you find?

   c. How do you feel?

4. **Write.** Imagine you are in this situation for three days. (At the end of the third day you will be **rescued**!) Write a journal entry for each day. Remember to use the ideas you took notes on in your "prewrite."

5. **Revise.** Reread your journal entries. Revise your journal if any ideas are not clear or complete.

   Use the **editing and proofreading symbols** on page 419 to help you mark any changes you want to make.

6. **Edit.** Use the **Writing Checklist** to help you find problems and errors.

7. Share your journal entries with a partner.

Writing Checklist
1. I wrote a journal entry for each of the three days.
2. I put a date at the top of each entry.
3. I described the setting.
4. I explained the problem I was facing.
5. I used the past progressive in my journal entry.

 **Writing Support**

Spelling

Commonly Confused Words: it's / its

   Some words sound the same but have different meanings and different spellings. These words often cause trouble for writers. When the writer uses the wrong word, the reader can become confused. It is important to learn the difference between commonly confused words.

It's and **its** are commonly confused words:

   it's = contraction of **it is**   **It's** important to check your writing for mistakes.

   its = possessive form of **it**   The dog has a collar around **its** neck.

Apply Check your journal entries for these commonly confused words. Make sure they are spelled and used correctly.

 Workbook
pages 206–208

 Independent Practice
CD-ROM/Online

Progress Check

How well did you understand this chapter? Try to answer the questions. If necessary, go back to the pages listed for a review.

Skills	Skills Assessment Questions	Pages to Review
Vocabulary From the Readings	What do these words mean?	
	• damage, force, freezing, injury / injuries, rescue, supplies	264
	• attitude, equipment, knowledge, skill, task	278
Academic Vocabulary	What do these academic vocabulary words mean?	
	• chronological, indicate	265
	• aid, contribute	276
Reading Strategies	What does chronological order mean?	265
	What does it mean to **think aloud**?	279
Text Genres	What is the text genre of *Shackleton and the Lost Antarctic Expedition*?	266
	What is the text genre of *Using Math to Survive in the Wild*?	279
Reading Comprehension	What is *Shackleton and the Lost Antarctic Expedition* about?	277
	What is *Using Math to Survive in the Wild* about?	283
Literary Element	What is a story's **setting**? What is the setting of *Shackleton and the Lost Antarctic Expedition*?	277
Spelling	Give the **ordinal number** for: 7, 3, 8, 1, 2, 10.	283
Writing Conventions	Rewrite these sentences using **capital letters for place names.** I live in new york. new york is in the northeast.	283
Listening and Speaking	**Phrases for Conversation**	
	What phrases can you use to ask for and give directions?	284
Vocabulary Development	What is an **adverb**? What are three adverbs that end with the suffix **-ly**? Use each in a sentence.	285
Grammar	When is the **present progressive tense** used? Give an example of a present progressive sentence.	286
	When is the **past progressive tense** used? Give an example of a past progressive sentence.	287
Writing Support: Spelling	Give a sentence with the commonly confused word **it's.** Give a sentence with the commonly confused word **its.**	289

Assessment Practice

Read this journal entry. Then answer Questions 1 through 4.

An Unbelievable Rescue

August, 1916

It's unbelievable that all my men are still alive! I don't have much time to write because we are sailing back to England—back to civilization. I have had an amazing adventure. Twenty-one months ago, five of my men and I left the rest of the crew on freezing Elephant Island and went to get help. I do not know how they survived with so few supplies. I can only tell our adventure. We sailed for 17 days over 800 miles of the worst seas to South Georgia Island. Unfortunately, we landed on the side of the island that had no people. Two of my men and I had to hike across 26 miles of mountains and glaciers. Finally, we arrived safely at the whaling station. The fishermen there were very surprised to see us. They happily loaned us a ship, and we set sail to rescue my crew.

Ernest Shackleton

1 **What does the word <u>rescue</u> mean in the title?**

> An Unbelievable Rescue

A equipment

B adventure

C saving

D supplies

2 **What event happened first in chronological order?**

A Shackleton began writing this passage.

B Shackleton and five other men left the rest of the crew on Elephant Island.

C Shackleton rescued his crew.

D Shackleton and five other men sailed 17 days over 800 miles.

3 **What is the setting of this passage?**

A a ship

B England

C fear

D a whaling station

4 **What word does the adjective <u>safely</u> modify in this sentence?**

> Finally, we arrived safely at the whaling station.

A Finally

B whaling

C we

D arrived

Writing on Demand: Survival Journal

Write a survival journal from the perspective of one of the crew members left on Elephant Island. Imagine you were left for 21 months without supplies. Write about one day on the island. Describe what you see, do, and eat. Only seals, penguins, fish, and whales can survive in this freezing environment. **(20 minutes)**

Writing Tip

Remember to give your thoughts and feelings as well as information about your survival.

CHAPTER 2

Objectives

Reading Strategies
Identify main idea and details; Describe mental images

Listening and Speaking
Create a "survival English" pamphlet

Grammar
Use comparative adjectives; Use superlative adjectives

Writing
Personal narrative: Write about a storm

Academic Vocabulary

focus	persuade
detail	recommend

Academic Content

Hurricanes and tornadoes
Storm safety

● **Chapter Focus Question**

How can big storms be a challenge to survive?

Reading 1 **Content:** Science

Textbook
The Fiercest Storms on Earth

Reading 2 **Literature**

Short story (excerpt)
Hurricane Friends
by Anilu Bernardo

The Fiercest Storms on Earth

● **About the Reading**

You are going to read a section from a science textbook about severe storms. You will learn what hurricanes and tornadoes are and how to survive them.

● Build Background

Hurricanes and Tornadoes

Hurricanes and tornadoes are two kinds of storms. However, they are very different. A hurricane looks like a very large group of slowly spinning clouds. It can cover hundreds of miles. A tornado is a smaller, fast-spinning cloud. It is usually dark gray. It looks like a funnel. Look at the pictures. Can you see these differences? You will learn about more differences between hurricanes and tornadoes in the reading.

Hurricane   **Tornado**

● Use Prior Knowledge

Explore What You Know About Storms

Brainstorm what you know about storms.

1. On a piece of paper, make a word web. In the center circle, write the word **storms.**

2. What words do you think of when you hear the word **storm**? Write them in the other circles.

3. Talk about your word web with a partner.

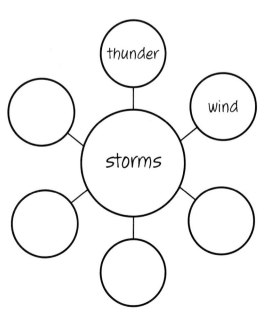

Key Vocabulary

- destroy
- energy
- flooding
- protect
- sink
- spin
- warning

● Vocabulary From the Reading

Learn, Practice, and Use Independently

Learn Vocabulary Read each sentence. Look at the **highlighted** word. Use the context (the words around the highlighted word) to figure out the meaning of the word. Use a dictionary if you need help.

1. The storm is very strong. I'm afraid it will **destroy** our house.
2. Electricity, battery power, and wind power are all sources of **energy.**
3. It rained all week. Now there is **flooding** in the town.
4. Sunglasses **protect** our eyes from the sun.
5. If you drop a stone in the water, it will **sink** to the bottom.
6. Children like to **spin** around and around until they feel dizzy.
7. The dark clouds are a **warning** that it is going to rain.

Practice Vocabulary What Key Vocabulary word does each picture show best? Write the word.

energy

✓Checkpoint

1. Name two things you can do to **protect** yourself from the sun.
2. Name two **warnings** a mother might give a young child.

Use Vocabulary Independently Write one sentence for each Key Vocabulary word. Use a dictionary or ask your teacher if you need help. Read your sentences to a partner.

Vocabulary Log

Workbook page 209

Independent Practice CD-ROM/Online

● Academic Vocabulary

Vocabulary for the Reading Strategy

Word	Explanation	Sample Sentence	Visual Cue
focus *noun*	a thing that is of great importance, an object of attention	The **focus** of the news report was the high price of gas.	
detail *noun*	smaller part of something larger and more important	The painting of the mountain scene shows many **details** that you can only see when you are close.	

Draw a picture and write a sentence for each word.

● Reading Strategy

Identify Main Idea and Details

The **main idea** is the most important idea in a paragraph, section, or reading. It is the **focus** of the paragraph, section, or reading. The **details** give the reader more information about the main idea. Facts, examples, and explanations are all kinds of **details.** As you read "The Fiercest Storms on Earth," look for main ideas and **details.**

1. Pause after you read each paragraph. Answer this question: What is the main idea of the paragraph?

2. Look for at least two **details** that support this idea.

3. After you finish the reading, you will complete a main idea and **details** chart for each section of the reading.

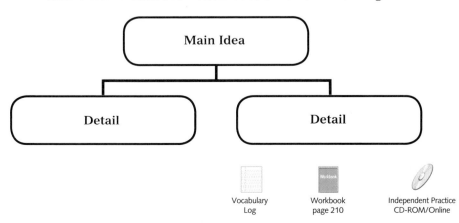

> **✓Checkpoint**
>
> **1.** What is a **main idea**? What are **details**?
>
> **2.** Explain the main idea and two **details** of an informational reading in a previous unit.

Vocabulary Log

Workbook page 210

Independent Practice CD-ROM/Online

● Text Genre

Informational Text: Textbook

"The Fiercest Storms on Earth" is from a science textbook. The purpose of textbooks is to teach students about academic subjects. Textbooks include many features to help students understand the information. As you read, look for these common textbook features.

Textbook	
headings	titles of major sections; heading words are usually larger and often in a different color than the rest of the text.
subheadings	titles that divide the major sections into smaller sections; subheading words are smaller than headings, but larger than the rest of the text; they are sometimes in a different color
graphics	visual features, such as pictures, photos, maps, graphs, and charts
captions	words that explain graphics

● Reading Focus Questions

As you read, think about these questions.

1. How does this reading relate to the theme of "survival"?
2. What do you think was the author's purpose for writing "The Fiercest Storms on Earth"?
3. How are hurricanes and tornadoes similar? How are they different?

✓Checkpoint

Name and explain two common **textbook** features.

Workbook
page 211

Independent Practice
CD-ROM/Online

The Fiercest Storms on Earth

1   What are hurricanes and tornadoes? What causes these storms? Why are they known as the fiercest storms on Earth?

Hurricanes—The Largest Storms

2   Hurricanes have different names in different parts of the world. In the Pacific Ocean they are typhoons, in the Indian Ocean they are cyclones, and in Australia they are willy-willies. Hurricanes are large, violent storms. They form over warm ocean water.

3   To be called a hurricane, the storm must have winds of at least 117 kilometers per hour (74 miles per hour). Some hurricanes have winds of more than 240 kilometers per hour (150 miles per hour)!

4   Hurricanes start as small thunderstorms over an ocean. Several of these storms may join to form a larger storm. This storm grows bigger as it takes in heat and moisture from the warm ocean water. As the storm grows, the wind increases. This causes the clouds to **spin**. The diagram on page 299 explains how a hurricane forms.

A large hurricane moves across open water toward Mexico.

---

fiercest most violent, most powerful

kilometers a distance; one kilometer is equal to 1,000 meters, or 0.62137 of a mile

miles a distance; one mile is equal to 5,280 feet, or 1.6 kilometers

moisture wetness, water

> **Reading Strategy**
>
> **Identify Main Idea and Details** How does this section heading help prepare you for the main idea of this section?

> **Reading Check**
>
> 1. **Recall facts** What is a cyclone?
> 2. **Recall facts** Where do hurricanes form?
> 3. **Explain** How do hurricanes start?

Reading Strategy

Identify Main Idea and Details What is the main idea of paragraph 5? Identify two **details** in this paragraph.

5 In the middle of a hurricane is a hole. This hole is called the eye of the hurricane. Within the eye the weather is calm. There is little wind and no rain. Sometimes people are fooled when the eye is **overhead**. They think the hurricane is over. But it isn't over. The other half of the storm is on its way.

6 Hurricanes are the largest storms on Earth. The storm can cover an area as wide as 600 kilometers (360 miles). This area is five times bigger than Washington, D.C.

Hurricanes on the Move

7 Once a hurricane forms, it begins to travel. As it moves, the winds blow harder. The winds can rip trees out of the ground. They can blow the roofs off houses. The winds can also produce giant ocean waves as tall as a house. These waves can wash away beaches and **sink** boats. The rain from a hurricane can also cause **flooding.**

This is a **satellite** photo of Hurricane Andrew. It shows the storm at three **locations** as it moved from Florida to Louisiana in 1992.

---

overhead above one's head

satellite human-made object in space that circles a larger object (such as the earth)

location place where something is

8 Luckily, hurricanes don't last very long once they reach land. When the storm moves over land or over cold ocean water, it loses its **source** of **energy** and dies down.

How a Hurricane Forms

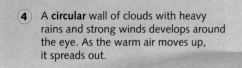

④ A **circular** wall of clouds with heavy rains and strong winds develops around the eye. As the warm air moves up, it spreads out.

⑤ In the eye the air **sinks** slowly, the winds are light, and there are no clouds.

③ Warm moist air **spirals** up around the eye.

Reading Strategy

Identify Main Idea and Details This diagram shows how a hurricane forms. Explain a few of the **details** of the diagram in your own words.

② Strong **surface** winds at the **base** of the hurricane blow into an area of low pressure.

① Warm ocean water provides the **energy**.

✓ Reading Check

1. **Recall facts** What provides hurricanes with their **energy**?

2. **Recall facts** What makes hurricanes die down?

3. **Analyze language** What two words on this page relate to circles?

---

source beginning, origin
surface top layer of something
base lowest part
spirals twists up or down in the shape of a circle
circular having a round shape

A funnel-shaped tornado

Destruction left by a tornado in Oklahoma

Twister!

9   Sometimes a thunderstorm gives birth to a tornado. Tornadoes are sometimes called twisters. A tornado is a **funnel-shaped** storm of **spinning** wind. The air in a tornado **spins** upward.

10   Tornadoes can develop without **warning**. They form when a **column** of warm air begins to **spin**. As air flows up into this swirling column, it **spins** very fast. This forms the well-known funnel-shaped cloud.

11   Even though tornadoes don't cover as much area as hurricanes, they can be just as dangerous. The speed of the winds in the center of a tornado can be as high as 500 kilometers per hour (300 miles per hour). This is twice the speed of the winds in the worst hurricane!

12   In tornadoes the air pressure is very low. The strong winds blowing into these low-pressure areas can sweep objects into the tornado, including dirt, trees, and roofs of buildings. The winds may be strong enough to move and **destroy** large trees, cars, trains, and houses.

Reading Strategy

Identify Main Idea and Details What is the main idea of paragraph 12? Identify two **details** in this paragraph.

Investigation
Compare hurricanes and tornadoes. What are some ways in which the two types of storms are similar? What are some ways in which they are different?

---

funnel-shaped in the shape of a utensil with a wide opening on top leading into a narrow bottom and used to control the flow of a liquid

column vertical row

Staying Safe in a Storm

13   In the past, people were not able to predict when storms, hurricanes, or tornadoes would occur. But today, scientists have tools, like weather satellites, to help them. These tools make it possible to better predict the weather. Here are some safety **precautions** you should follow for staying safe during a hurricane and during a tornado.

Reading Strategy

Identify Main Idea and Details What is the main idea of this page?

Staying Safe During a Hurricane

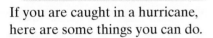

If you are caught in a hurricane, here are some things you can do.

- Get as far away from ocean beaches as possible. The huge waves **produced** by hurricanes are very dangerous.

- Stay inside in a basement, under a stairwell, or in another sheltered area.

- Stay away from windows. Glass can break in hurricane winds and injure people. It's a good idea to board up windows with plywood.

- Listen to local TV and radio stations for more information.

Staying Safe During a Tornado

If there is a tornado in your area, follow these precautions.

- If you are outside, try to stay in a **ditch** or other low area. This will help **protect** you from flying objects.

- If you are inside, try to stay in a basement or a storm cellar. If there is no basement or storm cellar, stay in a closet or bathroom.

- Stay away from windows and doors that lead outside. These can be blown apart by the winds of a tornado.

Reading Check

1. **Recall facts** What is a tool scientists use to help predict the weather?

2. **Recall facts** Where should you stay during a hurricane?

3. **Cause and effect** Why should you stay away from windows during a tornado?

---

precautions steps taken in advance to prevent harm

produced created

ditch long narrow hole dug in the earth, especially to hold or carry water

● Apply the Reading Strategy

Identify Main Idea and Details

Now complete the Reading Strategy graphic organizer.

1. Review the **Reading Strategy** on page 295.
2. Copy the main idea and **details** chart for each of these sections of the reading: Hurricanes—The Largest Storms; Hurricanes on the Move; Twister!; Staying Safe in a Storm.
3. Use the charts to list the main idea and **details.**

Section Heading: Hurricanes—The Largest Storms

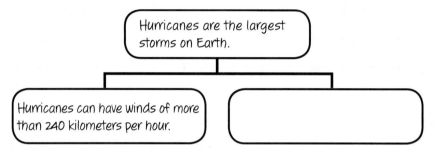

Hurricanes are the largest storms on Earth.

Hurricanes can have winds of more than 240 kilometers per hour.

● Academic Vocabulary

Vocabulary for the Reading Comprehension Questions

Word	Explanation	Sample Sentence	Visual Cue
persuade *verb*	to lead a person or group to believe or do something by arguing or reasoning with them	I am going to **persuade** my sister to take a walk so that she will be healthier.	
recommend *verb*	to tell others about something one likes; to advise someone to do something	This is a great book. I **recommend** you read it.	You should read this!

Draw a picture and write a sentence for each word.

✓Checkpoint

1. What have you **persuaded** someone to do?
2. What have you **recommended** that someone do?

Vocabulary Log

Reading Comprehension Questions

Think and Discuss

1. **Recall facts** What are some other names for hurricanes?
2. **Paraphrase** How do tornadoes form? Explain in your own words.
3. **Compare** How are hurricanes and tornadoes different?
4. **Make an inference** Why do you think the author called this reading "The Fiercest Storms on Earth"?
5. **Draw conclusions** What is the purpose of this reading: to entertain or to inform or to **persuade**? Explain.
6. **Consider ideas across texts** In *Shackleton and the Lost Antarctic Expedition,* you read about men shipwrecked in Antarctica. You imagined being lost in the forest in *Using Math to Survive in the Wild.* In "The Fiercest Storms on Earth," you learned about hurricanes and tornadoes. Which do you think would be hardest to survive? Explain your answer.
7. **Evaluate** Would you **recommend** "The Fiercest Storms on Earth" to a friend? Why or why not?
8. **Revisit the Reading Focus Questions** Go back to page 296 and discuss the questions.

Workbook page 212   Independent Practice CD-ROM/Online

Text Elements

Headings and Subheadings

Many informational texts have **headings** and **subheadings.** A heading is a title of a large section of text. It tells you the topic or subject of the section. Subheadings are titles of smaller sections within the larger section. Headings and subheadings help prepare you for each section of text.

1. Make a list with the heading and subheadings in "The Fiercest Storms on Earth."
2. How does each subheading prepare you for each section? Discuss your answer with a partner.

Heading:	"The Fiercest Storms on Earth"
Subheading:	
Subheading:	

✓ Checkpoint

Explain **headings** and **subheadings** in your own words.

Workbook page 213   Independent Practice CD-ROM/Online

Hurricane Friends

● About the Reading

You have read a textbook section about hurricanes and tornadoes. Now you will read a short story about a family who experiences and survives a hurricane.

● Build Background

Hurricane Andrew

"Hurricane Friends" is a short story about a family in Florida that lives through Hurricane Andrew. Hurricane Andrew was one of the worst hurricanes in United States history. It hit Florida on August 24, 1992. The storm had winds of 144 miles per hour. It caused over 25 billion dollars of damage. Over 30,000 homes were **destroyed.**

● Vocabulary From the Reading

Use Context Clues to Determine Meaning

Read the paragraph. Pay special attention to the **highlighted** words. Use the context to determine the meanings of these words. Discuss the meanings with a small group.

Key Vocabulary
amazed
concentrate
preparations
tool

The Big Storm

We heard that a big storm was coming. We spent all day making **preparations** for it. We made sure we had enough food and water. We used a hammer, a screwdriver, and other **tools** to get the house ready for the storm. We talked about the storm all day. It was hard to **concentrate** on anything else. Finally the storm came. We were **amazed** at how strong it was. We saw it blow cars over and rip trees out of the ground!

 ✓Checkpoint

1. What **preparations** do you make before a big storm?
2. Name two **tools.** Explain one or two things you can do with each **tool.**

Vocabulary Log

Workbook page 214

Independent Practice CD-ROM/Online

Reading Strategy

Describe Mental Images

Writers use words and descriptions that help the reader "see" the story. The pictures you "see" in your head are called **mental images.** As you read "Hurricane Friends," pay attention to the words and descriptions the author uses. Think about the images they create in your mind. Try to describe the images in your own words.

Text Genre

Short Story

"Hurricane Friends" is a **short story.** A short story has these features.

Short Story	
characters	people in a story
setting	where a story takes place
plot	events in a story that happen in a certain order
theme	the meaning or message of the story

Meet the Author

Anilu Bernardo was born in Cuba. She left the island with her family in 1961. The family came to the United States. Bernardo grew up in Miami, Florida. As a child, she wrote stories and poems in Spanish. Now she writes fiction for young adults. Bernardo always brings her bicultural experience to her stories.

Reading Focus Questions

As you read, think about these questions.

1. How does this reading relate to the theme of "survival"?
2. What do you think was the author's purpose for writing "Hurricane Friends"?
3. What do you think it is like to live through a hurricane?

Workbook
pages 215–216

Independent Practice
CD-ROM/Online

> **✓Checkpoint**
> 1. What is a **mental image**?
> 2. Name and describe two features of a **short story.**

Hurricane Friends

by Anilu Bernardo

1   Sunday morning the skies looked different. High gray clouds covered the clear blue. The wind was blowing, though it carried no rain, but a feeling of something worse to come made Clari **shudder.** Miami was now under a hurricane watch. This meant the storm was likely to hit Miami within twenty-four hours. Hurricane Andrew would land on South Florida that night.

2   Clari followed Papi around the outside of the house as he and Mami covered the windows with sheets of **plywood.** Clari helped bring **tools** that Papi needed from the garage. At lunch time, Clari made sandwiches, but Papi and Mami were too busy to stop and eat. They took bites as they worked.

3   The house was getting darker as the light was blocked from each window. It was an odd thing, Clari thought, to come into her room in the middle of the day and have it be dark as night.

4   The neighbors were busy as well. Everyone hurried to **protect** their windows and bring in loose things from the yards. The air was filled with sounds of electric drills and saws. Even some hammering could be heard. There were no children playing outside. Everyone was helping with **preparations.**

5   By afternoon, the wind had picked up. Now everyone shouted to be heard. The sky darkened and heavy gray clouds dropped sprinklings of rain. This was no ordinary rainstorm.

6   It was dark outside when they finished squeezing the cars into the crowded garage and closed the door. The family was in for the night and for the **duration** of the hurricane. Papi turned on the TV to hear news of the storm's movements. He lined up flashlights and batteries, candles and Clari's radio on the coffee table.

7   The wind **howled ferociously.** It puffed and pressed on the plywood covers like a giant wolf trying to blow the house down. They could hear things banging against the walls, and the cement tiles on the roof **rattled.**

shudder shake for a moment from fear

plywood material made of layers of wood pressed over each other for strength

duration time that something continues or exists

howled cried loudly, wailed

ferociously violently, fiercely

rattled shook and sounded like a rattle

8   Mami set out a game of **checkers**. But no one could **concentrate**.

9   Every television station had stopped regular programs for the weekend. The local news and weather announcers had been giving information on the hurricane and how to **protect** homes and families. Clari and her parents watched nervously and took in all their advice.

10   Clari lay on her mattress in the middle of the living room floor. She would not get a wink of sleep tonight.

11   The news was frightening. The hurricane whipped up winds of great speed and power. The palms seemed to be bent over by the force of the wind. Traffic signals and street lights were out in many parts of the city. Not a person was seen on the streets, only newsmen.

12   The wind beat ferociously at the house. It sounded like a **locomotive** coming at them at great speed. The cement tiles on the roof clattered like a thousand **castanets**. Papi feared they were losing some of them.

* * * * * *

Reading Strategy

Describe Mental Images What is your image of the streets outside? What words does the author use to help you imagine the street?

13   The winds died down slowly. Clari could tell by the quieting of the doors and roof tiles. After a while, there was little noise coming from the roof and only occasional **clattering** from the doors as gusts of wind threw final dying punches. There had been no other way to tell the hurricane had passed, as the **interior** of the house was as dark now as it had been all night.

14   Papi's watch told them it was eight-thirty in the morning. She had never spent a night like this before. She had not slept a wink. She hadn't even tried, though she admitted to herself she'd been too scared to close her eyes. The wonder was that she was not tired now. She was ready to go out and explore the neighborhood.

Reading Check
1. **Recall facts** Who were the only people on the streets?
2. **Understand figurative language** Why do you think the author compares the storm to a "locomotive coming at them at great speed"? How is the storm like this?

---

checkers a game with 12 round black and 12 round red pieces moved on a board
locomotive large railroad vehicle with an engine
castanets musical instrument made of a pair of shells, held in one hand
clattering loud sound of hard things hitting other hard things
interior inside

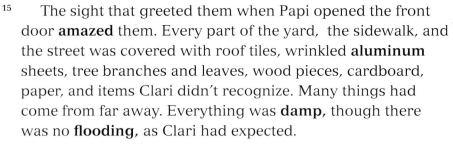

15   The sight that greeted them when Papi opened the front door **amazed** them. Every part of the yard, the sidewalk, and the street was covered with roof tiles, wrinkled **aluminum** sheets, tree branches and leaves, wood pieces, cardboard, paper, and items Clari didn't recognize. Many things had come from far away. Everything was **damp,** though there was no **flooding,** as Clari had expected.

16   The neighbors were coming out of their homes to **inspect** the damage. They looked around, **dazed** by the mess. None of the homes had electricity or phone service. The tiles of most roofs had been ripped off by the wind. The glass panes on many of the unprotected windows had broken, leaving rooms **soggy** and the furniture **destroyed.**

17   Clari couldn't believe the force of the wind. Cars that had not been stored in garages during the hurricane were **dented,** their windows **crushed.** There were large branches torn from trees. Two houses down, a neighbor's large mango tree was lying on the ground. Its roots were turned up, **bare** of soil.

18   After eating a quick, cold breakfast, the neighbors got together to pick up the trash on the street. When they finished, the families began the great task of cleaning up their houses and yards. It would take weeks, everyone agreed.

19   Papi removed some of the wood covering their windows and offered it to neighbors who had lost windows and had no way to cover them now. None of the stores had opened. Some were **destroyed.** There was no way to buy building supplies.

20   When the electric power was restored to the block, there was a moment of **triumph.** Neighbors carried the news happily to the street. Families ran in and out of their houses to test the lights.

Reading Strategy

Describe Mental Images What is your image of the damaged neighborhood? What words does the author use to help you imagine the neighborhood?

---

aluminum lightweight, silver gray metal with many uses

damp a little wet

inspect look at something closely

dazed stunned, unable to think clearly

soggy wet and soft, mushy

dented had depressions made by a blow

crushed smashed violently

bare uncovered, nude

triumph great success

After Reading 2

● **Reading Comprehension Questions**

Think and Discuss

1. **Recall facts** Does Clari sleep well the night of the hurricane? Why or why not?
2. **Identify mood** What is the mood of the story before the storm, during the storm, and after the storm?
3. **Compare and contrast texts** How are "Hurricane Friends" and "The Fiercest Storms on Earth" alike? How are they different?
4. **Relate your own experience to the reading** Have you ever experienced a hurricane or a big storm? If so, tell about it.
5. **Revisit the Reading Focus Questions** Go back to page 305 and discuss the questions.

Workbook
page 217

Independent Practice
CD-ROM/Online

Spelling

Silent *k* Words

Workbook
page 218

Independent Practice
CD-ROM/Online

Writing Conventions

Punctuation: Writing Numbers with Hyphens

Workbook
page 219

Independent Practice
CD-ROM/Online

Connect Readings 1 and 2

You have read two readings on the theme of survival. Use these activities to make connections between the readings.

1. Find related sentences in the readings.
   a. Read each sentence in the chart from "The Fiercest Storms on Earth."
   b. Scan (read quickly through) "Hurricane Friends." Look for one or more sentences related to the sentence from "The Fiercest Storms on Earth."
   c. Write the sentence(s) from "Hurricane Friends" next to the related sentence from "The Fiercest Storms on Earth."

The Fiercest Storms on Earth	Hurricane Friends
1. Some hurricanes have winds of more than 240 kilometers per hour (150 miles per hour)!	The hurricane whipped up winds of great speed and power. It sounded like a locomotive coming at them at great speed.
2. The winds can rip trees out of the ground.	
3. It's a good idea to board up windows with plywood.	
4. Listen to local TV and radio stations for more information.	

2. **Revisit the Chapter Focus Question** How can big storms be a challenge to survive? Use examples from the two readings in this chapter to answer this question.

Phrases for Conversation

Asking for Clarification

Could you repeat that, please?

Could you repeat what you just said?

Could you say that again, please?

Could you spell that, please?

Would you mind spelling that for me, please?

Listening and Speaking

Create a "Survival English" Pamphlet

Imagine you meet a visitor to the United States. This person does not speak English. How will he or she communicate? Create a "Survival English" document with English phrases the visitor needs to know.

1. With a small group, discuss these questions.
   a. Which of these categories of phrases are the most important to learn?
      - phrases for greetings
      - phrases for introductions
      - phrases for making requests
      - phrases for thanking
      - phrases for telling time
      - phrases for apologizing
   b. What other important categories of phrases should a visitor learn?

2. With your group, choose three or four of the categories of phrases you discussed. Work together to make a list of phrases for each category. If you don't understand a group member's suggestion, ask for clarification. Use the phrases in the **Phrases for Conversation.**

3. Create a "Survival English" document with your group's phrases. Include graphics for the phrases if appropriate.

4. Present your list of categories and phrases to the class. Use gestures to clarify your phrases.

5. Compare your document to the other groups' documents. Did you choose the same category of phrases? Did you come up with the same phrases for each category?

Reading Fluency

Adjusting Your Reading Rate to Scan

When you scan, you do not read every word. You look through a text quickly for key words or information. You must adjust your reading rate to scan.

Scan "The Fiercest Storms on Earth" (pages 297–301) for the answers to these questions. Be sure to keep your eyes moving while you scan for the answers.

1. A storm must have winds of at least how many kilometers per hour to be called a hurricane?

2. What is the hole in the center of a hurricane called?

3. What can be the speed of the winds in the center of a tornado?

4. What **tools** do scientists use to predict the weather?

● Vocabulary Development

Shades of Meaning in Related Words

As you learned in Unit 2, synonyms are words that have the same meaning. However, some words are related but have small differences in meaning. These words have different **shades of meaning.** It is important to be aware of the different shades of meaning of words as you read.

Look at the word pairs from the Chapter 2 readings. Their meanings are related, but they are also different.

Related Words	Related Meaning	Difference in Meaning
• **regular** • **ordinary**	normal	**regular:** usual **ordinary:** common; not special
• **damp** • **soggy**	wet	**damp:** a little wet **soggy:** wet and soft
• **strong** • **fierce**	having physical strength	**strong:** having physical strength **fierce:** powerful, having great physical strength

1. Work with a partner. Look at the pairs of words. Discuss these questions: How are the meanings of the words similar? How are they different?

   a. beautiful / handsome

   b. intelligent / clever

   c. see / watch

   d. difficult / challenging

   e. quietly / softly

   f. large / huge

2. Then look the words up in a dictionary or thesaurus. Check your ideas.

✓Checkpoint

1. Define **shades of meaning.**

2. How are the words *small* and *tiny* related? How do they have different shades of meaning?

Vocabulary Log

Workbook page 220

Independent Practice CD-ROM/Online

● **Grammar**

Comparative Adjectives: *-er* and *more*

Use comparative adjectives to compare two things.

Comparative Form of Adjectives: *-er*				
subject	*be*	**adjective + -er**	*than*	
Tornadoes	are	small**er**	**than**	hurricanes.

Notes

- For most one-syllable adjectives, add **-er** to form the comparative.

  tall / tall**er**   strong / strong**er**   fast / fast**er**

- For one- and two-syllable adjectives that end in **y**, change the **y** to **i** and add **-er.**

  happy / happ**ier**

Comparative Form of Adjectives: *more*				
subject	*be*	***more* + adjective**	*than*	
Hurricanes	are	**more** dangerous	**than**	regular storms.

Notes

- For adjectives with two or more syllables, put **more** in front of the adjective.

  expensive / **more** expensive

- Some adjectives have irregular comparative forms.

  good / **better**   bad / **worse**

Practice the Grammar Write the comparative form of each adjective.

1. funny   **3.** difficult   **5.** friendly   **7.** small

2. old   **4.** hungry   **6.** good   **8.** handsome

Use the Grammar Independently Compare two people or objects. Write five sentences. Use comparative adjectives. Read your sentences to your partner.

✓Checkpoint

1. What is a **comparative adjective?**

2. Create a comparative sentence about two foods.

Workbook
pages 221–222

Independent Practice
CD-ROM/Online

● Grammar

Superlative Adjectives: *-est* and *most*

Use superlative adjectives to compare three or more things.

Superlative Form of Adjectives: *-est*			
subject	*be*	*the* + **adjective** + *-est*	
Antarctica	is	**the** cold**est**	place on Earth.

Notes

- For most one-syllable adjectives, add **-est** to form the superlative.

  tall / tall**est**   strong / strong**est**   fast / fast**est**

- For one- and two-syllable adjectives that end in **y**, change the **y** to **i** and add **-est.**

  happy / happ**iest**

Superlative Form of Adjectives: *most*			
subject	*be*	*the* + *most* + **adjective**	
John	is	**the most** popular	boy in the class.

Notes

- For adjectives with two or more syllables, put **the + most** in front of the adjective.

  difficult / **the most** difficult

- Some adjectives have irregular superlative forms.

  good / **the best**   bad / **the worst**

Practice the Grammar Complete the sentences with the superlative form of each adjective.

1. The Nile is (long) ____ river in the world.
2. Hurricanes are (large) ____ storms on Earth.
3. Was Albert Einstein (intelligent) ____ person ever?
4. The Sears Tower is (famous) ____ building in Chicago.

Use the Grammar Independently Talk with your partner about your city. Use superlatives to discuss things like the tallest buildings, the most expensive restaurants, and the best shops.

Workbook
pages 223–224

Independent Practice
CD-ROM/Online

✓Checkpoint

1. What is a **superlative adjective**?

2. Create a superlative sentence about a food you like.

● **Writing Assignment**

Personal Narrative: Write About a Storm

Writing Suggestion

See **Milestones Handbook.**
pages 393–433

Writing Prompt

What is the worst storm you have experienced? Write about your memories of the storm. If you cannot remember a bad storm, interview someone else. Find out and write about the worst storm that that person has experienced. Use comparative and superlative adjectives.

Write Your Personal Narrative

1. **Read the student model.** It shows the first paragraph of a personal narrative.

2. **Think about the worst storm you can remember.** What kind of storm was it? Take time to remember the storm, the events of the storm, and how you felt during the storm.

Student Model

My Fiercest Storm

This is a story about the worst storm I can remember. I was about ten years old. I was at a playground near my grandmother's house. It was summer. It was a beautiful, sunny day. Suddenly, the sky got dark. Then it got darker. It was the blackest sky I could remember. My grandmother and I hurried home. We got home just in time.

3. **Write your personal narrative.**

   a. The first paragraph should give background information. Background information is general information, such as:
   - How old were you?
   - Where were you?
   - Who were you with?

b. The body of your personal narrative should be one or two paragraphs. It should tell the reader what happened before and during the storm. It should answer questions like:

- How did you find out about the storm?
- What **preparations** did you and others make?
- What was the storm like?
- How did you feel during the storm?

Be sure to use descriptive words. This will help your audience create mental images.
Use chronological order for the events.

c. Finish your narrative with a final paragraph. This paragraph should tell the reader what happened after the storm.

4. Revise. Reread your narrative. Revise your narrative if any ideas are not clear or complete.
Use the **editing and proofreading symbols** on page 419 to help you mark any changes you want to make.

5. Edit. Use the **Writing Checklist** to help you find problems and errors.

6. Share your personal narrative with a partner. Compare your experiences. Use comparative adjectives.

> ### Writing Checklist
>
> **1.** I included background information in my personal narrative.
>
> **2.** I used descriptive words.
>
> **3.** I used comparatives and/or superlative adjectives.
>
> **4.** I used **chronological** order.

 **Writing Support**

Mechanics
Commas

There are many uses for **commas** in writing. Here are two important uses.

- Use a comma between two or more adjectives that describe the same word but are NOT joined by the conjunction **and.**

  It was a beautiful, sunny day.

- Put commas between words or phrases in a series (a series has three or more items).

  She speaks English, Spanish, French, and Italian.

Apply Read your personal narrative. Check to make sure that you used commas correctly.

Workbook
pages 226–228

Independent Practice
CD-ROM/Online

Progress Check

How well did you understand this chapter? Try to answer the questions. If necessary, go back to the pages listed for a review.

Skills	Skills Assessment Questions	Pages to Review
Vocabulary From the Readings	Can you use these words in sentences?	
	• **destroy, energy, flooding, protect, sink, spin, warning**	294
	• **amazed, concentrate, preparations, tool**	304
Academic Vocabulary	What do these academic vocabulary words mean?	
	• **detail, focus**	295
	• **persuade, recommend**	302
Reading Strategies	What is the **main idea** of a reading? What are the **details**?	295
	How do authors create **mental images** in readers' minds?	305
Text Genres	What is the text genre of "The Fiercest Storms on Earth"?	296
	What is the text genre of "Hurricane Friends"?	305
Reading Comprehension	What is "The Fiercest Storms on Earth" about?	303
	What is "Hurricane Friends" about?	309
Text Elements	What are **headings** and **subheadings**?	303
Spelling	Pronounce these **silent _k_ words:** know, knee, knock, knife.	309
Writing Conventions	Write the words for these numbers. Use **hyphens:** 32, $\frac{1}{4}$, $\frac{1}{3}$, 55, $\frac{1}{2}$, 46.	309
Listening and Speaking	**Phrases for Conversation** What phrases can you use to ask for clarification?	310
Vocabulary Development	Name two words that are related but have different **shades of meaning.** Explain the different shades of meaning in these words.	311
Grammar	Give a sentence with a comparative adjective.	312
	Give a sentence with a superlative adjective.	313
Writing Support: Mechanics	What are two ways commas are used in writing? Write a sentence that includes one or more commas.	315

Assessment Practice

Read this passage. Then answer Questions 1 through 4.

Blizzards

1   A blizzard is a fierce winter storm. A blizzard gets its energy from high pressure air moving into a low pressure area. This causes snow to fall quickly and in large amounts. Strong winds blow. The temperature drops below freezing.

2   Blizzards can happen wherever snow falls. In North America, blizzards are most common in the Northeast. They occur in Canada, too.

3   One of the fiercest blizzards in U.S. history was the Great Blizzard of 1888. During that blizzard, 400 people died. Two hundred ships sank. Snow drifts were 15 to 50 feet high. The largest blizzard was the Storm of the Century in 1993. This blizzard dropped snow over 26 states in the United States. It went as far north as Canada and as far south as Mexico. Fewer people died than in most great blizzards, but all were amazed at how far the blizzard reached.

1   Read this phrase from paragraph 3.

> . . . all were amazed at how far the blizzard reached.

What does <u>amazed</u> mean?

A   very happy

B   very sad

C   very interested

D   very surprised

2   What is the main idea of paragraph 1?

A   Blizzards are fierce winter storms.

B   Blizzards can happen wherever snow falls.

C   A blizzard can cause a lot of damage.

D   A blizzard has strong winds.

3   What is the best subhead for paragraph 2?

A   Definition of a Blizzard

B   Locations of Blizzards

C   Famous Blizzards

D   Deadly Blizzards

4   What is the genre of this text?

A   diary entry

B   persuasive essay

C   informational text

D   personal narrative

Writing on Demand: Personal Narrative

Write about your experience with a storm. It can be a small storm or a fierce storm. Tell what you saw, what you did, and how you felt. **(20 minutes)**

Writing Tip
Use words and descriptions that help the reader see mental images.

Apply & Extend

Objectives

Listening and Speaking
Deliver a persuasive presentation

Media
Compare a survival story told in different forms of media

Writing
Expository writing: Write a "how-to" pamphlet

Projects

Independent Reading

● Listening and Speaking Workshop
Deliver a Persuasive Presentation

> **Topic**
>
> Deliver a persuasive presentation about the ten most important items needed to survive in the wild.

1. Brainstorm

With a small group, imagine being lost in the wild. Brainstorm a list of items to help you survive. Use a dictionary if necessary.

2. Plan

a. Discuss and choose the ten most important items from your list.

b. Put the items in order of importance.

c. Discuss these questions for each item. Take notes on group members' ideas.

- How do you use this item?
- Why is this item important?
- Why is it more important than other items?

d. Find or create visuals of each item. This will make your presentation more interesting.

3. Outline

a. Work with your group to write an outline for your presentation.

b. Include an introduction to your presentation. In your introduction, explain the purpose of the presentation.

c. Provide evidence for why each item is important for survival.

d. Use persuasive techniques to keep your audience's attention and to get them to accept the importance of the items. These techniques include word choice, repetition, and emotional appeal.

4. Practice

Have each member of your group present at least one item. Think about each part of the **Speaking Self-Evaluation** before you practice.

5. Present and Evaluate

Give the presentation. When the presentation is finished, ask your group members for feedback. Use the **Speaking Self-Evaluation** to evaluate your part of the presentation. Use the **Active Listening Evaluation** to evaluate and discuss your classmates' presentations.

Speaking Self-Evaluation
1. Our presentation begins with an explanation of its purpose.
2. I explained why the item(s) I presented is (are) important.
3. I spoke clearly and loudly enough for people to hear me.
4. I looked at the audience while I spoke.

Active Listening Evaluation
1. I understood the purpose of the presentation.
2. The presentation helped me understand the importance of each item.
3. The presentation was persuasive.
4. The presentation **persuaded** me that _____ .

● Media Workshop

Compare a Survival Story Told in Different Forms of Media

Some survival stories are very famous. There are informational texts about them. There are even movies about some of them. However, informational texts and movies often do not tell the same story in the same way.

1. Find and read an electronic or online encyclopedia article about Shackleton or another famous survival story.

2. Find and watch a movie about this same survival story. You may find the movie in your library or order it from your library network.

3. Think about the following questions.

   a. How is the movie different from the encyclopedia article? Are the facts the same? Is the story told differently? If so, in what way?

   b. Which presentation is more interesting? Why?

   c. What is the purpose of an encyclopedia article? Give examples from the encyclopedia article you read.

   d. What is the purpose of a movie? Give examples from the movie you watched.

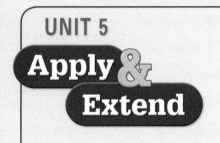
Writing Suggestion

See **Milestones Handbook**. pages 393–433

Writing Workshop

Expository Writing: Write a "How-To" Pamphlet

Expository writing is writing that gives information or explains something. "How-to" writing is writing that explains the process or steps for doing something.

> **Writing Prompt**
>
> Write a pamphlet about a disaster and how to survive it.

PREWRITE

1. Read the student model on the next page. It will help you understand how to write your pamphlet.

2. Choose a type of disaster for your pamphlet. Use the library and the Internet to learn more about the disaster. Research answers to these questions.

   a. What causes this disaster?

   b. What usually happens during this disaster?

   c. What precautions can a person take before this disaster?

   d. What tips can help someone survive this disaster?

   e. Are there any special tools, clothes, or equipment a person needs to survive this disaster or recover from this kind of disaster?

WRITE A DRAFT

1. The first part of your pamphlet should give information about the disaster. Explain:

   a. what the disaster is

   b. what causes the disaster

   c. what effects the disaster can have

   Try to use comparatives or superlatives in your description of the disaster.

2. The second part of your pamphlet should be a list of tips. The tips should be about preparing for and surviving this disaster. You can divide the tips into groups: how to prepare for this disaster, what to do during the disaster, and what to do after the disaster.

3. Include headings and subheadings for each section of your pamphlet.

Earthquakes: What Are They? What Causes Them? What Happens During One?

An earthquake is a sudden shaking of the earth. It is caused by the rocks shifting under the Earth's surface. Earthquakes can happen at any time without warning. Earthquakes can make buildings and bridges collapse. They can also lead to other disasters like landslides, avalanches, fires, and tsunamis. Earthquakes can cause many deaths and injuries. They can also cause a lot of damage to homes and property. It is important to be prepared for them.

Earthquake Safety Tips: Precautions to Take in Case of an Earthquake

- Make sure shelves are attached well to walls.
- Put the heaviest objects on the lowest shelves.
- Put objects that can break easily in low, closed cabinets.
- Hang mirrors and pictures away from places where people sit or sleep.
- Be sure to have emergency supplies in your house. For example, you should have a first aid kit, canned food, bottled water, and a flashlight with batteries.

What to Do During an Earthquake

- Go under a strong piece of furniture like a table or a desk. Stay away from bookcases or tall furniture that could fall on you.
- Stay away from windows. Windows often shatter during earthquakes. The glass can hurt you.
- Don't go outside during or right after an earthquake.
- If you are outside during an earthquake, do not try to enter a building. Try to get away from buildings, trees, and power lines. Crouch down and cover your head.
- If you are in a car, drive to a place away from buildings, trees, and power lines. Stop your car. Stay in your car. It will help protect you from falling objects.

What to Do After an Earthquake

- Put on long pants, a long sleeve shirt, heavy shoes, and heavy gloves. These clothes will help protect you from getting hurt by broken objects.
- After you have taken care of yourself, help injured or trapped people. Don't try to move injured people.
- Put out small fires so they won't spread. Fire is the most common danger after earthquakes.
- Be prepared for aftershocks. Aftershocks are smaller earthquakes that can follow major earthquakes. Sometimes aftershocks happen hours, days, or even weeks later.

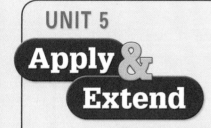
REVISE

1. Review your pamphlet. Make sure it explains the disaster, its causes, and its effects. Include headings and subheadings.

2. Exchange your pamphlet with a partner. Ask your partner to use the **Peer Review Checklist.** Your partner will point out errors and give suggestions.

3. Revise your draft to make it better. You may need to add or delete sentences. You may need to rearrange sentences to make your ideas clearer.

4. Use the **editing and proofreading symbols** on page 419 to help you mark the changes you want to make.

EDIT

1. Use the **Revising and Editing Checklist** to evaluate your essay.

2. Fix any errors in grammar, spelling, and punctuation.

Peer Review Checklist

1. The pamphlet gives a clear explanation of the disaster.

2. The pamphlet clearly explains the causes and effects of the disaster.

3. The pamphlet teaches useful tips for surviving the disaster.

4. The most useful thing I learned from the pamphlet is _____ .

5. The pamphlet would be better if _____ .

Revising and Editing Checklist

1. The first paragraph of my pamphlet explains the disaster.

2. I explained the causes and effects of the disaster.

3. I used capital letters and punctuation correctly.

4. I included headings and subheadings.

5. I used comparatives and/or superlatives correctly.

PUBLISH

1. Write your pamphlet in your best handwriting so that it is clear and easy to read. Or, if possible, use a computer to make your pamphlet look like a professional publication. If you use a computer, use a spell and grammar check.

2. Create a "cover" for your pamphlet with the name of the disaster. Also include a graphic (such as a photo or a drawing) to represent the disaster.

3. Present your pamphlet to the class. Read clearly and slowly enough so that everyone can understand you. Change the level of your voice to express the important ideas in your essay. Answer questions your classmates have about your pamphlet.

Build Your Knowledge

You may want to create and present your report using technology. Read and follow the steps for giving a technology presentation on page 429.

Projects

Choose one or more of the following projects to explore the theme of survival further.

PROJECT 1
Interview a Survivor

1. Find someone you know who has been in a survival situation.
2. Write a list of questions to ask this person.
3. Interview the person. Use the questions you prepared. Be sure to take notes on the interview.
4. Tell your class about the interview.

PROJECT 2
Create a Public Service Announcement

A public service announcement is a short announcement on television or radio. It teaches people about health or safety. Work with a small group to create a public service announcement about a disaster situation.

1. With your group, choose a disaster.
2. Use the Internet to research information about it.
3. Write a short script. The script should explain the disaster. It should also explain steps to take to stay safe during the disaster. The announcement should take only about one minute.
4. Choose a team member to be the announcer. Have the announcer give the announcement to the class. If possible, use a video recorder to record the public service announcement.

PROJECT 3
Create a Personal Survival Backpack

1. Imagine you are shipwrecked on a desert island. You have only one backpack or bag. What are the most important personal items you want to have in your backpack? Make a list of these items. For example, the items could include your favorite book, your favorite food, a portable DVD player, or photos of the people you love.
2. Put these items in a backpack or bag. (Remember: You can only take as many items as will fit in the backpack or bag!)
3. Bring the backpack or bag to class. Show your classmates each of the items in it. Explain why each item is so important to you.

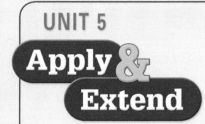

UNIT 5

Apply & Extend

Heinle Reading Library

Clara Barton and the American Red Cross by Eve Marko

This is Clara Barton's dramatic life story. Clara's wish to help people and her nursing skills led her to create the American Red Cross. From the Civil War battlefields to the flooded Ohio Valley, Clara helped victims of war and disasters survive and rebuild their lives.

● Independent Reading

Explore the theme of survival further by reading one or more of these books.

Shackleton and the Lost Antarctic Expedition by B. A. Hoena (author), Dave Hoover and Charles Barnett III (illustrators), Graphic Library, 2006.

In 1914 Ernest Shackleton and his crew set off to explore Antarctica. They were shipwrecked and never reached their goal. However, amazingly, they managed to survive. This book tells the story in graphic novel format. The dramatic illustrations and dialogue bring this exciting story to life.

Using Math to Survive in the Wild by Hilary Koll, Steve Mills, and Jonny Crockett, Gareth Stevens Publishing, 2006.

Imagine you are lost in a forest. You need to do many things. For example, you must build a shelter, find water, collect food, and cross a river. This book helps you understand how to use math to accomplish these things.

Hatchet by Gary Paulsen, Scholastic, 1999.

Brian Robeson is the only passenger on an airplane that crashes in the wilderness. Using only a hatchet and his intelligence, this 13-year-old boy survives for 54 days alone in the wilderness before he is rescued.

Julie of the Wolves by Jean Craighead George, HarperTrophy, 2005.

Julie, a 13-year-old orphan Eskimo, runs away. She is soon lost in the Alaskan wilderness. Julie has no food, no shelter, and no compass. Then a pack of wolves accepts her into their community. The wolves help her in her struggle to survive.

Island of the Blue Dolphins by Scott O'Dell, Scott Foresman, 1987.

Karana, a Native American girl, is left behind on her tribe's island. This story tells how Karana survives alone on the island for 18 years!

Milestones to Achievement

Writing: Revise and Edit

Read this rough draft of a student's personal narrative, which may contain errors. Then answer Questions 1 through 4.

Impossible Snow

(1) I live in South Padre Island, Texas. (2) It almost never snows here. (3) But the December before I turned seven, it snowed four whole inches. (4) That may not sound like a lot, but for us, it was incredible!

(5) I remember I was in the kitchen eating breakfast. (6) It was a quiet slow morning. (7) Then I heard my oldest brother yell. (8) "Snow! It's snowing! Quick! Come see!" (9) I dropped my spoon and ran to the kitchen window. (10) I couldn't believe my eyes. (11) Snow fell from the sky. (12) Real snow, not movie snow or book snow or dream snow, but real snow.

(13) I ran to the front door. (14) My brothers were already there, pulling on coats over their pajamas. (15) I found my coat, too. (16) Then we all ran outside to play. (17) We played in that snow all day.

(18) I think that was the happy day of my life. (19) Its crazy that frozen water could make a family so happy. (20) I can't wait for the next snowstorm.

---

1 How can you improve sentence 6?
A Add a comma after *quiet*.
B Add a comma after *slow*.
C Add commas after *quiet* and *slow*.
D Add commas before *quiet* and *slow*.

2 How can you improve sentence 11?
A Change *fell* to *is falling*.
B Change *fell* to *was falling*.
C Change *fell* to *fall*.
D Change *fell* to *falls*.

3 How can you improve sentence 18?
A Change *happy* to *happyer*.
B Change *happy* to *happier*.
C Change *happy* to *happyest*.
D Change *happy* to *happiest*.

4 How can you correct sentence 19?
A Change *Its* to *It's*.
B Change *happy* to *happyier*.
C Change *happy* to *happier*.
D Change *Its* to *its*.

Writing on Demand: Creative Writing

Write a three-paragraph short story about a person in a survival situation. **(20 minutes)**

> ## Writing Tip
> Use an appropriate organizational structure, such as **chronological** order, cause and effect, or compare/contrast.

● Reading

Read this short story. Then answer Questions 1 through 8.

Force to the Rescue

1   Greg lived near the ocean in Alaska. He raised and trained dogs—Siberian huskies. He then sold the dogs to people up and down the coast. On January 22, Greg was driving his boat through the ocean. He was taking a three-month-old puppy to a man and woman. The couple lived in a small town on an island. The weather was freezing. The ocean water was rough. The winds were fierce. Greg had to concentrate. The puppy stayed down in the bottom of the boat. He was afraid. Greg's own dog was standing out on the front of the boat, facing the wind. He wasn't afraid of an ocean storm. He was a tough, strong dog. He lived up to his name, Force. Everyone in the area knew Force.

2   Suddenly, Greg's boat hit some rocks. Greg knew this was an emergency. He called for help on his radio. The rescuers couldn't hear what Greg said. They had no knowledge of his location. Then the sound cut off. Rescuers jumped in their boats and searched everywhere. All they found was Greg's boat. It was destroyed. It was already sinking. After searching for three days, the rescuers sadly went home.

3   Two weeks later, a man and his father were fishing in a boat near a small island in the ocean. They heard a dog barking. The old man pointed to the shore. "Look, a dog!" The younger man looked up. He recognized Force at once. He called to him. The dog jumped in the water and swam quickly to the boat. The men were amazed that the dog was alive. His fur was matted and his leg was injured, but he led the men to Greg. Greg and the puppy had survived on the island. And Force's barking had led to his rescue!

1 What does the word <u>destroyed</u> mean in the following sentence from paragraph 2?

| It was destroyed. |

A running

B fixed

C wrecked

D empty

2 What does the word <u>knowledge</u> mean in the following sentence from paragraph 2?

| They had no knowledge of his location. |

A information

B sadness

C expression

D happiness

3 What is the main idea of this story?

A A dog is man's best friend.

B The ocean is fun but dangerous.

C A man raises Siberian huskies.

D A man and his dogs survive.

4 What happens last in this story?

A Greg's boat hits rocks.

B Greg's boat sinks.

C Fishermen find Greg and his dogs.

D Rescuers search for Greg and his dogs.

5 What is the setting of this story?

A a cool, breezy day

B a warm, rainy night

C the cold, Alaskan ocean

D a cold, Alaskan mountain

6 What is the theme of this story?

A conflict

B survival

C friendship

D discovery

7 Which sentence has a comparative adjective?

A The old man pointed to the shore.

B "Look, a dog!"

C The younger man looked up.

D He recognized Force at once.

8 How are the words <u>tough</u> and <u>strong</u> related in this sentence?

| He was a tough, strong dog. |

A They are both adverbs.

B They both modify the word *was*.

C They have shades of the same meaning.

D They are antonyms, or opposites.

Belonging

Explore the Theme

1. What does it mean to **belong**?
2. Describe the people and things in the pictures. How does each picture show **belonging** (or not belonging)?

Theme Activity

Look at the headings in the chart. With a partner, brainstorm a list of people or things that belong in each group.

family	baseball team	rock band	drama club
father	pitcher		

329

CHAPTER 1

Objectives

Reading Strategies
Make inferences;
Paraphrase

Listening and Speaking
Retell a story

Grammar
Learn the present
perfect tense; Learn
the past perfect tense

Writing
Business letter: Write
a letter of interest

Academic Vocabulary

insight | sequence
analyze | judgment

Academic Content

New Mexico
Biomes
Ecosystems

● **Chapter Focus Questions**
What gives people a feeling of belonging? What
makes animals belong in a certain place?

Reading 1 **Literature**
Novel (excerpt)
BLESS ME, ULTIMA
by Rudolfo Anaya

Reading 2 **Content:** Science
Textbook
Biomes and Ecosystems

BLESS ME, ULTIMA

● **About the Reading**
You are going to read an excerpt from a novel. It is
about Antonio Márez, a young Mexican-American boy,
on his first day of school.

● Build Background

Mexican Foods

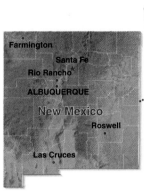

The setting of *Bless Me, Ultima* is New Mexico in the 1940s. New Mexico is a southwestern state in the United States. Over one-and-a-half million Mexicans lived in the United States at that time. However, many Americans did not know anything about Mexican culture. The main character in *Bless Me, Ultima* brings traditional Mexican foods to school for his lunch. In the 1940s, most Americans did not know Mexican foods.

Today Mexican food is very popular in the United States. Here are some foods mentioned in the story. Look at the foods. Which ones have you eaten? Where have you eaten Mexican food? Can you name other Mexican foods?

tortillas

chile peppers

beans

● Use Prior Knowledge

Think About Your First Day of School

In *Bless Me, Ultima,* Antonio Márez has a difficult time on his first day of school. Think of your first day at school this year. How did you feel? Put your feelings in a word web.

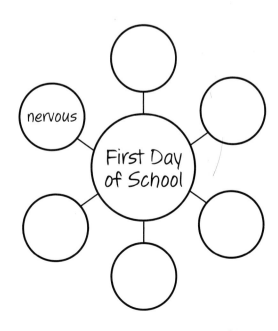

Key Vocabulary

custom
loneliness
pleased
point
protection
rude
weak

● Vocabulary From the Reading

Learn, Practice, and Use Independently

Learn Vocabulary Read each sentence. Look at the **highlighted** word. Read the context (the words around the highlighted word). Use the context to determine the meaning of the word.

1. In my country, it is a **custom** to bring gifts to a birthday party.

2. I had a feeling of **loneliness** every day until I made friends at my new school.

3. Marta was **pleased** that so many people came to her party.

4. When my teacher wants someone to answer, she says the person's name or she **points** with her finger.

5. The sun is dangerous. You need **protection.** Wear a hat and put on sunscreen.

6. Don't put your feet on the table. That's **rude.**

7. I feel sick and very **weak** today. I don't have the strength to walk to school.

Practice Vocabulary Copy the chart. Work with a partner. Write the Key Vocabulary word for each definition.

Word	Definition
protection	action taken against harm or loss, a defense
1.	not polite
2.	a condition of being alone and feeling sad
3.	not physically strong or not strong in character
4.	to indicate a place, direction, person, or thing, usually with a finger
5.	feeling happy or satisfied
6.	a regular practice that is special to a person, people, area, or nation

✓ Checkpoint

Write one sentence for each Key Vocabulary word. Read your sentences to a partner.

Use Vocabulary Independently Choose a Key Vocabulary word. Act it out for a partner. Your partner will say the word. Take turns until all the words have been acted out.

Vocabulary
Log

Workbook
page 229

Independent Practice
CD-ROM/Online

● Academic Vocabulary

Vocabulary for the Reading Strategy

Word	Explanation	Sample Sentence	Visual Cue
insight *noun*	the ability to see into or understand a complex person, situation, or subject	The professor gave us **insight** into how the heart works.	
analyze *verb*	to examine something in order to understand what it means	The doctor **analyzed** the x-ray to find the problem.	

Draw a picture and write a sentence for each word.

● Reading Strategy

Make Inferences

An **inference** is a guess. When you make an inference, you use information from the text and what you already know to make the guess. This helps you understand more about the reading than just the information on the page. Making inferences helps give you more **insight** into the characters and the story.

1. As you read *Bless Me, Ultima,* **analyze** the sentences. Do any sentences help you make an inference?

2. Look at the chart. After you read, you will look at the reading again. You will write sentences from the text in the first column. You will write inferences you made about these sentences in the second column.

Sentence from Reading	My Inference

✓Checkpoint

1. What is an **inference**?

2. How do you make an inference?

Vocabulary Log

Workbook page 230

Independent Practice CD-ROM/Online

● **Text Genre**

Novel

Bless Me, Ultima is a **novel.** A novel is a long work of fiction. Because a novel is longer than a short story, the reader learns a lot about the characters, especially the main character. The main character in a novel often goes through changes as the novel progresses. Look for these features in the main character of a novel.

Novel	
character traits	a character's qualities; the kind of person the character is
character motivation	the reason why a character does what he or she does
character changes	the ways a character becomes different as the story progresses

● **Meet the Author**

Rudolfo Anaya was born in 1937 in a small town in New Mexico. Anaya spoke Spanish at home. He did not learn English until he went to school. After college, Anaya worked as a middle school and high school English teacher.

● **Reading Focus Questions**

As you read, think about these questions.

1. How does the reading connect to the theme of "belonging"?

2. What do you think was the author's purpose in writing *Bless Me, Ultima*?

3. What makes a person feel like he or she belongs somewhere? What makes a person feel like he or she does not belong?

✓Checkpoint

1. Is a **novel** a work of fiction or nonfiction?

2. What are **character traits**?

Workbook
page 231

Independent Practice
CD-ROM/Online

BLESS ME, ULTIMA

by Rudolfo Anaya

1   On the first day of school I awoke with a sick feeling in my stomach. It did not hurt, it just made me feel **weak.** The sun did not sing as it came over the hill. Today I would take the goat path and **trek** into town for years and years of schooling. For the first time I would be away from the **protection** of my mother. I was excited and sad about it.

2   Somehow I got to the school grounds, but I was lost. The school was larger than I had expected. Its huge, yawning doors were **menacing.** I looked for Deborah and Theresa, but every face I saw was strange. I looked again at the doors of the **sacred** halls but I was too afraid to enter. My mother had said to go to Miss Maestas, but I did not know where to begin to find her. I had come to the town, and I had come to school, and I was very lost and afraid in the nervous, excited **swarm** of kids.

What inference can you make about these children?

---

trek travel with difficulty

menacing threatening to be harmful

sacred revered, respected

swarm crowd

Reading Strategy

Make Inferences
Who do you think Deborah and Theresa are? Why do you think this?

✓
Reading Check

1. **Recall facts** Where is the boy going today?

2. **Recall facts** How does the boy feel? What adjectives does the author use to describe the boy's feelings?

3. **Predict** What do you think is going to happen to the boy at school? Why do you think this? Confirm your prediction when you finish reading the story.

How does this school compare with Antonio's school?

3   It was then that I felt a hand on my shoulder. I turned and looked into the eyes of a strange red-haired boy. He spoke English, a **foreign tongue.**

4   "First grade," was all I could answer. He smiled and took my hand, and with him I entered school. The building was **cavernous** and dark. It had strange, unfamiliar smells and sounds that seemed to **gurgle** from its belly. There was a big hall and many rooms, and many mothers with children passed in and out of the rooms.

5   I wished for my mother, but I put away the thought because I knew I was expected to become a man. A **radiator** snapped with steam and I jumped. The red-haired boy laughed and led me into one of the rooms. This room was brighter than the hall. So it was like this that I entered school.

6   Miss Maestas was a kind woman. She thanked the boy, whose name was Red, for bringing me in, then asked my name. I told her I did not speak English.

7   "*¿Cómo te llamas?*" she asked.

8   "Antonio Márez," I replied. I told her my mother said I should see her, and that my mother sent her **regards.**

Reading Strategy

Make Inferences
What do you think "*¿Cómo te llamas?*" means? Why do you think this?

foreign tongue unfamiliar language

cavernous like a very large cave

gurgle make the sound of bubbling liquid

radiator set of metal pipes with hot steam running through them, used to heat rooms

¿Cómo te llamas? What is your name? (Spanish)

regards friendly greeting

9   She smiled. "Anthony Márez," she wrote in a book. I drew closer to look at the letters **formed** by her pen. "Do you want to learn to write?" she asked.

10   "Yes," I answered.

11   "Good," she smiled.

12   I wanted to ask her immediately about the **magic** in the letters, but that would be **rude** and so I was quiet. I was **fascinated** by the black letters that formed on the paper and made my name. Miss Maestas gave me a crayon and some paper and I sat in the corner and worked at copying my name over and over. She was very busy the rest of the day with the other children that came to the room. Many cried when their mothers left, and one wet his pants. I sat in my corner alone and wrote. By noon I could write my name, and when Miss Maestas discovered that she was very **pleased.**

13   She took me to the front of the room and spoke to the other boys and girls. She **pointed** at me but I did not understand her. Then the other boys and girls laughed and **pointed** at me. I did not feel so good. **Thereafter** I kept away from the groups as much as I could and worked alone. I worked hard. I listened to the strange sounds. I learned new names, new words.

How do you think these students feel?

> ### Reading Strategy
>
> **Make Inferences** Why do you think the boys and girls **pointed** and laughed at Antonio?

> ## ✓ Reading Check
>
> 1. **Recall facts** What did Antonio spend the morning doing?
> 2. **Recall facts** How does he feel when the other boys and girls laugh and **point** at him?
> 3. **Understand cause and effect** Why did Antonio stay away from the groups as much as he could after this?

---

formed shaped, made
magic charming quality
fascinated greatly interested
thereafter after that

Reading Strategy

Make Inferences Why did the children **point** and laugh again when they saw Antonio's lunch?

14   At noon we opened our lunches to eat. Miss Maestas left the room and a high school girl came and sat at the desk while we ate. My mother had packed a small jar of hot beans and some good, green **chile** wrapped in **tortillas.** When the other children saw my lunch they laughed and **pointed** again. Even the high school girl laughed. They showed me their sandwiches which were made of bread. Again I did not feel well.

15   I gathered my lunch and slipped out of the room. The strangeness of the school and the other children made me very sad. I did not understand them. I sneaked around the back of the school building, and standing against the wall I tried to eat. But I couldn't. A huge lump seemed to form in my throat and tears came to my eyes. I **yearned** for my mother, and at the same time I understood that she had sent me to this place where I was an **outcast.** I had tried hard to learn and they had laughed at me. I had opened my lunch to eat and again they had laughed and **pointed** at me.

---

chile a pepper with a hot, spicy taste, used fresh or dried in cooking

tortillas Mexican bread of corn meal or flour made in a thin layer and cooked on a grill

yearned felt a strong desire or need

outcast someone who is avoided or left alone by others

16   The pain and sadness seemed to spread to my **soul**, and I felt for the first time what the **grownups** call *la tristeza de la vida*. I wanted to run away, to hide, to run and never come back, never see anyone again. But I knew that if I did I would **shame** my family name, that my mother's dream would **crumble**. I knew I had to grow up and be a man, but oh it was so very hard.

◄ Reading Strategy

Make Inferences
What do you think Antonio's mother's dream is?

17   But no, I was not alone. Down the wall near the corner I saw two other boys who had sneaked out of the room. They were George and Willy. They were big boys, I knew they were from the farms of Delia. We banded together and in our **union** found strength. We found a few others who were like us, different in language and **custom**, and a part of our **loneliness** was gone. When the winter set in we moved into the auditorium and there, although many a meal was eaten in complete silence, we felt we belonged. We struggled against the feeling of **loneliness** that **gnawed** at our souls and we overcame it; that feeling I never shared again with anyone.

Do you think these children feel a sense of belonging?

---

soul part of a person that is not the body; the spirit, thoughts, emotions of a person

grownups adults

la tristeza de la vida the sadness of life (Spanish)

shame bring dishonor to

crumble fall into pieces

union coming together or uniting of people

gnawed bit or chewed on

✓ **Reading Check**

1. **Recall facts** What does Antonio want to do?
2. **Recall facts** Who are the boys Antonio becomes friends with?
3. **Identify main ideas** What is the main idea of the last paragraph?

● Apply the Reading Strategy

Make Inferences

Now complete the Reading Strategy chart.

1. Review the **Reading Strategy** on page 333.
2. Copy the chart on a piece of paper.
3. Look back at the reading. Find sentences that help you make inferences. Write these sentences in the first column of the chart.
4. Write your inferences about these sentences in the second column.

Sentence from Reading	My Inference
On the first day of school I had a sick feeling in my stomach.	Antonio probably does not want to go to school.

● Academic Vocabulary

Vocabulary for the Reading Comprehension Questions

Word	Explanation	Sample Sentence	Visual Cue
sequence *noun*	a connected series	A **sequence** of events led to the accident.	
judgment *noun*	the forming of an opinion after careful thought	The **judgment** of the court is that she is not guilty.	Not guilty.

Draw a picture and write a sentence for each word.

Checkpoint

Explain the meaning of **sequence** and **judgment**.

Vocabulary Log

Reading Comprehension Questions

Think and Discuss

1. **Recall facts** Who took Antonio to Miss Maestas?
2. **Determine sequence of events** When do the other students first **point** to and laugh at Antonio? When do they do this a second time?
3. **Describe** Use your own words to describe the school.
4. **Understand figurative language** The author describes the doors of the school as "huge" and "yawning" (paragraph 2). He talks about sounds that seem to come from its "belly" (paragraph 4). What is the author comparing the school to? Why?
5. **Make a judgment** After the children laugh and **point** at Antonio, he decides to stay away from them and work alone. Do you think this is a good decision? Why or why not?
6. **Relate to your own experience** Antonio feels alone even though there are kids all around him. Have you ever felt this way? If so, when? Use Key Vocabulary words in your explanation.
7. **Revisit the Reading Focus Questions** Go back to page 334 and discuss the questions.

Workbook
page 232

Independent Practice
CD-ROM/Online

Literary Elements

First-Person and Third-Person Narratives

Bless Me, Ultima is told by Antonio. Antonio is a character in the story. A story told by a character in the story is called a **first-person narrative.** In first-person narratives, the narrator refers to himself or herself as "I."

Other stories are told in the third person and called **third-person narrative.** In this kind of narrative, the narrator is not a character in the story. The narrator just tells the story. The characters in the story are referred to as "he," "she," or "they."

1. Look at the first paragraph of *Bless Me, Ultima*. Look for places where Antonio refers to himself as "I" or "me."
2. Look at the Table of Contents on pages vii–xii to review the readings in this book. Find another example of a first-person narrative. Find an example of a third-person narrative.

> ✓ **Checkpoint**
>
> What is a **first-person narrative** and a **third-person narrative**? Explain in your own words.

Workbook
page 233

Independent Practice
CD-ROM/Online

Biomes and Ecosystems

● About the Reading

In *Bless Me, Ultima,* you read an excerpt from a novel about a boy struggling to belong in a new environment. Now you will read a textbook selection about animals and the environments they belong in. Animals are usually born into and stay in the same environment all their lives.

● Build Background

The Difference Between a Biome and an Ecosystem

A **biome** is a large region that has its own kind of weather. Each biome is filled with plants and animals that belong in that biome. Most of these plants and animals could not survive in another biome. Imagine a polar bear in a forest or a monkey in the desert!

An **ecosystem** is much smaller than a biome. An ecosystem is all of the plants and animals that live together in a particular area. It is the relationship between these living things and their environment.

● Vocabulary From the Reading

Use Context Clues to Determine Meaning

Complete each sentence with the correct Key Vocabulary word.

1. Summer and autumn are my favorite _____.

2. We need to _____ the apple into two pieces, one for you and one for me.

3. I prefer the _____ in the South: hot and sunny.

Key Vocabulary
climate
divide
seasons

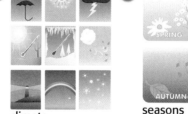
climate

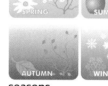
seasons

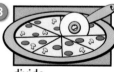
divide

✓ **Checkpoint**

1. What is your favorite **season**?
2. What is something you can **divide**?
3. What is the **climate** of your region?

Vocabulary Log

Workbook page 234

Independent Practice CD-ROM/Online

342 Unit 6 • Chapter 1

Reading Strategy

Paraphrase

When you **paraphrase**, you put a part of a text in your own words. As you read "Biomes and Ecosystems," follow these steps.

1. Stop reading when you come to a difficult sentence.
2. Read the sentence again. Look up unfamiliar words in a dictionary.
3. Say or write the sentence in your own words.

Text Genre

Informational Text: Textbook

"Biomes and Ecosystems" comes from a science **textbook.** Textbooks teach students about a specific content area. As you read, look for these common textbook features.

Textbook	
title	name of a reading
facts	information that can be proven
graphics	illustrations or charts that show information
captions	words that explain a picture or graphic

Build Your Knowledge

Before you read a text, look at the title, graphics, and captions. **Predict** what the reading is about. **Confirm** your prediction after you read. Making and confirming predictions will help you understand the text better.

Reading Focus Questions

As you read, think about these questions.

1. How does this reading connect to the theme of "belonging"?
2. What do you think was the author's purpose in writing "Biomes and Ecosystems"?
3. What kinds of biomes are there? Give an example of an animal that belongs in the desert biome. Explain one way that this animal can survive there.

✓Checkpoint

What does it mean to **paraphrase**? Explain how to paraphrase a part of a text.

Workbook
pages 235–236

Independent Practice
CD-ROM/Online

Biomes and Ecosystems

FOCUS QUESTION
Where do plants and animals live?

1 ecosystems
2 biomes
3 tundra
4 taiga
5 deciduous forest
6 rain forest
7 grassland
8 desert
9 community
10 population
11 species

1 | Ecosystems

2 | Biomes

3

5

7

8

Word Study
Word Origins

Deciduous comes from a Latin word, **decidere,** which means "to fall off."

Deciduous trees lose their leaves in the fall.

Deer antlers are **deciduous.** Deer lose their antlers each year.

Vocabulary in Context

A **biome** is an area where plants and animals live. Different plants and animals live in different biomes. Some live in dry **grasslands**. Others live in **deserts**. Some live in the cold **tundra** or **taiga**. Others live in wet **rain forests**. Many live in **deciduous forests**, where there are four **seasons**. Each of these large areas is a **biome**. The living and nonliving parts of a biome form an **ecosystem**. Plants and animals are living things. Nonliving things include rocks, water, and soil. An ecosystem can be large or small.

Living things in ecosystems are **divided** into smaller units. Each kind of living thing is called a **species**. All the members of a species living in an area form a **population**. Two or more populations of living things from the same area form a **community**.

Reading Strategy

Paraphrase
Paraphrase the first paragraph of the **Vocabulary in Context** box.

Viceroy butterfly

9

10

Florida panther

Armadillo

Roseate spoonbill

11

Florida panther

Raccoon

Florida panther

Sable palm

Florida panther

Florida panther

Indian blanket flower

Red grouper

✓ Check Your Understanding

1. Look at the pictures. What do all the Florida panthers in the picture form?
2. What things form an ecosystem?
3. Where do plants and animals live?

Critical Thinking Applying Information
4. What are some of the nonliving parts of a park ecosystem?

✔ Reading Check

1. **Recall facts** How many **seasons** are there in a deciduous forest?
2. **Recall facts** What forms a community?
3. **Analyze** What kind of biome would an elephant live in? A polar bear? A camel?

Reading Strategy

Paraphrase Paraphrase the **Desert Biomes** paragraph.

■ A Lizard and a Cactus Plant in a Desert Biome

■ A Kangaroo Rat in Its Habitat

Desert Biomes

A biome is a large area on Earth with a certain temperature and **rainfall.** Deserts are one kind of biome. Temperatures are from 20°C to 30°C. Rainfall is less than 25 cm a year. The living things there are **adapted** to that **climate.** Lizards and cactus plants are **equipped** to live in the desert. For example, cactus plants have special places for keeping water.

The Kangaroo Rat's Ecosystem

An ecosystem is made up of living things and nonliving things. Each species lives where it finds the things it needs. That place is its **habitat,** or home. The living things are adapted to live in that place. **Kangaroo rats** live in burrows (holes in the ground) in hot, dry, desert conditions. They do not have to drink water. They get all their water from seeds that they eat.

Word Study
Word Origins

Ecosystem is made up of two word parts.

- **Eco** comes from the Greek word **oikos,** which means "house."
- **System** comes from the Greek word **systema,** which means "to bring together."

An **ecosystem** brings together, or is made of, all the living and nonliving parts of a living thing's home.

● Reading Comprehension Questions

Think and Discuss

1. **Recall facts** How much rain falls each year in a desert biome?

2. **Understand word origins** What are the origins of the word *ecosystem*?

3. **Explain** How are kangaroo rats adapted to live in the desert ecosystem?

4. **Identify main idea and details** What is the main idea of the first paragraph of the **Vocabulary in Context** box? What are three details in the paragraph?

5. **Discuss** What is an ecosystem you know well? Describe the living and nonliving things in the ecosystem.

6. **Discuss** Why does the author write about the biome first and the ecosystem second?

7. **Revisit the Reading Focus Questions** Go back to page 343 and discuss the questions.

Workbook page 237 — Independent Practice CD-ROM/Online

Spelling

Silent **gh**

Workbook page 238 — Independent Practice CD-ROM/Online

Writing Conventions

Punctuation: Commas, Semicolons, and Dashes

Workbook page 239 — Independent Practice CD-ROM/Online

(S) Connect Readings 1 and 2

You have read two readings on the theme of belonging. Use these activities to make connections between the readings.

1. With a partner, use this chart to compare the two readings.

Reading title	What is the text genre?	Who or what is the reading about?	What is the purpose of the reading?	Which reading were you most interested in? Why?
BLESS ME, ULTIMA				
Biomes and Ecosystems				

2. **Revisit the Chapter Focus Questions** What gives people a feeling of belonging? Use examples from *Bless Me, Ultima*. What makes animals belong in a certain place? Use "Biomes and Ecosystems" to answer this question.

● Listening and Speaking

Retell a Story

Phrases for Conversation

Sequence Words

First, . . .
Second, . . .
Then, . . .
Next, . . .
After that, . . .
Finally, . . .

Imagine you want to tell the story of *Bless Me, Ultima* to a person who has not read it. Work with a partner to retell the story in your own words.

1. Discuss the important events and details.

   a. First, without looking back at the reading, discuss and take notes on the important events and details you remember.

   b. Talk about the main character's motivation and how he changes during the story. Take notes.

   c. Then, look back at the reading on pages 335–339. Skim (look quickly through) the reading to check your notes.

2. Retell the story to your class.

   a. Practice retelling the story, using the **Sequence** Words from the **Phrases for Conversation** box.

   b. Retell the story to your class. Take turns with your partner retelling different parts. Convey the story through your words, tone, and gestures. This will keep your audience's attention.

3. Your classmates will ask you questions to clarify information.

   a. Did you and your partner include all the important events and details from the story?

   b. Were there important events and details you forgot to include?

   c. Did you retell the story in the correct **sequence**?

● Reading Fluency

Paired Reading

Working with a partner can help you improve your reading fluency.

1. Find a partner. Read paragraphs 1 and 2 of *Bless Me, Ultima* (on page 335) silently.

2. Read the paragraph out loud three times while your partner listens.

3. During the third reading, your partner will take notes on your errors. After the reading, your partner will give you suggestions and feedback.

4. Now, change roles. Have your partner do the readings while you listen and take notes.

● Vocabulary Development

Frequently Used Foreign Words in English

Many words we use frequently in English come from other languages, in particular, many words for foods. When people from different countries came to the United States, they brought foods from their countries. As these foods became popular in the United States, the names of the foods became part of the English language.

Look at this sentence from *Bless Me, Ultima*. Can you find the words that come from Spanish?

> My mother had packed a small jar of hot beans and some good, green chile wrapped in tortillas.

If you chose *chile* and *tortillas,* you are correct!

1. Work with a partner. Guess the language that each food word comes from. Use a dictionary to check your guesses.

   a. taco   **f.** enchilada

   b. sushi   **g.** bagel

   c. spinach   **h.** tea

   d. pizza   **i.** soy

   e. croissant   **j.** pasta

2. Work with a partner. Choose one of the food words above. Don't tell your partner the word. Tell the language the word is from and what the food is like. Your partner will guess the word.

> It is a French word. It is a kind of bread. It has flour and lots of butter. You can put jam on it.

> It's a croissant!

✓ Checkpoint

1. How have some **foreign words** come into the English language?

2. What are some examples of foreign words that are frequently used in English?

Vocabulary Log

Workbook page 240

Independent Practice CD-ROM/Online

● Grammar

The Present Perfect Tense

Use the **present perfect tense** to say that something happened in the past when the exact time is not important.

I **have visited** Spain and Italy.
She **has read** that book.

Use the **present perfect tense** with **for** and **since** to talk about something that started in the past and continues to the present. Use **for** to talk about a period of time. Use **since** for a specific time.

John **has lived** in Florida **for** ten years.
They **have been** sick **since** Monday.

The Present Perfect Tense			
subject	***has / have***	**past participle**	
I / You / We / They	**have**	**gone**	to Europe.
He / She / It	**has**		

Practice the Grammar

A. Use the phrases to write sentences about things you have done in this chapter.

1. read a short story

2. learn about biomes and ecosystems

3. practice making inferences

4. answer questions

B. Complete these sentences with information about yourself.

1. I have lived in this town/city for…

2. I have lived here since…

3. I have been in class since…

Use the Grammar Independently

Write five sentences about things you have done in your life. Read your sentences to the class.

I have ridden on a camel.

Grammar Expansion

The Present Perfect—Negative and Question Forms

Workbook pages 242

Independent Practice CD-ROM/Online

✓ Checkpoint

1. When should you use the **present perfect tense**?

2. Give an example of a sentence with the present perfect tense.

Workbook page 241

Independent Practice CD-ROM/Online

● Grammar

The Past Perfect Tense

Use the **past perfect tense** to talk about one action or event that took place before another event took place in the past.

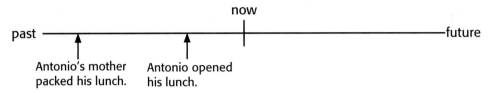

now

past ———————————————————————— future

Antonio's mother packed his lunch.

Antonio opened his lunch.

Antonio opened his lunch. (simple past)
Antonio's mother **had packed** his lunch earlier that morning. (past perfect)

The Present Perfect Tense			
subject	***had***	**past participle**	
I			hard before the test.
He / She	**had**	**studied**	
You / We / They			

Note

Pronouns with **had** can be contracted: **I'd, he'd, she'd, you'd, we'd, they'd.**

Practice the Grammar Copy these sentences from *Bless Me, Ultima.* Complete each sentence with the past perfect tense of the verb.

1. (expect) The school was larger than I _____.
2. (pack) My mother _____ a small jar of hot beans.
3. (try) I _____ hard to learn.
4. (laugh) They _____ at me.
5. (open) I _____ my lunch to eat and again they had laughed and **pointed** at me.
6. (sneak) I saw two other boys who _____ out of the room.

Use the Grammar Independently Write five sentences about things that had already happened before you arrived in class today.

The teacher had turned on the lights.

Workbook
page 243

Independent Practice
CD-ROM/Online

Grammar Expansion

The Past Perfect—
Negative and Question
Forms

Workbook
page 244

Independent Practice
CD-ROM/Online

✓ *Checkpoint*

1. When should you use the **past perfect tense**?

2. Give an example of a sentence with the past perfect tense.

● **Writing Assignment**

Business Letter: Write a Letter of Interest

Writing Suggestion

See **Milestones Handbook**.
pages 393–433

Writing Prompt

Volunteering is a good way to feel like you belong to your community. It can also help prepare you for a future career. Think about an organization or place you would like to be a part of. Write a letter to express your interest in volunteering there. Explain why you want to volunteer. Also explain why your interests and experience would make you a good volunteer. Use the present perfect to tell about your experience.

Write Your Letter of Interest

1. **Read the student model.** It will help you understand the assignment. Pay attention to the format of the letter.

Student Model

your address

407 Bell Street
Miami, Florida 33016

the date

April 5, 2008

the address of the place you are writing to

American Society for the Prevention of Cruelty to Animals
302 Atwood Avenue
Miami, Florida 33011

Dear Sir or Madam:

body

I am very interested in doing volunteer work with your organization. I have always loved animals. I have had many animals. Right now I have a dog, two cats, and three fish. I take care of all of these animals myself. I have also taken care of a few stray animals, and I have found them homes. One day I want to be a veterinarian.

I hope you will let me volunteer at the ASPCA. I think I can be very helpful to your organization. I also think I would learn a lot from working at the ASPCA.

closing

Sincerely,

signature

Michelle Saint-Hubert

Workbook
page 245

2. **Choose a place where you would like to volunteer.** You may want to volunteer at one of these places in your community.

- a hospital
- a park
- a library
- a senior center
- another place in your community

3. **Write your letter.** Remember to tell about

- why you are interested in volunteering there
- your related interests
- your related experience

4. **Revise.** Reread your letter. Check for parts that are not clear or complete.
    Use the **editing and proofreading symbols** on page 419 to mark any changes you want to make.

5. **Edit.** Use the **Writing Checklist** to help you find problems and errors.

Writing Checklist

1. I clearly stated my purpose (why I want to volunteer).

2. I wrote about my interests and experience.

3. I used the present perfect tense to talk about my experience.

4. I formatted my letter correctly.

Writing Support

Format

Format of a Business Letter

1. When you write a **business letter,** make sure to include

- your address
- the full date (do not use abbreviations)
- the address of the place you are writing to
- a greeting (also called a salutation)

Use a colon (:) after the greeting in a business letter.

- a closing
- your signature

2. Be sure to capitalize

- the month
- the names of businesses and organizations
- all first and last names and titles
- the first letter of the greeting
- the first letter of the closing

Apply Check your letter. Have you used the correct business letter format?

Workbook
pages 246–248

Independent Practice
CD-ROM/Online

Progress Check

How well did you understand this chapter? Try to answer the questions. If necessary, go back to the pages listed for a review.

Skills	Skills Assessment Questions	Pages to Review
Vocabulary From the Readings	What do these words mean? • **custom, loneliness, pleased, point, protection, rude, weak** • **climate, divide, seasons**	332 342
Academic Vocabulary	What do these academic vocabulary words mean? • **analyze, insight** • **judgment, sequence**	333 340
Reading Strategies	What does it mean to **make an inference**? What does it mean to **paraphrase**?	333 343
Text Genres	What is the text genre of *Bless Me, Ultima*? What is the text genre of "Biomes and Ecosystems"?	334 343
Reading Comprehension	What is *Bless Me, Ultima* about? What is "Biomes and Ecosystems" about?	341 347
Literary Elements	What is a first-person narrative? What is a third-person narrative? What kind of narrative is *Bless Me, Ultima*?	341
Spelling	Pronounce these **silent gh** words: night, bought, daughter, right.	347
Writing Conventions	When can you use a **semi-colon**? A **dash**?	347
Listening and Speaking	**Phrases for Conversation** What words can you use to indicate **sequence**?	348
Vocabulary Development	What are three examples of frequently used **foreign words in English**?	349
Grammar	When is the **present perfect tense** used? Give an example of a present perfect tense sentence.	350
	When is the **past perfect tense** used? Give an example of a past perfect tense sentence.	351
Writing Support: Format	Describe how to format a **business letter**.	353

Assessment Practice

Read this passage. Then answer Questions 1 through 4.

New Places

1   My parents thought it would be easiest if we moved to the United States in the summer. That sounded good. But this summer has been the hardest of my life.

2   After we moved into our apartment, my brother and I couldn't wait to go to the city pool. We walked through the gate and were amazed. Parents and children were running everywhere. I stayed close to my brother for protection. I felt a sudden loneliness. The sounds of English came loud and fast. I wanted to turn and run, but I looked at my brother. He smiled. I took a deep breath. Together we dove into the crowd and then into the pool.

1 What does the word <u>loneliness</u> mean in this sentence from paragraph 2?

> I felt a sudden loneliness.

A happiness

B confusion

C fear

D sadness about being alone

2 What inference can you make from the following sentence?

> I stayed close to my brother for protection.

A The narrator is older than the brother.

B The narrator and the brother are twins.

C The brother is older than the narrator.

D The narrator can't swim.

3 Which line shows you the story is a first-person narrative?

A Parents and children were running everywhere.

B My brother pulled my hand.

C The sounds of English came loud and fast.

D He smiled.

4 How does the narrator change at the end of the story?

A The narrator starts to have fun.

B The narrator wants to go home.

C The narrator is rude.

D The narrator learns to swim.

Writing on Demand: Business Letter

Your school is having an International Day celebration. You want local businesses to donate prizes for the best food. Write a business letter asking for donations. **(20 minutes)**

> **Writing Tip**
> Remember to clearly state your purpose for writing your letter.

CHAPTER 2

Objectives

Reading Strategies
Summarize; Relate your own experiences to a reading

Listening and Speaking
Interview an immigrant

Grammar
Learn about complex sentences with time clauses

Writing
Biography: Write a short biography

Academic Vocabulary

organize	process
brief	authentic

Academic Content
Ellis Island, New York
U.S. immigration
Vietnam

● **Chapter Focus Question**
How do immigrants find a sense of belonging in a new country?

Reading 1 **Content:** Social Studies
Informational text
If Your Name Was Changed at Ellis Island
by Ellen Levine

Primary source document
I Was Dreaming to Come to America
Memories selected by Veronica Lawlor

Reading 2 **Literature**
Novel (excerpt)
Seedfolks
by Paul Fleischman

If Your Name Was Changed at Ellis Island

● **About the Reading**
You are going to read an informational text. It is about the experience of immigrants who arrived at Ellis Island in New York. Immigrants are people who come to another country to live.

Ellis Island
in New York Harbor

● Build Background

Ellis Island

Ellis Island, in New York Harbor, was the most important immigration station in United States history. It opened in 1892 and closed in 1954. During those years, over 12 million people entered the United States through Ellis Island. Today, more than 100 million Americans (or over 40 percent of the U.S. population) are related to immigrants who passed through Ellis Island. The main building on Ellis Island is now a museum.

The Statue of Liberty and Ellis Island

One of the first things the immigrants saw as they arrived in New York Harbor was the Statue of Liberty. How do you think immigrants felt as they passed the Statue of Liberty on their way to Ellis Island?

● Use Prior Knowledge

Brainstorm Reasons for Immigration

What are some reasons why people immigrate (come to a different country)? Brainstorm ideas with a partner. Copy the picture of the Statue of Liberty's head. Write your ideas in the crown.

Before Reading 1

Key Vocabulary

- avoid
- familiar
- million
- nation
- roots
- stranger

● Vocabulary From the Reading

Learn, Practice, and Use Independently

Learn Vocabulary Read the paragraph. Pay attention to the **highlighted** words. Use the context to determine the meanings of these words. Discuss the meanings with a small group.

My grandmother was born in Ireland. She came to America when she was 18. It was difficult to be an immigrant. She had moved 3,000 miles from home. However, it felt like a **million** miles to my grandmother. She had left everything **familiar** to her including her town, her family, and her friends. She didn't know anyone here. Everyone was a **stranger.** She was shy. At first, she tried to **avoid** talking to people. However, soon she put down **roots** in America. She got married and had children. She and my grandfather worked hard to make a good life in America. People like my grandparents helped make America a great **nation.**

Practice Vocabulary Write the Key Vocabulary word for each definition.

Word	Definition
million	1,000,000 of something
1.	to stay away from, to not do something
2.	an independent country with its own government
3.	connections to a place
4.	known about
5.	an unfamiliar person

Use Vocabulary Independently Write one sentence for each Key Vocabulary word. Read your sentences to a partner.

✓Checkpoint

Draw pictures to represent two Key Vocabulary words. Your partner will guess the words. Take turns.

Vocabulary Log

Workbook page 249

Independent Practice CD-ROM/Online

● Academic Vocabulary

Vocabulary for the Reading Strategy

Word	Explanation	Sample Sentence	Visual Cue
organize *verb*	to put in order, to arrange	I organize my socks by color.	
brief *adjective*	short in length or time	Her speech was very brief.	

Draw a picture and write a sentence for each word.

● Reading Strategy

Summarize

When you **summarize** a reading or a section of a reading, you give only the most important ideas. A **summary** is brief. Summarizing helps you remember the important information in a reading. Use this strategy after you read *If Your Name Was Changed at Ellis Island*.

1. Reread each page. Take notes on the most important ideas on each page. Do not include any details.
2. **Organize** your notes. Make sure they are in a logical order (an order that makes sense).
3. Write the main ideas in your own words and in as few words as possible. This is your summary.

Page	Notes	My Summary
page 361		
page 362		
page 363		
page 364		

✓**Checkpoint**
What is a **summary**? How do you create a summary?

Vocabulary Log

Workbook page 250

Independent Practice CD-ROM/Online

● **Text Genre**

Informational Text and Primary Source Documents

If Your Name Was Changed at Ellis Island is an **informational text.** An informational text includes facts and details.

I Was Dreaming to Come to America is a collection of **primary source documents.** Look at the information about this kind of document.

Primary Source Document	
types of primary source documents	diaries, letters, speeches, interviews
who creates them	people who lived during a certain time in history and who have direct knowledge of the events of that time
purpose for reading them	to help us understand the time in history when they were created

● **Meet the Author**

Ellen Levine was born in New York City. Levine is a writer and teacher. She has taught adults and teenagers in English as a Second Language programs. She writes both fiction and nonfiction, but most of her books have been nonfiction. Levine says, "I enjoy learning new things and meeting new people, even if they lived 200 years ago."

● **Reading Focus Questions**

As you read, think about these questions.

1. How does this reading connect to the theme of "belonging"?

2. What do you think was the author's purpose in writing *If Your Name Was Changed at Ellis Island*?

3. What was it like to be an immigrant arriving at Ellis Island?

✓**Checkpoint**

1. Name two kinds of **primary source documents.**

2. What is the purpose for reading a primary source document?

Workbook
page 251

Independent Practice
CD-ROM/Online

If Your Name Was Changed at Ellis Island

by Ellen Levine

1   America has always been a **nation** of immigrants. Even the first Americans were immigrants. They were groups of people who probably crossed the **Bering Strait** over a strip of land. This strip connected North America with Asia thousands and thousands of years ago.

2   When the thirteen **colonies** were first **settled,** most immigrants came from England, Holland, and France. Soon there were Scandinavians, Welsh, Scots, Scotch-Irish, Irish, and Germans. In 1643, there were at least eighteen different languages spoken in the streets of America.

3   By the end of the 1800s, Italians, Poles, Armenians, Russians, and others from southern and eastern Europe poured into America. On the west coast, Chinese and Japanese immigrants arrived.

Immigrants on a ship headed to Ellis Island

4   It was the greatest human **migration** in history. We don't know exactly how many people came. For long periods no records were kept. We do know that nearly 35 **million** people came to America between 1820 and 1924. In 1924, **strict** laws were passed to limit the number of immigrants entering the country.

> **Reading Strategy**
>
> **Summarize** Summarize paragraph 4.

5   For most immigrants, the trip was difficult and often dangerous. They traveled for weeks or months. Then they arrived in a place where they didn't speak the language. They often had nowhere to live and little money. Yet they poured into America.

6   For these immigrants, America was their destination. Ellis Island was their first stop.

> **Reading Check**
>
> 1. **Recall facts** Where did the first Americans probably come from?
> 2. **Evaluate** How does the picture help you understand the text better?

Bering Strait stretch of water that separates Alaska from Eastern Siberia
colonies groups of people living in an area of land governed by a distant country
settled moved into by people making a home there
migration the act of moving from one country or region to settle in another
strict severe

7   Ellis Island was an immigration center in New York Harbor. **Millions** of immigrants passed through Ellis Island. They were examined by doctors and legal inspectors. Some were allowed to enter right away. Some were held for a while. Some were sent back.

8   Most immigrants to America came through Ellis Island, but not all. Some entered through other east coast ports in Boston, Philadelphia, or Baltimore. Some entered through southern or southwestern ports like New Orleans and Galveston. Others entered through west coast cities like San Francisco. In 1907, more immigrants came to the United States than at any other time. There were seventy immigration stations. But ninety percent of all the **newcomers** passed through Ellis Island.

Reading Strategy

Summarize Summarize paragraph 9.

9   Not all immigrants who arrived in New York had to go through Ellis Island. People with the most expensive tickets on the ship were lucky. Immigration inspectors examined them on the ship. If they passed the inspection, they entered the country when the boat **docked** in New York. The poor immigrants with cheap tickets were taken to Ellis Island.

Legal inspectors processing an immigrant

---

newcomers recent arrivals

docked approached a dock and then tied up to it

10 Why did people leave their homelands? Some people left because of terrible events like an earthquake or **famine.** In Ireland, for example, a terrible disease in the mid-1800s destroyed the potato crop. Nearly 2 **million** people died of **starvation.** Almost as many people left for America.

11 **Millions** of immigrants **fled** for other reasons. In the late 1800s and early 1900s, thousands of Russian Jews were killed in **massacres.** More than 2 **million** Jews left Russia and eastern Europe because of these massacres.

12 Thousands of people fled their country for other reasons. Many left to **avoid** serving in their government's army. Some left because of sickness at home. A deadly **flu epidemic** in Turkey, for example, sent many people from their homes.

13 Most people left because they couldn't **earn a living** in their country. Newly invented factory machines replaced many workers. New farm machinery also put many small farmers out of work. As people left the countryside for the cities, they lived in crowded and poor conditions. In America, they hoped to find work and a better life.

> ◁ **Reading Strategy**
>
> **Summarize** Summarize paragraph 13.

Just Off the Ship, by Martha Walter

✓ Reading Check

1. **Recall facts** Why did so many Irish people come to America in the mid-1800s?

2. **Recall facts** What other country had a famine in the 1800s?

3. **Understand cause and effect** What caused many workers to be unable to make a living in their country anymore?

---

famine serious lack of food
starvation the state of being extremely hungry and having no food
fled ran away
massacres events when many people are brutally killed
flu short for *influenza*—a contagious illness spread by viruses
epidemic situation where a disease spreads quickly among many people
earn a living get enough money from working to pay for the things needed to live

14   Many people called America the "Golden Land." They believed it was a place where you could get a good job, go to a free school, and eat well. There was a **saying** in Polish that people came to America *za chlebem*—"for bread." One person added that they came "for bread, with butter."

Reading Strategy

Summarize Summarize paragraph 15.

15   Some people came to look for work. **Wages** were higher in America than in their home countries. Until the late 1800s, businesses often sent **agents** overseas to encourage workers to migrate. If you agreed to work for their companies, they paid your way to America.

16   Many people came because there was a lot of cheap land. In 1862, the U.S. government passed a law called the Homestead Act. Immigrants could **stake a claim** to 160 **acres** of land. They needed to live on and work the land for five years. Then they would pay a small amount of money. Then the land would be theirs.

17   Some new western states advertised in European newspapers about their growing towns and cheap farmland. They wanted new settlers. Often the advertisements were not true. They showed pictures of towns that were not real. They gave descriptions of farm fields where forests stood. But people came anyway. They were searching, always searching, for a better life.

Immigrants arriving in New York City

---

saying familiar statement expressing something generally accepted as wise or true

wages money paid for work done

agents people who do business for others

stake a claim demand or ask for ownership, especially of a piece of land

acres square pieces of land measuring 69.57 yards on each side

I Was Dreaming to Come to America

Memories selected by Veronica Lawlor

The following memories were written by immigrants who arrived at Ellis Island in the early 1900s.

Immigrant children at Ellis Island

1   I feel like I had two lives. You plant something in the ground, it has its **roots,** and then you **transplant** it where it stays **permanently.** That's what happened to me. You put an end and forget about your childhood; I became a man here. All of a sudden, I started life new, **amongst** people whose language I didn't understand. It was a different life; everything was different but I never **despaired,** I was **optimistic.**

2   And this is the only country where you're not a **stranger,** because we are all **strangers.** It's only a matter of time who got here first.

> Lazarus Salamon
> Hungary
> Arrived in 1920, age 16

3   My father left when I was two years old for America. I didn't know what he looked like. I didn't have the least idea. Then I saw this man coming forward and he was beautiful. I didn't know he was my father. He was tall, **slender,** and he had brown, wavy hair, and to me he looked beautiful. He looked very **familiar** to me. Later on I realized why he looked **familiar** to me. He looked exactly like I did.

> Katherine Beychok
> Russia
> Arrived in 1910, age 10

> **Reading Strategy**
>
> **Summarize** Summarize paragraph 3.

> ✓ **Reading Check**
>
> 1. **Recall facts** How old was Lazarus Salamon when he came to America?
>
> 2. **Make an inference** What did Katherine Beychok's hair look like? How do you know?

---

transplant uproot carefully and plant somewhere else

permanently forever

amongst (British English spelling) surrounded by

despaired felt sadness without hope of relief

optimistic expecting the best

slender thin

● **Apply the Reading Strategy**

Summarize

Now complete the Reading Strategy chart.

1. Review the **Reading Strategy** on page 359.
2. Draw the chart on a piece of paper.
3. Reread each page of the reading. Take notes on the most important ideas on each page.
4. **Organize** your notes.
5. Write the main ideas in your own words and in as few words as possible. This is your summary.

Page	Notes	My Summary
Page 361	• America has always been a **nation** of immigrants. • Nearly 35 **million** people came to America between 1820 and 1924. • For most, the trip was difficult and often dangerous. Yet they poured into America. • Ellis Island was their first stop in America.	Immigrants have always come to America. **Millions** of immigrants came to America between 1820 and 1924. The trip to America was difficult but many immigrants came anyway. They arrived first at Ellis Island.

● **Academic Vocabulary**

Vocabulary for the Reading Comprehension Questions

Word	Explanation	Sample Sentence	Visual Cue
process *noun*	a series of actions that brings about a result	The **process** of finding a job can take a long time. First, you write a resumé. Then, you go for an interview. Hopefully, then you get the job!	
authentic *adjective*	real, not fake	The store clerk checks all $100 bills to make sure they are **authentic**.	authentic fake

Draw a picture and write a sentence for each word.

✓**Checkpoint**

Explain the meanings of **process** and **authentic** in your own words.

Vocabulary Log

Reading Comprehension Questions

Think and Discuss

1. **Recall facts** Where did most of the immigrants come from when the colonies were first settled?

2. **Explain steps in a process** What steps could immigrants follow to get their own land through the Homestead Act?

3. **Analyze photos** How does the look and feel of the photos add to the effect of the reading?

4. **Discuss** Do you think it is easier to come to a new country as a young person or as an older person? Why? Use Key Vocabulary words in your answer.

5. **Discuss** The two memories in *I was Dreaming to Come to America* are **authentic.** How do we know they are authentic? Why is it important to read authentic texts?

6. **Revisit the Reading Focus Questions** Go back to page 360 and discuss the questions.

Workbook
page 252

Independent Practice
CD-ROM/Online

Text Elements

Photos and Captions

Informational texts about times in modern history often include **photos.** Photos help you see things you read about in the text and sometimes give you more information.

Photos in informational texts usually have **captions.** Captions are explanations of the photos.

Look at the photos on each page of the reading. Then make a chart like the one here.

Page	Photo Description	Related Text	Extra Information from the Photo
page 361	A black and white photo of a ship of immigrants.	We do know that nearly 35 **million** people came to America between 1820 and 1924. They poured into America.	The immigrant ships were very crowded.

√Checkpoint

1. What are **photos** and **captions**?

2. How can photos help you understand a text better?

Workbook
page 253

Independent Practice
CD-ROM/Online

Seedfolks

About the Reading

In *If Your Name Was Changed at Ellis Island,* you read an informational text about immigration to the United States. You also read immigrants' memories of arriving at Ellis Island in *I Was Dreaming to Come to America.* Now you will read a short story about Kim, a Vietnamese girl who immigrated to the United States.

Build Background

Community Gardens

Community gardens usually begin with an empty piece of land. This land is divided up and assigned to people who want to garden. People grow flowers and fresh fruits and vegetables in community gardens. Community gardens also bring people in the community together. There are about 10,000 community gardens in the United States.

Vocabulary From the Reading

Use Context Clues to Determine Meaning

Use the context of the sentences to determine the meaning of the **highlighted** word. Discuss the meanings with a small group.

1. Firefighters show their **bravery** every time they enter a burning building.
2. We own a small **lot** next to our house. We park our car there.
3. The bus was late. However, she waited with **patience** until it came.
4. The **soil** near the beach is sandy and rocky.

Key Vocabulary

bravery

lot

patience

soil

✓Checkpoint

1. Name a situation that calls for **bravery.**
2. Name a situation when you need **patience.**

Vocabulary Log

Workbook page 254

Independent Practice CD-ROM/Online

Reading Strategy

Relate Your Own Experiences to a Reading

Relate your own experiences to the experiences of the characters in a reading. This will help you understand the character and the story better.

As you read *Seedfolks,* think about these questions: How are you similar to Kim, the main character? Do you have the same feelings? Have you had the same experiences? How are you different?

Text Genre

Novel

You are going to read an excerpt (a part) from a **novel** called *Seedfolks.* A novel is a long work of fiction. A novel includes the features below. Look for these features as you read the excerpt from *Seedfolks.*

Novel	
character	a person in the story
setting	where and when the story happens
details and descriptions	information that helps the reader imagine a story and makes the story real and interesting

Meet the Author

Paul Fleischman is the author of many award-winning books for young readers. His father, Sid Fleischman, is also a well-known writer. Fleischman says that words have always been his world. "We grew up knowing that words felt good in the ears and on the tongue, that they were as much fun to play with as toys."

Reading Focus Questions

As you read, think about these questions.

1. How does this reading connect to the theme of "belonging"?
2. What do you think was the author's purpose in writing *Seedfolks*?
3. What can a person do to create a feeling of belonging in a new place?

Workbook
pages 255–256

Independent Practice
CD-ROM/Online

✓Checkpoint

1. What does it mean to **relate your own experiences to a reading**?
2. How can a reader do this?

Seedfolks

by Paul Fleischman

1   The sidewalk was completely empty. It was Sunday, early in April. An icy wind **teetered** trash cans and turned my cheeks to **marble.** In Vietnam we had no weather like that. Here in Cleveland people call it spring. I walked half a block, then crossed the street and reached the **vacant lot.**

2   I stood tall and **scouted**. No one was sleeping on the old couch in the middle. I'd never entered the **lot** before, or wanted to. I did so now, picking my way between tires and trash bags. I nearly stepped on two rats **gnawing** and froze. Then I told myself that I must show my **bravery.** I continued further, and chose a spot far from the sidewalk and hidden from view by a **rusty** refrigerator. I had to keep my project safe.

Reading Strategy

Relate Your Own Experiences to a Reading The girl is scared but tries to be brave. Have you ever felt like this? If so, when?

Why do you think it is warmer in Vietnam than in Cleveland, Ohio?

---

teetered rocked back and forth dangerously

marble type of stone that is cut and polished for use in floors, walls, statues, and decoration

vacant empty

scouted looked for and collected information

gnawing biting or chewing something over a period of time

rusty covered with rust

3   I took out my spoon and began to dig. The snow had melted, but the ground was hard. After much work, I finished one hole, then a second, then a third. I thought about how my mother and sisters remembered my father, how they knew his face from every angle and held in their fingers the feel of his hands. I had no such memories to cry over. I'd been born eight months after he'd died. Worse, he had no memories of me.

Reading Strategy

Relate Your Own Experiences to a Reading The girl digs the holes even though it is hard work. Have you ever worked hard at a task even though it was difficult? If so, when and why?

Women Gardening, by Tilly Willis

Compare and contrast this scene with the scene in the story.

Reading Check

1. **Recall facts** When did the girl's father die?

2. **Make predictions** What do you think the girl is going to do with the holes she is digging? Confirm your prediction after you finish the story.

4

I dug six holes. All his life in Vietnam my father had been a farmer. Here our apartment house had no yard. But in that vacant **lot** he would see me. He would watch my beans break ground and spread, and would notice with pleasure their **pods** growing **plump**. He would see my **patience** and my hard work. I would show him that I could **raise** plants, as he had. I would show him that I was his daughter.

5

My class had **sprouted** lima beans in paper cups the year before. I now placed a bean in each of the holes. I covered them up, pressing the **soil** down firmly with my fingertips. I opened my **thermos** and watered them all. And I **vowed** to myself that those beans would **thrive.**

Reading Strategy

Relate Your Own Experiences to a Reading The girl is gardening to make her father proud of her. Have you ever done something to make someone proud of you? If so, what?

Epilogue

Kim's idea to grow plants in the vacant **lot** gives her neighbors the idea of starting a community garden. This garden not only changes the **lot,** but it brings a sense of community to the whole neighborhood.

Lima bean plant

Lima bean flower

Lima bean seed pod

---

pods long, narrow cases in which seeds grow on certain plants, such as peas and beans

plump round in shape

raise grow and care for

sprouted grown

thermos container used to keep drinks hot or cold

vowed promised

thrive grow strong and healthy

After Reading 2

● Reading Comprehension Questions

Think and Discuss

1. **Recall facts** What country is Kim from? Where does she live now?
2. **Summarize** Summarize the story. Use Key Vocabulary words.
3. **Identify mood** What is the mood of this story?
4. **Identify similarities across texts** In what ways is this story similar to *Bless Me, Ultima* (page 335)? Think about elements like theme, characters, and settings.
5. **Revisit the Reading Focus Questions** Go back to page 369 and discuss the questions.

Workbook
page 257

Independent Practice
CD-ROM/Online

Spelling

Silent **l**

Workbook
page 258

Independent Practice
CD-ROM/Online

Writing Conventions

Punctuation: Colons and Dashes

Workbook
page 259

Independent Practice
CD-ROM/Online

(S) Connect Readings 1 and 2

In this chapter, you have read selections on the theme of belonging. Use these activities to make connections between the readings.

1. Compare the readings by discussing these questions in a small group.

   a. Do you think the character in *Seedfolks* came to America through Ellis Island? Why or why not?

   b. In *If Your Name Was Changed at Ellis Island*, the author says that many people called America the "Golden Land." Do you think the character in *Seedfolks* thinks of America as the "Golden Land"? Why or why not?

   c. A **symbol** is something that represents something else. For example, a flag can be symbol of a country. Discuss these questions about symbols in a small group.

      • What do you think seeds and planting are symbols of in *Seedfolks*?

      • How are these same symbols used in Lazarus Salamon's letter in *I Was Dreaming to Come to America*?

2. **Revisit the Chapter Focus Question** How do immigrants find a sense of belonging in a new country? Use examples from *If Your Name Was Changed at Ellis Island*, *I Was Dreaming to Come to America*, and *Seedfolks* to answer the question.

Phrases for Conversation

Interrupting

Excuse me . . .

Pardon me . . .

I'm sorry to interrupt, but . . .

Could I ask you a question about that?

Requesting Information

Please, could you tell me . . . ?

Would you mind telling me . . . ?

I wonder if you could tell me . . . ?

● **Listening and Speaking**

Interview an Immigrant

1. Interview someone who immigrated to the United States. Ask questions such as:
   a. Where did you come from?
   b. When and why did you come to the United States?
   c. What was the most difficult thing about coming to the United States?
   d. What was the best thing?
   e. How has your life changed?
2. Take notes on the interview.
3. You may need to interrupt the speaker or request more information. Use the phrases from the **Phrases for Conversation** box.
4. Report back to your class on your interview.

● **Reading Fluency**

Rapid Word Recognition: Words Ending in Silent *e*

Good readers recognize words quickly. This helps them read fluently. Below is a list of key words from the readings with a silent -**e** at the end. After each key word there is a line followed by other words. As quickly as possible, point to the word that matches the key word. See how many words you can point to in 10 seconds or less. Your partner will time you.

1.	froze	safe	face	place	hole	froze
2.	face	hole	safe	froze	face	place
3.	safe	place	face	hole	froze	safe
4.	place	froze	place	safe	face	hole
5.	hole	face	hole	froze	place	safe
6.	safe	froze	face	safe	place	hole
7.	hole	hole	safe	place	froze	face
8.	froze	safe	place	froze	face	hole
9.	place	froze	hole	face	place	safe
10.	face	safe	face	place	froze	hole

Finally, read the 10 words in the first column aloud. Your partner will time you. Count how many words you read correctly in 15 seconds.

Vocabulary Development

Denotative and Connotative Meaning

A word's **denotative meaning** is the meaning you find in the dictionary. The denotative meaning of the word *mother* is *female parent*.

A word's **connotative meaning** is the feelings you connect to the word. This includes more than the word's dictionary meaning. The connotative meaning of the word *mother* includes ideas like *love, comfort,* and *protection*.

Authors choose words carefully. The connotative meanings of the words they choose give the reader additional information about the characters and events in the story. When you read, pay attention to the words the author chooses.

1. Work with a partner. Read these sentences from *Seedfolks*.

    a. The sidewalk was completely **empty.**

    b. An icy wind turned my cheeks to **marble.**

    c. I nearly stepped on two **rats.**

    d. I thought about how my mother and sisters remembered my **father.**

2. Look up the meaning of the **bold** words in a dictionary.

3. Copy the chart. Write the dictionary definition of each word in the "Denotative" column.

4. Talk with your partner about the connotative meaning of each word.

5. Write your ideas about the connotative meaning of each word in the "Connotative" column.

6. Share your ideas with the class.

	Denotative	Connotative
a. empty		
b. marble		
c. rat		
d. father		

✓ Checkpoint

Choose two Key Vocabulary words from this chapter. Explain the **connotative** and **denotative meanings** of these words.

Vocabulary Log

Workbook page 260

Independent Practice CD-ROM/Online

Grammar

Complex Sentences with Time Clauses

Use **complex sentences with time clauses** to talk about an event and when the event happened in a single sentence. Use time words to clarify the order of events.

Time Word	Meaning
before	earlier in time
after	later in time
when	at that time
while	during that time

A complex sentence is a sentence that includes a **main clause** and a **subordinate clause.**

- A main clause is an independent clause that can stand alone as a complete sentence.
- A subordinate clause is a dependent clause. It cannot stand alone.

A time clause tells **when** something happens. It is a kind of subordinate clause. A time clause has a subject and a verb, but it is not a complete sentence. It must be used with a main clause to form a complete sentence.

Main Clause	Time Clause
The woman came to the United States	**after** her husband found a job there.
Many immigrants did not speak English	**before** they arrived in the United States.
My mother came to America	**when** she was 16 years old.
She lived with her aunt	**while** she looked for a job.

Notes

1. When a complex sentence begins with the main clause, no comma is used between the clauses.

> My mother came to America when she was 16 years old.

2. When a complex sentence begins with the time clause, put a comma at the end of the time clause.

> When she was 16 years old, my mother came to America.

Practice the Grammar Copy these sentences about Kim from *Seedfolks*. Then <u>underline</u> the main clause and circle the time clause in each sentence.

1. The girl's father died before she was born.
2. Before the girl's family moved to Cleveland, they lived in Vietnam.
3. She almost stepped on two rats when she entered the vacant **lot.**
4. The girl tried to be brave while she looked for a place to plant her beans.
5. The snow had melted before she started to dig.
6. After she dug the holes, the girl covered them up.
7. She watered the beans after she covered them up.
8. While she planted the beans, she thought about her father.

> ### Grammar Expansion
>
> Complex Sentences with Other Kinds of Dependent Clauses;
> Compound Sentences with Two Independent Clauses
>
>
>
> Workbook   Independent Practice
> pages 263–264   CD-ROM/Online

Use the Grammar Independently Write complex sentences with time clauses about your life. Then share your sentences with a partner.

<u>I was born</u> after <u>my family moved to the United States.</u>

1. _____ after _____ .
2. Before _____ , _____ .
3. When _____ , _____ .
4. _____ while _____ .

> ### ✓Checkpoint
>
> 1. Give an example of a **complex sentence with a time clause.**
> 2. Identify the main clause and the time clause in your complex sentence.

● **Writing Assignment**

Short Biography

A **biography** is the story of a real person's life. Biographies are usually written in chronological order.

Writing Suggestion

See **Milestones Handbook**.
pages 393–433

Writing Prompt

Write a short biography about an immigrant. Include complex sentences with time clauses.

Write Your Short Biography

1. **Read the student model.** It will help you understand how to write your biography.

2. **Choose a person to write about.** You can write about the person you interviewed for the **Listening and Speaking** activity, or you can write about a new person.

3. **Interview the person.** Find out about the most important events in this person's life and take notes. For example:
   a. the person's birth date
   b. when the person came to the United States
   c. when the person got married

Student Model

Biography of Elena Arias

Elena Arias was born in Lima, Peru, in 1980. In 1999, she came to the United States. In 2000, she went to work in a restaurant. While she was working at the restaurant, she took English classes. She studied English and worked in the restaurant for one year. After she had learned enough English, she went to cooking school for two years. She got a job in another restaurant when she finished school in 2003. In 2005, she started her own Peruvian restaurant. She met Jorge Sanchez while she was working in the restaurant. Elena and Jorge got married in 2008. Elena says, "I love to cook, and I can make my living by cooking in my restaurant. I'm very lucky."

Workbook
page 265

4. **Create a timeline.** Organize the dates chronologically in a timeline.

5. **Write your short biography.** Make sure to include all the information from your timeline. Give more information and details about these events to make the biography more interesting. Another way to make the biography more interesting is to use direct quotations. (See the **Writing Support** box below.)

6. **Revise.** Check your biography for problems or errors. Revise it if any ideas are not clear or complete.

   Use the **editing and proofreading symbols** on page 419 to mark any changes you want to make.

7. **Edit.** Use the **Writing Checklist** to help you find problems and errors.

> ### Writing Checklist
>
> 1. I wrote about the most important events in the person's life.
>
> 2. I wrote about these events in chronological order.
>
> 3. I included complex sentences with time clauses.
>
> 4. I punctuated direct quotations correctly.

 **Writing Support**

Mechanics
Direct Quotations

Direct quotations are a person's exact words. Use direct quotations to make your writing more interesting.

> Levine says, "I enjoy learning new things and meeting new people, even if they lived 200 years ago."

To write direct quotations:

- Put quotation marks (". . .") around the words the person says.
- Use a capital letter with the first word of the direct quotation.
- If the quotation comes before the name of the speaker, place a comma (,) after the quote and before the closing quotation mark.

   > "When I first came to America, I was scared," says Bing Li.

- If the quotation comes after the name of the speaker, place the comma after the name and before the opening quotation mark.

   > Bing Li says, "When I first came to America, I was scared."

Apply Read your biography. Can you make it more interesting by adding one or more direct quotations?

Workbook
pages 266–268

Independent Practice
CD-ROM/Online

Progress Check

How well did you understand this chapter? Try to answer the questions. If necessary, go back to the pages listed for a review.

Skills	Skills Assessment Questions	Pages to Review
Vocabulary From the Readings	What do these words mean?	
	• **avoid, familiar, million, nation, roots, stranger**	358
	• **bravery, lot, patience, soil**	368
Academic Vocabulary	What do these academic vocabulary words mean?	
	• **brief, organize**	359
	• **authentic, process**	366
Reading Strategies	What does it mean to **summarize** a text?	359
	How can you **relate your own experiences to a reading**?	369
Text Genres	What is the text genre of *If Your Name Was Changed at Ellis Island*?	360
	What is the text genre of *I Was Dreaming to Come to America*?	360
	What is the text genre of *Seedfolks*?	369
Reading Comprehension	What are *If Your Name Was Changed at Ellis Island* and *I Was Dreaming to Come to America* about?	367
	What is *Seedfolks* about?	373
Spelling	Pronounce these **silent *l*** words: could, half, walk, Lincoln.	373
Writing Conventions	Give a sentence with a colon and a sentence with dashes.	373
Text Elements	How can **photos** and **captions** help you understand a text?	367
Listening and Speaking	**Phrases for Conversation**	
	What phrases can you use for interrupting someone and for requesting information?	374
Vocabulary Development	What is a word's **connotative** meaning? What is a word's **denotative** meaning?	375
Grammar	Give an example of a **complex sentence with a time clause**.	376
Writing Support: Mechanics	What is a **direct quotation**? Give an example in writing.	379

Assessment Practice

Read this passage. Then answer Questions 1 through 4.

The Cat Family

1   The leopard, cheetah, and jaguar all belong to the cat family. They are all large, spotted cats. They differ in where they live and how they move and hunt.

2   Leopards live in Asia and Africa. Jaguars live in the Americas. They live as far north as the southern United States and as far south as Argentina. Most jaguars live in Central America and Brazil. Cheetahs live mostly in African nations.

3   Leopards can climb trees to catch monkeys. They can also lie and wait for animals to pass by. Jaguars are also good climbers. Unlike most cats, jaguars are also good swimmers. Cheetahs can run 70 miles per hour. They are the fastest animals in the world.

---

1 Read this sentence from the passage.

> **Cheetahs live mostly in African nations.**

What does <u>nations</u> mean?

A towns   C wild areas

B countries   D plains

2 Which is the best summary of paragraph 2?

A Large, spotted cats live in many parts of the world.

B Bobcats, ocelots, and lynx are smaller spotted cats.

C Jaguars, cheetahs, and leopards live in zoos.

D All big, spotted cats hunt.

3 Which would be the best photo for this passage?

A a picture of a monkey in a tree

B a picture of a tiger swimming

C pictures of a leopard, a jaguar, and a cheetah

D pictures of jaguars, ocelots, and bobcats

4 What is the genre of this text?

A diary entry

B persuasive essay

C informational text

D personal narrative

Writing on Demand: Short Biography

Write a short biography of someone who moved from one place to another. This could be from one country to another or from one neighborhood to another. Write about the important events of his or her life. **(20 minutes)**

> **Writing Tip**
> Use complex sentences with time clauses (*before, after, when, while*) to clarify the order of events.

Apply & Extend

Objectives

Listening and Speaking
Deliver an informational presentation

Media
Become aware of advertisements in everyday life

Writing
Write a personal narrative

Projects

Independent Reading

Build Your Knowledge

See pages 422–423 in the **Milestones Handbook** for information about how to use reference materials and their organizational features.

● Listening and Speaking Workshop

Deliver an Informational Presentation

> **Topic**
>
> An informational presentation gives facts and details on a certain topic. Your group will prepare and deliver an informational presentation about a biome.

1. Choose a Biome You Want to Learn More About
Reread "Biomes and Ecosystems" (pages 344–346). Choose a biome from the reading that you want to learn more about. Form a group with other students who want to learn about this biome.

2. Create a List of Questions
What information will help your audience understand this biome? Make a list of questions, including the following.

a. Where can this biome be found?

b. What kinds of plants and animals live in this biome?

c. How are the plants and animals adapted to live in this biome?

3. Research Information for Your Presentation

a. Find information about your biome in the "Biomes and Ecosystems" reading. Take notes on this information.

b. Find more information about your biome in your science textbook, on the Internet, or at the library. Summarize the facts and information you find.

c. Find visuals (photos, illustrations, or charts) to make your presentation more interesting.

4. Organize Your Presentation
Work with your group to write an outline for your presentation.

5. Practice
Decide which members of your group will present each part of the presentation. Think about each part of the **Speaking Self-Evaluation** before you practice.

6. Present and Evaluate
Give your presentation. When you are done, ask your class for feedback. Use the **Speaking Self-Evaluation** to evaluate your presentation. Use the **Active Listening Evaluation** to evaluate and discuss your classmates' presentations.

● Media Workshop

Become Aware of Advertisements in Everyday Life

What are some of the groups, clubs, or places you belong to? What are the places you go to every day? Do you see advertisements there? Look carefully. You may be surprised at how many advertisements you see and the places where you see them. For example, there may be advertisements on your school supplies. Some sports fields have advertisements on scoreboards or walls. Some supermarkets even have advertisements on fruit!

1. Keep a list of advertisements you see throughout one day. Take notes on the time and place where you saw them.

2. Bring your list to class the next day. Compare your list with your classmates' lists. Discuss these questions.

   a. Did you see more advertisements than you expected to see?
   b. What were the most common places to see advertisements?
   c. Did you see advertisements in surprising places? If so, where?
   d. What kinds of graphics did the advertisements use? How did they affect the message?

Monday
Time: 7:30 AM
Place: bus
Advertisement(s) for: sneakers, bank, fast food
restaurant, lawyer

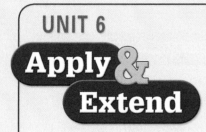

Apply & Extend

Writing Suggestion

See **Milestones Handbook**.
pages 393–433

● Writing Workshop

Personal Narrative

When you write a **personal narrative,** you tell a true story from your own life. You describe the thoughts and feelings you had during a certain event in your life. Personal narratives are always written in the first person.

> **Writing Prompt**
>
> Write a personal narrative about a time when you felt like you did not belong somewhere.

PREWRITE

1. Read the student model on the next page. It will help you understand how to write a personal narrative.
2. Think of a time in your life when you felt you did not belong. This should be a memory that is important to you. It should be an experience that you remember well.
3. Think about these questions. Take notes on your ideas.
   a. Where were you?
   b. Who else was there?
   c. Why did you feel you did not belong?
   d. What other thoughts and feelings did you have?
   e. How did this experience end?

WRITE A DRAFT

1. Start with an introduction. This paragraph should briefly introduce the narrative you will tell. For example, you can tell the reader where and when the experience happened and how old you were at the time.
2. Next, tell the story in a few paragraphs. Make sure your narrative has a beginning, a middle, and an end.
3. Be sure to include sensory details and concrete language to make the narrative more interesting for your audience.
4. Use direct quotations to bring your narrative to life. Remember to use a capital letter for the first word of a direct quotation.
5. Write the conclusion. The conclusion should tell how you changed and what you learned from the experience. It should summarize what the experience meant to you.

Alessandro Sabato

A New Neighborhood

Until I was 12, my family lived at 134 Jerome Street, Apartment 4E. I knew all the places in my neighborhood. I had lots of friends. I felt like I belonged. When I was 12, we moved to a new neighborhood. It was about 20 miles away. This experience was very hard for me.

Suddenly, everything was different. I did not know anyone, and I did not have any friends. I spent a lot of time in my room in our new apartment. The thing I missed most was playing basketball. I had always played basketball after school with my friends. One day after school, I took a basketball to the basketball court near our new apartment. I was going to practice by myself. When I got there, I saw a group of boys playing. They looked older than I am. They ignored me. I was a little afraid of them. I did not want them to tease me. So I stayed quiet and just watched.

The next day after school, I went to the park with my basketball again. The same kids were there again. Again, I watched the other kids play. The same thing happened on the third day. However, on that day one of the kids looked at me and said, "Are you going to join the game? Or are you just going to sit there forever?"

I am a very good basketball player. I scored a lot of points. As we played, I realized I was having fun. The next week, I joined the game every day after school. By the end of the week, the other kids did not seem like strangers anymore.

I remember that day really well. It was the day I started to feel like part of my new neighborhood. It was the day I realized that I can belong in more than one place.

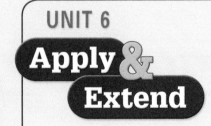
REVISE

1. Review your narrative.
   a. Does the beginning draw the reader in?
   b. Are the ideas clear and in the right order?
   c. Are the sentences varied?
2. Exchange your narrative with a partner. Ask your partner to use the **Peer Review Checklist** to review your narrative. Your partner will point out errors and give suggestions for making your draft better.
3. Revise your draft. Add, delete, or rearrange sentences to make your ideas clearer.
4. Use the **editing and proofreading symbols** on page 419 to help you mark the changes you want to make.

EDIT

1. Use the **Revising and Editing Checklist** to evaluate your narrative.
2. Fix any errors in grammar, spelling, and punctuation.

Peer Review Checklist

1. The writer told about a time he or she did not fit in.
2. There is a beginning, a middle, and an end to the narrative.
3. The writer wrote about his or her thoughts and feelings.
4. The writer included details to make the narrative interesting.

Revising and Editing Checklist

1. I told the story in chronological order.
2. I wrote the narrative in the first person.
3. I used direct quotations with correct punctuation.
4. I used the present perfect and/or the past perfect tense correctly.
5. I used capital letters and punctuation correctly.

PUBLISH

1. Write your narrative in your best handwriting. Be sure it is clear and easy to read. Or use a computer. If you use a computer, use a spell check and a grammar check.
2. Read your narrative to the class. Read clearly and slowly enough so that everyone can understand you. Change the level of your voice and use appropriate gestures to express the important ideas in your narrative.

● Projects

Choose one or more of the following projects to explore the theme of belonging further.

PROJECT 1
Create a Class Immigration Map

1. Find out what country or countries your family came from.
2. Make a list of all the students in class and the countries each student's family came from.
3. Find an outline map of the world on the Internet. Print it out.
4. Use a marker to color in the countries the families came from.
5. For each of the countries, draw one star for each student whose family came from that country.
6. Hang the map in your classroom.

PROJECT 2
Join a Group or a Club

1. Choose a group or club at school or in your neighborhood that you are interested in.
2. Join this group.
3. Report back to your class on these items.
   a. Explain why you chose this group or club.
   b. Explain the process involved in joining the club.
   c. Every few weeks, give an update on what you have done with your group.

PROJECT 3
Plan a Town

A well-planned town gives people a sense of community and belonging.

1. Work with a partner. Imagine you are town planners.
2. Discuss this question: What kinds of shops, areas, and facilities give people a sense of belonging? Take notes on your ideas.
3. Draw a map of your town. Label the shops, areas, and facilities on your map.
4. Show the map to your class. Describe your town. Explain how each place on the map will help give its citizens a sense of community and belonging.

Apply & Extend

Heinle Reading Library

Jane Eyre
by Charlotte Brontë

In a specially adapted version by Malvina G. Vogel

Since she lost her parents, Jane has known nothing but unkindness and loneliness. Jane uses her intelligence and spirit to overcome hardships and to find her place in the world.

Build Your Knowledge

Seedfolks, by Paul Fleischman, is a collection of 13 vignettes by different characters. Read these vignettes and write a report where you compare the characters. Include information on their character traits and motivations.

● Independent Reading

Explore the theme of belonging further by reading one or more of these books.

Bless Me, Ultima by Rudolfo Anaya, Warner Books, 1999.

Antonio Márez is a young Mexican-American boy who struggles to find his identity and place in the world. Antonio questions who he is, where he comes from, and who he wants to become. Antonio is guided through these questions by Ultima, an elderly woman who lives with his family.

If Your Name Was Changed at Ellis Island by Ellen Levine (author) and Wayne Parmenter (illustrator), Scholastic Paperbacks, 1994.

Ellis Island was the main immigration port for the United States from the 1880s to the 1910s. This book tells what immigrants experienced when they came to Ellis Island. It also includes stories of real individuals who passed through Ellis Island.

Seedfolks by Paul Fleischman, HarperTeen, 2004.

A young Vietnamese-American girl plants a few beans in a vacant lot. This simple action slowly changes her urban neighborhood. One by one, neighbors of many ethnicities come together to create a community garden. As they do this, they also create a sense of community and belonging.

Stargirl by Jerry Spinelli, Knopf Books for Young Readers, 2002.

Stargirl Caraway is a new 10th grader at school. She is not like the other students. She dresses in strange clothes. She dances when there is no music. At first, Stargirl's differences make her popular. However, soon her classmates turn against her. Stargirl reminds the reader that being true to yourself is more important than being accepted by others.

Pictures of Hollis Woods by Patricia Reilly Griff, Orchard Books, 2005.

Hollis Woods is an orphan. She dreams of finding a family and a place where she belongs. When a retired art teacher takes Hollis into her home, Hollis thinks she may have finally found that place.

MILESTONES TRACKER

● Writing: Revise and Edit

Read this rough draft of a student's business letter, which may contain errors. Then answer Questions 1 through 4.

(**1**) 653 Beachside Boulevard
(**2**) California 90254

(**3**) April 15, 2009

(**4**) Angela's Jewelry
(**5**) 3 Ayala Lane
(**6**) San Francisco, California 90334

(**7**) Dear Ms. Hernandez:

(**8**) I attend Bay Side School. (**9**) We are having a Heritage Day—a special day to celebrate different cultures. (**10**) We will have games, art, and music. (**11**) We invite musicians from San Francisco to perform.

(**12**) We are writing to local businesses, asking if they can give us prizes for the games. (**13**) Would you be willing to donate some of your jewelry? (**14**) When we are downtown my friends and I shop at your store a lot.

(**15**) I hope you will consider our request. (**16**) You would help make this year's Heritage Day a success. (**17**) Thank you for your consideration.

(**18**) Sincerely,

(**19**) *Sarah Chin*

1 **How can you improve line 2?**
  A Add a comma after *California.*
  B Move line 2 after line 4.
  C Give an apartment number.
  D Give a city name.

2 **How can you correct sentence 11?**
  A Change *invite* to *have invited.*
  B Change *invite* to *am inviting.*
  C Change *invite* to *had invited.*
  D Change *invite* to *has invited.*

3 **How can you correct sentence 14?**
  A Add a comma after *when.*
  B Add a comma after *downtown.*
  C Add a comma after *I.*
  D Add a comma after *shop.*

4 **What sentence can you add after sentence 15?**
  A We will have a sign that says, prizes donated by Angela's Jewelry.
  B "We will have a sign that says, prizes donated by Angela's Jewelry."
  C We will have a sign that says, "Prizes donated by Angela's Jewelry."
  D We will have a sign that says "prizes donated by Angela's Jewelry."

Writing on Demand: Business Letter

Write a thank-you letter to Angela's Jewelry. Describe what happened at the celebration. Talk about the prizes. (**20 minutes**)

> **Writing Tip**
> Review business letter format on page 353.

● Reading

Read this informational text. Then answer Questions 1 through 8.

Lalo Delgado

1 Abelardo Delgado—whose nickname was "Lalo"—was a community leader, poet, teacher, and family man. As an immigrant to the United States, Lalo had to work hard to achieve his goals. He was born in Chihuahua, Mexico, in 1930. When he was 12, he moved to El Paso, Texas. There, Lalo studied hard and graduated from high school with honors. He wanted to go to college, but he didn't have enough money. Lalo went to work in construction and in restaurants.

2 In 1955, Lalo's life as a community leader began. He started working with young people at the community center in El Paso. He helped them get an education and jobs. After much patience and hard work, Lalo himself was able to go to college in 1958. He studied Spanish at the University of Texas. Throughout the 1960s, Lalo continued his community building. He worked with César Chávez. They helped farm workers get protection and rights.

3 While he worked to improve communities, he also wrote poetry. He wrote about how hard it was to be an immigrant. He wrote love poems to his wife. While they were engaged to be married, he sent her a dollar every day to buy a wedding dress. On each dollar, he wrote a poem. In the late 1960s, he began to publish his poems.

4 Then, Lalo Delgado used his love of poetry to teach others. He taught at universities throughout the nation. He helped many universities develop Mexican-American Studies programs.

5 While he divided his time between building, helping, and teaching his community, Lalo was still devoted to his family. He was married for 51 years. He had 8 children, 19 grandchildren, and 4 great-grandchildren. When he died in 2004, he was celebrated as a wonderful husband, father, poet, teacher, and activist.

1 What does the word protection mean in the following sentence from paragraph 2?

> They helped farm workers get protection and rights.

A security

B happiness

C money

D jobs

2 What does the word divided mean in the following sentence from paragraph 5?

> While he divided his time between building, helping, and teaching his community, Lalo was still devoted to his family.

A left

B took

C spent

D split

3 How did Lalo build his community?

A by being an immigrant

B by graduating with honors

C by working with young people and farm workers

D by being a good husband

4 How was Lalo a leader in education?

A He graduated with honors.

B He studied Spanish at the University of Texas.

C He helped poor youths get an education.

D He helped to start Mexican-American Studies programs at universities.

5 In what voice is this narrative written?

A first-person

B second-person

C third-person

D fourth-person

6 What photo would be best for this passage?

A a picture of Mexico

B a picture of Lalo Delgado

C a picture of the University of Texas

D a picture of César Chávez

7 Which is a complex sentence with a time clause?

A He helped many universities develop Mexican-American Studies programs.

B While he divided his time building, helping, and teaching his community, Lalo was still devoted to his family.

C He was married for 51 years.

D He had 8 children, 19 grandchildren, and 4 great-grandchildren.

8 What is the meaning of the word rights in this sentence from paragraph 2?

> They helped farm workers get protection and rights.

A freedoms given by law

B the opposite of left

C correct

D to make straight

Grammar Reference

○ Nouns

- **Nouns** name a person, place, or thing.
- **Singular nouns** are nouns that name one person, place, or thing.
- **Plural nouns** are nouns that name more than one person, place, or thing.

Regular Plural Nouns

Singular	Plural	Spelling Rule
book	book**s**	most nouns: add **-s**
bus lunch	bus**es** lunch**es**	nouns that end in **s, x, z, ch, sh**: add **-es**
baby family	bab**ies** famil**ies**	nouns that end in a **consonant + y**: change the **y** to **i** and add **-es**
loaf knife	loa**ves** kni**ves**	nouns that end in **f** or **fe**: change the **f** or **fe** to **-ves**

Irregular Plural Nouns

Some nouns are irregular in the plural form.

Singular	Plural	Singular	Plural
man	**men**	child	**children**
woman	**women**	mouse	**mice**

Possessive Nouns

- To show possession with **names** and **singular nouns,** use an apostrophe + **s** (**'s**).
- To show possession with **plural nouns ending in s,** use only an apostrophe (**'**).
- To show possession with **irregular plurals,** use an apostrophe + **s** (**'s**).

Statement	Sentence with Possessive Noun
Sara has a nice apartment.	Sara**'s** apartment is nice.
The boy has a TV in his room.	The boy**'s** TV is in his room.
The girls have a big bedroom.	The girls**'** bedroom is big.
The men have blue hats.	The men**'s** hats are blue.

Count and Noncount Nouns

- **Count nouns** are nouns you can count. They are singular or plural.
- You use **a, an, the,** or a **number** with count nouns.
  > I have **one egg.** I have **12 carrots.**
  >
  > I made **a salad.** I made it with **a tomato** and **an onion. The salad** was delicious.
- **Noncount nouns** can't be counted. They are singular. Don't use **a, an,** or **numbers.**
  > I like **juice.** I eat **cheese.** I always drink **milk.**

Compound Nouns

A **compound noun** is a noun that is made up of two or more words. Most compound nouns are formed by nouns modified by other nouns or by adjectives.

> tooth + brush = toothbrush
>
> soft + ball = softball
>
> hand + shake = handshake

Articles

There are three articles: **a, an,** and **the.** Articles are used with nouns.

Indefinite Articles: a, an

- Use **a** and **an** with singular and plural count nouns when the noun is not specific.
- Use **a** before a word beginning with a consonant sound.
  > I have **a** cousin in Chicago.
- Use **an** before a word beginning with a vowel sound.
  > I have **an** uncle in Tampa.

Definite Article: the

- Use **the** before a specific noun.
  > I do not usually like rice, but **the** rice your mother makes is great.

- Use **the** before names of:

regions of countries that are directions	I live in **the** South.
mountains, lakes, and islands	We go camping in **the** Rockies.
that are plural	**The** Caribbean Islands are beautiful.
large bodies of water and deserts	**The** Pacific is the largest ocean.

- Do not use **the** before names of:

continents, countries, states, cities	South America is very large.
	Miami is in Florida.
exception: the United States	I live in **the** United States.
mountains, lakes, and islands	Mount McKinley is in Alaska.
that are singular	My aunt is from Puerto Rico.

○ Pronouns

A **pronoun** takes the place of a noun or refers to a noun.

My brother is sick today. **He** has a cold.

Subject Pronouns

- **Subject pronouns** take the place of subject nouns.

Subject Pronoun	Sentence	Subject Pronoun	Sentence
singular		plural	
I	**I** am Mario.	we	**We** are in class.
you	**You** are a student.	you	**You** are students.
he	**He** is a teacher.	they	**They** are in the office.
she	**She** is a lawyer.		
it	**It** is my pen.		

Object Pronouns

- **Object pronouns** take the place of object nouns.
- They show to whom something happened or who received something.
- They come after a verb or preposition.

Object Pronoun	Sentence	Object Pronoun	Sentence
singular		plural	
me	Min likes **me.**	us	They live next door to **us.**
you	Fatima works with **you.**	you	Ben helps **you** on Mondays.
him	Cosima knows **him.**	them	The teacher helps **them** every day.
her	Javier is walking with **her.**		
it	Victor bought **it.**		

Possessive Pronouns

Possessive pronouns tell who owns or has something.

Possessive Pronoun	Sentence	Possessive Pronoun	Sentence
singular		plural	
mine	This book is **mine.**	ours	That car is **ours.**
yours	**Yours** is on the table.	yours	Where did you park **yours**?
his	Matteo is reading **his.**	theirs	They brought **theirs** last week.
hers	Irina doesn't have **hers.**		
its	The cat has its food. The dog wants **its.**		

Adjectives

- **Adjectives** describe nouns.
- Adjectives can come before nouns: I have a **loud** voice.
- Adjectives can come after the verb **be:** My voice is **loud.**

Comparative Adjectives

Comparative adjectives compare two things.

Adjective	Comparative	Spelling Rule
tall	tall**er**	most one-syllable adjectives: add **-er**
dry happy	dr**ier** happ**ier**	one- and two-syllable adjectives that end in **y:** change the **y** to **i** and add **-er**
careful difficult	**more** careful **more** difficult	two or more syllable adjectives: put **more** in front of the adjective

Irregular comparatives

good / **better**
bad / **worse**

Superlative Adjectives

Superlative adjectives compare three or more things.

Adjective	Superlative	Spelling Rule
tall	**the** tall**est**	most one-syllable adjectives: add **-est**
dry happy	**the** dr**iest** **the** happ**iest**	one- and two-syllable adjectives that end in **y:** change the **y** to **i** and add **-est**
careful difficult	**the most** careful **the most** difficult	two or more syllable adjectives: put **most** in front of the adjective

Irregular superlatives

good / **the best**
bad / **the worst**

Possessive Adjectives

Possessive adjectives tell who something belongs to. They come before nouns.

Possessive Adjective	Sentence	Possessive Adjective	Sentence
singular		**plural**	
my	I am a student. **My** name is Matt.	**our**	We are in school. **Our** teacher is Mr. Dunn.
your	You are a teacher. **Your** class is in Room 21.	**your**	You are good students. **Your** grades are excellent.
his	Sam is a student. **His** teacher is Mrs. Martin.	**their**	Mrs. Ho and Mr. Dunn are teachers. **Their** students are in class.
her	Meg is in class. **Her** books are here.		
its	The computer is in the office. **Its** screen is on.		

○ Prepositions

- **Prepositions** and the words that follow them can tell *where, when,* and *how* something happens.
    She is playing **in** the park. (where)
    They go to school **at** 7:00. (when)
    Mary walks **with** energy. (how)
- A **prepositional phrase** is a preposition and the words that follow it.
    She put the plate **on the table.**

Common Prepositions		
about	below	of
above	between	on
against	by	over
around	for	through
at	from	to
before	in	under

○ Conjunctions

- **Conjunctions** can join words, phrases, or clauses (parts of a sentence with a subject and a verb).
- Conjunctions can join two independent clauses (clauses that can stand alone). Use these conjunctions: **and, or, but, so.**
    Maria did her homework, **and** I helped her.
    We can eat at home, **or** we can go to a restaurant.
    I want a glass of milk, **but** we don't have any.
    It's raining, **so** you need your umbrella.
- Conjunctions can join an independent clause (a clause that can stand alone) with a dependent clause (a clause that cannot stand alone). Use these conjunctions: **before, when, after, because, although.** The dependent clause can come first or second.
    Before I came here, I lived in Haiti.
    I learned English **when** I came to the United States.
    After I learned English, I made lots of friends.
    He took the job **because** he wanted the experience.
    I walked to the mall **although** it is a mile away.

*For more about clauses, see page 410.

○ Adverbs

- **Adverbs** describe verbs, adjectives, or other adverbs. They often answer the questions "how?" or "how frequently?"
    It snows **often** in Boston.
- Many adverbs end with **-ly.**
    The man spoke **softly.**

○ Interjections

- **Interjections** are words that express strong feelings.
- They are often followed by an exclamation point.
    Hooray! It's snowing.

○ Verbs

A **verb** is an action word.

Simple Present Tense

Use the **simple present tense** to tell about an action that generally happens or is true now.

Simple Present Tense of *be*	
singular	**plural**
I **am** Mario.	We **are** in class.
You **are** a student.	You **are** students.
He **is** a teacher.	
She **is** a lawyer.	They **are** in the office.
It **is** my pen.	

Contractions

I am = I'm
you are = you're
he is = he's
she is = she's
it is = it's
we are = we're
they are = they're

Simple Present Tense of Regular Verbs				
affirmative		**negative**		
subject	**verb**	**subject**	**verb**	
I You We They	**read.**	I You We They	**do not**	**read.**
He She It	**read<u>s</u>.**	He She It	**does not**	**read.**

Contractions

do not = don't
does not = doesn't

Present Progressive Tense

- The **present progressive tense** of a verb tells about an action happening right now.
- The present progressive uses **am, is,** or **are** and the **-ing** form of a verb.

Present Progressive Tense					
affirmative			**negative**		
I	**am**		I	**am not**	
He She It	**is**		He She It	**is not**	
We You They	**are**	**walking.**	We You They	**are not**	**walking.**

Present Progressive: *-ing* Spelling Rules

Present Progressive: *-ing* Spelling Rules	
rule	**examples**
Add **-ing** to the end of most verbs.	ask → ask**ing** go → go**ing**
For verbs that end in **e**, drop the **e** and add **-ing.**	dance → danc**ing** invite → invit**ing**
For verbs with one syllable that end in a vowel + a consonant, double the consonant and add **-ing.**	stop → sto**pping** run → ru**nning**
Do not double the consonant **w, x,** or **y.**	draw → draw**ing** fix → fix**ing** play → play**ing**
Double the consonant for verbs with two syllables that end in a consonant + vowel + consonant, with the stress on the last syllable.	begin → begi**nning** admit → admi**tting**

Present Perfect Tense

- Use the **present perfect tense** to say that something happened in the past, when the exact time is not important.
- It is also used to talk about something that started in the past and continues to the present.
- The present perfect tense uses **have/has** and the past participle of a verb.
- The past participle of regular verbs ends in **-ed** or **-d:** walk**ed,** danc**ed.**
- See page 401 for a list of irregular past participles.

Present Perfect Tense					
affirmative			**negative**		
I	**have**		I	**have not**	
He She It	**has**	already **walked.**	He She It	**has not**	already **walked.**
We You They	**have**		We You They	**have not**	

Contractions

have not = haven't
has not = hasn't

- Use the **present perfect tense** with *for* and *since* to talk about something that started in the past and continues to the present.

> John **has lived** in Florida for ten years.
> They **have been** sick since Monday.

Irregular Past Participles

Base	Past Participle	Base	Past Participle
be	been	leave	left
become	become	lie	lain
begin	begun	lose	lost
break	broken	make	made
bring	brought	mean	meant
build	built	meet	met
buy	bought	pay	paid
choose	chosen	put	put
come	come	read	read
cost	cost	ride	ridden
cut	cut	run	run
do	done	say	said
draw	drawn	see	seen
drink	drunk	sell	sold
drive	driven	send	sent
eat	eaten	sing	sung
fall	fallen	sit	sat
feel	felt	sleep	slept
find	found	speak	spoken
fly	flown	spend	spent
get	gotten	stand	stood
give	given	swim	swum
go	gone	take	taken
grow	grown	teach	taught
have	had	tell	told
hear	heard	think	thought
hold	held	understand	understood
keep	kept	wear	worn
know	known	win	won
lay	laid	write	written

Imperatives

- Use the **imperative** to give instructions, directions, or orders.
- The imperative is the base form without a subject. The implied subject is *you*.
- Strong orders end with an exclamation point (**!**).

Imperatives		
simple present	**imperative**	**negative imperative**
You turn left at the library.	**Turn** left at the library.	**Do not (Don't) turn** left at the library.
You take the bus.	**Take** the bus!	**Do not (Don't) take** the bus!

Simple Past Tense

Use the **simple past** tense of a verb to tell about an action that happened in the past.

Simple Past Tense of Regular Verbs

- Add **-ed** or **-d** to form the simple past tense of a regular verb.
- Contraction: **did not = didn't**

Verb	Simple Past	Affirmative Sentence	Negative Sentence
play	play**ed**	Sue **played** volleyball last week.	Sue **did not play** volleyball last week.
dance	dance**d**	I **danced** yesterday.	I **did not dance** yesterday.

Simple Past Tense of Irregular Verbs

Irregular verbs have special forms.

Base	Simple Past	Base	Simple Past	Base	Simple Past	Base	Simple Past
be	was/were	eat	ate	leave	left	sing	sang
become	became	fall	fell	lie	lay	sit	sat
begin	began	feel	felt	lose	lost	sleep	slept
break	broke	find	found	make	made	speak	spoke
bring	brought	fly	flew	mean	meant	spend	spent
build	built	get	got	meet	met	stand	stood
buy	bought	give	gave	pay	paid	swim	swam
choose	chose	go	went	put	put	take	took
come	came	grow	grew	read	read	teach	taught
cost	cost	have	had	ride	rode	tell	told
cut	cut	hear	heard	run	ran	think	thought
do	did	hold	held	say	said	understand	understood
draw	drew	keep	kept	see	saw	wear	wore
drink	drank	know	knew	sell	sold	win	won
drive	drove	lay	laid	send	sent	write	wrote

Simple Past Tense of *be*

Simple Past Tense of *be*		
subject	simple past of *be*	statement
I He She It	**was** **was not**	I **was** at school yesterday. She **was not** at school on Monday.
We You They	**were not** **were**	We **were not** thirsty. You **were** hungry.

Contractions
was not = wasn't
were not = weren't

Past Progressive Tense

- The **past progressive** form of a verb tells about an action that was happening at a particular time in the past or when something else happened.
- The past progressive uses the simple past tense of **be** and the **-ing** form of a verb.

Past Progressive Tense					
affirmative			negative		
I	**was**		I	**was not**	
He She It	**was**	eat**ing** dinner when a fire engine went by.	He She It	**was not**	eat**ing** dinner at 8:00 last night.
We You They	**were**		We You They	**were not**	

Past Perfect Tense

- Use the **past perfect tense** to talk about a past action or event that took place before another event took place in the past.
- The past perfect tense uses **had** and the past participle of a verb.
- See page 401 for a list of irregular past participles.

Past Perfect Tense					
affirmative			negative		
I	**had**		I	**had not**	
He She It	**had**	**studied** hard before the test yesterday.	He She It	**had not**	**studied** hard before the test yesterday.
We You They	**had**		We You They	**had not**	

Contractions
I had = I'd
you had = you'd
he had = he'd
she had = she'd
we had = we'd
they had = they'd

Future Tense

The **future tense** describes events in the future.

Future Tense with *will*

- One way to show the future tense is to use **will** before the main verb.
- Use **will** with all subject nouns and pronouns.

Future Tense with *will*	
affirmative	**negative**
I **will** go to the mall tonight.	I **will not** go to the mall tonight.
You **will** go at noon.	You **will not** go at noon.
He **will** buy a hat tomorrow.	He **will not** buy a hat tomorrow.
She **will** go next Tuesday.	She **will not** go next Tuesday.
It **will** be fun.	It **will not** be fun.
We **will** pay now.	We **will not** pay now.
They **will** use a credit card.	They **will not** use a credit card.

Affirmative Contractions

I will = I'll
you will = you'll
he will = he'll
she will = she'll
it will = it'll
we will = we'll
they will = they'll

Negative Contraction

will not = won't

Future with *going to* + verb

- You can also show the future time by using **be** + **going to** before the main verb.
- This is more informal than **will.**

Future Tense with *be + going to*	
affirmative	**negative**
I **am going to** go to the mall tonight.	I **am not going to** go to the mall tonight.
You **are going to** go at noon.	You **are not going to** go at noon.
He **is going to** buy a hat tomorrow.	He **is not going to** buy a hat tomorrow.
She **is going to** go next Tuesday.	She **is not going to** go next Tuesday.
It **is going to** be fun.	It **is not going to** be fun.
We **are going to** pay now.	We **are not going to** pay now.
They **are going to** use a credit card.	They **are not going to** use a credit card.

Future Perfect Tense

- Use the **future perfect tense** to say that something will be completed in the future or at the time of another action in the future.

Present Perfect Tense					
affirmative			**negative**		
I	**will have**	already **eaten** by 8:00 tonight.	I	**will not have**	already **eaten** by 8:00 tonight.
He/She/It	**will have**		He/She/It	**will not have**	
We/You/They	**will have**		We/You/They	**will not have**	

○ Question Types

- There are two types of questions: *yes/no* **questions** and **information questions.**
- The answer to a *yes/no* question is either *yes* or *no.*
- The answer to an information question is a piece of information.

Yes/No Questions with *be*

Simple Present

To ask *yes/no* questions with **be,** put **am, is,** or **are** before the subject.

Present Progressive

- To ask *yes/no* questions with **be,** put **am, is,** or **are** before the subject.
- Use the **-ing** form of the verb after the subject.

Simple Past

- To ask *yes/no* questions with **be,** put **was/were** before the subject.
- Use the base form of the verb after the subject.

Future

- To ask *yes/no* questions with **be,** put **will** before the subject.
- Use the base form of the verb after the subject.

	statement	*yes/no* question	short answer
Yes/No Questions with be			
Simple Present	The kitchen **is** big.	**Is** the kitchen big?	Yes, **it is.** No, **it isn't.**
	The rooms **are** small.	**Are** the rooms small?	Yes, **they are.** No, **they aren't.**
Present Progressive	She **is being** serious.	**Is** she **being** serious?	Yes, **she is.** No, **she isn't.**
Simple Past	The window **was** open.	**Was** the window open?	Yes, **it was.** No, **it wasn't.**
	The doors **were** closed.	**Were** the doors closed?	Yes, **they were.** No, **they weren't.**
Future	You **will be** here tomorrow.	**Will** you **be** here tomorrow?	Yes, I **will.** No, I **won't.**
	My parents **will be** busy this weekend.	**Will** my parents **be** busy this weekend?	Yes, they **will.** No, they **won't.**

Simple Present

- To ask *yes/no* questions with all verbs except **be,** put **do** or **does** before the subject.
- Use the base form of the verb after the subject.

Present Progressive

- To make *yes/no* questions with all verbs except **be,** put **am, is,** or **are** before the subject.
- Use the **-ing** form of the verb after the subject.

Simple Past

- To ask *yes/no* questions with all verbs except **be,** put **did** before the subject.
- Use the base form of the verb after the subject.

Future

- To make *yes/no* questions with all verbs except **be,** put **will** before the subject.
- Use the base form of the verb after the subject.

Yes/No Questions with Verbs Except *be*			
	statement	*yes/no* question	short answer
Simple Present	He **likes** the house.	**Does** he **like** the house?	Yes, he **does.** No, he **doesn't.**
	They **study** in the kitchen.	**Do** they **study** in the kitchen?	Yes, they **do.** No, they **don't.**
Present Progressive	You **are sitting** in the living room.	**Are** you **sitting** in the living room?	Yes, I **am.** No, I'm **not.**
	She **is learning** how to drive.	**Is** she **learning** how to drive?	Yes, she **is.** No, she **isn't.**
Simple Past	You **ate** in the kitchen.	**Did** you **eat** in the kitchen?	Yes, I **did.** No, I **didn't.**
	You **read** a book in the living room.	**Did** you **read** a book in the living room?	Yes, we **did.** No, we **didn't.**
Future	He **will graduate** in 2010.	**Will** he **graduate** in 2010?	Yes, he **will.** No, he **won't.**
	We **will have** a test on Friday.	**Will** we **have** a test on Friday?	Yes, we **will.** No, we **won't.**

Information Questions

- Information questions start with a question word.
- Another name for information questions is **wh-** questions because most question words begin with **wh-** (**who, what, when, where, why**).
- The answer to an information question is a specific piece of information.

	Question Word	**Helping Verb**	**Subject**	**Main Verb**	
Simple Present	Who	do	you	see	in the picture?
Simple Past	What	did	you	see	at the museum?
Present Progressive	Why	are	you	watching	the movie?
Future Tense	Where	will	you	see	your friends?

○ Frequently Misused Verbs

Certain verbs are frequently misused.

Misused Verbs	**Example**
lie = to rest in a horizontal position	Present: I **lie** in my bed to take a nap. Past: The cat **lay** in the shade.
lay = to put something down	Present: **Lay** your keys on the table. Past: We **laid** a new rug on the floor.
sit = to take a sitting position	Present: I **sit** in the first row in class. Past: She **sat** quietly for 15 minutes.
set = to put or place something	Present: Please **set** the dish on the table. Past: I don't know where I **set** my keys.
rise = to go or get up	Present: My father usually **rises** at 6:00. Past: Yesterday, he **rose** at 7:00.
raise = to lift or bring something up	Present: **Raise** your hand if you have a question. Past: I **raised** my voice so the teacher could hear me.

○ Complete Sentences

- A sentence is a group of words. The words express a complete thought.
- A complete sentence has a subject and a verb.
- The subject tells who or what the sentence is about. The subject can be a noun or a pronoun.
- The verb tells about the subject.
- A complete sentence begins with a capital letter.
- A complete sentence ends with a punctuation mark:
  a period (**.**), a question mark (**?**), or an exclamation point (**!**).

Complete Sentences	Incomplete Sentences
My brother is in your math class.	Julien your brother. (no verb)
She needs a pen.	Exercises every day. (no subject)

Subject-Verb Agreement

- The **subject** and **verb** in a sentence must **agree** in number.
- When a subject is singular, the verb must be a singular form.
- When the subject is plural, the verb must be a plural form.

Subject-Verb Agreement	
singular subject + singular verb	**plural subject + plural verb**
She is a doctor.	**They are** teachers.
The man cooks breakfast every day.	**The children cook** dinner on the weekend.

Agreement with Compound Subjects

- A **compound subject** has two or more parts.
- The subjects are combined with conjunctions, such as **and** and **or.**
- If the conjunction is **and,** the verb is usually plural.
  - Alex and Bob **play** soccer.
- If the conjunction is **or,** the verb agrees with the subject closest to the verb.
  - A pen or a pencil **is** required.
  - A book or two notebooks **are** required.

Declarative Sentence

- A **declarative sentence** states (or "declares") an idea, fact, or information.
- A declarative sentence usually ends in a period (**.**).
    > My grandmother is a wise woman.
    > John and Johanna are twins.

Interrogative Sentence

- An **interrogative sentence** asks a question.
- An interrogative sentence usually ends in a question mark (**?**).
- An interrogative sentence can ask for a *yes/no* answer or for specific information.
    > Do you like tacos? (Answer: *yes* or *no*)
    > Where were you born? (Answer: a specific place)

Imperative Sentence

- An **imperative sentence** gives an order or command.
- An imperative sentence does not include a subject. It uses the base form of the verb.
- An imperative sentence ends in a period (**.**) or an exclamation point (**!**).
    > Please shut the door.
    > Be careful!

Exclamatory Sentence

- An **exclamatory sentence** shows strong feeling.
- An exclamatory sentence ends in an exclamation point (**!**).
    > I really like my English class!
    > Hurry up! We're late!

○ Sentence Types

Clauses

- Most sentences are made of **clauses.** Clauses have at least one **subject** and one <u>verb</u>.
     Raoul <u>did</u> his homework.
- An **independent clause** can stand alone as a sentence. It expresses a complete thought.
     Raoul did his homework.
- A **dependent clause** cannot stand alone as a sentence. It must be used with an independent clause.
     <u>Before he went to bed</u>, <u>Raoul did his homework.</u>
        [dependent clause]   [independent clause]

Sentence Types

There are different sentence types. Using different types of sentences can make your writing more interesting.

Simple Sentence	Feature	Example
	one independent clause (there is no dependent clause)	Raoul got up early.

Compound Sentence	Feature	Example
	two independent clauses joined by a conjunction such as **and, but, or, nor, so, yet** (there is no dependent clause) NOTE: A comma links the two independent clauses.	Raoul got up early, **and** then he left for school.

Complex Sentence	Feature	Example
	an independent clause and at least one dependent clause	Although he went to bed late, Raoul got up early.
	an independent clause and a dependent clause joined by relative pronouns such as **who, that, which, whose, where**	Raoul read the book **that** his English teacher assigned.

Compound-Complex Sentence	Feature	Example
	at least two independent clauses and at least one dependent clause	Because I am a good student, some people expect me to speak perfectly, and other people expect me to write perfectly.

How to Use a Dictionary and a Thesaurus

○ How to Use a Dictionary

A good dictionary is an important reference tool. A dictionary can help your writing because it helps you to understand and select appropriate words for your writing.

Dictionaries are available in printed book form, on CD-ROM, and online.

Features of a Dictionary

- Word entries are organized alphabetically from A to Z.
- An entry starts with a headword. The headword shows how the word is broken into syllables.
- After the headword, you will find the pronunciation and syllable stress. Dictionaries use symbols to represent sounds. These symbols are used to help you pronounce the word in a way that most people will understand. The pronunciation also shows which syllable is stressed.
- Next, you'll find grammatical information. For each word, there is an abbreviation that tells you the part of speech—noun, pronoun, adjective, verb, adverb, preposition, conjunction, or interjection—that the word represents.
- Next is the definition—what the word means. When there are multiple meanings, the meanings are numbered.
- Entries often include an example sentence to show how to use the word in context.
- Some dictionaries also include the origin of the word. English has been spoken for about 1,500 years, so knowing word origins helps you understand when a word came into the language and where it came from.
- Some dictionaries also include synonyms (words with similar meanings) and antonyms (words with opposite meanings).

> **mile•stone** /'maɪl,stoʊn/ *n.*
> **1** a marker, such as a stone that indicates the distance in miles: *Many years ago, the main road between Boston and New York had milestones next to it.* **2** an important achievement, event: *Getting her college degree was a milestone in her life.*
> [from Old English]
> *synonym* accomplishment, achievement, event

pronunciation
part of speech
definition
example sentence
origin
synonym

○ How to Use a Thesaurus

A thesaurus is another important reference tool.

- A thesaurus includes words and their **synonyms**—words that have the same or similar meanings.
- Some thesauruses also include **antonyms**—words that have opposite meanings.
- It may also include related words or concepts.
- Thesauruses are available in printed book form, on CD-ROM, and online.
- Use a thesaurus to help you vary your word choices and make your writing more interesting.
- When you know the meaning of the synonym or the antonym of an unknown word, you can determine that word's meaning.

> **sympathy** *n.*
> **1** understanding, concern. *antonym* indifference **2** accord, support of someone/something. *antonym* hostility
> *Related words* humanity, kindness, pity

synonyms
antonym
related words

Spelling

Spelling Rules

i before *e* except after *c* or when pronounced *ay*

- **i** before **e**: fri**e**nd, bri**e**f, ni**e**ce, fi**e**rce
- after **c**: rec**ei**ve, c**ei**ling
- pronounced *ay*: **ei**ght, n**ei**ghbor, w**ei**gh, th**ei**r

q and *u*

- Always put the letter **u** after the letter **q**: **qu**ick, **qu**estion, **qu**iz.

Noun Plurals

- Add **-s** to form the plural of most nouns.
  - paper / paper**s**
- For nouns ending in **-s, -x, -z, -ch, -sh**: add **-es.**
  - gas / gas**es**   box / box**es**   sandwich / sandwich**es**   dish / dish**es**
- For nouns ending in consonant + **y**: change the **y** to **i** and add **-es.**
  - family / famil**ies**
- For nouns ending in **-f** or **-fe**: change the **-f** or **-fe** to **-ves.**
  - loaf / loa**ves**   life / li**ves**
- For nouns ending in vowel + **o**: add **-s.**
  - radio / radio**s**
- For nouns ending in consonant + **o**: add **-es.**
  - tomato / tomato**es**

Suffixes

- When adding a suffix that begins with a vowel: drop a final silent **-e.**
  - combine / combin**ation**   remove / remov**able**
- When adding a suffix that begins with a consonant: keep the final silent **-e.**
  - achieve / achiev**ement**   care / car**eful**
- When adding a suffix to a one-syllable word that ends in vowel + consonant: double the consonant.
  - hit / hi**tting**   stop / sto**pped**
- Change a final **y** to **i,** except when adding **-ing.**
  - day / da**ily**   try / tr**ied**   play / pla**ying**

Frequently Misspelled Words

address	broccoli	embarrass	government	jewelry	library	necessary	prejudice	scissors	through
arctic	calendar	exercise	height	judgment	mathematics	neighbor	raspberry	separate	truly
beginning	definite	fascinate	humorous	ketchup	miniature	occasion	receive	sincerely	until
believe	desperate	February	independent	knowledge	misspell	piece	rhythm	special	Wednesday
bicycle	disastrous	foreign	jealous	leisure	mysterious	precede	science	thorough	weird

Homophones

- **Homophones** are words that have the same pronunciation but different spellings and meanings.

Homophone	Example
to = part of a verb infinitive; also a preposition	I want **to** read my book. I went **to** the store for my grandfather.
two = the number 2	My **two** shoes are beside the bed.
too = also	My books are at home. My notebook is, **too.**
it's = it is	I lost my backpack. **It's** not in my bedroom.
its = possessive adjective	I like that house and especially **its** porch.
their = possessive adjective	**Their** room is usually messy.
they're = they are	**They're** always quiet.
there = place	My house is over **there** by the shopping mall.
your = possessive adjective	When is **your** birthday?
you're = you are	**You're** the best teacher in the school.

Other homophones

buy (to purchase) / **by** (a preposition) / **bye** (short form of good-bye)

fir (tree) / **fur** (animal hair)

hair (on your head) / **hare** (animal)

pair (two) / **pear** (fruit)

peace (quiet; no war) / **piece** (part of something)

scene (part of a play) / **seen** (past participle of the verb *see*)

write (form letters or words) / **right** (correct; a direction)

Homographs

- **Homographs** are words that are spelled the same but have different meanings.
- They may or may not have the same pronunciation.

Homograph	Example
dove = a small bird	A white **dove** flew by.
dove = past tense of the verb *dive* (different pronunciation)	I **dove** into the swimming pool.
just = fair and reasonable	My mother is a **just** person.
just = a short time ago (same pronunciation)	The baby **just** fell asleep.
tear = rip	He has a **tear** in his shirt.
tear = water from the eye (different pronunciation)	There are **tears** in her eyes.
well = in good health	Marco doesn't feel **well.**
well = a hole made in the ground to reach water, oil, etc. (same pronunciation)	There is no water left in the **well.**

Roots, Prefixes, Suffixes

Common Greek and Latin Word Roots

Greek Root	Meaning	Example
astro	star	astronaut
auto	self	automatic
biblio	book	bibliography
bio	life	biology
meter	measure	speedometer
micro	small	microscope
sphere	ball	hemisphere
tele	from afar	telephone

Latin Root	Meaning	Example
centi	hundred	centipede
contra	against	contrary
dict	say, speak	dictate
fract	break	fraction
man	hand	manual
pop	people	population
struct	build	construct
vid/vis	see	video/visual

Prefixes

- A **prefix** is a group of letters added to the beginning of a word.
- The word it is added to is called the **root word.**
- The prefix changes the meaning of the root word.

Prefix	Meaning	Example
anti-	against	antifreeze
bi-	two	bicycle
dis-	not, opposite	dislike
inter-	between	international
mid-	middle	midway
mis-	not, incorrectly	misunderstand
over-	over	overlook
pre-	before	preview
re-	back, again	rewrite
super-	above	superstar
un-	not	unhealthy

Suffixes

- A **suffix** is a group of letters added to the end of a root word.
- A suffix changes the meaning of the root word.

Suffix	Meaning	Example
-able	can be done	removable
-en	made of	wooden
-er, -or	one who	worker, actor
-ful	full of	careful
-ist	one who	dentist
-less	without	fearless
-ment	action or process	enjoyment
-ness	condition of	kindness
-ous	possessing the qualities of	gaseous
-tion	act, process	attraction

Syllabication

- A **syllable** is a unit of pronunciation.
- A syllable contains only one vowel sound.
- A word can have one or more syllables.
- Dividing words into syllables helps you learn how to pronounce them.

Closed Syllables

- A closed syllable ends in a consonant.
- A closed syllable has one vowel.
- The vowel sound in a closed syllable is short.
     sat, run, nap/**kin**, **sub**/**ject**

Open Syllables

- An open syllable ends in a vowel.
- The vowel sound in an open syllable is usually long.
     me, no, she, mu/sic, **ta**/ble, **o**/pen

Final -e Syllables (VCe)

- A final **-e** syllable ends in a vowel (V), a consonant (C), and a final **-e.**
- The final **-e** is silent and makes the earlier vowel long.
     make, cute, hope a/**lone,** in/**side**

Vowel Digraphs (Vowel Teams)

- A vowel digraph (or vowel team) is created when two vowels together form one vowel sound in the same syllable.
- The vowel sound in a vowel digraph syllable is long.
     boat, meat, ex/**plain,** re/**peat,** **sea**/son

r-Controlled Vowels

- **r**-controlled vowels contain a vowel followed by an **r.**
- The vowel sound is affected by the **r.**
- When dividing a word into syllables, the vowel and the *r* usually stay in the same syllable.
     car, her, bird, but/**ter,** en/**ter, per**/son

Consonant + -le

- A common syllable spelling pattern is a consonant + **-le.**
- The **e** is silent.
- The syllable appears at the end of a word.
     ta/**ble,** cir/**cle,** ti/**tle**

Punctuation

Period (.)

Declarative Sentence	A statement is called a declarative sentence. Put a period at the end of a declarative sentence.	Today is the first day of school.
Abbreviations	An abbreviation is a short form of a word. Put a period at the end of an abbreviation.	Tuesday → Tues. inch → in.

Question Mark (?)

Questions	A question is also called an interrogative sentence. Put a question mark at the end of a question.	What is your name? Are you going to the party?

Exclamation Point (!)

Exclamations and Emphasis	An exclamation point at the end of a sentence shows strong feelings or surprise. Use exclamation points with exclamatory sentences and with imperative sentences for emphasis.	The burrito was delicious! Don't eat the lettuce! I didn't wash it yet!

Comma (,)

Items in a Series	Use a comma after each part of a series. A series has three or more parts.	I have a pen, a pencil, and a book.
In Dates	Use a comma after the day in a date.	September 13, 2009
In Addresses	Use a comma before an apartment number. Use a comma after a city.	126 First St., Apt. 3A Santa Ana, CA 92701
In Letters	Use a comma after the greeting and the closing in a friendly letter.	Dear Aunt Mary, Your friend,
In Compound Sentences	Use a comma to link independent clauses in a compound sentence joined by conjunctions: **and, but, or, nor, for, so, yet.** The comma comes before the conjunction.	I like apples, but I prefer strawberries. You need to leave now, or you'll miss the bus.

Apostrophe (')

Contractions	An apostrophe takes the place of missing letters in contractions.	it is → it's he will → he'll
Possessives	An apostrophe + **s** indicates possession. If the word is singular and ends in **s,** add **'s.** If the word is plural and ends in **s,** just add an apostrophe.	the girl**'s** book Lois**'s** book the boys**'** house

Quotation Marks (" ")

Quotations	Quotation marks show the exact words people say. Put quotation marks where the speaker's words start and stop. Put a comma between the quote and the speaker of the quote.	"Let me clean the car," Ramón said. Ramón said, "Let me clean the car."
Titles	Use quotation marks for titles of articles in newspapers and magazines, poems, songs, and short stories.	Did you read the article "New Park Opens" in *The Daily News*? My favorite poem is "The Road Not Taken," by Robert Frost.

Parentheses (( ))

Extra Information	Parentheses are curved signs that give extra information or an explanation in a reading.	You use it to access (make use of) hundreds of Web sites.

Semicolon (;)

To Connect Independent Clauses	Use a semicolon to connect two independent clauses when there is no conjunction (such as **and, but, or, nor**).	Some people like country music; some people don't.

Colon (:)

In Time	Use a colon to separate hours from minutes.	10:15 AM 9:33 PM
In Letters	In a business letter, use a colon after the greeting.	Dear Mr. Best:
A List	Use a colon to introduce a list.	Kim enjoys lots of physical activities: hiking, swimming, soccer, and baseball.

○ Italics

- When using a computer, use *italics* in the situations below.
- When using handwriting, use <u>underlining</u>.

For Emphasis	Use italics for words you want to emphasize.	Do you *really* want to go?
Titles of Documents	Use italics for titles of: documents, newspapers, magazines, books, movies.	*The Constitution* *The Sunday News* *Fun Magazine* *The Pearl*
Foreign Words	Use italics for foreign words in an English sentence.	In Turkish, the first two numbers are *bir* and *iki*.

Capitalization

First Word in Sentence	Use a capital letter for the first word in a sentence.	**A** word problem uses words and data.
First Word in a Quoted Sentence	Use a capital letter for a quotation that is a complete sentence. Do not use a capital letter for the second part of a quoted sentence that is interrupted.	He said, "**W**e are leaving at 4:00." "We are leaving," he said, "at 4:00."
Pronoun "I"	The subject pronoun **I** always has a capital letter.	Mario is hungry, but **I** am not.
Proper Nouns	The names of the days and months always begin with capital letters. The names of people and titles always begin with capital letters.	My birthday is **T**uesday, **M**arch 24th. My father's name is **D**r. **I**brahim.
Nationalities, Languages, Academic Courses, Organizations, Holidays, Historical Events, and Special Events	Use capital letters for the names of nationalities, languages, academic courses, organizations, holidays, historical events, and special events.	**A**merican **S**panish **A**lgebra I **T**he **A**merican **R**ed **C**ross **F**ourth of **J**uly **B**attle of **G**ettysburg **W**inter **C**oncert
Specific Places and Geographical Names	Use capital letters for street names. Use capital letters for the names of cities, states, countries. Use capital letters for the names of mountains, rivers, lakes, and oceans.	**F**ifth **A**venue, **E**ast **S**treet **S**acramento, **C**alifornia **U**nited **S**tates the **R**ocky **M**ountains, the **H**udson **R**iver, **L**ake **E**rie, the **P**acific **O**cean
Titles of Works	Capitalize the first word and the important words in the titles of books, magazines, newspapers, works of art, musical compositions.	*Before We Were Free* *Scientific Magazine* *Community Newspaper* *Mona Lisa* "Symphony No. 5"

Editing and Proofreading Symbols

Symbol	Meaning
⌧	insert a paragraph indent
∽	transpose (move around) letters, words, or sentences
Sp	check spelling
∧	insert word, words, or punctuation mark
ℓ	delete/take out
⌃	insert a comma
⊙	insert a period
⌃	insert a semicolon
⊙	insert a colon
⌄⌄ ⌄⌄	insert quotation marks
≡	make a capital
⧸	make lowercase
#	insert a space
⌒	close up the space

Revising and Editing Checklist

1. **Development of Ideas/Content**
   a. Did I choose an appropriate form of writing (e.g., personal letter, letter to the editor, review, poem, report, narrative) for my purpose?
   b. Is the purpose of my writing clear?
   c. Is my writing focused on the topic I chose to write about?
   d. Did I support my ideas with details, facts, examples, and explanations?
   e. Did I write appropriately for my audience?

2. **Organization**
   a. Is my writing clear and logical?
   b. Do I have a strong, interesting beginning that gets the reader's attention?
   c. Did I group related ideas? Did I use transition words correctly?
   d. Did I maintain a consistent focus?
   e. Do my ideas progress logically? Can I improve the progression?
   f. Can I improve the meaning and focus of my writing by adding, deleting, consolidating, clarifying, and rearranging words and sentences?
   g. Do I have a strong ending that summarizes my topic?

3. **Sentence Structures**
   a. Are my sentences complete? Do they have a subject and a verb?
   b. Did I use declarative, interrogative, imperative, and exclamatory sentences appropriately?
   c. Did I make sure that there are no run-on sentences or fragments?
   d. Did I use different types of sentences—simple, compound, complex, and compound-complex?
   e. Can I revise to connect short, related sentences with appositives, participial phrases, adjectives, adverbs, conjunctions, transitions, and prepositional phrases?

4. **Paragraph Structure**
   Single Paragraph
   a. Does my paragraph have a topic sentence?
   b. Did I support my topic sentence with facts and details?

   Multi-Paragraph
   a. Did I provide an introductory paragraph?
   b. Did I establish and support a central idea with a topic sentence at or near the beginning of the first paragraph?
   c. Did I include supporting paragraphs with simple facts, details, and explanations?
   d. Did I provide details and transitional expressions that link one paragraph to another in a clear line of thought?
   e. Did I conclude with a paragraph that summarizes the points?

5. **Grammar and Usage (see pages 394–410)**
   a. Is my writing in the right tense (for example, present or past tense)?
   b. Did I use subject pronouns and object pronouns correctly?
   c. Did I use the pronouns *she*, *her*, or *hers* for women and girls, and *he*, *him*, or *his* for men and boys?
   d. Do my verbs agree with their subjects? Did I use singular verb forms with singular subjects and plural verb forms with plural subjects?
   e. Did I use articles, nouns, adjectives, and compound words correctly?
   f. Did I use correct verb forms (regular and irregular) and appropriate verb tenses?

6. **Word Choice**
   a. Did I choose exact and descriptive words?
   b. Did I use a dictionary, thesaurus, or glossary to help me choose better words?
   c. Did I eliminate extra words so that my writing is not wordy?

7. **Writing Conventions**
   Form
   a. Did I write my name and the date?
   b. Did I write a title and underline it?
   c. Did I leave margins at the top and bottom and on both sides of the paper?
   d. Did I use correct spacing between letters in words and words in a sentence?
   e. Did I indent the first line of each paragraph?
   f. Did I use my best handwriting or, if I used a computer, did I create an attractive presentation?
   g. Did I need to include a bibliography? If so, did I correctly cite my references?

   Spelling (see pages 412–413)
   a. Did I check the spelling of all words I'm not sure about?
   b. If I wrote my paper on a computer, did I use the spell check?

   Punctuation (see pages 416–417)
   a. Did I punctuate each sentence with the right punctuation mark?
   b. For direct speech, did I use quotation marks and commas correctly?
   c. Did I use apostrophes correctly in contractions and possessives?
   d. Did I use parentheses for extra information?
   e. Did I use commas, colons, and semicolons correctly?

   Capitalization (see page 418)
   a. Did I capitalize the pronoun "I" and the names of proper nouns?
   b. Did I start each sentence with a capital letter?

8. **My Own Criteria**
   What are some things you want to look for in your writing?
   a.
   b.
   c.

○ The Research Process

STEP 1 Identify a topic.

Choose a topic that is specific, not general. It is difficult to research and write about a general topic.

General Topic	Specific Topic
Rain Forests	The Climate of the Rain Forests
	Ways to Save the Rain Forests

STEP 2 Frame a central question or questions about your topic.

Your questions guide your research. As you find out information, write new questions and revise your original questions, as necessary.

STEP 3 Use references.

Find out more about your topic by using a variety of reference resources.

Reference	Description	How to Use It
computer catalog	database of all books in the library	Type in keywords to find books and other references related to your topic. Ask the librarian for help, if necessary.
books	books with information related to your topic	Look at the table of contents, preface, appendix, and index to locate content related to your topic. Also look at citations, end notes, and bibliographic entries that provide more information.
encyclopedias	collection of articles on thousands of topics; often include illustrations, photos, charts, and maps	Print encyclopedias: Look up topics in alphabetical order; they often have cross-references to related topics. CD-ROM or online encyclopedias: Type in keywords related to your topic, then click on the articles; links within the articles indicate cross-references.
atlas	collection of maps that show location of places or other features, such as geographic, economic, or political features	Print atlas: Look at the table of contents or index to locate information related to your topic. CD-ROM or online atlas: Type in keywords related to your topic, then click on the links.
almanac	yearly publication that includes lists, tables, and brief articles relating to a topic	Print almanac: Look at the table of contents or index to locate information related to your topic. CD-ROM or online almanac: Type in keywords related to your topic, then click on the links.

Reference	Description	How to Use It
dictionary	list of words in alphabetical order with pronunciation, part of speech, meanings, and often word origins	Print dictionary: Look up the word alphabetically. CD-ROM or online dictionary: Type in the word.
thesaurus	dictionary of synonyms (words with the same or similar meanings); often includes antonyms (words with opposite meanings)	Print thesaurus: Look up the word alphabetically; use the head words (words at the top of the page) to guide you. CD-ROM or online thesaurus: Type in the word.
magazine	a weekly or monthly publication that includes articles, stories, essays, and photos	Use an electronic database at the library to locate magazines with articles about your topic. Use the table of contents of the magazine to find the article. Current issues are usually on display. Older ones will be in the electronic archives.
newspaper	a daily or weekly print paper containing news articles	Use an electronic database at the library to locate articles about your topic. Current issues are usually on display. Older ones will be in the electronic archives.
Internet	a computer network of electronic information	Type keywords into a browser. Scan the links to find sites that seem useful.

STEP 4 Take notes on note cards.

Note cards help you keep track of the information you find and the sources of the information.

Use note cards to organize this information.

a. Follow the format below to record the information that answers your questions.

b. Paraphrase or summarize the information from your source. Use your own words.

c. If you cite words directly from the source, you must use quotation marks.

d. Provide the complete source information. See page 424 for how to cite sources.

TOPIC: _____

Question: _____
(What do you want to know?)

Paraphrase or summarize your source:
OR **"Quote" your source:**

Source:

When citing sources using handwriting, use underlining as shown below.
When using a computer, use *italics*.

Citations for Reference Sources

reference	how to cite
book	Author. <u>Title of Book</u>, City of Publication: Publisher, Year. **Example:** Roper, Edward R. <u>Rain Forest</u>, New York: Omni Publishing, 1998.
encyclopedia	Author of Article, "Title of Article." <u>Title of Book</u>. City of Publication: Publisher, Year. **Example:** Alpert, Louis C. "Inca." <u>Encyclopedia Americana</u>, International Edition. 1999.
magazine or newspaper	Author of Article. "Title of Article." <u>Title of Magazine or Newspaper</u> Date: Page(s). **Example:** Tyler, Dawn. "On the Sands." <u>Hawaii Living</u> February 1998: 20-23.
Internet article	Creator's Name (if given). "Title of Article." <u>Web Page Title</u>. Institution or Organization. Date of access. <URL address>. If you cannot find the information, use the web address as the citation. **Example:** Likakis, Angela. "The World of Science." <u>Science News</u>. Science Resource Center. InfoSci. February 28, 1998. <http://infosci.thinkgroup.com/itweb/boston_massachusetts>

STEP 5 Write your research paper.

a.   Organize your note cards in logical sequence.

b.   Create an outline from your notes. See page 425 for how to create an outline.

c.   Use your outline to draft your paper.

d.   Revise and edit your paper. Use the Research Paper Checklist on page 426.

e.   Incorporate visuals.

STEP 6 Create a title page, table of contents, and bibliography.

a.   The first page should include the title of your research paper, centered on the page. Include your name and the date in the bottom right-hand corner.

b.   At the beginning of your research paper, make a "Table of Contents" to show the organization.

c.   At the end of your paper, start a new page with the title "Bibliography."

d.   In your bibliography, list all your sources. Use the correct citation format. List your sources in alphabetical order.

Research Paper Outline

1. Sort your note cards before you do your outline.
2. Organize topics and subtopics into a logical order.
3. Write a topic or a thesis.
4. List major headings after a Roman numeral and a period.
5. List subtopics after a capital letter and a period.
6. List supporting details and examples after a number and a period.

Title

I. Topic 1 or Thesis
  A. Subtopic 1
    1. Detail/Example
    2. Detail/Example
  B. Subtopic 2
    1. Detail/Example
    2. Detail/Example

II. Topic 2 or Thesis
  A. Subtopic 1
    1. Detail/Example
    2. Detail/Example
  B. Subtopic 2
    1. Detail/Example
    2. Detail/Example

III. Topic 3 or Thesis
  A. Subtopic 1
    1. Detail/Example
    2. Detail/Example
  B. Subtopic 2
    1. Detail/Example
    2. Detail/Example

IV. Topic 4 or Thesis
  A. Subtopic 1
    1. Detail/Example
    2. Detail/Example
  B. Subtopic 2
    1. Detail/Example
    2. Detail/Example

V. Conclusion (restate thesis)

○ Research Paper Checklist

1. Research
    a. I framed a central question.
    b. I researched my question using a variety of reference materials.
    c. I took notes with information from these sources.
    d. I revised my research questions and added new ones as needed.
    e. I organized my information in an outline.
    f. I used at least three sources.

2. Reference Materials
    a. I evaluated each reference source for credibility.
    b. I did not plagiarize. I summarized and paraphrased, or I quoted my sources.
    c. I documented sources for all information that is not my own opinion.
    d. When I used exact words from a source, I put them in quotation marks and cited where they came from.

3. Organization
    a. I stated my thesis clearly in the introduction.
    b. I stayed focused on my topic and thesis.
    c. I combined short, related sentences with appositives, participial phrases, adjectives, adverbs, and prepositional phrases.
    d. I used transitional words between paragraphs.
    e. I summarized and answered my thesis question in the conclusion.

4. Writing
    a. I checked my spelling with a dictionary or with the computer's spell check.
    b. I checked my punctuation in every sentence.
    c. I checked my choice of words.
    d. I checked my verb tenses and subject-verb agreement.

5. Form
    a. I wrote an interesting title that reflects the subject.
    b. I wrote my name and date.
    c. I used correct margins on each page.
    d. I used double spacing on the computer.
    e. I indented each paragraph.
    f. I used correct capitalization and punctuation.
    g. I cited my sources correctly.

6. Evaluation
    a. I thought about how well I answered my research questions.
    b. I thought about questions for further research.

Technology Guide

O The Computer

You can use a computer to help you work. You can also use a computer to help you find information. A computer is made up of **hardware** and **software.** Hardware is the part of the computer that you can touch. Software is the instructions that make the computer work.

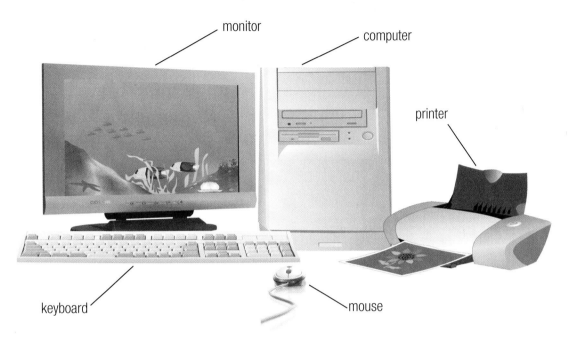

monitor

computer

printer

keyboard

mouse

Computer Hardware

1. The most important part of a computer is the box that contains the computer's memory. Your information is stored in the computer's memory.
2. You give information to the computer by typing on a keyboard or by clicking a mouse.
3. You see the information on the monitor. The monitor looks like a television screen.
4. You can use a printer to print the information on paper.

Computer Software

Software is made to do a special kind of job. For example, there is software that helps you write and edit your writing (word processing). There is software that makes it easy to create presentations. Other software lets you find information on the Internet. These pieces of software are also called **programs** or **applications.**

◯ Word Processing

A word processing program is a tool for writing. You can use it to:

- correct mistakes, move text around, and add or delete text.
- do spelling and grammar checks to help you find and correct errors.
- find synonyms by using a thesaurus in the program.
- create visuals.
- choose text features such as **boldface type** and *italic type*.

How to Create a Document

Anything that you write in a word processing
program is called a **document.**

1. Make sure that the computer is on.
2. Find the **icon** (the little picture) for your word
   processing program on the screen.
3. Use the mouse to move the arrow onto the word
   processing icon and click on the program to
   open it. Different computers do this in different
   ways. Ask someone to help you.
4. When the program opens, you can start typing.
5. You can learn how to use special keys on the
   keyboard. For example, if you press the key
   marked **Tab** when you are at the beginning
   of a line, the computer will make a paragraph
   indent. The **Shift** keys make capital letters.

tab—makes a
paragraph indentation

shift—makes
capital letters

6. Look at the icons in this illustration. You can
   click on these icons with the
   mouse to make special effects
   such as **bold** or *italic* type.
   (The icons on your program
   might be different from these.)
7. VERY IMPORTANT: The
   computer will not "remember"
   your work by itself. You have to
   save it to the computer's
   memory. There is a
   Save icon that will make the
   computer do this. When you click on the Save icon the first time,
   the computer will ask you to name your document. As you write,
   save your work often.
8. When you have finished your first draft, use the spelling and
   grammar checks to find and fix errors. You can add text features
   and visuals if you like. Print your work or send it to someone by e-mail.

Saves your
document.

Checks spelling
and grammar.

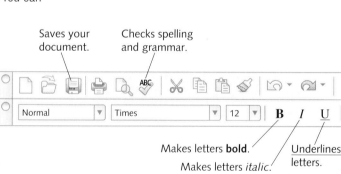

Makes letters **bold**.
Makes letters *italic*.

Underlines
letters.

○ Technology Presentations

Using media such as video, graphics, and slides on a computer can make your oral presentations clearer and more interesting.

STEP 1 Plan the media parts of your presentation.

1. Plan, organize, and prepare your presentation. Take notes on how technology could help make your points.
   a. Is there a video that would help show your idea? Could you make one?
   b. Would music add to your presentation? What kind? Where can you get it?
   c. Should you show charts and visuals on the computer?
2. Make note cards. Use one card for what you will say and another card for the technology parts. Put the cards in order.

Card 1 My speech	**Card 2 Media**	**Card 3 My speech**
Sports	Play video of sports scenes in town.	Sports are fun.
Important in our community		Teamwork
Most people like some kind of sport.		Healthy
Introduce video.		

STEP 2 Prepare the media parts of your presentation.

1. Find or create the images and sounds that you want to use. Look in the "Clip Art" section of your software or scan art or photos into your program.
2. If available, use the presentation software on your computer to organize the images and sounds.

STEP 3 Practice your presentation.

1. Practice your technology presentation out loud.
2. Ask a partner to watch your presentation and give suggestions for improvement.

STEP 4 Give your technology presentation to your audience.

1. Set up your equipment early to be sure that everything is working.
2. After your presentation, ask the audience to evaluate your presentation.

○ How to Use the Internet

Key Definitions

Internet	millions of computers connected together to exchange information
Web sites	locations on the Internet
browser	software that lets you see Web sites
keywords	words typed into a search engine to find information on a certain topic
link	takes you to another Web site or to another place on the same Web site when you click your mouse on it

address bar—
Type Web
addresses here.

search box—
Type your
keywords here.

Click here
to start
your search.

Do Research on the Internet

1. Open your browser. Ask your teacher or a classmate how to do this.
2. Type keywords for your topic in the "search" box. Click on the button that says "go" (or "start" or "search").
3. Look at the list of Web sites that comes up on the screen. Choose one of the sites that seems interesting and click on it.
4. On a Web site, there are pages of information. Sometimes there are links to take you to other Web sites.
5. If you already know the exact address of a Web site, you can type it into the address bar. For example, http://visions.heinle.com.

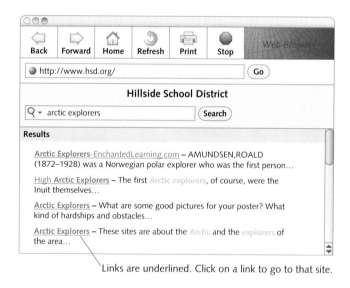

Links are underlined. Click on a link to go to that site.

Use Information from the Internet

Many Web sites have good information. Others may have mistakes, or they may tell only one side of an issue. You must evaluate the information that you find on the Internet. Ask your teacher or another adult for suggestions of sites that you can trust. Use other resources to check the information you find on the Internet.

How to Use E-Mail

Key Definitions

e-mail	software that lets you type a message and send it to someone else who has e-mail
e-mail address	where the e-mail system sends the message
inbox	a list of who sent you messages and what the messages are about

Read an E-Mail Message

1. Open the e-mail program. Ask your teacher or a classmate how to do this. See if there are any new messages in your inbox.
2. Open a message. Programs do this differently. Usually you double click the mouse on the message.
3. Read the message.
4. If you want to keep the message, do not do anything. The computer will save it in your inbox. If you want to discard the message, click on the "delete" button on the toolbar.
5. To send an answer back, click on the "reply" button. Write your message and click "send."

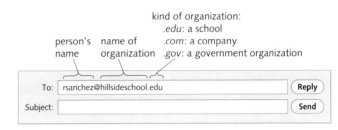

Send an E-Mail Message

1. Open your e-mail program.
2. On the toolbar, click on the "new message" button.
3. Type in the address of the person you are writing to.
4. Type in a subject that tells what the message is about.
5. Type your message.
6. Click on the "send" button.

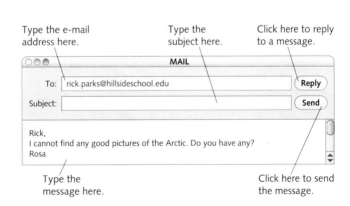

○ **Print Letters**

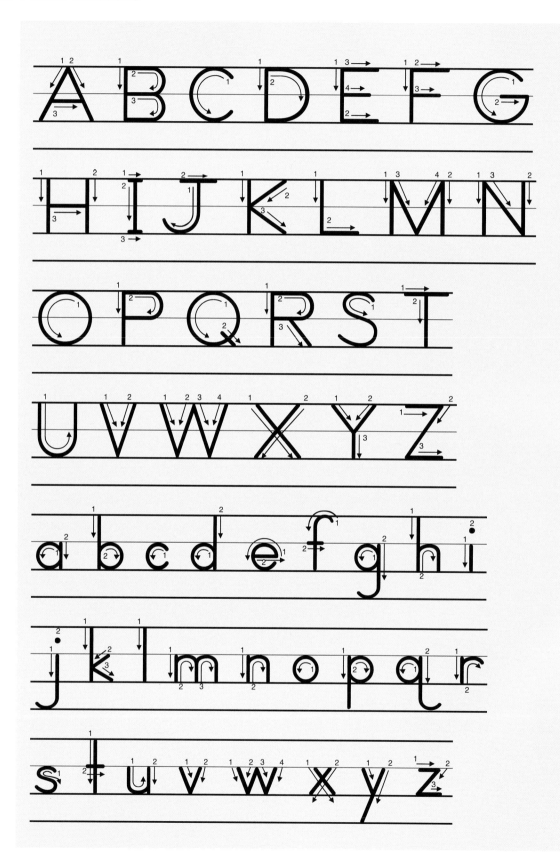

○ Cursive Letters

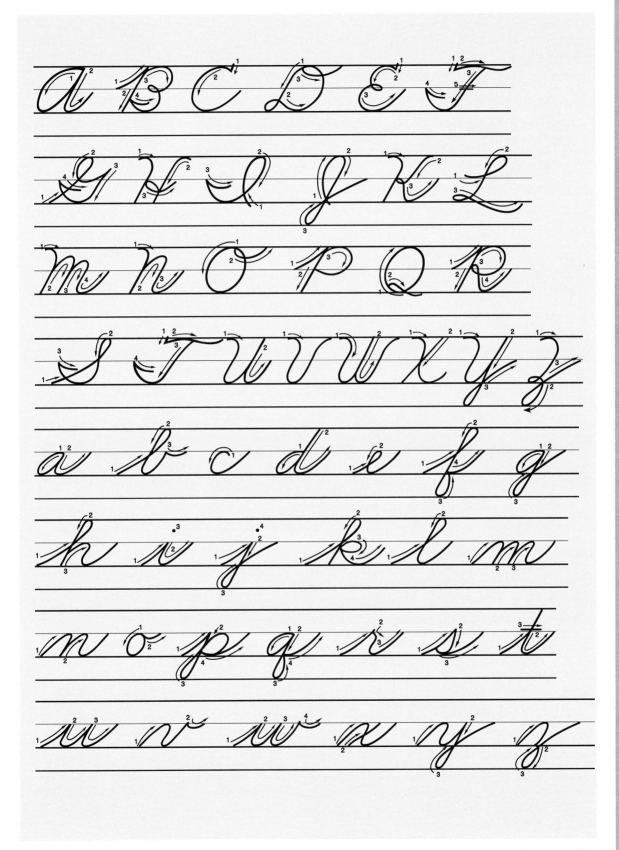

GLOSSARY

Glossary
Key Vocabulary, Academic Vocabulary, Literary/Text Element Terms

The definitions included in this Glossary represent how the words are used in this student book. Many words have multiple meanings. These additional meanings can be found in a dictionary.

Glossary Pronunciation Key

• The pronunciation of each listing is shown in parentheses after the listing.
• The words below are examples of how each letter and sign are pronounced.
• The symbol (′) appears after a syllable with heavy stress.
• The symbol (′) appears after a syllable with light stress.

For example: **pronunciation** (prə nun′sē ā′shən)

a	map, flag	k	keys, sink	ŧʜ	the, mother
ā	gate, play	l	library, animal	u	run, son
ä	art, barn	m	math, room	ü	school, rude
â	fare, scared	n	nice, green	u̇	could, pull
b	book, tub	ng	sing, hang	v	value, weave
ch	chair, teacher	o	hot, closet	w	watch, shower
d	desk, bald	ō	motive, polar	y	yes, employer
e	net, pen	ô	war, story	z	zip, stanza
ē	heal, scene	ȯ	fall, cause	zh	visual, conclusion
ėr	nurse, germ	oi	soil, annoy	ə	a in ability
f	fact, sofa	ou	proud, brown		e in liberty
g	go, bag	p	pillow, lamp		i in pencil
h	helmet, holiday	r	ruler, hair		o in dictionary
i	miss, image	s	sunny, class		u in injury
ī	wise, rhyme	t	time, weight		
j	jacket, subject	th	theme, truth		

How to Use the Glossary

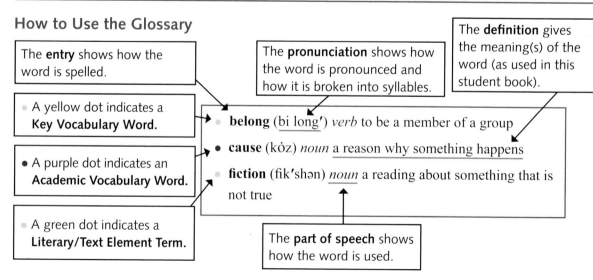

The **entry** shows how the word is spelled.

The **pronunciation** shows how the word is pronounced and how it is broken into syllables.

The **definition** gives the meaning(s) of the word (as used in this student book).

• A yellow dot indicates a **Key Vocabulary Word.**
• A purple dot indicates an **Academic Vocabulary Word.**
• A green dot indicates a **Literary/Text Element Term.**

• **belong** (bi long′) *verb* to be a member of a group
• **cause** (kȯz) *noun* a reason why something happens
• **fiction** (fik′shən) *noun* a reading about something that is not true

The **part of speech** shows how the word is used.

434   Glossary

A

- **act** (akt) *noun* a group of two or more scenes that make up a major part of a play
- **actual event** (ak′chü əl i vent′) *noun* a thing that really happened
- **advice** (ad vīs′) *noun* directions or opinions as given to someone about what to do
- **affect** (ə fekt′) *verb* to change, to have an impact on
- **aid** (ād) *verb* to assist or help
- **amazed** (ə māz′d) *verb* to be surprised or impressed
- **analyze** (an′l īz) *verb* to examine something in order to understand what it means
- **ancestor** (an′ses′tər) *noun* your parents, grandparents, great-grandparents, etc.
- **annoy** (ə noi′) *verb* to cause a little bit of anger
- **apology** (ə pol′ə jē) *noun* an expression of regret for doing something wrong
- **attitude** (at′ə tüd) *noun* a feeling about or toward someone or something
- **authentic** (ȯ then′tik) *adjective* real, not fake
- **avoid** (ə void′) *verb* to stay away from, to not do something

B

- **belong** (bi long′) *verb* to be a member of a group
- **biography** (bī og′rə fē) *noun* the story of a person's life that is written by another person
- **blame** (blām) *verb* to say someone is responsible for something bad
- **bottom** (bot′əm) *noun* the lowest part of something

- **bragging** (brag ing) *verb* to praise one's own successes
- **bravery** (brā′vər ē) *noun* unafraid of danger
- **brief** (brēf) *adjective* short in length or time
- **bud** (bud) *noun* a young, not fully grown leaf or flower
- **burn** (bėrn) *verb* to be on fire

C

- **caption** (kap′shən) *noun* words that explain the information in a photograph, illustration, or chart
- **cast of characters** (kast ov kar′ik tərz) *noun* the people in a play
- **cause** (kȯz) *noun* a reason why something happens
- **ceremony** (ser′ə mō′nē) *noun* a formal event, usually with rituals (plural: ceremonies)
- **character** (kar′ik tər) *noun* a person in a story, who may be imaginary or real
- **character changes** (kar′ik tər chānj es) *noun* the ways in which a character becomes different as a story progresses
- **character motivation** (kar′ik tər mō′tiv ā shən) *noun* the reason why a character does what he or she does
- **character trait** (kar′ik tər trāt) *noun* a character's qualities; the kind of person the character is
- **characterization** (kar′ik tə rez ā shən) *noun* the way an author creates a character, describing his or her words, thoughts, actions, and what the character looks like
- **chronological** (kron′ə loj′ə kəl) *adjective* describes events arranged in the order in which they happen over time

- **circular** (sėr′kyə lər) *adjective* having a round shape or design
- **climate** (klī′mit) *noun* the type of weather that a place has
- **climax** (klī′maks) *noun* when a conflict grows to an exciting or high point, when things start to change
- **comfort** (kum′fərt) *verb* to make pain or worry less bad
- **compare** (kəm pâr′) *verb* to look for ways that things are the same or different
- **complex** (kəm pleks′) *adjective* having many parts or details that make something hard to understand or work with
- **compromise** (kom′prə mīz) *verb* to reach an agreement where each side gets some, but not all, of what it wants
- **concentrate** (kon′sən trāt) *verb* to think hard about something
- **conclusion** (kən klü′zhən) *noun* a judgment or an opinion that you make from information you know
- **confirm** (kən fėrm′) *verb* to make sure something is right by checking it
- **conflict** (kon′flikt) *noun* a problem or struggle at the center of a story
- **connotative meaning** (kən nō tā′tiv mē′ning) *noun* the feeling you connect to a word
- **consist** (kən sist′) *verb* to be made up of something
- **contrast** (kən trast′) *verb* to look for ways that things are different
- **contribute** (kən trib′yüt) *verb* to give; to participate positively in something
- **crop** (krop) *noun* plants grown by farmers for food

- **custom** (kus′təm) *noun* a regular practice that is special to a person, people, area, or nation

- **damage** (dam′ij) *verb* to hurt (someone's property, reputation, etc.)
- **definition** (def′ə nish′ən) *noun* the meaning of a word
- **denotative meaning** (di nō′ tā′tiv mē′ning) *noun* the meaning of a word that you find in the dictionary
- **description** (di skrip′shən) *noun* details about the times and places in a person's life that help the reader imagine a story
- **design** (di zīn′) *verb* to draw sketches or plans
- **destroy** (di stroi′) *verb* to pull or break down; to ruin
- **detail** (di tāl′) *noun* a smaller part of something larger and more important
- **develop** (div el′əp) *verb* to turn into something more complete, greater, better, or bigger
- **dialogue** (dī′ə lȯg) *noun* the words characters say to each other
- **direct quotation** (də rekt′ kwō tā′shən) *noun* a person's exact words
- **disappear** (dis′ə pir′) *verb* to go out of sight
- **distance** (dis′təns) *noun* the amount of space between two points
- **distinguish** (dis ting′gwish) *verb* to see or understand how things are different
- **divide** (də vīd′) *verb* to separate (into parts), break up

---

- A yellow dot indicates a **Key Vocabulary Word.**
- A purple dot indicates an **Academic Vocabulary Word.**
- A green dot indicates a **Literary/Text Element Term.**

E

- **effect** (ə fekt′) *noun* a result
- **energy** (en′ər jē) *noun* the power to do work or be active
- **engineer** (en′jə nir′) *noun* a person trained in science and mathematics who plans the making of machines, roads, and bridges, etc.
- **entertain** (en′tər tān) *verb* to amuse, to give enjoyment
- **environment** (en vī′rən mənt) *noun* the air, land, and water that people, other animals, and plants live in; surroundings
- **equal** (ē′kwəl) *adjective* being the same; equivalent; alike
- **equipment** (i kwip′mənt) *noun* useful items needed for a purpose, such as work or sports
- **evaluate** (i val′yü āt) *verb* to study and make a judgment about something
- **event** (i vent′) *noun* an important thing that happens in a person's life
- **evidence** (ev′ə dəns) *noun* words or things that show something is true
- **examine** (eg zam′ən) *verb* to look at closely
- **example** (eg zam′pəl) *noun* something that shows or explains a fact
- **exercise** (ek′sər sīz) *noun* a problem for students to solve by themselves
- **experiment** (ek sper′ə mənt) *noun* a test done to see if something works or happens

F

- **fact** (fakt) *noun* a statement that is true
- **factory** (fak′tər ē) *noun* a building or group of buildings where people work, usually with machines, to make things

- **familiar** (fə mil′yər) *adjective* known about
- **fiction** (fik′shən) *noun* a reading about something that is not true
- **figurative language** (fig′yər u′tiv lang′gwij) *noun* words or writing that expresses ideas in imaginative ways, such as comparing two things that are not alike
- **first-person narrative** (fėrst pėr′sən nar′ə tiv) *noun* a story told by a character in a story, who usually refers to himself or herself as "I"
- **flood** (flud′) *verb* when dry land is covered with water
- **focus** (fō′kəs) *verb* to center one's attention on something or someone
- **force** (fôrs) *verb* to use power to make someone do something
- **free-verse poem** (frē vėrs pō′əm) *noun* a poem with lines that do not end with rhyming words
- **freeze** (frēz) *verb* to become very hard or turn into ice because of very cold temperatures
- **freezing** (frēz′ ing) *adjective* to have a temperature that is below the freezing point (32°F/0°C); very cold
- **frozen** (frō′ zn) *adjective* changed into a solid state by very cold temperatures

G

- **generation** (jen′ə rā′shən) *noun* a group of people born during the same time period
- **germ** (jėrm) *noun* a very small living thing that can cause illnesses or disease
- **gradually** (graj′ü əl′lē) *adjective* to happen slowly or by small steps
- **graph** (graf′) *noun* a drawing that shows changes in quantities

- **graphic** (graf′ik) *noun* an illustration or chart that shows information
- **graphic novel** (graf′ik nov′əl) *noun* a book with text and art in comic-book style
- **grateful** (grāt′fəl) *adjective* thankful

H

- **heading** (hed′ing) *noun* titles used to separate sections of a text
- **heal** (hēl) *verb* to cure; to become well or to make someone become well
- **hero** (hir′ō) *noun* a person who is famous for doing something brave or good
- **honest** (on′ist) *adjective* truthful and trustworthy
- **honor** (on′ər) *verb* to show respect or to give recognition
- **hope** (hōp) *verb* to want something to happen

I

- **illustration** (il′ə strā′shən) *noun* art or a photo that helps the reader understand something described in a reading
- **image** (im′ij) *noun* a picture you make in your mind
- **indicate** (in′də kāt) *verb* to show where or what something is
- **inference** (in fėr′ens) *noun* a guess based on some information
- **inform** (in fôrm′) *verb* to give information about something
- **informational text** (in′fər mā′shən′ əl tekst) *noun* a form of non-fiction
- **inheritance** (in her′ə təns) *noun* something, often money or land, passed down to someone by a relative

- **injury** (in′jər ē) *noun* hurt or damage (plural: injuries)
- **insight** (in′sīt′) *noun* the ability to see into or understand a complex person, situation, or subject
- **invention** (in ven′shən) *noun* something useful created by someone

J

- **judgment** (juj′mənt) *noun* the forming of an opinion after careful thought

K

- **knowledge** (nol′ij) *noun* information about or familiarity with something

L

- **lifestyle** (līf′ stīl) *noun* the way in which a person lives
- **link** (lingk) *noun* a connection to another part of a Web site or another Web address
- **locate** (lō′kāt) *verb* to find by searching
- **located** (lō′kā′ted) *verb* to be placed
- **loneliness** (lōn′lē nes) *noun* a condition of being alone and feeling sad
- **lot** (lot) *noun* a piece of land

M

- **machine** (mə shēn′) *noun* a piece of equipment that uses power to do work
- **manufacture** (man′yə fak′chər) *verb* to make something for sale using tools or machinery
- **melt** (melt) *verb* to change something from a solid to a liquid state by warming it

---

- A yellow dot indicates a **Key Vocabulary Word.**
- A purple dot indicates an **Academic Vocabulary Word.**
- A green dot indicates a **Literary/Text Element Term.**

- **merchant** (mėr′chənt) *noun* a person or business that buys and sells goods
- **million** (mil′yən) *noun* 1,000,000 of something
- **misunderstanding** (mis′un′dər stan′ding) *noun* a mistaken idea; an argument, or disagreement
- **mixture** (miks′chər) *noun* a combination of things, especially foods or chemicals
- **modal** (mō′dul) *noun* a special "helping" *verb*, such as can, could, should, or must, that is used with another verb to express an idea
- **modern** (mod′ərn) *adjective* related to today's life; current; new
- **mood** (müd) *noun* the feeling a writer wants the reader to get from a reading
- **moral** (môr′əl) *noun* an idea about correct living and how to behave, usually shown by a story

- **narrator** (nar′āt ėr) *noun* the character who describes the scene in a reading and gives background information
- **nation** (nā′shən) *noun* an independent country with its own government
- **nonfiction** (non fik′shən) *noun* a reading about something that is true
- **novel** (nov′əl) *noun* a long work of fiction
- **numeral** (nü′mər əl) *noun* a symbol that represents (stands for) a number

O

- **opinion** (ə pin′yən) *noun* something that someone thinks or believes and cannot be proven to be true or false
- **organize** (ôr′gə nīz) *verb* to put in order, to arrange

- **outline** (out′līn′) *noun* a summary of the main ideas of a reading

- **paraphrase** (par′ə frāz) *verb* to put part of a reading in your own words; to take complex ideas and simplify them
- **patience** (pā′shəns) *noun* the ability to accept discomfort, pain, or troubles while waiting calmly for something to change
- **peace** (pēs) *noun* a time of quiet and cooperation between people or nations
- **personal narrative** (pėr sə nəl nar′ə tiv) *noun* a true story that you write about your own life
- **personality** (pėr′sə nal′ə tē) *noun* the way a person thinks, feels, and acts
- **personification** (pər son′ if ik ā′ shən) *noun* when an author gives human qualities to nonhuman characters
- **perspective** (pər spek′ tiv) *noun* a way of seeing things
- **persuade** (pər swād′) *verb* to lead a person or group to believe or do something
- **photo** (fō′ tō) *noun* a picture
- **play** (plā) *noun* a theatrical production, such as a drama or musical
- **pleased** (plēzd) *adjective* feeling happy or satisfied
- **plot** (plot) *noun* events in a story that happen in a certain order
- **poetry** (pō′i trē) *noun* poems in general or as a form of literature
- **point** (point) *verb* to indicate a place, direction, person, or thing, usually with a finger
- **predict** (pri dikt′) *verb* to say what will happen in the future

preparation (prep'ə rā' shən) *noun* making something ready

primary source document (prī'mer'ē sôrs dok'yə mənt) *noun* diaries, letters, speeches, and interviews that are created by a person who lived during a certain time in history and has direct knowledge of that time

process (pros'es) *noun* a series of actions that brings about a result

product (prod'əkt) *noun* anything that is manufactured or grown for sale

protect (prə tekt') *verb* to defend against harm or loss

protection (prə tek'shən) *noun* action taken against harm or loss, a defense

proud (proud) *adjective* pleased or satisfied with someone's success

pure (pyür) *adjective* not mixed with other things

purpose (pėr'pəs) *noun* a goal; a reason for doing something

R

ratio (rā'shē ō) *noun* a relationship between two numbers

realize (rē'ə līz) *verb* to understand; to see that something is true

recognize (rek' əg nīz) *verb* to remember someone or something when you see or hear that person or thing

recommend (rek'ə mend') *verb* to tell others about something one likes

reflect (ri flekt') *verb* to think deeply about

refugee (ref'yə jē') *noun* a person trying to leave bad living conditions (such as oppression, war, or hunger)

region (rē'jən) *noun* a geographical area of a country

relative (rel'ə tiv) *noun* a person connected by blood or marriage to someone

remind (ri mīnd') *verb* to cause someone to remember

rescue (res'kyü) *verb* to save from danger

resolution (rez' ə lü' shən) *noun* how a conflict is resolved in a story

revise (ri vīz') *verb* to change something already written in order to make corrections or to improve it

rhyme (rīm) *noun* words that have the same ending sound

rhyming poem (rīm ing pō'əm) *noun* a poem with lines that end with rhyming words

rhythm (riŦH'əm) *noun* a regular beat, especially in music or movement

role (rōl) *noun* a part or job one takes in a group

roots (rütz) *noun* connections to a place

rude (rüd) *adjective* not polite

S

safe (sāf) *adjective* protected

scared (skârd) *verb* to cause fear

scene (sēn) *noun* a part of a play that happens in one place and at one time

season (sē'zn) *noun* a time of year, such as spring or summer, or the time for a certain activity or sport

segregation (seg'rə gā'shən) *noun* the separation of a group from a larger group

sensory language (sen'sər ē lang'gwij) *noun* words that help you see, hear, smell, touch, and taste what a poet is describing

A yellow dot indicates a **Key Vocabulary Word.**
A purple dot indicates an **Academic Vocabulary Word.**
A green dot indicates a **Literary/Text Element Term.**

- **sequence** (sē′kwəns) *noun* a connected series of events
- **serious** (sir′ē əs) *adjective* thoughtful and quiet
- **setting** (set′ing) *noun* where a story happens
- **short story** (shôrt stôr′ē) *noun* a piece of fiction that is shorter and usually simpler than a novel
- **shrink** (shringk) *verb* to make or become smaller
- **similar** (sim′ə lər) *adjective* almost the same
- **simplify** (sim′plə fī) *verb* to make something less complex or less difficult to understand
- **sink** (singk) *verb* to go or fall below the surface of water
- **skill** (skil) *noun* ability to do a particular thing well because of practice, talent, or special training
- **slave** (slāv) *noun* a person who is owned by someone else
- **soil** (soil) *noun* the top layers of earth in which plants grow
- **speculate** (spek′yə lāt) *verb* to think about and make a guess
- **spin** (spin) *verb* to turn around in a small circle
- **stage directions** (stāj də rek′shəns) *noun* notes within a play that tell characters how to speak and move
- **stanza** (stan′zə) *noun* a group of lines in a poem
- **steep** (stēp) *adjective* at an angle at which one could easily fall
- **story** (stôr′ē) *noun* a piece of fiction written or told out loud
- **stranger** (strān′jər) *noun* an unfamiliar person

- **stuck** (stuk) *adjective* attached with glue, tape, or a pointed object
- **subject** (sub′ jikt) *noun* what a text is about
- **summarize** (sum′ə rīz′) *verb* to give only the most important ideas of a reading
- **supply** (sə plī) *noun* a quantity of goods (plural: supplies)
- **support** (sə port′) *verb* to hold up, to keep from falling or slipping
- **surprised** (sər prīzd′) *adjective* to feel pleasure or shock due to an unexpected event
- **symbol** (sim′bəl) *noun* something that represents something else
- **synonym** (sin′ə nim) *noun* a word that has a similar meaning to another word

T

- **task** (task) *noun* an assignment; a job to be performed
- **technology** (tek nol′ə jē) *noun* science and theoretical engineering used in practical applications
- **text** (tekst) *noun* written material
- **textbook** (tekst′bük′) *noun* a book that teaches students about a specific content area
- **theme** (thēm) *noun* the meaning or message of a story
- **thesaurus** (thi sôr′əs) *noun* a reference book or online resource that lists synonyms for words
- **third-person narrative** (thėrd pėr′sən nar′ə tiv) *noun* a story told by a narrator who is not a part of the story
- **tone** (tōn) *noun* the author's attitude toward his or her subject and audience

tool (tül) *noun* an implement used to make or repair things

tradition (trə dish′ən) *noun* the passing of customs and beliefs from one age group to another (parents to children)

traditional (trə dish′ə nəl) *adjective* a customary way of celebrating a religious or cultural event and belief

trust (trust) *verb* to have faith in someone

truth (truth) *noun* accuracy, correctness

upset (up set′) *verb* to hurt emotionally

violence (vī′ə ləns) *noun* a strong force that hurts someone or something

visual (vizh′ü əl) *noun* photographs, illustrations, and charts that give readers more information about a text

visualize (vizh′ ü ə līz) *verb* to make a picture in your mind

warning (wôr′ning) *noun* a danger sign; a statement that something bad might happen

weak (wēk) *adjective* not physically strong or not strong in character

Web address (web ə dres′) *noun* the location of a Web site on the Internet

wisdom (wiz′dəm) *noun* knowledge usually gained from experience

wise (wīz) *adjective* showing good judgment based on experience

wonder (wun′dər) *verb* to express an interest in knowing

words in bold (wėrdz in bōld) *noun* heavy, dark type for important words

writing style (rī′ting stīl) *noun* the author's way of using language, including word choice, grammar, sentence length, and punctuation

- A yellow dot indicates a **Key Vocabulary Word.**
- A purple dot indicates an **Academic Vocabulary Word.**
- A green dot indicates a **Literary/Text Element Term.**

Index of Skills

Text Genres

Reading

Independent Reading

Reading Fluency

Reading Strategies

Readings

Meet the Author

Research and Technology

Viewing and Representing

Vocabulary and Concept Development

Academic Vocabulary

Key Vocabulary

Language Functions

Vocabulary Development

Writing

Penmanship

Writing Applications

Text Credits

Unit 1 **Chapter 1** pp. 9–13, MY KOREAN NAME by Leonard Chang from HIGHLIGHTS FOR CHILDREN, August 1999. Copyright © 1999 by Highlights for Children, Inc., Columbus, Ohio. Reprinted by permission. pp. 18–20, HOME LIFE IN ANCIENT GREECE by Melanie Ann Apel from HOME LIFE IN ANCIENT GREECE. Copyright © 2004. Reprinted by permission of Rosen Publishing. **Chapter 2** pp. 35–39, GENES: A FAMILY INHERITANCE from YOUR GENES from Science Museum website (ScienceMuseum.org.uk). Reprinted by permission of Science Museum. pp. 44–46, Excerpted from PRIDE OF PUERTO RICO: THE LIFE OF ROBERTO CLEMENTE, text copyright © 1988 by Paul Robert Walker, reprinted by permission of Harcourt, Inc. This material may not be reproduced in any form or by any means without the prior written permission of the publisher.

Unit 2 **Chapter 1** pp. 73–77, THE STRONGEST ONE from PUSHING UP THE SKY by Joseph Bruchac, copyright © 2000 by Joseph Bruchac, text. Used by permission of Dial Books for Young Readers, a Division of Penguin Young Readers Group, a Member of Penguin Group (USA) Inc., 345 Hudson Street, New York, NY 10014. All rights reserved, pp. 82–84. CIRCLES AND CIRCUMFERENCE from PRENTICE HALL MATHEMATICS, Course 1 © 2004 by Pearson Education, Inc. or its affiliate(s). Used by permission. All rights reserved. **Chapter 2** pp. 99–103, EUREKA! from EUREKA!: GREAT INVENTIONS AND HOW THEY HAPPENED by Richard Platt. NY: Kingfisher Knowledge/Houghton Mifflin, 2003. Copyright © 2003 by Richard Platt. Reprinted by permission of Houghton Mifflin Company. All rights reserved. p. 108, THE FIRST BOOK from ON THE BUS WITH ROSA PARKS, W.W. Norton & Co., Inc. © 1999 by Rita Dove. Reprinted by permission of the author. p. 109, UNFOLDING BUD by Naoshi Koriyama. Reproduced with permission from the July 3, 1957 issue of The Christian Science Monitor (www.csmonitor.com). Copyright © 1957 The Christian Science Monitor. All rights reserved.

Unit 3 **Chapter 1** pp. 137–141, DRAGONWINGS from DRAGONWINGS by Laurence Yep. NY: HarperCollins, 1977. Copyright © 1992 by Laurence Yep. First appeared in America Theatre Magazine. Now appears in Norton Anthology of Children's Literature. Reprinted by permission of Curtis Brown, Ltd. p. 146, DA VINCI'S DREAMS by Nick D'Alto. Adapted from ODYSSEY'S November 2001 issue: Looking at Leonardo's Science, © 2001, Cobblestone Publishing, 30 Grove Street, Suite C, Peterborough, NH 03458. All rights reserved. Used by permission of Carus Publishing Company. **Chapter 2** pp. 161–165, MARTIN LUTHER KING JR. DAY from MARTIN LUTHER KING JR. DAY by Mir Tamim Ansary. Copyright © 1999 Reed Educational & Publishing Group. Published by Heinemann Library. p. 170, DREAMS copyright © 1994 by The Estate of Langston Hughes, from THE COLLECTED POEMS OF LANGSTON HUGHES by Langston Hughes, edited by Arnold Rampersad with David Roessel, Associate Editor. Used by permission of Alfred A. Knopf, a division of Random House, Inc. and Harold Ober Associates. pp. 171–172, THE DREAM ON MY WALL and THE STUDENT TEACHER by Jane Medina from THE DREAM ON BLANCA'S WALL: POEMS IN ENGLISH AND SPANISH. Reprinted by permission of Boyds Mills Press, a Highlights Company.

Unit 4 **Chapter 1** pp. 199–207, SUZY AND LEAH from SUZY AND LEAH. Copyright © 1993 by Jane Yolen. Reprinted by permission of Curtis Brown, Ltd. pp. 212–214, THE KIDS' GUIDE TO WORKING OUT CONFLICTS from THE KIDS' GUIDE TO WORKING OUT CONFLICTS by Naomi Drew, M.A. Reprinted by permission of Free Spirit Publishing, Inc. **Chapter 2** pp. 229–233, THE CIVIL WAR: BACKGROUND TO THE CONFLICT from Chapter 13 in HARCOURT BRACE SOCIAL STUDIES: United States, Grade 5 (2000 National Edition), copyright © 2000 by Harcourt, Inc., adapted by permission of the publisher. This material may not be reproduced in any form or by any means without the prior written permission of the publisher. pp. 238–240, THE QUARREL BETWEEN WIND AND THUNDER reprinted with the permission of Margaret K. McElderry Books, an imprint of Simon & Schuster Children's Publishing Division, from HOLD UP THE SKY AND OTHER NATIVE AMERICAN TALES by Jane Louise Curry. Text copyright © 2003 by Jane Louise Curry. All rights reserved.

Unit 5 **Chapter 1** pp. 267–275, SHACKLETON AND THE LOST ANTARCTIC EXPEDITION from SHACKLETON AND THE LOST ANTARCTIC EXPEDITION by B.A. Hoena. Copyright © 2006 by Capstone Press. All rights reserved. pp. 280–282, USING MATH TO SURVIVE IN THE WILD from USING MATH TO SURVIVE IN THE WILD. Special permission granted by, and published and copyrighted by, Gareth Stevens, Inc., a Weekly Reader company. All rights reserved. **Chapter 2** pp. 297–301, THE FIERCEST STORMS ON EARTH from DISCOVERYWORKS, Grade 4 by Badders et al. Copyright © 1996 by Silver Burdett Ginn, Inc. Reprinted by permission of Houghton Mifflin Company. All rights reserved. pp. 306–308, HURRICANE FRIENDS is reprinted with permission from the publisher of FITTING IN by Anilu Bernardo. Copyright © 1996 Arte Publico Press-University of Houston.

Unit 6 **Chapter 1** pp. 335–339, BLESS ME, ULTIMA from BLESS ME, ULTIMA by Rudolfo Anaya. Copyright © Rudolfo Anaya 1974. Published in hardcover and mass market paperback by Warner Books Inc. 1994; originally published by TQS Publications. Reprinted by permission of Susan Bergholz Literary Services, New York, NY, and Lamy, NM. All rights reserved. pp. 344–346, BIOMES AND ECOSYSTEMS from GATEWAY TO SCIENCE: Vocabulary and Concepts, 1st Edition by Collins, 2008. Reprinted with permission of Heinle, a division of Cengage Learning: www.cengagerights.com. Fax 800-730-2215. **Chapter 2** pp. 361–364, IF YOUR NAME WAS CHANGED AT ELLIS ISLAND from IF YOUR NAME WAS CHANGED AT ELLIS ISLAND by Ellen Levine. Copyright © 1993 by Ellen Levine. Reprinted by permission of Scholastic Inc. p. 365, LAZARUS SALAMON, HUNGARY and KATHERINE BEYCHOK, RUSSIA from I WAS DREAMING TO COME TO AMERICA by Veronica Lawlor, copyright © 1995 by Veronica Lawlor. Used by permission of Viking Penguin, a Division of Penguin Young Readers Group, a Member of Penguin Group (USA) Inc., 345 Hudson Street, New York, NY 10014. All rights reserved. pp. 370–372, SEEDFOLKS from SEEDFOLKS by Paul Fleischman, illustrated by Judy Pedersen. Text copyright © 1997 by Paul Fleischman. Used by permission of HarperCollins Publishers and Paul Fleischman.

Illustrator Credits

Greg Copeland/illustrationOnline: pp. 44–46, 238–240; **Tommy Hunt/illustrationOnline:** pp. 133, 137–141; **Ed Sauk/illustrationOnline:** pp.9–13; **John Schreiner/** **illustrationOnline:** p.102; **Richard Waldrep/illustration Online:** pp. 194, 199–207. Contributing Illustrators: **Nesbitt Graphics, Inc.** and **Value Chain International, Ltd.**

Photo Credits